An OP

THE SECOND
A SHORT HISTORY

R. A. C. Parker is a Fellow of Queen's College, Oxford. His other publications include *Chamberlain and Appeasement: British Policy and the Coming of the Second World War* (1993).

THE SECOND WORLD WAR

A SHORT HISTORY

Revised edition

R. A. C. PARKER

Oxford   New York

OXFORD UNIVERSITY PRESS

Oxford University Press, Great Clarendon Street, Oxford OX2 6DP
Oxford New York
Athens Auckland Bangkok Bogotá Buenos Aires Calcutta
Cape Town Chennai Dar es Salaam Delhi Florence Hong Kong Istanbul
Karachi Kuala Lumpur Madrid Melbourne Mexico City Mumbai
Nairobi Paris São Paulo Singapore Taipei Tokyo Toronto Warsaw
and associated companies
in Berlin Ibadan

Oxford is a registered trade mark of Oxford University Press

First published as Struggle for Survival 1989
First issued as an Oxford University Press paperback 1990
Reprinted six times
First issued as an Oxford University Press paperback,
with the title Second World War 1997

British Library Cataloguing in Publication Data

Data available

Library of Congress Cataloguing in Publication Data

Data available

ISBN 0-19-289285-1

3 5 7 9 10 8 6 4

Printed in Great Britain by
Cox & Wyman Ltd,
Reading, Berkshire

PREFACE

THIS book is a short history of the Second World War. It deals not only with military history, how the war was won and lost, but also analyses its causes and consequences. Such a study compels rigorous selection because it concerns most of world history from 1939 to 1945 and in some years before and after.

I have chosen, therefore, to examine only the decisive episodes of the war: those that changed its course and determined its outcome. For example, as the Australian government complained at the time, the hard offensive fighting, in the most arduous conditions, of the Australian forces in the south-west Pacific area had little bearing on the operations planned against the Japanese home islands. The same is true of the Burma campaign of the British and Imperial 14th Army which, although bringing victory over some of the best Japanese troops, became no more than a brilliant sideshow in the war against Japan, whatever its significance in rebuilding British influence in south-east Asia.

Some British writers treat American contributions to wartime strategic debates with condescension. I have tried to escape any British prejudices in considering the conduct of the allies.

The war changed the lives of a larger number of men, women, and children than any other single set of events. Effectively to illustrate the diverse and erratic impact of war on individuals would need many volumes of personal experiences. I have isolated aspects of the war that affected whole national, ethnic, or social groups. The experience of the populations in countries fought over, or occupied by the enemy, differed so much from those who escaped invasion that generalizations on the social effects of war are impossible; in particular, English-speaking societies escaped many of the hardships endured in continental Europe and east Asia. I have pointed to some of the more important ways in which human lives could be affected but, ideally, every society needs its own detailed analysis. I did not forget the sufferings that statistics can muffle and I hope the reader will be able to sense the miseries of this war. I have devoted a chapter to the unique experience of the European Jews.

The effects of the war still dominate world affairs. This book endeavours to show their variety and importance by reviewing a sample of the most far-reaching and durable.

A decision is now forced on writers touching on Chinese history: whether or not to adopt the new system of transliteration of Chinese names in which, for example, Peking becomes Beijing and Mao Tse-tung Mao Zedong. It seems best to retain the usage of the participants in the Second World War, who would have been puzzled by the substitution of Jiang Jieshi for the familiar name of the 'Generalissimo', Chiang Kai-shek.

Any author of a study of so intense and wide-ranging a subject emerges burdened by debts to the work of others. A book-list is appended and it includes some, but not all, of my sources. I am grateful to everyone whose work I have used and to Miss Pat Lloyd, secretary.

ALASTAIR PARKER,
1989

CONTENTS

LIST OF PLATES

LIST OF MAPS

Hitler, Germany, and the origins of the European war

TWO separate wars made up the 'Second World War': a European war and a Far Eastern War. After 1941 the United States and the United Kingdom took part in both, while their enemies waged separate wars and, until the last days, the Soviet Union fought only in Europe. These two wars were caused by the conflicts between the actions of the rulers of Germany and Japan on one side and, on the other, what the governments and the politically influential sections of the populations of Britain, France, and the United States thought acceptable. In 1939 the government of Poland chose to fight, encouraged by Britain and France, rather than risk the loss of Polish independence; in 1940 Mussolini voluntarily brought Italy into the European war, but only because he supposed that it was already won. The numerous other countries who fought, or were fought over, had no choice. Towards the end of the war more states joined in against Germany in order to qualify themselves as founder members of the United Nations: their participation was usually only nominal.

The actions of Germany and Japan, and the reactions to them of Britain, France, Poland, and the United States explain the Second World War. Most important is to study Germany; the German government started the war in Europe. Unless this German-made war had already broken out, the Japanese could not have attacked the British Empire and the United States. The paradox of Nazi rule in Germany was that Hitler's government was both unrepresentative and popular. Only a very small proportion of Germans would have approved in advance Hitler's expansionist, violent, and murderous actions, yet his dictatorship seems to have won the support of the majority for several years and nearly complete acquiescence almost until the end. German support for Hitler depended on ignorance by Germans of what his regime would bring. Those German national objectives which most Germans desired would certainly have been difficult to attain; they need not have produced a great European war. For that to happen, the special ferocity and recklessness given to German foreign policy by the Nazis was necessary. Hitler's foreign activities were approved, at least before 1941, because their apparent aims corresponded to those of most politically minded Germans, in spite of the fact that Hitler's real objects went much further: to win a self-inflicted struggle for survival.

Hitler and the Nazis came to power because of the support registered by German voters in 1932 (37 and 33 per cent of the votes cast in the two Reichstag elections) and because powerful non-Nazi politicians preferred to try to work with and to exploit the Nazis rather than to ally with the socialists in combatting them. Resentment and fears generated by economic crisis and alleged political injustices explain mass support for this nationalist and authoritarian party. It was critical for the success of the Nazis, and for Hitler's eventual winning of German acquiescence in an aggressive foreign policy, that Germans thought their economic and political grievances to be consequences of the imposition and enforcement of the Treaty of Versailles by predatory foreigners. Few Germans felt any particular 'guilt' for the First World War, and they did not feel that its painful consequences, embodied in the Versailles treaty, represented a justified retribution. 'Reparations', the obligation to repay the damage done to the allies during the war, inspired special anger because they were thought to be unjust as well as ruinous. Germans blamed both the great inflation of 1923, which eventually made German currency worthless and so brought economic life to a halt, and the slump after 1929, which culminated in the unemployment of nearly half the industrial labour force in 1932, on the vengeful policies of foreigners, especially the French. The inflation was, in fact, largely due to German resistance to reparations, and the slump to the withdrawal of capital by American investors, whose motives contained no particular hostility to Germany, and to the rigorously deflationary policies of the German government. However, foreign attitudes, especially as shown in the Franco-Belgian occupation of the Ruhr in 1923, and in French reluctance to co-operate in easing pressure on German banks in 1931, lent apparent justification to the belief that Germany's economic disasters were due to foreign malice.

The frontiers laid down in the Treaty of Versailles gave more reasons for xenophobic nationalism. Some Germans disliked the continued separation of German-speaking Austrians from Germany and the rule of Czechs over Germans following the breakup of the Habsburg monarchy and the creation of Czechoslovakia. Many more Germans thought it wrong that Poles should govern Germans in reborn Poland. Other aspects of Versailles, like the loss of German colonies, irritated special-interest groups, while an extremely influential section of German society resented the treaty limitations on the size and equipment of the German army.

Support for the Nazis resulted from their expressions of hatred towards foreigners but also from the panic aroused by the economic catastrophe of the depression years, 1929–32. The Nazis accused both socialists and capitalists, and denounced both as unpatriotic, internationally-minded tools of alien malevolence and exploitation. Socialist subversion, the Nazis argued, brought German defeat in 1918, and thereafter agents of capitalist liberalism, notably Stresemann, the apostle of German fulfilment of the Treaty of Versailles during the years 1924–9, truckled to allied dictation. In its second economic catastrophe of the inter-war years, Germany was harder hit by the great depression than any other large industrial country. By 1932, the depression made the Nazis the strongest political party. Few working men turned to the Nazis: the combined votes of the Socialists (SPD) and the Communists (KPD) remained constant during the party's rise. Mass support came principally from the middle class and the peasantry. The middle class found it easy to believe that the depression was the result of socialistic ideas, particularly embodied in supposedly selfish and short-sighted trade unions. Working-class resistance to downward pressure on wages and to reductions in public spending on social welfare was, the middle classes readily supposed, foolish and harmful to everyone, and postponed the recovery which the reduction of wage costs and the maintenance of confidence in the currency would bring.

The Nazis' alleged appeal to the working class was more truly an effective appeal to the others: they claimed to be classless, to stand for a state and a government above class conflict and for an end to the wastefulness of industrial disputes. Hence their appeal to men of impartiality and moderation. Against the most extreme advocates of class conflict, the Communists, the Nazis promised the most vigorous struggle, a welcome prospect to those who were frightened by the fragility of the social framework, and who feared its overthrow. The Nazis' insistence on the need for self-sacrificing co-operation for the general good gave their cause a reforming, even high-minded, aspect which made it easier for enemies of socialism to feel themselves disinterested.

The Nazis were supported by a disproportionate number of young voters, probably because of their opposition to class-based parties. Only one non-socialist party kept intact its voting strength, the Centre party, which itself had a classless aspect through its association with the Catholic church. The Nazis' claim to be detached from class conflict was strengthened by their hostility to the individualistic excesses they attributed to international capitalism. In a time of deep economic recession, an attack on successful capitalists as conspiratorial scoundrels had wide appeal, especially to debtors, and, therefore, to struggling peasants and smallholders hard hit by falling prices and by the tendency of Weimar governments, especially Brüning's, to favour grain growers at the expense of livestock producers. It was clear that the Nazis would discriminate against Jews but few voters can have imagined the organized murders arranged by the wartime German government. In 1932 anti-Semitism probably alienated more Germans than it attracted. However, it appealed, with some success which it is impossible to assess with precision, to peasants who resented their indebtedness to moneyed men, to small shopkeepers who disliked the competition of large stores, and to professional men—lawyers or doctors, for instance—who attributed their competitive failures or lack of employment to unfair advantages conferred on Jews by the supposed cohesiveness of their culture or religion. Votes for the Nazis expressed the fears and hatreds brought about by deprivation or the fear of deprivation. The Nazis encouraged and exploited suspicion between socially distinct groups, while they themselves claimed to stand for a united nation.

However, in all the elections before Hitler became Chancellor, a majority voted against the Nazis. An armed seizure of power would have been impossible against the police and the army, whose obedience could certainly be counted on by Field Marshal Hindenburg, the President, and by ministers approved by him. For the Nazis to come to power constitutionally, the help of non-Nazis was needed. In 1930 Brüning was appointed Chancellor when the previous German government split because of disagreement on whether government spending should be cut by reducing the cost of defence or of poor relief. Hindenburg and his advisers expected Brüning to avoid dependence on Socialist support in the Reichstag so that he could maintain, or even increase, spending on defence. However, when it became clear that he could get no co-operation from the Nazis, Brüning was forced, after all, to rely on the 'toleration', the half-concealed support, of the Socialists.

In 1932 Socialists in the provincial governments began to insist that the Nazis should be curbed, especially the violence of the SA, the Nazi storm-troops. They compelled the government to attack the SA, thus obliging Brüning to work with their party against the Nazis. This collaboration was embodied in the presidential election of 1932, when Hindenburg was backed by the Socialists in order to keep Hitler in second place. Hindenburg and his closest advisers, who wanted above all to weaken Socialism and strengthen the army, attempted to escape from this unwelcome alliance by discovering another method of collaborating with the Nazis. To do so, they ousted Brüning and tried another Chancellor, Franz von Papen. He suppressed the government of Prussia, in which Socialist ministers held key positions, withdrew the measures against the SA, and offered Hitler the Vice-Chancellorship. But Hitler refused to accept a subordinate position and denied Papen Nazi votes in the Reichstag. Nor was the army willing to accept a military dictatorship presided over by Papen since, according to its political mouthpiece, General von Schleicher, it was not strong enough simultaneously to combat the Nazis, the Socialists, and the Communists. Instead Schleicher himself became Chancellor and tried to work with the trade unions and to split the Nazis in order to weaken Hitler. He failed, and by January 1933 the choice was between either renewed dependence on the Socialists, or military rule, or acceptance of Hitler's terms. President Hindenburg was persuaded, principally by Papen and General Blomberg, that the interests of the army and of German conservatives could be pursued even if Hitler became Chancellor.

After Hitler had become Chancellor, successfully insisting on Nazi control of the Prussian and Reich ministries of the interior and police, he exploited his position to use an expanded SA to intimidate civilian politicians while offering flattery and bribes to Hindenburg and the army leadership, promising the army expansion and continued independence. He succeeded in securing the dissolution of all other parties, while the passing of the Enabling Act gave a legal gloss to his dictatorship. His great problem in 1933 and early 1934 was that to intimidate civilian politicians he had to bully some groups who had social and political connections with the army. Worse still, the leaders of the SA, and many of its members, wanted a radicalization of German society, with higher status and superior employments for themselves. SA officers, they claimed, should have a standing equal to that of army officers, but the regular army feared that it might be swamped. In the summer of 1934, therefore, Hitler was compelled to choose—either to use the SA to carry out a social revolution and bring new men to power and influence, or to suppress the pretensions of its leaders and work with the existing owners of wealth, property, and influence. In June 1934 an uncertain number of the SA leadership, probably between one and two hundred, were killed, together with some old foes of Hitler, like Schleicher.

From then until 1938 followed the period of normalization and relative respectability. Order returned. Jews were discriminated against by legislative prohibitions rather than by open brutality. Violence against political enemies of the Nazis was hidden behind the fences of concentration camps. Henceforward, Nazi Germany was run by two only partially interlocking sets of rulers: the established civil service, judiciary, teachers, army officers, businessmen, and police on the one side, and on the other, the party, with its own hierarchies and spheres of influence. These two sets of rulers tolerated each other without mutual liking or respect, and thus the Third Reich combined orderly, old-fashioned, conservative, honesty and efficiency in many aspects of government and in the armed services, with the powerful influence of brutal, lawless, often corrupt and sometimes incompetent, party-dominated mechanisms. Hitler's laziness and intellectual incoherence helped to make him politically dominant: by avoiding choices between conflicting purposes and methods he strengthened his position as arbiter. Nazi zealots and, though with less reason, conservatives, and even those who believed in legality, could all continue to regard Hitler as their ally against the others. The effect, combined with the way in which Hitler's oratorical genius made him the only possible chief of Nazism, was to establish him as a true dictator, an absolute ruler—not in the manner of Philip II of Spain or Napoleon, of a hard-working administrator inquiring into every aspect of the empire he ruled, but in the sense that he was always the ultimate last resort, the final adjudicator between conflicting subordinates and overlapping jurisdictions.

By 1939, when the European war broke out, support for Hitler inside Germany had increased still further. At first Hitler's government simply continued the credit-creation schemes of Papen and Schleicher, but after a few months they were extended, large-scale public works programmes were added and, from 1934 on, rearmament increased. Compulsory military service was restored in 1935. By 1936, therefore, unemployment had nearly disappeared. So extensive had been the resources unused in the depression that the German economic revival was able to provide for the whole labour force in the later 1930s a standard of living equal to that of a fully employed worker in 1932, greater profits, increased incomes for agricultural producers, and armaments production outstripping that of any other country. There were, of course, no elections or free votes to test opinion, but it seems clear that, by the end of 1938, a substantial majority of Germans had accepted the regime. Hitler could try to secure his foreign aims as master of a powerful, united country.

What were these aims? An answer must be sought with care since in them, if they existed, are to be found the causes of the Second World War. Several serious historians believe the enquiry to be futile for one of two reasons. One is that Hitler, whatever his subjective wishes might be, should be regarded as a product of ineluctable social and economic forces, derived from the workings of capitalism, which necessarily led to Nazi dictatorship and European war. It is certainly true that Hitler could not have come to power without the world slump, which was itself a consequence of the way in which capitalist economies were organized. And it is true that the regime, in most of its aspects, proved compatible with German business interests. However, German capitalism did not require the war. On the contrary, the nationalistic foreign policy pursued before 1939 provided the basis for stable German prosperity, but only if Hitler agreed to check rearmament. Primary producers, in south-east Europe and South America, as well as industrialized countries, especially the United Kingdom, were ready to meet German economic needs. A revival of co-operation with the Soviet Union proved possible in 1939. If it is true that 'capitalism' dictated the destruction of the Soviet Union, its alleged puppet demonstrated implausible ineptitude in simultaneously taking on the British Empire and the United States. There were more effective and less hazardous ways of pursuing the interests of capitalists than the path followed by Hitler's Germany after 1939.

The second reason for denying that Hitler had 'plans' or 'aims' is that it is difficult to fit his actions into any clear pattern, and that his own justifications of his actions and expositions of his purposes are incoherent and inconsistent. It is possible to conclude that a mindless urge to violence moved Hitler and the Nazis, or that their dominance in Germany, together with Hitler's dictatorship, needed the justification of an endless struggle against enemies whose identity at any moment was determined by accidental circumstances. This interpretation has much to support it. Hitler's personal popularity inside Germany rested in large part on his theatrical performance in the role of saviour of the German people from dangerous foes. By 1938, it can be argued, new enemies were required. This line of argument fits the extraordinarily confused and muddled nature of the regime. As 'Führer', Hitler ran his government through subordinate but competing individuals and organizations, and acted as an evasive arbitrator, interfering with reluctance, and trying to avoid committing himself to any definite view. Discussions of general policy seldom took place, or, if they did, were in unrecorded conversations between Hitler and a few trusted intimates. The Führer's decisions, therefore, came arbitrarily, without debate, without their being deduced from general principles or explained as methods of reaching agreed objectives. Hitler's notorious unwillingness to take decisions reinforces the impression given by the lack of guiding principles behind them that his actions were responses to changing circumstances, and made only to ensure the survival of the regime.

There can be no conclusive way of refuting the argument that Hitler needed continuing foreign crises and emergencies, for we cannot know what would have happened if he had tried to rule without them. Certainly it would have been possible for Hitler to try a different course in 1939: to restrict armaments, peacefully to win concessions at the expense of Poland, to secure trading concessions and foreign loans and so consolidate the position of Germany as the strongest European power. The difficulty in thinking of Hitler as the ruler of such a peaceful and conservative Germany comes not only from the difficulty of securing support for dictatorship in such tranquil conditions but even more from that of believing that he himself would have accepted them. It is more likely that Hitler sincerely believed that he should lead Germany in what he thought to be an inevitable national and racial struggle for existence and that, as it happened, the resulting continuous state of crisis offered justification for Nazi dictatorship.

In Hitler's writings and recorded private utterances two themes constantly recur: the need to 'solve the Jewish problem' and the need to secure 'living space' for the Germans. Defeating the Jews would safeguard the racial purity of Germans, while 'living space' would strengthen them in the struggle for survival, which Hitler assumed to be taking place between competing races and nations. His detailed ideas of how these objectives should be attained were vague and inconsistent. 'The Jew' must be fought—but the 'final solution', mass murder, did not emerge before 1941. 'Living space' meant land for the settlement of German peasants, and a source of raw materials for German industry. Hitler advocated armed expansion to create a German-dominated European land mass capable of self-sufficiency in war and of supporting a struggle against any eventual national rivals. This required expansion in 'the east' which usually seemed to mean European Russia. Most historians agree that the great object of Hitler's life was the destruction of the Soviet Union and German exploitation of Russian resources. Even here, however, Hitler was inconsistent; in early 1939 he was apparently trying to work with Poland against the Soviet Union, but for a few months in 1939 and 1940 he seems to have made a serious attempt to co-operate with the Soviet Union on the basis of agreed spheres of influence, and was even ready to make do for 'living space' with the German share of Poland. Certainly Ribbentrop, his Foreign Minister, was allowed to work along these lines. By contrast, at the end of 1940, Hitler decided to conquer Russia and exploit as 'living space' both Russia and Poland.

The conquest of 'living space', and indeed the 'struggle' which, according to Hitler, Germany could not escape, required military power. Before 1939 he consistently urged acceleration and extension of the pace and scale of German rearmament. In August 1936 he put his thoughts into writing—a rare event after his coming to power—in an exposition of the purposes of the Four-Year Plan, a set of economic measures designed to make Germany as self-sufficient as possible. Hitler ended: 'The German army must be fit for operations in four years' time; the German economy must be ready for war in four years' time.' No priorities were worked out between army, air force, and navy or between civilian production and that for the armed forces. Neither was any strategy for expansion worked out. Here as elsewhere Hitler's aims were sought by a series of improvisations. It was a political and strategic improvisation which began the European war: the attack on Poland in 1939.

Hitler's leaning towards armed aggression, linked with his assumption of the inevitability of a constant struggle for existence amongst nations and races was certain to bring war. That it came how and when it did was mainly the result of British policy. British governments were not at all opposed to rising German prosperity; indeed they assumed that German prosperity was one of the conditions of British prosperity. German complaints against the Treaty of Versailles received widespread sympathy in Britain. In the 1920s, and even in the early 1930s, Britain pressed France to agree to concessions to Germany on 'disarmament' (which meant permitting some German rearmament) and on reparations. Britain did little to help France maintain the territorial provisions of the treaty. Most people in Britain would have welcomed a strong, prosperous, peaceful Germany. Nazi Germany acquired strength and prosperity but its peacefulness was far from certain. To British governments it seemed very threatening. The fear was not of a direct threat to British interests; although the Nazis maintained, and even encouraged, the demand of some non-Nazi groups for the return of Germany's pre-war colonies, Hitler did not stress this demand, or treat it as incompatible with the Anglo-German understanding he claimed to desire. German trading methods impinged on British trade in south-eastern Europe and in Latin America but the impact on the overall level of British trade was much too small to provoke armed resistance to Germany. Indeed British ministers seem to have thought a purely economic dominance by Germany in south-eastern Europe an acceptable price for peace.

However, German preparation for war, and what could be discerned of the intentions of the Nazi regime, suggested an armed bid for eastern-European expansion. Hitler hoped that the British would give him a free hand in the east in return for German acceptance of the British Empire and of things as they were outside Europe and, perhaps, in western Europe too. The snag about this from the British point of view was that Hitler and Nazi Germany, unless checked, seemed likely to become politically dominant in eastern Europe. If British disinterest compelled France also to abandon eastern Europe, the Soviet Union would be isolated, and since it was not thought able to fight Germany alone, it would either face destruction or would have to collaborate in whatever might be Hitler's designs. Then, in western Europe, France could not defend its own independence and would face the same choice. The warlike Nazi government would then organize Europe to make Germany militarily even more powerful. Against such a German-organized Europe, Britain would be hard to defend for long, and would in turn become dependent on German goodwill. The British government was bound to try to stop this process if it could, so in 1939 it encouraged two allies, France and Poland, to risk war in order to check Hitler's advance. This was the reason for the outbreak of the European war—the British government was interfering in Europe to maintain a balance of power.

British governments, however, even in 1939, did not think mainly in these terms, nor could they have secured mass support had they seemed to do so. Governments believed that they were trying to maintain peace, thought carefully about how this was to be done, and generally did not find it necessary to explain even to themselves that peace must be maintained on terms that left British independence and welfare safe from foreign threat. This, like most of the really important objects of policy, was taken for granted. There was little discussion of what the loss of British independence would mean in practice: perhaps the most likely event was thought to be an armed and irresistible German demand for the return of pre-1914 colonies. The Nazi threat seemed more extensive than that, yet it was difficult to explain exactly what was threatened. This vagueness about what constituted the British interests that needed defence facilitated an expression of policy in the high-minded terms that most of the articulate section of the electorate required. The rule of law, the frustration of aggression, the upholding of the principles of the covenant of the League of Nations, and the rights of weaker nations were to be secured by peaceful means. All this was encapsulated in the aim of 'European appeasement', a concept which commanded general support until the methods employed by Chamberlain in 1938 to attain it began to bring it into disrepute. Appeasement meant getting a peaceful Germany. To do this British governments mixed conciliation and coercion, attempts to arrange the peaceful solution of legitimate German grievances with threats of resistance to German aggression. As time went on, more and more policy-makers, and observers of events lost faith in the possibility of making durable bargains with Hitler, and the element of coercion in British policy increased.

The concessions offered to Germany at first were surprisingly meagre: from 1933 to 1935 the legalization of German rearmament in return for agreed limits on German military strength, and, in 1936 and 1937, attempts to secure German peaceableness in return either for the giving up of the 'demilitarized zone'—that is to say the prohibition of military activity in the Rhineland area of Germany (something the Germans, in any case, seized for themselves in March 1936)—or by a very limited restoration of pre-war German colonies. This confidence in the ease with which Germany could be pacified came from the belief that French insistence on Germany's obedience to the Treaty of Versailles had been the original cause of Nazi aggressiveness; once French governments had been bypassed, or induced to be less rigid, all should be well.

This conviction was shaken in 1935, with the open rearmament of Germany in clear breach of the treaty, and in 1936 with the forcible remilitarization of the Rhineland. Early in 1936 the British government agreed to rearm for possible war. In 1936 and 1937, however, it continued to look for some inducement to persuade the German authorities to become peaceful and to limit their armaments. This inducement was still to be found in colonial concessions. Only in 1938 did the British government, firmly led by Neville Chamberlain as Prime Minister, take up the new line of interfering in central and eastern Europe to arrange political concessions to German desires. British appeasers were pursuing incompatible objects. They hoped to change Europe sufficiently to make it acceptable to Hitler (or, failing that, to other Germans capable of restraining Hitler) and simultaneously to prevent unchallengeable domination of Europe by German military power. It did not matter much to the British what the details of the necessary changes in central and eastern Europe might be, yet the pursuit of this type of 'appeasement' made Britain the main obstacle to German expansion.

In March 1938 Hitler and Goering (who still held the first place in the competition for influence that revolved round the Führer) used force to secure the incorporation of the Austrian republic into Germany. Almost immediately the Sudeten Germans, who lived in the western border areas of Czechoslovakia, one of the new states created at the end of the First World War, were encouraged to demand the solution of their grievances, real and imaginary. A first-class international crisis was in prospect. If Germany attacked Czechoslovakia, France was bound to help it, and then the Soviet Union was bound by treaty also to help Czechoslovakia. And if France were at war with Germany, Britain would almost certainly be drawn in.

The British Cabinet considered two ways of stopping this chain of events. One was to add a British promise of help if Czechoslovakia were attacked, but this idea was rejected. Chamberlain and the Foreign Secretary, Lord Halifax, felt that it might precipitate an avoidable war, while other ministers were swayed by the fear that British defences against German air attack were not yet sufficiently powerful to risk war. Instead they agreed to encourage a solution of German grievances against Czechoslovakia. Hitler would be warned that Britain might help the Czechs if Germany attacked; Beneš, the president of Czechoslovakia, was to be told that Britain might not help if he were unreasonable. The French government was persuaded to say the same.

In September 1938 Hitler threatened war if German grievances were not put right at once. The British Prime Minister flew to meet Hitler at Berchtesgaden, where he promised to try to arrange the peaceful transfer of the Czech territory inhabited by Germans. The French were persuaded to join in compelling the Czechoslovak government to agree, and Chamberlain returned finally to settle everything with Hitler at Godesberg. Here Hitler, trying to isolate Czechoslovakia for total destruction, demanded a speeding-up of the transfer. Chamberlain was then obliged by the British cabinet to make Hitler retreat, by a threat of war, sufficiently to make possible the Munich agreement for a slightly delayed cession of German-inhabited territory by Czechoslovakia. Though it was not, therefore, a total triumph for Hitler, the agreement looked like an Anglo-French surrender.

This culmination of 'appeasement' has aroused enormous controversy. 'Munich', it is claimed, made war more likely. By 'standing up to Hitler' Britain and France would have forced him to accept defeat, or, if he had tried to go to war, he would have been overthrown. Well-placed German soldiers were ready, so the British were informed, to eject Hitler from power if his claims on Czechoslovakia were forcibly resisted by the western allies. Instead, the Munich settlement reinforced Hitler's prestige and made any moves to restrain him less likely in the future. In other ways Germany gained strength for further threats and aggressive action, particularly by an increase in industrial capacity as well as by the neutralization of the Czechoslovak army. The conduct of the allies in pressing Czechoslovakia into surrender made it more difficult to rally future resistance to Germany; indeed, it is possible that Munich caused Stalin to abandon his attempts to organize opposition to Hitler, and persuaded him instead to lead the Soviet Union into the Nazi–Soviet pact of August 1939. The neglect of Soviet interests—Russia was left out of the Munich negotiations—caused much criticism in the west at the time, especially because it went with neglect of the League of Nations and of the doctrine of 'collective security'. The League had wide support in Britain, especially among liberals, progressives, and socialists, as a means of preventing war either through conciliation or coercion. But British governments deliberately avoided the League (and the Soviet Union, which was prominent in the League after 1935), because they thought that it would make it more difficult to reach settlements with Hitler.

The most effective answer Chamberlain could have made to these criticisms was that 'standing up to Hitler', with or without the League and the Soviet Union, involved a serious risk of war, which German conspirators might not be able to prevent. The chances that Germany might win a war begun in 1938 seemed greater than if war were postponed. The reason was that German air attack on Britain might inflict 'a knock-out blow'. In 1939 British defences against air attack would be greatly strengthened by extended radar and many more single-seat monoplane fighter aircraft. This argument did not, then or later, prevent impassioned hostility to Chamberlain. One reason is that it was clear before Munich, and clearer still afterwards, that Chamberlain was not thinking of how, most effectively and safely, to coerce Hitler, but, on the contrary, believed, with only occasional doubt, that he had dis-covered a method of securing peace by agreement. Munich showed the way to 'peace in our time'. After Munich, therefore, Chamberlain disliked and resisted those preparations for war which he thought, by provoking Hitler, might make peaceful solutions more difficult. He did not fully share the rising scepticism that followed Munich about the possibility of peace with Nazi Germany.

There were several grounds for this scepticism. First, Hitler made clear, in angry reaction to the acceleration in British rearmament that the Cabinet compelled Chamberlain to announce after Munich, that he objected to British interference in continental Europe. Then, the violent attacks on Jews in Germany in the 'Kristallnacht', 9–10 November 1938, aroused distaste for the Nazi regime and lack of confidence in its trustworthiness. In January 1939 plausible evidence accumulated that Hitler resented British interest in peace-keeping in Europe so strongly that he was considering a pre-emptive strike against Britain, perhaps preceded by the invasion of the Netherlands. Above all, in March 1939 German troops occupied what remained of the Czech provinces of Czechoslovakia and gave Slovakia a tenuous independence. After this most politicians and, so far as one can tell, most British citizens, were convinced that maximum preparation for war, through accelerated rearmament and the encouragement of alliances against Germany, was the only possible way of averting war, either by inspiring fear in Hitler, or as some ministers and officials hoped, by causing German moderates— soldiers, businessmen, and bankers—to restrain Hitler, perhaps with the help of Goering.

The general British conviction in the summer of 1939 that a limit, backed by a clear threat of force, should be put to Hitler's forceful expansion was a consequence of the failure of the determined attempt at peaceful co-operation with Germany. It is hard to see that any British government could have avoided some such attempt, nor can it easily be believed that British opinion could have been persuaded to accept the risk of another European war without it. The conviction that more force was needed was shared by Chamberlain, but he still hoped, and even expected, that he could guide Germany, including even Hitler himself, back to peaceful compromise. Hence his agreement to the British pledge, given at the end of March 1939, that any armed attack on its territory which the Polish government resisted as a threat to Poland's independence would bring the United Kingdom to its aid. On the other hand, he tried hard, but unsuccessfully, to prevent acceptance by the British Cabinet of an Anglo-French attempt to secure a Russian alliance, which he believed would actually lessen the chances of a German renunciation of the use of force by provoking resentment against 'encirclement'. It is possible that Chamberlain's attitude to the negotiations caused Stalin finally to decide to make a bargain with Germany rather than to join in resistance to Hitler.

In the winter of 1938/9 conversations took place between Beck, the

Polish Foreign Minister, Ribbentrop, his German counterpart, and Hitler himself. The Germans asked for relatively minor concessions from Poland to settle Polish–German differences. Danzig, established in 1919, in spite of its overwhelmingly German population, as a separate 'free city' under the League of Nations, would return to Germany, and the Polish Corridor, a strip of territory designed to give Poland secure access to Danzig and the sea, which separated East Prussia from the rest of Germany, was to be crossed by a road over which Germany should have extraterritorial rights. In return there were hints that Germany would assist an expansion of Polish influence or territory at the expense of the Soviet Union. What Poles objected to was that Poland would become a dependent satellite of Germany; only by avoiding the extremes of hostility or close friendship either with Germany or the Soviet Union could Poland maintain independence. The Polish government refused Hitler's offers. Hence, in the spring of 1939, Poland ceased to be a possible ally of Hitler's and became an object of conquest. The British guarantee of assistance to Poland meant that European war would begin if German forces attacked.

Having ceased to try for Polish aid against the Soviet Union, Hitler began to seek Soviet help against Poland. On 23 August the Nazi–Soviet pact was signed: it included secret provisions for Soviet spheres of interest in the countries bordering on the Soviet Union and, as became evident in September, arrangements for the partition of Poland. Hitler imagined that the failure of Britain and France to secure Soviet help would cause them to abandon Poland, but two days later Britain signed the formal Anglo-Polish alliance. Evidently surprised, Hitler postponed the German attack to give himself time to persuade the British to abandon its ally. His suggestion was the old one: that Britain should cease to interfere in eastern Europe while, in return, Germany would support the perpetuation of the British Empire.

On the British side the reaction, with some doubts on Chamberlain's part, was to believe that Hitler was being compelled to back down and that a continued British refusal to abandon Poland was the only way to prevent a war. But the British government was not bluffing: if its threats failed to deter Hitler then it intended to carry them out. For Hitler, however, it was impossible to climb down, especially since the British this time insisted that he could have no concessions without giving some serious guarantees that German policy was ceasing to be warlike. If Britain were to deny him a free hand in the east, Hitler must fight sooner or later, and he was more likely to secure the support of public opinion for a war in resisting British interference in a solution of German grievances against Poland than in any other context.

Both Hitler and the British, therefore, felt driven into war in September 1939. Their objects were incompatible: Hitler wished to remodel eastern Europe in a way that required the use of powerful armed forces, and success would make Germany dominant in Europe. The British government must resist this, if it could, unless Nazi Germany could be trusted never to exploit this dominance to limit British independence. But Hitler's Germany seemed peculiarly predisposed to use force to impose its wishes on foreign countries and to regard their independence as a threat, and by the summer of 1939 the government and, it seems, the majority of the British people, thought Hitler a menace to British safety. This was an unsurprising effect of strident Nazi praise of violence, coupled with well-publicized displays of strength, and the use of armed force to break treaties in the Rhineland, Austria, and Czechoslovakia.

Britain declared war on 3 September 1939 to prevent German domination of Europe. However, it was not the result merely of an impersonal calculation of forces: the power that threatened to dominate Europe was one whose conduct, even before the war, suggested that its dominance might be intolerable. The conduct of the rulers of Germany during the war brought added retrospective justification to the British decision.

The German attack on Poland was the occasion, not the cause, of Britain's going to war, though it was the German propensity to launch such attacks which caused the war. By then the British government knew that neither British nor French action could prevent the rapid conquest of Poland. The Polish government and people, on the other hand, expected much more from the western allies. The Poles were profoundly attached to national independence and readier than most national groups to take risks in its defence. Whatever their allies might do, it would have been difficult for any Polish government to give in to the Germans. A heroic defeat and the maintenance of national self-respect would have been more acceptable. No one, however, can have anticipated the frightful suffering they had to endure between 1939 and 1945.

Among the belligerents of 1939, the average Frenchman probably went most reluctantly to war. For most Germans an attack on Poland had some appeal; the French were faced only with the prospect of defeating German power. That they had to do this meant that victory in the First World War had proved useless. There was nothing to gain in a new war and, as 1914–18 suggested, much to lose even in victory. A declining birth-rate gave France a population structure poorly adapted for war, and it had suffered more than any other great power during the previous struggle. The Treaty of Versailles, France's pre-war alliances with Belgium, Czechoslovakia, and Poland, and its links with Yugoslavia and Romania had supposedly made France safe. Faced with Hitler, French governments insisted that Versailles should be upheld, but were reluctant to risk war to enforce it. French governments, therefore, did nothing to conciliate Germany by concessions but, on the other hand, willingly exploited pretexts for inactivity when Hitler seized what he wanted by direct action. This was the pattern followed at the time of German rearmament in breach of the treaties, when the German air force was re-created, at the time of the unilateral German remilitarization of the Rhineland, and of the invasion of Austria. This process of no concession but no resistance led to a steady weakening of France compared with Germany and an increasing divergence between those who favoured a definite choice of one course or the other as more likely to bring France a tolerable future.

In 1938 the Daladier government, which was in power from April 1938 until March 1940, was deeply divided over Czechoslovakia. It was not too difficult to agree that a firm attitude should be shown to Hitler—most French politicians rejected Chamberlain's belief that concessions would make him less dangerous—the difficulty was to work out what to do if Hitler used force. The problem was particularly acute since France was bound by treaty to defend Czechoslovakia against German attack. Within the government the Foreign Minister, Georges Bonnet, and, more indecisively, the Prime Minister, Edouard Daladier, favoured giving way in the last resort rather than war; others, like Reynaud and Mandel, disagreed and argued for war, or rather, argued that willingness to go to war provided the only chance in the long run of avoiding it. In 1938 Chamberlain's determination to seek agreement with Hitler enabled Bonnet and Daladier to persuade their colleagues to retreat and to abandon the Czech alliance while the British took the blame.

The loss of Czechoslovakia worried the chiefs of the French armed forces, especially their head, General Gamelin. To compensate they asked for a serious British land contribution in a possible war, more than the two divisions which were all the British would promise in 1938. As a result of the fear of a German attack in the Low Countries—acute early in 1939—and of the German occupation of Prague in March, the French got the British to agree to conscription in peacetime and to the creation of a far larger army—thirty-two divisions—than had been contemplated before. This went with a British promise to defend France against any attack. By these concessions, British ministers hoped to stiffen French resolve, though Chamberlain hoped also to secure influence over French policy in order to induce French ministers to be conciliatory towards Italy.

After March 1939, and the German occupation of Prague, it was clear to the French, too, that Hitlerian domination of eastern Europe could only be stopped by force. France was bound by treaty to defend Poland in case of German attack, a commitment which had been reasserted in 1936, and renewed in 1939 when Gamelin encouraged Polish resistance to German demands by promising a French attack to draw strength away from any German attack on Poland. The French government believed that it was highly desirable to get a new Russian alliance with a Russian promise of help to defend Poland. The threat of British, French, and Russian action might deter the Germans. Bonnet himself was eager for alliance, but when the negotiations failed he reverted to his position of the year before: if Germany climbed down, excellent; if not, France should do so. Thus Bonnet believed that, in the last resort, Poland should be induced or compelled to make concessions in order to avoid the embarrassment involved in another French desertion of an ally.

In 1939 Daladier, though still hesitant, was readier to face the risks of war than in 1938. After Munich, Bonnet had attempted to improve relations with the German government: Ribbentrop, the Nazi Foreign Minister, came to Paris in December 1938, and a friendly declaration was issued. The implication, which Ribbentrop later claimed Bonnet had explicitly accepted in private, was that the French were giving a free hand in the east to Hitler. The events of the first half of 1939, however, emphasized the disadvantages of such a bargain. The seizure of Prague advertised Hitler's untrustworthiness. At the beginning of 1939, Italian claims to French territory were noisily revived, and the 'Pact of Steel' between Italy and Germany, made in April 1939, added the threat of German support for Italian claims.

It seemed, therefore, increasingly unsafe for France to permit Hitler to dominate eastern Europe. Especially after the failure of negotiations for a Soviet alliance, however, resistance to Hitler meant a risk of immediate war. At the end of August, when a German attack on Poland became imminent, the French government reconsidered the whole sombre situation. Bonnet suggested that the French guarantee to Poland against attack should be abandoned. Gamelin, on the other hand, made the case for honouring the guarantee by a declaration of war. If Poland resisted, fighting in the east could be expected to go on long enough to make it impossible for Germany to attack France in 1939, and so enable the French forces to benefit from increasing arms production. The firm British attitude meant that France was, this time, sure of assistance, and the British Expeditionary Force would make it easier to defend France in 1940. Without Russian aid, France could not spare enough forces from the German front to knock out Italy at the start of the war. In the last week of August, therefore, information that Italy would stay neutral confirmed Gamelin's reasoning. For Gamelin the loss of the Russian alliance made it the more necessary to seize the momentary advantages of Italian neutrality and British determination to fight. Daladier's hesitations and those of other French ministers were overcome by the determination shown by the Polish and British governments: if France were ever to fight for its independence against German expansion, August 1939 seemed the best time to do it.

Governments conducted foreign affairs and assembled military strength, launched attacks and declared war. They felt themselves responsible for maintaining the safety and independence of their populations and were therefore probably more sensitive about threats to them than most ordinary citizens. It is difficult to assess how far the four governments that went to war in 1939 had the support of their populations. Acquiescence, at least, was general: a reluctant acquiescence in a war thought of as defensive, even by Germans, who saw it as brought about by western interference in a belated German attempt to right one of the wrongs of Versailles. Enthusiasm was everywhere absent: 1914–18 was too recent.

In Britain there seems to have been more positive support for war than in France; as war approached, the British government felt that it must appear to be standing firm or risk the hostility of public opinion as represented in Parliament. In France, on the other hand, Daladier felt it essential to make it seem that every chance of a peaceful solution was being explored. This was shown in the difference in response to last-minute Italian attempts to prevent war. The efforts made for many years by British governments to redress German grievances by peaceful means had by 1939, it seems, convinced British opinion that Hitler must be stopped, if necessary by force. French opinion, used to governments which proclaimed their vigilant defiance of Germany, was perhaps less readily convinced that the path of peaceful negotiation had been explored sufficiently to justify the alternative of war. However, opinion polls in both countries suggested more or less reluctant support for resistance. In July 1939 'Yes' votes to the question whether war on Germany should follow a German attack on Poland were given by 76 per cent of respondents in both Britain and France: a remarkable coincidence.

Poland was invaded at dawn on 1 September 1939. The British declaration of war was held up, by French desire for delay, until 12 noon on 3 September, and the French followed at 5 p.m.

2

German conquest of Poland, Norway, the Low Countries, and France

THE war began with the German attack on Poland. The Germans intended to conquer Poland quickly before autumn rain made movement difficult and before the French could attack in the west. Polish commanders hoped to resist German attacks until the French offensive they counted on drew German troops away. Gamelin, the Commander-in-Chief of French land forces in time of war, had promised a French attack beginning on the sixteenth day of mobilization, which pointed to 12 September. That Poland chose to fight Germany had one immediately satisfactory result: French mobilization proceeded undisturbed. Thereafter, British and French strategists hoped for protracted Polish resistance in order to delay German concentration against their armies in the west until the British Expeditionary Force in France had been expanded and fully trained. They feared, however, that the resistance of the main Polish armies would not last long. Estimates varied from six weeks to three months. Afterwards a guerrilla war might be kept going, with Russian aid, in eastern Poland. The Nazi–Soviet pact removed that hope.

Poland was defended by thirty regular infantry divisions plus ten of reserves. Mobile forces consisted of eleven brigades of horsed cavalry and one armoured brigade. British pressure on the Poles at the end of August to delay their mobilization in order not to give the Germans an excuse to attack meant that the reserve divisions were not ready in time. The Germans employed fifty-five divisions. Of these, twenty-four were infantry divisions of the 'first wave', containing four-fifths regular soldiers and one-fifth reservists recently released from active service. Fifteen were infantry divisions of categories 2 or 3, with regular cadres and high-quality young reservists. All ordinary German infantry divisions marched on foot, with transport and artillery drawn by horses. The remaining sixteen divisions were about to open a new chapter in the history of warfare. They included all the best units: many contained only regular soldiers and they were all fully mechanized. Six were panzer divisions. These were made up of heavy and medium tank units with motorized infantry and artillery. Their role was breakthrough and exploitation: the overrunning of defences followed by fast-moving attacks on lines of communication, supply, and command. The other ten were motorized infantry divisions to be used for rapid consolidation of newly-captured key positions. The slower-moving infantry divisions occupied ground and dealt with pockets of isolated enemy troops left by the advancing panzers.

Polish dispositions were not suited to meet this type of attack. The Polish command had two options: one was to keep armoured and other mobile divisions in reserve ready to carry out prompt counter-attacks against any breaches in defensive deployments, but for this option the Poles were totally unequipped; the only other was to establish defensive positions in great depth, to prevent an armoured breakthrough. Polish strategy made this difficult, as the Polish command tried to defend the whole of an extremely long frontier, from Slovakia to East Prussia. Apparently, the intention was to attempt a fighting retreat from advanced positions, holding on to territory, especially the manufacturing areas, as long as possible, until the French attack in the west reduced German strength in the east. The result was to facilitate the German object of breakthrough and envelopment.

German success was helped by overwhelming air superiority: about 2,000 German aircraft against about 600, mostly obsolete, Polish aircraft. The Polish air force, with inadequate early-warning systems, was largely destroyed on the ground. The Luftwaffe was able to support the ground troops and to attack Polish headquarters and communications. Within a week, all the defending armies, except one, had been broken into separate fragments, and several Polish divisions had been encircled. The counter-attack launched on 10 September by the one intact Polish army led only to its own encirclement. Two weeks after the beginning of the invasion, most of the Polish fighting forces were contained in detached pockets, the largest around Kutno, Radom, and Warsaw. Warsaw surrendered, after obstinate resistance, on 27 September, but some Polish units continued fighting until 6 October.

By then, an event ominous for Britain and France had taken place. Russian troops began to advance into Polish territory on 17 September. Poland was about to be partitioned between Germany and the Soviet Union. It became clear that Germany and the Soviet Union had reached some kind of bargain which implied Soviet support for Germany, as distinct from a strict neutrality which would have kept German troops in Poland to watch the Red Army. Stalin was giving Hitler a free hand in the west. Moreover, Soviet supplies of minerals and raw materials seriously

POLAND: FRONTIERS in 1939 and the SOVIET-GERMAN PARTITION

lessened the effect of the allied maritime blockade of Germany.

Allied strategy was therefore brought into question. Anglo-French strategy was one of delay. The allied staffs had agreed that, as time passed, the ability of Britain and France to defend themselves against attack would increase, while economic blockade and, later, aerial bombardment, would erode German power and morale. Eventually Hitler would be overthrown by discontented Germans or, in the last resort, an allied invasion would topple his enfeebled regime. There was much to be said in favour of this strategy. Hitler himself seems to have made the same basic assumption, that time was not on his side. He was eager to launch an early attack on France, imposed the idea on his generals, and initially ordered it to begin on 12 November 1939. It was postponed twenty-nine times before the eventual date of 10 May 1940. In some respects, British and French strength was increasing faster than that of the Germans. In the first six months of 1940 the combined Anglo-French production of tanks was 1,412 compared with a German total of 558. In the months from January to May 1940 Anglo-French aircraft production was 6,794, against a German total of little over one-half that figure. The British government and its military advisers continued to have faith in the passive strategy of defence against German attack, and reliance on blockade to make the success of such an attack less and less likely.

The French were much less complacent. Co-operation between the Soviet Union and the Germans would allow a German attack in the west to be made using all the best units of the German army. Meanwhile, in the French view, Soviet help for Hitler made ineffective the blockade of Germany. To the French, Germany was growing stronger, while the British land contribution to the defence of France increased very slowly. Unless something were done, the French believed, to counter the Soviet contribution, France might be overwhelmed before Anglo-French strength could catch up. The British, on the contrary, thought that the Nazi–Soviet understanding would not last for long and that, in the meantime, the blockade of Germany still had some effect. The British ministry of economic warfare insisted that time favoured the allies and that Germany could not overcome increasing economic problems. Above all, the British had more confidence that France could be defended than the French themselves had. The French prime ministers, first Daladier and then Reynaud, and the service chiefs, Gamelin for the army, Darlan for the navy, and Vuillemin for the air force, eagerly sought extra ways of weakening Germany to reduce the weight of attack the Germans could mount against France. They pressed four schemes on the British. One was to stir up fighting in south-eastern Europe and to build up an allied force at Salonika to foster it. Two more schemes were intended to reduce Soviet help for Germany. At the end of November 1939 the Soviet government, exploiting the acquiescence in territorial expansion given by Germany in the Nazi–Soviet agreement, attacked Finland. French ministers were especially eager to support Finnish resistance. A third suggestion was to bomb Russian oilfields in the Caucasus. The final proposal was to interrupt the supply of high-grade iron ore from northern Sweden to Germany. The first three ideas caused controversy between Britain and France. Anglo-French interference in south-eastern Europe, the British thought, was risky without Italian support. They did not wish to drive Mussolini into a decision, which might go the wrong way, on war for or against Germany; indeed, the British government, especially Chamberlain himself, regarded Italian neutrality as helpful. The British totally disagreed with the French view that it might be sensible to risk war with the Soviet Union. The British believed that Nazi–Soviet co-operation would not last; the French feared it might last long enough to see the defeat of France. The British, therefore, were reluctant whole-heartedly to support Finland and managed to shelve the alarming French schemes for bombing Russian territory.

The only agreed suggestion was to cut off German supplies of Swedish iron-ore. At first an excuse for sending allied troops along the railway across northern Norway and Sweden was to be found on the pretext of bringing aid to Finland. Those troops could then seize the iron-ore fields and the export routes from them. After Finland surrendered, on 12 March 1940, a new device was worked out. The British agreed to lay mines in Norwegian territorial waters to block the ice-free route used by iron-ore carriers going to Germany. If, as was hoped, the Germans retaliated by invading the Scandinavian countries, then an allied expedition could at once seize the northern territories, with the iron-ore fields. In the end, Hitler acted first with his own preventive invasion.

Bickerings between the British and French continued. Together with French political changes, they caused delay to the allied operations in Norway. The allegedly more energetic Reynaud had succeeded Daladier as Prime Minister on 21 March. However, at first he had to retain the latter as minister of national defence. Daladier's ill-will obstructed Anglo-French agreement. On 8 April 1940 the British began mine-laying around the Norwegian coast; but pre-emptive action had already begun. German supply ships had left port for Norway on 3 April, and four fast warships with troops on board, followed on 6 April. The British, therefore, immediately called off mine-laying, abandoned their plan to land troops in Norway, and ordered out all available warships to attack the German ships at sea. British soldiers already embarked for Norway were disembarked and did not sail until 12 April. In consequence, the allies were faced with the need to dislodge German forces who had had time to establish themselves in Denmark and Norway and who, using warships as troop transports, had arrived as far north as the iron-ore port of Narvik. British troops landed in central Norway and were turned out again. Further north, Anglo-French forces recaptured Narvik, with much difficulty, and then left it after the German attack on France. In central Norway, German air power hampered troops and endangered warships; in the far north, British naval superiority only slowly counter-balanced the German advantage of first occupation. In the whole campaign the Germans were helped by their success in decoding a high proportion of signals in the main British naval cipher. The resulting German seizure of Norway safeguarded iron-ore supplies and helped naval war against Britain. British failure in Norway brought about the fall of the Chamberlain government.

- Railways from the Swedish iron-ore mines

| 0 | 100 | 200 | 300 | 400 | 500 | 600 km |

| 0 | 100 | 200 | 300 | 400 miles |

N

FINLAND

Narvik
Kiruna
Gallivare

Lulea

Trondheim

NORWAY

SWEDEN

Helsinki

SHETLANDS

ORKNEYS

USSR

DENMARK

GREAT
BRITAIN

NETHERLANDS

BELGIUM

'GREAT
GERMANY'

LUX.

SLOVAKIA

FRANCE

HUNGARY

RUMANIA

SWITZ.

ITALY

YUGOSLAVIA

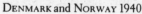

DENMARK and NORWAY 1940

The next great turning-point of the war began on 10 May 1940, when the Germans attacked Holland, Belgium, Luxemburg, and France. The events of the next six weeks determined the broad outline of the entire war. The defeat of France made possible the German attack on Russia; that Britain fought on enabled the United States to intervene in Europe. The historian of the Second World War must, therefore, take special care to analyse and explain these events.

It had been taken for granted that the German attack on France would come through Belgium and Luxemburg. An attack across the Franco-German frontier into Alsace-Lorraine was unlikely because it offered less opportunity for encircling manœuvres to secure a quick decision, and because of the French fortifications behind the frontier—the so-called Maginot Line. This had been designed to prevent a sudden German incursion into France before French mobilization could be completed, and to economize on the forces needed to defend that part of the French frontier in order to concentrate more resources further north, for the French army, of course, did not rely solely on the Maginot Line for the defence of France.

The virtual certainty that a German land attack would go through Belgium raised political and strategic problems for the French authorities. In 1936 the Belgian government declared Belgian neutrality in any European war, and gave up the alliance with France made after the First World War. The Belgian hope was that a firmly declared intention to deny Belgium to French armies would remove any motive for a pre-emptive German attack. This made sense, provided that the next European war began in the east and that Germany welcomed Belgian neutrality as a means of hampering French interference. However, if Germany were at war with France but at peace in the east, then a German attack on Belgium was nearly certain. Even so, the Belgian government did not change its attitude: French troops would not be allowed in until German troops had entered Belgium. Very secret and limited Franco-Belgian and Anglo-Belgian military contacts took place to work out what should happen then, but nothing more.

Two options were open to the defenders of France in case of German attack through Belgium. One was to leave the Belgians to their fate and defend the French frontier. The advantage was that well-prepared positions could be constructed there. There were, however, great disadvantages. All Belgian resources would be lost, a much longer line would have to be defended, and the Germans would come dangerously close to some of the most highly industrialized parts of France.

Moreover, German use of Belgian ports would seriously worsen the naval threat to British sea communications. It is not surprising that the French command chose the second option, to advance into Belgium once the German attack had begun. There remained disagreement about how far the allies should go forward. General Gamelin, the commander of all French land forces and supreme allied commander, encouraged by recent assurances that Belgian forces would co-operate both in advance preparations and in operations when the time came, imposed a highly venturesome solution, 'Plan D'. Most of his subordinates preferred 'Plan E', under which the bulk of the defending forces would remain on the frontier. Only the allied left wing on the Franco-Belgian frontier, which meant the British Expeditionary Force, would move forward to the line of the Scheldt from Tournai to Ghent and Antwerp, covering only the western extremity of Belgium. Gamelin favoured 'Plan D', to defend the line of the river Dyle from Wavre to Louvain and Antwerp, and then on a line, in advance of Gembloux, to the Meuse line from Namur to Sedan. Most of Belgium, including Brussels, would then be denied to the Germans. Gamelin supported, too, an adventurous addition, a plan to dispatch a highly mobile French army to enter Dutch territory in order to hold, with possible Dutch assistance, the mouths of the Scheldt. On 10 May 1940 'Plan D', with this 'Breda variant', went into effect.

The size and equipment of the allied forces that faced the German attack in the west in 1940 gave them a reasonable chance of successful defence: the assumption that the Germans were overwhelmingly superior in numbers or equipment is incorrect. On 10 May the German army in the west had 136 divisions, of which eighty-nine were then in the front-line armies. Of the infantry divisions, forty-six were 'first-wave' divisions—about four-fifths of their personnel, of nearly 18,000 men in each division, were regulars. There were six motorized infantry divisions and ten panzer divisions. The six panzer divisions that had fought in Poland now had a reduced tank strength and a doubled establishment of motorized infantry. The four newly created panzer divisions had a still smaller tank strength. In practice, the tank strength of the panzers in May 1940 averaged about 250. Of the 2,500 or so tanks, over half were obsolescent and highly vulnerable light tanks, the PzKw marks I and II. The panzer divisions also each included four battalions of motorized infantry, a motorcycle battalion, and a motorized artillery regiment, plus anti-tank and reconnaissance battalions and engineer, signal and service units.

The French army had the equivalent of ninety-one divisions, of which three were armoured, three were 'light mechanized divisions' (DLM), and five cavalry. Thirty-one of the infantry divisions, the 'A' divisions, had a preponderance of regulars in their strength of about 16,500 men. By May 1940 seven infantry divisions were motorized. The Light Cavalry Divisions were largely mechanized and partially armoured. The DLMs bore more resemblance to the German panzer divisions of 1940 than did the French armoured divisions, the *Divisions Cuirassées de Réserve*. The DLMs had a full strength of 200 tanks, of which about half were H-35s, equivalent to the German PzKw mark III, or Somuas, comparable to the heaviest German tank of 1940, the PzKw IV. They included three battalions of motorized infantry, motorcycle squadrons, and reconnaissance battalions, field and anti-tank artillery, engineers, anti-aircraft, and signal units, and so, like the German panzers, they were effective combinations of all arms. Their numerical strength was similar, somewhat over 10,000 men. French armoured divisions, the DCRs, had a strength of 156 tanks of which about ninety were H-39s and 66 the *Char B*. The latter, though slow, and with dangerously short range, was more heavily armoured and effectively gunned than any German tank. The DCRs were smaller units than the DLM, with about 6,500 men. They had only one battalion of motorized infantry, no reconnaissance or motor-cycle units, one company of engineers and signals personnel, and artillery both field and anti-tank. On 10 May only the 1st and 2nd armoured divisions were complete and up to strength. A considerably higher proportion of German armour, therefore, was organized in mobile divisions than was the case in the French army, where more tanks were allotted to direct support of infantry battalions. It is obviously wrong, however, to imagine that the French high command was ignorant of the value of armoured divisions.

The British had ten infantry divisions, slightly smaller than French and German divisions—about 13,600 men. Five of them were largely made up of regular soldiers. Five were territorial divisions, made up of volunteers who had engaged in part-time training as civilians with regular cadres. All the British divisions had motor transport for equipment and supplies but most did not have lorries for their infantry. Some of the territorial divisions were under strength, incompletely trained, and short of transport. There were two light-armoured reconnaissance brigades of fifty-six light tanks each, four regiments each with twenty-eight light tanks, and an army tank brigade with 100 infantry tanks. The latter were 'Matildas', slow, but so heavily armoured as to be invulnerable to all enemy weapons except field artillery or 88-mm anti-aircraft guns adapted to an anti-tank role. Matildas armed with two-pounder guns were, in 1940, superior in all short-range tank-to-tank combat. After the battle had begun a British armoured division arrived, but never fought as a complete division. At full strength it had 312 medium 'cruiser' tanks and supporting arms, including two motorized infantry battalions. With ten Belgian divisions added to the British and French, allied ground troops were equal in numbers to the German attackers. In numbers of troops of the best quality, the Germans were superior, with nearly one million men in preponderantly regular divisions compared with about 650,000 in the British and French forces. Total numbers of tanks were about equal, but the Germans had about 1,200 of their heavier combat tanks available in mobile units on 10 May, compared with about 850 in similar British and French units.

In the air the allies were inferior: there were 1,046 French aircraft in first-line service on the north-eastern front, plus 416 British and about 300 Belgian and Dutch aircraft. The Germans had available more than 3,000. The disparity was made even worse by the comparative quality of the aircraft employed. The Germans had at least 2,000 up-to-date machines, while most of the French and British were obsolete or obsolescent, partly because the British insisted on reserving their main bomber force for possible strategic attack on the Ruhr region, and on holding back most of their best fighter squadrons for home defence.

German superiority in numbers and equipment was not great enough to bring about the defeat of France in 1940. This was achieved by tactical surprise and superior German organization. It is often claimed that there were more profound causes: for instance, that democratically governed countries tend to produce inferior armies than do authoritarian or dictatorial regimes. The evidence accumulated since the French Revolution does not convincingly support this view. It is possible that societies where the armed forces are regarded with particular respect may have especially effective soldiers, and perhaps such societies are especially prone to authoritarianism. However, such societies might do even better if democratically governed so that war might be based on consent. The German government would certainly have been less aggressive if democracy had survived in Germany; indeed, a general European war would have been impossible. It is hard to say how far Hitler's zeal for armed struggle infected the Germans he ruled; though German victory over France was popular enough in Germany, what evidence there is suggests that it was mainly because it seemed likely to bring a rapid end to an unpopular war.

BELGIUM and NE FRANCE: GERMAN BREAKTHROUGH 1940

Many writers have suggested that the workings of French democracy had introduced so great a degree of dissension as to make it difficult for French citizens to work together to defend their country. Some of the political right, it is alleged, were ready to welcome military defeat in order to end dangers of left-wing dominance. It is true that the defeat when it came was exploited by the Vichy regime in this way. That consequence of the defeat was, however, not necessarily one of its causes. Only a tiny minority of the right wanted France to be conquered, though once it had happened defeat was promptly blamed on the left. On the left, complete pacifism, steadily eroded by Nazi conduct, was rare after March 1939. It is true that the Communists became hostile to the war after the Nazi–Soviet pact, but the effect was to weaken the party more than to weaken France, for except among the most dedicated militants, the new party line was accepted with great reluctance. On the civilian side, French military production had reached a high level by the outbreak of war.

So, it must be asked if the defeat can reasonably be attributed to strictly military causes. We have already seen that allied armies began to advance to a line of defence in Belgium and Holland as soon as those countries appealed for aid against the Germans on 10 May 1940. Among them were the bulk of the best and most mobile units available, including almost the whole of the British Expeditionary Force. The French high command supposed that the main weight of the German attack would be north of Namur in the Belgian plain. Strong French forces, plus the British, were to move to the line Namur–Wavre–Louvain–Antwerp–Breda. The Belgians were to delay the German advance to this position and then fall back to hold the Louvain–Antwerp sector. The French 7th Army included one DLM and two motorized infantry divisions as well as four other infantry divisions, two of which were held in reserve. The Belgian army had six divisions on the front to be held, the British moved up four, with four in reserve. The French 1st Army was very strong. Six infantry divisions, all regular divisions, half of them motorized, moved forward to defensive positions north of Namur. The two DLMs were pushed ahead of the main body and used as cavalry to co-operate with the Belgian covering forces in delaying the German approach to the main line of resistance. Then, in theory, they were to be withdrawn into reserve for possible counter-attacks. North of Namur, then, the French and the British employed twenty-nine divisions, of which three were armoured and five motorized, while the infantry were regulars or high-quality reservists. These reinforced the bulk of the Belgian army. Against them (and the Dutch army) the Germans placed Army Group B with twenty-eight divisions, of which three were panzers and two motorized infantry. South of Namur against the French defences in the sector Namur–Sedan–Longwy, the Germans put Army Group A of forty-four divisions, with a spearhead of seven panzer and three motorized divisions. In defence against this formidable German force were deployed, behind a light cavalry screen, thirteen French infantry divisions, one of which was a regular motorized division, but three of which were series 'B' divisions made up of the lowest category of reservists. This German concentration of highly mobile divisions, prepared to break through the defences in the Meuse between Namur and Sedan, resulted from a change of plan.

The original German plan was to make Army Group B the more powerful and to use it on the northern flank to sweep west and south. Allied dispositions could have countered such a manœuvre with success. However, the influence of Rundstedt, commanding Army Group A, and his Chief of Staff, Manstein, with some support from Hitler, caused Brauchitsch and the army high command to recast the plan and give nearly all the mobile and armoured divisions to Army Group A. They would strike for the coast to separate the allied forces in Belgium from those in France and cut the supply lines of the northern armies.

The Germans achieved surprise. Both the date of the attack and the point of their principal effort were unexpected. Repeated last-minute cancellations of previous attacks meant German advanced forces were in position well before 10 May. Behind them, the location of the heavy concentration of German armour in the area Bonn–Euskirchen gave no indication which part of the allied front north of the Maginot Line was principally threatened. High-level German signals were not being successfully decoded by the allies at the critical moment. On their side, by contrast, German success in decoding French signals from the Ministry of War meant that their high command was forewarned of Gamelin's intention to advance to the Dyle and knew the allied strength and dispositions. It was no accident that the Germans attacked weak sectors of the French front. The invaders advanced faster than the French had anticipated; by the end of 13 May German troops had crossed the Meuse, south of Namur, around Sedan, near Dinant, and at Monthermé. At Sedan and Dinant tanks began to cross on 14 May, at Monthermé on 15 May.

The unexpected strength of the German forces in an unexpected sector could be countered only by rapid reaction and redeployment by the French. At this stage inferior staff work and inadequacies in the higher commands brought defeat. The effects were most decisive in the handling of the French armoured formations. The two 'light mechanized divisions' which had gone ahead to cover 1st Army's advance through Belgium were to have been withdrawn into reserve after this task was accomplished. In fact, infantry divisions managed to get the tank units split up to stiffen their defences, and these two excellent, well-trained, and powerful divisions were not available again as mobile fighting organizations until 21 May, after much wear and tear.

On 10 May the three armoured divisions were concentrated in reserve near Reims. Next day the 1st Armoured Division was ordered to Charleroi. Early on 14 May it was told to counter-attack the Dinant bridgehead. But it could not complete the move to its assembly area until night, and supplies for refuelling were delayed until midday on 15 May. By that time the division was under attack from the 7th Panzer. By next day only seventeen tanks remained, and the division was no longer an effective fighting force: lack of fuel explained a high proportion of the losses, while other tanks had lost their way. The 2nd Armoured Division was also ordered to Charleroi and moved on 13 May. Next day Georges, the French Commander-in-Chief in the north-east, changed its destination to Signy l'Abbaye to use it against the Sedan breakthrough. Unfortunately the tanks and artillery had gone by rail to points further north than the wheeled vehicles. By the evening of 15 May, advanced German armour had separated the two parts of the division which ceased for some time to be fit for battle. On 13 May, the 3rd Armoured and the 3rd Motorized Infantry Division were ordered to concentrate south of Sedan. By dawn on the 14th they were at Le Chesne under orders to attack northwards 'with the utmost vigour and determination'. They were not fuelled and ready to advance until 4 p.m. Then the corps commander postponed the attack and ordered 3rd Armoured to take up defensive positions. Next morning Georges intervened to insist on the attack. However, the armour could not be reassembled on that day, and on 16 May the attack was given up because of breakdowns.

In war between comparable forces victory goes to the side which suffers fewer delays and confusions and in which the chain of command is more lucid and effective. The best French troops and their equipment and morale were fully equal to those of the best German troops. They were defeated because too often they were not in the right place at the right time.

At the end of 14 May, Corap, commanding the 9th Army, faced with German crossings at Dinant and Sedan, ordered a general withdrawal and an attempt to hold a line further back. The process accelerated the collapse of his weaker static divisions, and on 15 May German armoured forces began to break out. On 16 May their forward elements had got 35 miles beyond the Meuse crossings; by 18 May, 80 miles; and, on 20 May, they reached the sea after covering 135 miles in a week. The northern French, British, and Belgian forces were separated from the bulk of the French armies. The panzers' advance was extremely daring: they were stretched out in long columns along the roads, moving fast, with only motorized infantry keeping pace. The slower-moving marching infantry, relying on horsed transport, followed. Meanwhile the Germans were vulnerable to counter-attack, but the allies had no suitable forces immediately available. What could have been done was shown by the attacks that were made. From the south of the German corridor to the sea the hastily improvised and incomplete 4th Armoured Division, commanded by de Gaulle, attacked on 17 May, reached Montcornet, and interrupted German road traffic. Having no infantry, however, de Gaulle was compelled to withdraw. On 19 May he attacked again with similar immediate results, which again could not be exploited for want of infantry and artillery support. From the north the British Tank Brigade, with two battalions of infantry and supporting artillery, attacked on 21 May to the south of Arras, their right being covered by what its commander could assemble of the 3rd French DLM. The British met Rommel's 7th Panzer Division, and withdrew the same day, after worrying the Germans. Hitler himself was told that strong British forces had attempted to break through to the south, and had temporarily succeeded in pushing the Germans back in several places.

These attacks, especially the British, inspired caution on the German side. However, a large-scale combined allied attack from north and south against the German corridor never took place. Orders for it were issued by Georges on 18 May, by Gamelin on 19 May, and again by his successor in overall command, Weygand, on 21 and 22 May. By the end of 25 May the idea had been abandoned. On the night of 23 May, Lord Gort, the British Commander-in-Chief, withdrew British forces (5th and 50th Divisions) from Arras. Next day General Besson, in command of the proposed French attack in the south, argued that the British withdrawal had permitted German reinforcement against his forces and so made his attack impossible. In spite of this, preparation continued to be made for an allied attack from the north, and in the morning of 25 May, Anglo-French conferences confirmed that three French divisions, with tanks, would co-operate with two British infantry divisions and the British tank brigade in an offensive to start on the evening of 26 May. However, later on 25 May Gort received news that Belgian retreats were opening a gap into which the Germans could advance and cut off the British from the coast. Gort ordered his British divisions earmarked for the allied attack from the north against the German corridor to fill this gap instead. Thus he kept open his line of retreat and saved the British army from possible annihilation. He informed the French only after he had given the orders. This was the end of all prospect of defeating the German incursion. Blanchard, in command in the north, called off the attack and directed that a bridgehead covering Dunkirk was to be formed and 'held with no thought of retreat'. British intentions were different. On the evening of 26 May the British Admiralty gave the order 'Operation DYNAMO is to commence'. The men of the British Expeditionary Force were to be brought home from Dunkirk.

Gort was not hopeful. He was not certain that he could get his forces safely back to the coast nor that they could be taken off if they got there. The Germans shared his view. Partly because of their confidence that the BEF was trapped, they inadvertently facilitated its escape. On 23 May, Rundstedt halted the advance of the forward panzer divisions now moving eastwards towards the Belgian coast and its hinterland. One reason was to allow infantry divisions to close up in order to guard against any more allied counter-attacks; the other was to avoid further weakening of the German armoured divisions which would be needed for the second phase of the French campaign. Offensive action by ground troops against the allied forces north of the German penetration was to be left to Army Group B. Hitler approved the decision and ordered renewed attacks only on 27 May. It was a mistake and not, as many writers claim, a deliberate gesture to conciliate the British: on 24 May Hitler had ordered the 'annihilation' of allied forces in the northern pocket, and the Luftwaffe was to prevent the escape of British forces. Though the British had begun to make contingency plans to take off the BEF as early as 19 May, the success of the evacuation remained long in doubt. On 28 May, Churchill believed that 50,000 men could certainly be got away but that 100,000 would be miraculous. Next day, Ironside, the Chief of the Imperial General Staff, thought there was 'very little chance of the whole BEF coming off'.

It was under these gloomy auspices that the British government considered whether or not to try to make peace with Hitler. Already, on 15 May, Churchill had felt it necessary to warn President Roosevelt: 'if necessary, we shall continue the war alone', and, he went on, 'we are not afraid of that'. On 25 May the service chiefs produced a formal report for the Cabinet on the prospects of continuing the war alone against Germany, and, very likely, against Italy too. They reckoned that the air force and navy together could prevent a landing in England that would be powerful enough and sustained for long enough to defeat Britain. If, on the other hand, the German army established itself ashore, all would be over: the British had only three-and-a-half fully equipped and trained divisions and two armoured brigades, while the Germans would have seventy available divisions. Air superiority must be retained. Without it the navy could not hold off invasion indefinitely. The Luftwaffe might try to win air superiority by bombing aircraft factories; the morale of the workers might then be decisive. Oddly the paper made no mention of the danger that brought Britain nearest to defeat—submarine attack on merchant shipping. The service staffs thought the supply of Britain principally to be endangered by air attack on the ports, and still underestimated the submarine. The conclusions of the paper were even more optimistic on the prospects of defeating Germany. Relying on evidence from the Ministry for Economic Warfare, the paper asserted that there would be a widespread shortage of food in Europe by the end of

1940. By the middle of 1941 Germany, lacking some key raw materials, would find it difficult to maintain weapons production, and by the end of that year shortage of oil would 'force Germany to weaken her military control in Europe'. These events could happen even sooner as a result of British bombing. Everything rested, though, on one underlined assumption: that the United States should be 'willing to give us full economic and financial support, *without which we do not think we could continue the war with any chance of success*'.

When Churchill put some supplementary questions to the Chiefs of Staff, he set out some of the peace terms he supposed Hitler would impose on Britain: 'terms . . . which would place her entirely at the mercy of Germany through disarmament, cession of naval bases in the Orkneys, etc.' So far as Hitler's real terms can be discovered, they seem to have been, as one Cabinet minister put it later in the summer, that he 'was prepared to call it off provided he could keep what he had got' with perhaps a colony or two. Still, it is hard to believe that Hitler would have allowed the Royal Navy and the Royal Air Force to remain effective.

The War Cabinet accepted the opinion of the Chiefs of Staff that Britain could continue the fight alone. Its discussion on whether or not to make peace came about indirectly as the result of a French request that the British should join in making offers to Mussolini to persuade him to stay out of the war. Mussolini, the Cabinet thought, would then try to act as an intermediary between Hitler and the western powers, so that negotiations with him might lead to peace negotiations with Germany. Discussion stretched over three days, from 26 to 28 May. Churchill, with some inconsistencies, took an increasingly defiant and belligerent line. At one moment he wished to wait until after the Dunkirk evacuation: 'The operation might be a great failure. On the other hand . . . we might save a considerable portion of the Force. . . . This would afford a real test of air superiority.' At another he said he would be prepared to consider peace terms and cede some overseas territories provided the essentials of British strength were retained. More and more eloquently and firmly, however, Churchill argued that acceptable terms were unobtainable from Hitler, that even to discuss terms would weaken the will to fight, and that it would be better 'if the worst came to the worst . . . to go down fighting'.

The change of government of 10 May 1940 now showed itself decisive. The House of Commons debate following the allied defeat in Norway had brought about Chamberlain's resignation as Prime Minister in favour of someone who could bring the Labour Party into a coalition government. The Labour Party vetoed Chamberlain but were ready to accept Halifax or Churchill. Halifax failed to seize the succession, which Chamberlain tried to win for him, and Churchill became Prime Minister. He kept Chamberlain and Halifax in his war Cabinet as representatives of the Conservative Party, which had the majority in the House of Commons. Now Halifax, who retained for the time being his old office as Foreign Secretary, wished to use Italy to open negotiations with Hitler. He thought that Hitler would not necessarily make excessive demands for peace, and he was obviously irritated by Churchill's frequent use of emotional rhetoric. He even hinted at resignation. The difference between them could not be solved by logic nor by any available evidence: Churchill believed that merely to discuss terms with Hitler would be intolerable, and that any such discussion would mean acceptance of defeat and therefore of Hitler's terms. Halifax thought terms could be considered and rejected if they impaired British independence. Churchill countered that 'we should then find that all the forces of resolution which were now at our disposal would have vanished', and declared that 'we should get no worse terms if we went on fighting, even if we were beaten, than were open to us now'.

Halifax was alone, however; only Chamberlain gave him any support, and then no further than to urge sympathetic treatment of a request from the despairing French. The Labour Party members, Attlee and Green-wood, backed Churchill. So did Archibald Sinclair, brought in to speak for the Liberal Party. During the third day of the War Cabinet's discussion Churchill got warm support when he talked to ministers outside that small body. He seems to have been surprised by the enthusiasm he aroused when he promised that there was no question of negotiation. Thereafter he did not waver, in public or in private, from a determined assertion that peace with Hitler was intolerable and that resistance to Germany would be hard and painful but that it could be and would be successful.

The prime minister thus expressed, and strengthened, 'forces of resolution' which, paradoxically, grew as German successes multiplied. The war was begun because Nazi Germany might threaten British independence: German conquest of Poland, Denmark, Norway, Lux-emburg, Holland, and Belgium, and the dramatic breakthrough to the English channel confirmed German power and ruthlessness. Hitler must be checked or Britain's independence would be gone.

Meanwhile, more soldiers were getting away from Dunkirk, most from the harbour, many from the beaches. 765 British ships went to Dunkirk, two-thirds of them civilian. From 27 May to 4 June, 338,000 men were taken off, nearly 140,000 of whom were French. The French authorities ordered their troops to leave only on the fifth day of evacuation. Until then they clung to the hope of maintaining a large bridgehead, a futile hope because it could not have been supplied. As a result, the French played the main part in preventing the Germans from wiping out the allied pocket, and in the closing stages of withdrawal the rearguard was entirely French. This was a valuable service, since it turned out to be the British troops that mattered for the future of the war. Many of the best soldiers of the British army had gone to France. Even with their equipment and vehicles lost, their return greatly strengthened the British defence against invasion: the more troops the British could re-equip and assemble, the larger any German descent on the British coast would have to be and the more vulnerable to British naval and air attack.

In France, General Weygand was organizing his last line of defence, one which he expected to hold only briefly. He had at his disposal the four armoured divisions that had failed to halt the original German breakthrough but they had less than one-third of their original strength. By a considerable feat of organization three enfeebled mobile divisions were rebuilt with personnel evacuated from Dunkirk and brought back from England, and two more created from the remains of the cavalry divisions that had fought in Belgium. But now that most of the best French divisions had been lost, Weygand had only about forty-five divisions, many under strength, to try to hold the Somme–Aisne line 'without thought of retreat' against ninety-five divisions, including ten panzers, briefly rested and hastily brought up to strength. In a five-day battle, from 5 to 9 June, the 'Weygand line' was broken, and a brief French stand on the Seine–Marne line quickly failed. After 12 June the Germans pursued the beaten French to the Loire and beyond, isolating French forces still holding the Maginot Line, broken through at only two points.

Would France remain in the war? Metropolitan France might be overrun, but the French Empire remained, with some soldiers available, some air force units, and a powerful navy. A few units could still be shipped overseas from France. After Finland's surrender to the Soviet Union on 13 March 1940, Daladier had fallen as Premier to be replaced by Reynaud, the advocate of more vigorous prosecution of the war. In fact this did not lead to anything more than heightened rhetoric and increased quarrelling between Reynaud and Daladier, whose political strength caused him to be retained in the government, and intensified intriguing by Reynaud against Gamelin, Daladier's protégé. Reynaud got rid of Gamelin only on 19 May, in the middle of the battle; his replacement, Weygand, was militarily a sound choice, but politically disastrous. At the same time Reynaud brought Marshal Pétain into his government, apparently to inspire confidence in victory. He proved inappropriate for this purpose. Reynaud was intelligent, liberal-minded, passionately anti-Nazi, and an eloquent exponent of out-and-out struggle against Hitler's Germany. He was ambitious and well to the right in politics. His connections and associates included people for whom sustained resistance to Hitler was less overwhelming a priority than it was to him, and who were readier to count the cost.

With rising emphasis, Weygand told the government that there must be an armistice. Reynaud wanted him to surrender the armies in France, leaving the government to carry on the war from outside France. Weygand refused, and insisted that the government must be responsible for an armistice. Within Reynaud's government, Chautemps suggested that the Germans should be asked their terms. He argued, as Halifax had done a few weeks before at the time of Dunkirk, that harsh terms could be rejected after scrutiny. Reynaud failed to win enough support to defeat Chautemps, and resigned on 16 June 1940.

He was succeeded by Marshal Pétain who showed no hesitation in accepting defeat. Indeed he seemed almost to relish it as a suitable punishment for alleged French self-indulgence and as a means of constructing a new France based on self-sacrifice and a call to duty. Moreover, Pétain argued that the French government should not go overseas to continue the fight from the empire. This would be desertion, an abandonment of the French people to the enemy. Weygand wanted a French constitutional authority to be maintained in France, with armed forces at its disposal which would be preserved from the defeat, presumably by agreement with the Germans, in order to forestall disorder in France and a possible revolutionary take-over. The Communists, of course, now members of an illegal organization, were opposed to the war against Germany, because of the Nazi–Soviet pact. They might be expected to work against a continued struggle and so, perhaps, to win German support. In any case, both Pétain and Weygand thought that British resistance would soon be overwhelmed. Continued French resistance would therefore do no more than help the British to secure from the Germans better terms than the French, who had borne the brunt of the struggle. Pétain offered himself to France as its saviour and the Franco-German armistice was signed on 21 June.

The willingness of the French government to come to terms gave Hitler two enormous advantages. He could govern France by indirect rule through a government set up in the unoccupied zone of France—the whole of northern France and the Atlantic coast, including the railway to Spain, was occupied by German forces—and he could prevent the French fleet from joining the Royal Navy. On 18 June General de Gaulle, a recently appointed junior minister in Reynaud's government, taken from the successful command of the 4th Armoured Division, broadcast from London an appeal to the French to continue the fight. In contrast to Pétain, de Gaulle believed that the world war was only beginning, that the democracies would win it, and that France should be among the victors. Few responded. Governing officials in most of the French empire, including Morocco, Algeria, and Tunisia, however reluctantly, followed the lead of the legal authority, placing, as they saw it, the preservation of French unity before the need to defeat Hitler.

British control of the Mediterranean, the defence of Egypt and the Suez Canal, with Palestine, and the oilfields beyond, was further jeopardized by the Italian declaration of war on 10 June 1940. It is difficult confidently to ascribe any ideas or aspirations to Mussolini beyond that of power for himself. Dictator of Italy since 1925, he expressed many ideas at one time or another but their lack of consistency and their bombastic emptiness weaken their credibility. He came to power as the leader, or more accurately as the spokesman, of the Fascists, an association of bands of violent political groups engaged in physical and moral intimidation of left-wing organizations and trade unions in town and countryside, especially in areas north of Rome. Some old-fashioned liberal politicians found it congenial to collaborate with the Fascists against Socialists and the Christian progressive party, rather than to work with these groups against the Fascists. Later on, Mussolini secured the support of the Church, of industrialists and businessmen, and of peasant proprietors, pleased by the destruction of agrarian unions and the high prices for their produce associated with the search for national self-sufficiency.

High-handed and sometimes violent, authoritarian Fascist dictatorship was justified by a classless appeal to nationalism and incoherent calls to 'greatness'. If Mussolini himself had any consistent aims, which is uncertain, national self-assertion was certainly one of them. Its appeal to Italians was limited compared with patriotic responses aroused in Germany, Britain, and France. The Italian population was, on average, considerably poorer and less educated, and the concept of Italian nationhood had comparatively restricted appeal. Still, national triumphs were approved by Fascists and by Monarchist conservatives, provided they could be secured without excessive sacrifices. National triumphs would strengthen Mussolini personally and perhaps help him to attack surviving non-Fascist institutions, like the monarchy itself.

Such considerations confirmed Mussolini's own inclination towards foreign adventure. The outbreak of war in September 1939 made him restless. Neutrality was not a suitable posture for a man of virility and violence. On the other hand, Britain and France together were alarmingly strong in the Mediterranean. The dramatic German victory of May 1940 precipitated a decision, and on 26 May Mussolini chose war. A few days later he told Hitler that Italy would declare war on 5 June, a date postponed, at Hitler's request, to 10 June. There followed eleven days of complete lack of success against France before the armistice. Yet it was not that Mussolini wished only to join the peace conference. On the contrary, he wanted the war to go on, and looked forward to Italian participation in armed encounters. Evidently he was ignorant of the weakness of the Italian armed services.

The wartime strength of the Italian army was large, on paper: seventy-three divisions, fifty-three in Italy and twenty in the empire. But only nineteen divisions were complete. There were three armoured divisions, but Italian tanks were either very light or mainly obsolete. Italy had 3300 military aircraft, but only 1800 were immediately usable and only about 1100 were reasonably modern. In theory the navy was a formidable force, with two battleships and two more nearly complete, seven heavy cruisers, twelve light cruisers, fifty-nine destroyers, sixty-seven motor torpedo boats, and no less than 115 submarines. However, most of the equipment, and the training of the ships' companies, were defective. The submarines were slow, noisy, shallow-diving, and of limited endurance. Individual officers and men were brave, and the mass of the soldiers were patient and good-humoured. However, most officers were self-centred, self-indulgent, and professionally ignorant. Italy lacked a traditional military class from which able officers could be drawn. Among the ranks, there was little of the national patriotism which, in the German army, overcame regional peculiarities. Metropolitan Italy was vulnerable and had to defend an overseas empire in Albania, Libya, the Dodecanese, recently-conquered Ethiopia, Italian Somaliland, and Eritrea. Mussolini, however, was not thinking of defence but of a 'war of a few months' in which Italy would take the offensive to create a satellite state at the expense of Yugoslavia, extend Albania at the expense of Greece, and above all drive the British out of Egypt and secure control of the Mediterranean and a safe route to east Africa through the Suez Canal. These ambitions proved absurd, but British force was required to make them so.

3

Britain alone

ON 18 June 1940 Churchill announced: 'the Battle of France is over; I expect that the Battle of Britain is about to begin.' Could Britain continue to resist? Would the population accept the immediate risks of making the attempt?

In May 1940 disaster followed disaster as the French army was baffled and outmanœuvred. It was a coincidence which brought Churchill to power when the battle began; the result was to give the government's voice a special quality at a moment when crisis made the British public receptive to leadership. Already on 10 May, when he became Prime Minister, he had much support: his pre-war allegations of inadequacies in rearmament, especially in the air, and his prophecy that the destruction of Czechoslovakia would rapidly follow its supposed salvation at Munich were remembered and conferred on Churchill a novel reputation for prescience and wisdom. His zeal for active war-making and his energy as a minister were sensed by the public as well as by politicians. At this moment of national decision three characteristics of Churchill's speeches gave them exceptional power. From the start he foretold hardships and dangers. In his first speech as Prime Minister, on 13 May, he told the House of Commons, 'I have nothing to offer but blood, toil, tears, and sweat. We have before us an ordeal of the most grievous kind. We have before us many, many long months of struggle and of suffering.' A second quality was the combination of uplifting calls to duty with cloudy but encouraging visions of a better future. Thus he declared on 18 June:

The whole fury and might of the enemy must very soon be turned on us. Hitler knows that he will have to break us in this island or lose the war. If we can stand up to him, all Europe may be free, and the life of the world may move forward into broad, sunlit uplands; but if we fail, then the whole world, including the United States, including all that we have known and cared for, will sink into the abyss of a new dark age made more sinister and perhaps more protracted by the lights of a perverted science. Let us therefore brace ourselves to our duties and so bear ourselves that if the British Empire and its Commonwealth last for a thousand years, men will still say 'This was their finest hour'.

The imprecision of these speeches avoided the detail of methods of defence or discussion of precise war aims. Matters were kept on a high emotional plane and so Churchill forestalled cool, reasoned controversy, which might be incompatible with self-sacrificing belligerence. Above all, their literary merit made sure that his speeches were listened to and remembered. The rolling magnificence of the language partly created, partly expressed the belief that the decision to fight on was the only possible response to French defeat:

We shall go on to the end. We shall fight in France, we shall fight on the seas and oceans, we shall fight with growing confidence and growing strength in the air, we shall defend our island, whatever the cost may be. We shall fight on the beaches, we shall fight on the landing grounds, we shall fight in the fields and in the streets, we shall fight in the hills; we shall never surrender . . .

Churchill made exhilarating the prospect of peril: 'rhetoric', as he later wrote, 'was no guarantee of survival', but it helped.

Hitler hoped for a compromise peace. Its terms were never made clear: probably Britain would have to recognize German dominance in continental Europe and return former German colonies while Germany would permit, and even assist, the continued existence of the British empire. Churchill's belief that the Germans would insist on disarming Britain in order to ensure fulfilment of such terms was almost certainly correct. We do not know, for the question never arose. After the fall of France, German peace feelers were brushed aside with scant evidence of interest in them from anyone other than R. A. Butler and the Duke of Windsor, who counted for little, and one or two quickly restrained British diplomats. Meanwhile, the German navy, army, and air force were tentatively considering the invasion of England. At the end of June, Jodl, of the German armed services High Command, drew up a paper on the continuation of the war against Britain, while Hitler decided that a display of force might be needed to bring the British to reason; it might even have to be used. On 2 July Hitler ordered plans to be made for invasion. Next day a ferocious act of war displayed the determination of the British government. The French fleet at Mers-el-Kébir, near Oran, was bombarded by British warships. Under the Franco-German armistice, French warships were to be disarmed under German or Italian supervision. Though the French naval Commander-in-Chief, Darlan, assured the British that French ships would never be used against them, the British government wished to be certain that they would not fall intact into enemy hands. The stakes were high, for the French navy was powerful and effective. If, by force or fraud, the Germans won control of

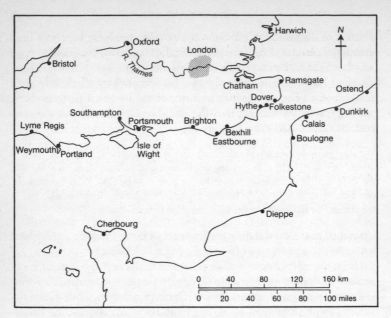

SE ENGLAND and the CHANNEL: THE INVASION COAST 1940

its warships, Britain's capacity to fight on would have been jeopardized. In less than ten minutes the British force put out of action three major French warships, including the modern battle-cruiser *Dunquerque*, and killed more than 1,250 French sailors. However, another battle-cruiser, the *Strasbourg*, escaped to Toulon. (All warships there were scuttled by the French authorities when the Germans seized the harbour at the end of 1942.) Churchill was moved to tears while explaining the action in the House of Commons. A few months later, Roosevelt's associate, Harry Hopkins, declared that it was this action that convinced the President that Britain would fight to the end.

On 17 July the German army produced its invasion plan: thirteen divisions in the first wave were to be followed by six panzer and three motorized divisions, followed by seventeen more infantry divisions. An airborne division would help the first wave. Landings would take place between Ramsgate and Bexhill, between Brighton and the Isle of Wight, and between Weymouth and Lyme Regis. Ninety thousand men would take part in the initial assault, and by the third day 260,000 would be ashore. The German naval authorities objected that they would find it difficult to assemble the necessary ships and impossible to protect them over so wide a frontage, with landings at several points over a 200-mile stretch of coastline. The navy wanted to limit landings to a 50-mile front between Folkestone and Eastbourne. Brauchitsch, the Commander-in-Chief of the German army, insisted on an additional landing near Brighton to outflank any British attempt to hold a line between Chatham and Brighton. The final plan involved landings in three sectors, between Folkestone and Brighton, over about 75 miles. More than 80,000 men would land in the first two hours, and within three days 125,000 men would be ashore. Parachutists would drop behind Hythe. Ten complete divisions were to arrive in the first eleven days, followed by the second wave of six panzer and two motorized divisions (one of which would be the SS Death's Head Division) within four weeks, and another nine divisions two weeks later. Eight further divisions were in reserve. The operation, SEALION, was to be ready from 15 September.

It is not surprising that the German army felt confident of success provided it could get ashore and be supplied. By September the British had twenty-seven infantry divisions, but only four were fully equipped (including one Canadian division) and a further eight reasonably equipped. In addition there were eleven brigades. Field artillery, machine guns, and anti-tank guns were in seriously short supply; priority in equipment had gone to the Expeditionary Force, which had left most of it at Dunkirk. Training was defective. Two armoured divisions and two tank brigades had to take their share of only 600 modern cruiser and infantry tanks in the whole country. The German Army Command had much respect for the qualities of British troops, who would fight 'with tenacity and determination', but very little for 'the British operational command, possessing little flexibility', and ineffective in mobile warfare. The Home Guard, of 500,000 uniformed volunteers, was mainly armed with old American rifles and organized for local defence. The Germans, in July, rated its combat value as 'slight'; by September it was perhaps more effective.

General Jodl thought of the invasion as 'a river crossing in force on a broad front . . . the role of artillery will fall to the Luftwaffe'. The German air force was therefore to compensate for German naval inferiority. The naval staff was gloomy: 'measured against the strength of the enemy the various operational possibilities available to the Navy . . . are infinitesimally small.' In home waters the Royal Navy had ready five capital ships (three battleships and two battle-cruisers), ten cruisers, and fifty destroyers. The German navy, much weakened by losses in the Norwegian campaign, could muster five cruisers, of which four would try to distract the British by escorting a mock invasion convoy towards the coast between Aberdeen and Newcastle, while the heavy cruiser *Hipper* and, if it were repaired in time, the pocket battleship *Admiral Scheer* were to raid merchant shipping. Ten destroyers, fifty motor torpedo boats, and twenty-seven submarines would attempt to interrupt the approach of British warships and protect the troop-carrying vessels. These were a cumbersome assortment: for the first landings 1,130 barges and 1,028 motor boats and fishing vessels, with 390 tugs or trawlers for towing the barges that were insufficiently powered. In support were 170 larger merchant ships. The navy intended to lay minefields to create a protected route but the naval staff was sceptical about their value in the channel. Indeed, the German Naval Command doubted the entire venture: 'even if the Luftwaffe, after defeating the enemy air force over the Channel, is available in undiminished strength, it will be possible for the enemy fleet to break into the area of transit.' Everyone agreed that the Luftwaffe must defeat the Royal Air Force and win air superiority over the Channel as a necessary condition of a successful invasion. Then German bombers might be able to attack British warships without interference from British fighters. RAF Fighter Command must be worn down. German air strategy was obvious. Bombers should make daylight attacks on important targets that the RAF would be compelled to defend. German fighter aircraft would then attack British fighters. The Germans hoped that the RAF would feel compelled to challenge German fighters in a direct struggle.

The Germans began, towards the end of July 1940, with attacks on British coastal shipping and British southern ports. The Luftwaffe then had available three air fleets based on northern France, the Low Countries, northern Germany, Denmark, and Norway. Together they could put in the air about 900 long-range bombers, 250 dive-bombers, 190 twin-engined fighters, and about 630 single-seat fighters. Against this the RAF could put up about 600 single-seat fighters. Fighter Command had the disadvantage, as the defender, that the Germans could choose the area of combat for any given day. On the other hand, the RAF was fighting over British soil or accessible parts of the Channel. British pilots who parachuted from their aircraft could often be returned to action; Germans generally became prisoners or were drowned.

The fighter aircraft mainly involved were the single-seat types, the Messerschmitt 109 and British Hurricane and Spitfire. The German twin-engined fighter, the Messerschmitt 110, had a longer range but was unwieldly and outclassed by both British types. The Me 109E, the version prominent in the Battle of Britain, was as fast as the Spitfire and considerably faster than the Hurricane. It climbed at a higher rate but was less manœuvrable than the Hurricane and Spitfire except in one respect: if the British aircraft went into a dive after using most of their fuel, their engines, with float carburettors, cut out, so that the Me 109, with fuel injection, could dive to escape pursuit or to attack. At high altitudes the Me 109 was much superior until, in early August 1940, Spitfires and Hurricanes were equipped with new three-bladed propellers. The British had one immense advantage: their well-integrated system of fighter control. From a chain of radar stations, supplemented by observer posts, reports of approaching aircraft went to fighter command and sector stations. Thence squadrons of fighters from each sector were directed at the enemy by radio telephone. British fighters concentrated as far as possible on the German bombers. As a result German fighters were forced into the tactically weak position of close escort to their bombers.

Between 10 July and 12 August the Luftwaffe concentrated its attacks on shipping, destroying about 30,000 tons. However, this was from traffic in the Channel of nearly one million tons every week. The RAF lost 148 aircraft, the Germans 298, of which 105 were fighters. The Luftwaffe began the main battle on 13 August, 'Eagle Day'. Now all three German air fleets came into action. Attacks began on airfields and aircraft factories. This phase continued until 6 September, with a period of reduced activity from 19 August to 23 August. In late August the German commanders reduced the proportion of bombers to fighters in order more effectively to challenge the British fighter defence.

This was the critical stage of the battle, when the Luftwaffe came closest to defeating RAF Fighter Command. Shortage of fighter aircraft was prevented by the special efforts given to manufacture under the aegis of Churchill's flamboyant nominee to the newly-created Ministry of Aircraft Production, Lord Beaverbrook. He gave priority to fighter aircraft and brought an unexpected rise in production. During August, 390 Spitfires and Hurricanes were lost while 414 new machines were produced. Even so, in the most dangerous period, between 24 August and 6 September, 295 fighters were lost and 171 badly damaged, while output of new and repaired Spitfires and Hurricanes in those two weeks was 269. The German side, however, was worse off: in August, 231 Me 109s were lost while 160 were produced. British aircraft production now exceeded that of Germany, a result of the priority given to the RAF by the Baldwin and Chamberlain governments before the war and of the priority given to fighters by the latter, of the work of Inskip as

Minister for Co-ordination of Defence, Kingsley Wood as Air Minister, and Sir F. Lemon as Director of Production at the Air Ministry. They provided the capacity; Beaverbrook now got the most out of it.

Shortage of pilots became more urgent than shortage of aircraft. Between 24 August and 6 September, Fighter Command lost 231 pilots killed or wounded, nearly a quarter of its opening strength and nearly double the rate at which new pilots were coming from the operational training units. Towards the end of August, fifty-three new pilots had to be brought in from outside Fighter Command and given a six-day conversion course. Average skills among pilots declined as pilots were lost or withdrawn for rest, or to act as instructors, and losses increased. However, in early September the numerical strength of Fighter Command was higher than it had been at the end of July. Nevertheless, British control of the air over the Straits of Dover was put in grave peril by the German strategy of this period. The Germans made sustained attacks on airfields in south-east England, including the sector-stations which directed fighter squadrons to their targets. Sector operations rooms were vulnerable—they were above ground, often in flimsy buildings. There was a danger that airfields in the south-eastern corner of England would become unusable and that fighter squadrons would be forced to go north and west of London. In case of invasion, the RAF would then be less able to interfere with German bombers attacking British warships. At this critical moment, the Luftwaffe shifted its attacks further inland, and the British forward airfields recovered. This German mistake was the result of over-confidence. During the battle both sides consistently exaggerated the losses of the enemy, and by early September the Germans supposed that the front-line squadrons of Fighter Command must be crippled. All they needed to do was to force into action the squadrons that had been held back in reserve further inland and defeat them. Attacks on London would draw them out. Moreover, the bombing of London might well end the war and make invasion unnecessary, except perhaps as a final stroke to finish off a collapsing enemy.

On 7 September more than 300 German bombers, escorted by 600 fighters, were sent to attack London. British ground forces were kept at eight hours' notice for action. The attack on London helped to convince the British command that a higher degree of readiness was needed. There was only one way to bring it about: just after 8 p.m. the signal CROM-WELL—'invasion imminent'—went out to eastern and southern commands and GHQ Reserve. When nothing happened there spread among the British defenders comforting rumours of disasters alleged to have overwhelmed an attempted German invasion. On 9 September London was attacked again. In three days the Luftwaffe lost eighty-four aircraft. Evidently the RAF was still in the fight, and on 11 September, and again on 13 September, Hitler postponed the decision to invade. On 15 September 220 German bombers attacked London, with diversionary attacks on Southampton and Portland. The RAF had one of its best days: sixty German aircraft were lost compared with twenty-six from Fighter Command. On 17 September Hitler postponed the invasion, while leaving open the possibility of October. On 12 October he postponed it until spring 1941. It was never revived. Between 10 July and 31 October, Fighter Command lost 792 aircraft, the Luftwaffe 1389. In the whole course of the battle, 2,945 RAF aircrew were involved: 507 were killed and about 500 wounded. The figures justify Churchill's famous remark: 'Never in the field of human conflict was so much owed by so many to so few.'

The 'Battle of Britain', the German daytime attempt to destroy Fighter Command and so win air superiority over the Channel, was accompanied by the beginnings of 'the Blitz', the popular English name for the German campaign of night-bombing. Small-scale and scattered night-bombing had gone on since July as the Germans sought experience and tested their navigational systems. Heavy attacks began from 28 to 31 August with four attacks on Liverpool. About 160 bombers were sent there each night. The advantages and disadvantages of night-bombing were immediately evident. The defence was weak: only seven bombers were lost. Much damage was done: on 31 August 160 fires were started in the commercial centre. On the other hand few bombs hit the docks. Indeed, the majority of bombs dropped were nowhere near Liverpool, even of those dropped by crews who claimed to have hit the target. Strong diversionary attacks elsewhere led to widespread and often pointless bombardment. German commanders were trying to attack military objectives, not to terrorize civilians, but the precision required was seldom possible. Later on, successful British interference with navigational guidance systems made matters worse. Bombers could be induced by false signals to release their loads on open country. On 8 May 1941 crews who imagined they had bombed Derby had in fact bombed Nottingham and those crews who should have bombed Nottingham bombed open country as far east of Nottingham as Nottingham is from Derby. From 7 September, however, after a few more attacks on other towns, especially Liverpool, Bristol, and Swansea, German bombers attacked London. Over a continuous period of 68 nights, with only one night undisturbed, London was bombed. The panic flight from London, which pre-war British governments had feared, did not take place. Morale was not broken, though it would be wrong to follow British wartime propaganda and imagine a universal spirit of dauntless defiance. The 'knock-out blow' failed as a war-winner.

In early November 1940 the Luftwaffe ceased its exclusive concentration on London and began to visit a selection of British industrial centres, eventually including sixteen towns. On 14 November the largest attack made outside London—with 450 aircraft—took place against Coventry. Weaker local government and a more concentrated target made the effects more severe than in most of the individual London raids.

Between November 1940 and mid-May 1941, after which German attention moved to the eastern front, over 20,000 tons of high explosive and 80,000 canisters of incendiaries were dropped on Britain. London was not neglected and, though now spared continuous attack, the heaviest German raid ever carried out was directed at London on 19 April 1941, when over 700 aircraft carried more than 1,000 tons of high explosive and 4,000 canisters of incendiaries to the capital. Some aircraft made double or even treble journeys, partly to conceal the beginnings of the transfer of the Luftwaffe to the east. At the end of the campaign Hitler's titular deputy, Rudolf Hess, dropped in to try to find someone with sufficient authority and good sense to make peace with Germany. He failed. The bombing of Britain, though causing severe loss and injury—about 42,000 were killed and at least 50,000 seriously wounded—did no more than cause transient checks to war production. The only exception was the slowing down of the production of aero-engines through one successful raid on a component factory.

It was another method of defeating Britain that came nearest to success: sinking cargo ships in order to deprive it of imports of food and raw materials. The weapons were submarines, surface warships, aircraft, and mines. In the period between the outbreak of war and the end of May 1940, 562 British, allied, and neutral merchant ships, totalling 1,750,000 tons, were sunk. The German occupation of Norway and France immensely strengthened the campaign. In the next period of the same number of months, from June 1940 to February 1941, there were lost 1,377 ships of 5,300,000 tons. In the next four months, March to June 1941, the average loss continued and 582 ships of 2,160,000 tons were sunk. In April 1941, 688,000 tons were lost, an annual rate of over 8 million tons, which could not have been endured. Losses began to exceed building. From the end of September 1940 to the end of June

1941, British dry-cargo merchant shipping fell by 2,890,000 tons from 17,718,000 tons to 14,828,000 tons. Fortunately there was a great accretion of chartered or requisitioned foreign shipping, which brought the total under British control to 22,459,000 tons at the end of September 1940. However, that figure fell to 21,115,000 by the end of June 1941, a net loss of well over one million tons. In the first year of the war British imports had been 44.2 million tons while in the second year they fell to 31.5 million tons. This was endurable (in 1942 it proved possible to survive with 22.9 million tons), but the trend was alarming. In the first half of 1942 tankers under British control fell by 400,000 (dw) tons, about six per cent of the total.

In August 1940 German long-range aircraft, the Focke-Wulf *Kondors*, were based near Bordeaux and later also at Stavanger in Norway. At that time armed escort for convoys could be provided by the British only as far west as 17 degrees, about 300 miles west of Ireland. The long range of the Focke-Wulfs meant that they were able to bomb totally defenceless British vessels. In January and February 1941, forty-seven ships of 168,000 tons were sunk by only fifteen aircraft. Merchant ships were armed—by the spring of 1941 over 4,000 had some anti-aircraft weapons. Ships converted into improvised aircraft-carriers began to come into service after April 1941. Fifty merchant ships were equipped to catapult Hurricanes into the air for once-only attacks on the Focke-Wulfs. Fighter bases were established in the Hebrides and Iceland. Another method of attack, mine-laying, caused acute problems when the magnetic mine was first exploited. But that, and the acoustic mine that followed, were successfully countered so that mine warfare turned into a matter of numbers: provided enough minesweepers were available, swept channels could be maintained.

Surface raiders had been the threat which had most preoccupied the pre-war Admiralty. They came in two types: converted merchantmen, which were highly vulnerable to British warships, and German warships which might require heavy naval concentrations to counter. The Germans employed one battleship, two battle-cruisers, three 'pocket battle-ships' (extra-heavy cruisers), and two heavy cruisers, plus seven armed merchantmen. Before June 1941 they sank about 900,000 tons but the most dramatic raid inflicted no loss at all on allied merchant shipping. On 21 May 1941 the most powerful warship afloat, the *Bismarck*, accompanied by the heavy cruiser, *Prinz Eugen*, set out into the Atlantic from Norway. The Royal Navy dispatched many ships to search and destroy. Actively involved in combat were three battleships, one battle-cruiser, two fleet aircraft-carriers, one cruiser, and five destroyers. The battle-cruiser *Hood*, the largest ship in the British fleet, was blown up, but the *Bismarck* was sunk on 27 May.

Only in July 1940 did Hitler give sufficient priority to U-boat building to enable the German navy to aim to procure twenty-five submarines a month in 1941. From January 1941 the number of operational U-boats began to increase, and by July the January figure of 22 had been trebled. In October 1940 an increased number of British escort vessels enabled convoying to be extended to 19 degrees west, about 400 miles west of Ireland. German submarines were able to strike well beyond this limit. Even against escorted convoys they had great successes. Until effective ship-borne anti-submarine radar was evolved, British detection equipment worked only against submerged vessels. German submarines moved faster on the surface than the convoys. They operated in night attacks on the surface against convoys whose positions had previously been established. In April 1941, when fuelling bases in Iceland were ready, the British were able to extend convoy protection to 35 degrees west, more than half-way across the Atlantic. The U-boat commander, Admiral Dönitz, responded by developing 'wolf-pack' tactics in which groups of submarines were assembled to engage in sustained attacks on a convoy.

In the battle between surface raiders or submarines against merchant ships and their escorts, victory needed numbers and skill, but knowledge of where to find or to evade the enemy could be decisive. Such knowledge made it easier to get to the right place with the right forces at the right time and to know where dangers were lurking. The outcome of the 'Battle of the Atlantic' mainly depended on code-breaking. Submarines and convoys moved slowly, so there was time to act on advance knowledge of their intentions. Their orders had to come by radio and could be intercepted. High-level German radio signals were coded by the Enigma machine, a battery-powered electro-mechanical apparatus. Striking a letter-key arranged as on a typewriter closed an electric circuit which lit up a letter on a display panel. The path of the circuit depended on the choice of three out of five internally-wired wheels, on the positioning of the wheels in relation to each other, and to which of twenty-six plugs a plug corresponding to each letter on the keyboard was attached. All these settings were changed every day or every two days. When a letter was struck one of the wheels moved one place, thus constantly changing the circuit activated by any individual letter on the keyboard. If properly used, Enigma was secure: the signals of some German organizations were never decoded. Sometimes, however, messages were coded by Enigma which were also sent in lower-grade ciphers which themselves could be broken, and sometimes repetitions of formulae in numerous messages, or repeated use of the same arrangement of the wheels, enabled the settings of the machine to be worked out. For operational use much depended on how quickly this could be done. From 1940 to the end of the war the Luftwaffe Enigma was read more or less promptly. More dramatic in its immediate effect on operations was the breaking of the German 'Home Waters' Enigma at the beginning of June 1941. All signals to U-boats became accessible, and they were tightly controlled by Dönitz from his Paris headquarters. Now convoys were often rerouted to evade German wolf packs and, if warships were available, or aircraft within range, submarines could be hunted. For the moment British supply lines were safe. In July 1941 shipping losses from submarine attack fell to less than one-third of those in June despite the increasing number of U-boats. The Battle of the Atlantic appeared to have been won by the British.

Against Italy the British defence was equally successful. The Italian east-African empire in Somaliland, Eritrea, and Ethiopia, cut off from Italy, was conquered. Marshal Graziani, with overwhelming numerical strength, but with forces weak in equipment and training, reluctantly invaded Egypt in September 1940 from the Italian colony of Libya, but soon halted. In November 1940 British naval torpedo-carrying aircraft (in an operation which aroused much interest in Japan), put out of action half the Italian fleet of battleships at anchor in Taranto. In December, with two infantry divisions and a tank regiment, General O'Connor launched a British attack on Graziani's forces. Success followed success, and by early February 1941 the British had destroyed ten Italian divisions and captured 130,000 prisoners at the cost of less than 500 killed and 1,500 wounded. General Wavell, the British Commander-in-Chief in the Middle East, was able to eject a pro-German government which had seized power in Iraq and take Syria from the French authorities there who had remained loyal to Pétain's government at Vichy. In Syria the British were helped by some of the small number of French soldiers who had rallied to de Gaulle in order to continue the war on behalf of 'Free France'.

In October 1940 Italian troops from Albania, which Mussolini had occupied in 1939, invaded Greece. Soon the Greek army forced them into retreat. Hitler decided on German intervention to ensure that British air-bases were kept out of Greece, from whence the Romanian oilfields might be bombed, and to help the Italians to remain in Libya. On

EASTERN MEDITERRANEAN

4 November 1940 Hitler decided upon an invasion of Greece and on 11 January 1941 directed German ground forces to Libya. Rommel, the successful commander of a panzer division in France, arrived in Libya on 12 February. At nearly the same time, Churchill decided that the victorious British troops should renounce the chance of conquering the whole of Libya in favour of an expedition to aid the Greeks against the impending German attack.

The Germans first persuaded Romania and Bulgaria to admit their troops. Resistance to this process from Yugoslavia, after an internal *coup*, was crushed by a hastily prepared campaign, which lasted one week, and on 6 April 1941 the Germans invaded Greece. The British force, of two divisions, one Australian and one New Zealand, and an armoured brigade, found it difficult to co-operate with the Greek army, and the Germans were stronger. By 30 April British forces had left Greece, again losing much equipment and 11,000 men.

A few days earlier, Hitler had agreed to a parachute and airborne attack on Crete to protect the Aegean Sea, keep British bases out of range of Romanian oilfields, and give Goering's Luftwaffe forces a chance to distinguish themselves. This they did, capturing the island and inflicting heavy losses on British warships sent to intercept sea-borne landings, sinking three cruisers and five destroyers, and damaging many others. The lesson of the Norwegian campaign in 1940 was even more clearly illustrated: control of the sea could not be held by ships against dominant air power.

In June 1941 British forces were still established in Egypt and controlled the Middle East and beyond. Rommel's first offensive in March and April 1941 had driven the British out of Libya, except Tobruk, but the Egyptian frontier line was held and Wavell counter-attacked, though without success, in May and June. This desert campaign caught the attention of the British public. It was the first encounter in which British ground troops fought alone against Axis forces, while the glamour of a star began to be attached to Rommel. Yet it was not a matter of life and death like the Battle of Britain or the Battle of the Atlantic. Loss of the oil of Iraq and Iran, which might have followed a British defeat in Egypt, would not have forced a British surrender. As it was, by the summer of 1941 virtually no oil came to Britain from the Persian Gulf—the journey was too long. Already in the first half of 1941, at least 82 per cent of British oil imports came from the western hemisphere. Middle Eastern defeat, it is true, would have had evil effects, and would have meant increased dependence on the United States for oil supplies to India and the east and so compelled an even greater degree of reliance on it for the maintenance of the British Empire. As it was, however, that dependence was substantial enough.

Between June 1940 and June 1941 Britain could stand alone only with American help. This would come if the President were convinced that it was worthwhile to back Britain rather than concentrate resources on the direct defence of the United States, and if he could find sufficient support to make it politically possible. The determined nature of British resistance and Churchill's defiant rhetoric enabled both conditions to be fulfilled, the first, perhaps, more easily than the second. The most urgent British needs, in the summer of 1940, were arms to replace some of the losses in France and warships to escort convoys of merchant vessels. As soon as he became Prime Minister, Churchill asked Roosevelt for '40 or 50 of your older destroyers', and repeated the request until on 2 September 1940 it was agreed that ninety-nine-year leases of air and naval bases in the British West Indies and Newfoundland should be given to the United States in return for fifty First-World-War American destroyers. The British bought 500,000 rifles, 85,000 machine guns, 900 field guns, 25,000 automatic rifles, and 21,000 revolvers, which had been in US army stores, and collected them from American ports in June. They also took over French contracts to buy aircraft from US factories. Thereafter the British government gave orders for machinery and weapons to sustain expanding British forces, so building up American capacity for arms manufacture. In the autumn a contract was given to Henry Kaiser for the building of sixty merchant ships, the foundation for an essential war industry. In the later part of 1940, more than half of all British imports came from Canada and the United States. Canada provided finance by interest-free loans or gifts, but supply from the United States was a very different matter. Everything had to be paid for, as loans to belligerent states, or their citizens, were forbidden by US statute law.

By the end of 1940, British commitments in the United States amounted to 10 billion dollars. There was no way for the British to find this sum. The first year of war showed an adverse balance of payments for the sterling area of nearly 2 billion dollars, and exports necessarily continued to fall—by the end of 1940, they were less than half the pre-war level. Early in 1940, gold reserves were worth about 1.8 billion dollars and sterling area gold production might add 200 million dollars per annum. Marketable dollar securities might fetch up to 4 billion dollars. At the time of Dunkirk the British government gave up the attempt to fight the war on its own resources. Churchill wrote to Roosevelt in May 1940: 'We shall go on paying dollars for as long as we can, but I should like to feel reasonably sure that when we can pay no more you will give us the stuff just the same.' Spending continued with intermittent and vague encouragement from Washington. By November 1940 about 2 billion dollars were left, mostly in investments which were not readily saleable. On 8 December 1940 Churchill signed an elaborate letter to Roosevelt, now re-elected President for a third term. To avoid defeat Britain needed more merchant ships and the United States must build them and help to protect them. To make victory possible Britain must have the benefit of a greatly increased American production of aircraft. American production of weapons should be enlarged to help to equip the British army. 'The moment approaches when we shall no longer be able to pay cash for shipping and other supplies.' Almost immediately Roosevelt set in train the political processes which brought the Lend-Lease Act into law in March 1941. The United States were to become 'the arsenal of democracy' and dollars would not be needed by those who fought the Nazis.

Britain's success in defending herself during the year when she fought alone had two main effects on the course of the war. Britain continued to contribute material resources and a highly organized, skilled, and determined population. Secondly, her continued fight both accelerated and facilitated American participation in the struggle against Hitler. British resistance to Germany made it prudent for America to bring aid not far 'short of war' and so to become involved in the European conflict before Hitler could organize his continental conquests, and it meant that American power could effectively be brought to bear on the other side of the Atlantic by way of a well-equipped, secure, and conveniently situated base.

4

Operation BARBAROSSA: the German attack on the Soviet Union

IN 1940 Hitler made his most important decision, to attack Russia. If he had any settled aims, this was one of them. In 1924, in *Mein Kampf*, Hitler had urged territorial expansion and insisted that 'when we speak of new lands to give living space to the German people in the struggle for existence we must first think of Russia and her border states'.

On 2 June 1940 Hitler opined that Britain would soon be ready for 'a reasonable peace', and then 'at last he would have a free hand' for his 'great and true task: the conflict with Bolshevism'. On 30 June he explained that 'a demonstration of our military power' would make Britain give way 'and leave our rear free for the East'. The army General Staff began on 3 July to study an attack on Russia. On 21 July Hitler set out his views to the armed forces' commanders on the problems caused by British resistance. Perhaps, he thought, Spain, Italy, Russia, and Germany should combine against the British Empire. More congenial would be a compromise with Britain, followed by a war of conquest against Russia. However, the military soon persuaded Hitler that to attack Russia in autumn 1940 was impossible, and preparations were therefore ordered for an attack on Russia at the earliest practicable date—May 1941. On 31 July Hitler told Brauchitsch, the army Commander-in-Chief, and Halder, the Chief of Staff, that if it were required, the defeat of England might take up to two years (using submarine and air attack). If Russia were smashed, however, England's last hope would go and Germany would be 'the master of Europe and the Balkans'. When Russia was knocked out, Japan's importance would increase and the United States would then find it more difficult to maintain England's hopes. Halder's notes indicate Hitler's conclusion: 'The quicker we smash Russia the better . . . Ukraine, White Russia, Baltic states to us.'

The unexpected and successful persistence of the British forced Hitler to choose between continued co-operation with the Soviet Union, at least until Britain capitulated, and the alternative of a two-front war. In favour of working with Russia was the proved willingness of the Soviet government to fulfil German demands for food and minerals, and the obvious difficulty of 'destroying' the Soviet Union. The Germans, for instance, never worked out what to do, after victory, with the land beyond the Urals. A well-disposed British Empire could help to keep Asiatic Russia in check, and this was another reason for compelling the British to see reason before ending the German understanding with the Soviet Union.

There were, however, convincing reasons for immediate war with Russia. In 1940, evidence accumulated that Roosevelt had decided that American resources should be used to defend British independence. In 1941, Hitler believed, American strength would be negligible, in 1942 significant, and thereafter formidable. It was not certain that he could beat Britain in 1941. By then the British would have equipped thirty to thirty-five divisions against an invasion and 'on the spot that means a great deal'. For 1942, therefore, there was the prospect of a hard struggle with the Anglo-Saxon powers. Meanwhile, the Soviet Union would grow stronger and Germany, involved in the west, would become highly vulnerable to Russian threats. On the other hand, if Russian forces could be destroyed in 1941, Germany would then, in control of all the resources of continental Europe, face the Anglo-American coalition with confidence. Moreover, in 1941 Britain would be weakened by submarines and surface ships while Japan would be freed from fear of Russia and enabled to threaten American interests in the Far East. On the assumption that the Soviet army could be destroyed in a single campaign, these arguments were powerful. Hitler and his advisers made that assumption. Perhaps the war was inevitable anyway. For a state which based its legitimacy, inside and outside its borders, on superior force, there could be no security as long as any rival force existed.

In spite of all these motives for action, and in spite of his dreams of settling nordic peasants in eastern cornfields, Hitler hesitated. Near the end of his life, on 26 February 1945, he explained:

I adhered to the hope that an entente, at least honestly sincere, if not unreservedly friendly, could be established between the Third Reich and Stalin's Russia. I imagined that after fifteen years of power, Stalin, the realist, would have rid himself of the nebulous Marxist ideology and that he was pursuing it merely as a poison reserved exclusively for external use . . . we could have created a situation in which a durable entente would have been possible—by defining precisely the zones of influence to be attributed to each party, by rigorously restricting our collaboration to the field of economics and in such a manner that both parties would have derived benefit therefrom. An entente, in short, watched over by an eagle eye and with a finger on the trigger.

In October 1940 Hitler took up the scheme, favoured by his Foreign Minister, Ribbentrop, and the naval chiefs, for an anti-British combination of Spain, France, Italy, Germany, Russia, and Japan. Russia would expand towards the Persian Gulf, Japan southwards, Germany would dominate eastern and south-eastern Europe, Italy could have Egypt, Spain would join in attacking Gibraltar and, with France, secure northwest Africa against the British and Americans. Somehow the competing claims of Spain, France, and Italy were to be reconciled. Stalin was asked to send Molotov, his close associate, to confer in Berlin, and Hitler went off in his special train to talk to Franco, the Spanish dictator, Pétain, the chief of the new French state, and Mussolini.

Quite soon it all went wrong. Franco declined to enter the war, while Pétain, though more amenable in theory, evaded definite plans for fighting the British. Mussolini launched his futile and unhelpful invasion of Greece. Above all, Stalin proved, from Hitler's point of view, an awkward ally. He refused to have his attention directed to the Persian Gulf and continued to take an interest in south-eastern Europe. Stalin responded to German victories in 1940 by pushing Soviet frontiers further to the west: in June and July the Red Army occupied the Baltic states and took Bessarabia and northern Bukovina from Romania. All this was broadly in line with the Nazi–Soviet bargain of August 1939. However, when Molotov came to Berlin on 12 November 1940, he let out, as Hitler put it, many cats from his sack. He asked for more of Romania, a free hand in Finland, the right to protect Bulgaria, a Russian base in the Turkish straits, and a recognition of Soviet interest in Hungary, Yugoslavia, Greece, and German-occupied Poland, as well as in Sweden and the narrow waters at the entrance to the Baltic. Hitler, though taking the precaution of ordering continued studies of a possible attack on Russia, regardless of Molotov's visit, had seen it as a test of whether Russia and Germany stood 'back to back' or 'face to face'. Hitler still also kept open the possibility of an invasion of England in the spring of 1941, which, if seriously meant, implied a renewed understanding with Russia.

The Soviet reply to the German proposals that Molotov took from Berlin came on 26 November 1940. It insisted that German troops should immediately be withdrawn from Finland which 'belongs to the Soviet Union's sphere of influence', that there should be a mutual assistance pact between the Soviet Union and Bulgaria which 'is situated inside the security zone of the Black Sea boundaries of the Soviet Union', that the Soviet Union should have a base within range of the straits, and that the area south of the Caucasus was to be the centre of the 'aspirations of the Soviet Union'. On these terms, and provided Japan gave up claims to coal and oil in Northern Sakhalin, Stalin would accept a four-power agreement with Germany, Italy, and Japan.

With this Soviet reply, Hitler ceased to look for a compromise, and on 5 December he told his service chiefs to attack Russia the following May. On 17 December he explained to General Jodl that 'we must solve all continental European problems in 1941 because from 1942 the United States would be able to interfere'. The fact that Britain had kept the war going meant that the approach of effective American interference had been accelerated and, in consequence, Hitler had at once to find a durable solution for the Russian problem. On 13 December 1940, he signed the order for operation BARBAROSSA. Preparations were to be complete by 15 May 1941. The main Russian forces were to be destroyed by a series of deep encirclements as far east as possible. The final aim was to form a barrier against Asiatic Russia along a line from Archangel to the Volga. After BARBAROSSA, the new Europe would be guarded in the west by defensive positions in Europe and north-west Africa. The Germans and Italians would clear the British from the Mediterranean and the Near East and occupy the oil fields of Iraq and Iran. The Azores would be taken as bases for eventual air attacks on the United States. The German army would be reduced in size but made more mobile, with a basis of thirty-six armoured or motorized divisions.

While Hitler counted his chickens, Stalin contemplated the impending collapse of his policy, and perhaps of the regime, with apparent disbelief. We know less about the motives and thought of the Soviet government than of any other of the great powers involved in the war. It is not even clear who ruled Russia; Stalin was evidently the ultimate maker of decisions but we do not know whose advice he sought. We are especially ignorant about the years immediately before the war. With little documentary guidance, all that can be done is to look for the motives most likely to explain the actions of the Soviet government. Explanations can only be tentative. In 1939, before the German invasion of Poland began the war, Stalin could choose either to ally with Britain and France to resist German expansion or, while encouraging the western powers to fight Germany, keep the Soviet Union out of war and extract a price from Hitler for Soviet neutrality or co-operation. It may be that Stalin made his deal with Hitler because he thought that Britain and France were seeking the Soviet alliance only in order to help them to intimidate Germany into an accommodation with themselves, a bargain which might leave the Soviet Union alone to face a reinforced Germany. It is also possible that Stalin never intended to fight Germany and used the hope of a Russian alliance to encourage Britain and France to resist Hitler in 1939, while encouraging the Germans to attack Poland and risk war with the western powers, by secretly offering the Germans the prospect of Soviet neutrality. If Britain and France fulfilled their pledge towards Poland when Germany attacked, then Stalin would be able to watch the mutual weakening of the capitalist powers; if they did not, then he would have done well to sell his neutrality in advance while it was marketable at the highest price.

Conveniently, Stalin had little need to justify his foreign policy. He did not need to worry about a 'public opinion'. Russians who were educated and ambitious were likely to be members of a party which, in the 1930s, had become more and more amenable to Stalin's dictation, while those who were outside it were either ignorant or subdued. The only exception might have been the Red Army, but that, too, had been very effectively subdued in the army purge of 1937. The Soviet Union, therefore, could pursue policies more decisively and subtly prescribed by *raison d'état* than any other power. Stalin offered vital economic aid to Germany in return for the partition of Poland and a free hand in extending his control into Finnish territory, all three Baltic states, and part of Romania. Russian claims in Poland and bases and land in Finland were secured before the German attack on France. The rest was hurriedly seized in June and July 1940. The defeat of France must have been very bad news for Stalin—instead of the imperialists slowly wearing each other down, Hitler, the puppet of the most formidable imperialists, would have his hands free for the east. Britain's continued resistance was more reassuring and might, Stalin perhaps believed, make Russian neutrality continue to be valuable to the Germans. Stalin demonstrated his reliability and value to the Germans by prompt delivery of supplies to the Reich, while attempting to bargain by setting out his maximum demands.

There is evidence, much of it from the period after his death when Stalin was discredited by his successors, which suggests that he was surprised by the German attack. If so it is odd, since he received warnings from several reliable sources. Perhaps he thought that the massive German troop movements of the spring of 1941 were either an elaborate manœuvre to deceive the British into relaxing their guard against invasion (a cover story put out by the Germans themselves) or a diplomatic bluff, a means of strengthening the bargaining position of the

Germans. Probably he thought it inconceivable that Hitler would risk a protracted war on two fronts.

On his side, Hitler did not expect it to be protracted. On 27 March he told his generals that the start of BARBAROSSA would be delayed for up to four weeks because of the need to crush Yugoslavia before the invasion of Greece. Until then preparations for BARBAROSSA were due to be complete by 15 May; the attack began on 22 June. It is not certain that the assault could have started earlier even if there had been no Balkan operations. Training and movement of some of the forces might have delayed the date. Furthermore, the spring period of slush and mud lasted longer than usual in 1941, and the River Bug was still too wide, early in June, for a crossing to be secured. In any case, though the delay came to seem important later, it did not matter to the German command at the time. It was assumed that German forces could begin to be withdrawn from Russia and prepared for operations against the Anglo-Americans in August—so that ten weeks were thought sufficient to defeat and round up the main Russian forces.

By any standard of military accomplishment, except that required by BARBAROSSA, the achievement of the German army in Russia was incomparable. This superb instrument, the most effective land force ever known, won the biggest victories in the history of war. As exponents of modern warfare, the Germans were on average far superior to their opponents, but their superiority was not great enough for them to defeat the Soviet forces and to conquer European Russia. This was the decisive campaign; more than anything else the survival of the Soviet Union determined the pattern of the Second World War and of the post-war world. It was the successful resistance of the Soviet Union and the victory of the Russian armies that enabled the Anglo-American coalition to join in defeating Hitler, with much less suffering to their peoples and in a few years, rather than in the decades of struggle that might otherwise have been required.

German strength was based on a well-educated society whose history meant that scientists, technologists, and especially soldiers secured respect and high status. The Nazis weakened German education and science by anti-intellectualism and anti-Semitism, but accumulated intellectual capital could not be dissipated in the brief years of Nazi dominance. On the other hand, the Nazi regime succeeded in one of its objects—that of reducing suspicion between classes by distracting attention from the continuing inequalities in German society, and so reinforced the cohesion of Germans. A high degree of cohesion in a nation is an essential condition of military effectiveness because it facilitates a sense of mutual loyalty and obligation among the troops and between officers and men. Nazi dominance left the independence of the army largely intact, at least until 1944. As it expanded in size, that army was able to use its own methods of recruitment, promotion, and training. The wartime army was distinguished by the high quality of leadership at the level of higher command, among officers at every level, and among NCOs. The prestige of the army had meant that the cadres of the wartime army had been drawn from men of high potential. The General Staff corps continued to attract men of real intellectual ability. Discipline could be based on consent, in the sense that officers and NCOs could secure obedience by their skill, so that German army discipline did not stifle individual initiative. German soldiers combined ready obedience to orders with the ability individually to work out the correct response to unexpected situations. The different arms were trained in habits of flexible co-operation. Germans were not supermen: they were capable of fear, panic, and disorder, but the average military skill of the German soldier was the highest in the world. To support it German industry provided well-designed and reliable equipment. Even so, only a portion of the German army was highly mobile—the panzer and motorized divisions (the latter were subsequently renamed 'panzer-grenadier' divisions). In fluid warfare these units dominated the battlefield.

The Red Army was formed from an agglomeration of diverse peoples. The Soviet Union included many nationalities, often mutually uncomprehending or hostile. Red Army soldiers varied enormously in education: illiteracy and ignorance coexisted with intellectual ability and sophisticated knowledge. Rigid and harsh discipline based on unquestioning obedience was common, yet muddle, inefficiency, and drunkenness were often tolerated. Staff work was poor, communications primitive, co-operation between various arms was inadequate, the chain of command cumbersome. Intellectual initiatives were rare. The Soviet regime, as it had developed under Stalin in the 1930s, did not encourage the taking of responsibility. The great military purge at the end of the 1930s fostered a frightened conformity among senior officers—possibly only about half their number remained alive. The Red Army was inflexible, slow-moving, and prone to disorganization. Individual officers and men were baffled by the unexpected. Some served the regime only through compulsion and surrendered as soon as the chance came, though many others fought tenaciously from the start.

The six months' campaign of 1941 can be summarized very simply: the immense German superiority was not quite great enough. There were 208 German divisions in 1941, of which 167 were at full strength. The invasion of Russia was entrusted to 146 divisions. In addition, there were the equivalent of fourteen Romanian divisions, while the Finnish army manned its own sector of the eastern front. The Red Army in the border region included 150 divisions, with twenty more against Finland. These were, as the Germans expected, seriously under strength: the establishment of a rifle division was 14,500 officers and men but most had under 9,000. However, there were far more of them than the German planners expected: in the interior and the Far East there were another 133 divisions. German mobile divisions were intended to bring victory and there were seventeen panzer and twelve motorized divisions in the van of the invasion. The Russians, however, were already creating twenty new mechanized corps; only half were equipped in June 1941, but their full strength of each corps of 1,000 tanks and 17,000 men would make them formidable instruments. The invading army had 3,350 tanks. The Red Army had about 20,000 tanks, nearly all of them obsolete and three-quarters unserviceable at the moment of invasion, but there were nearly 1,500 new tanks among them—the heavy KVs and the T-34—the most successful tank of the entire war—which caused surprise and dismay to the Germans since they were invulnerable to the current German tanks and all except a few of the heaviest anti-tank weapons. The Soviet air force, about 8,000 strong in June 1941, also included large numbers of obsolete machines, but against the German combat strength of 2,000 modern aircraft, quantity production was beginning of effective fighters and ground-attack types. Russian artillery was excellent in equipment and men—after the NKVD (the state police) and the air arm, it had first call on the best recruits.

The German attack had three powerful thrusts: Army Group North, with six mobile and twenty-three infantry divisions, was to attack towards Leningrad; Army Group Centre, with fifteen mobile divisions and thirty-five infantry divisions, to drive on Moscow; and Army Group South, with eight mobile and thirty-three German and fourteen Romanian infantry divisions, to advance into the Ukraine and towards the Caucasus. The plan was to defeat the bulk of the Red Army in the first three weeks in a series of envelopments. Panzer groups were to break through and encircle Russian armies, and then German infantry, following on foot, would kill or capture the surrounded Russians. Then the Baltic states and Leningrad would be captured, Moscow and its defenders encircled and destroyed, and finally a line reached from the Caucasus and the Volga to

Archangel. In the closing phase, in the autumn of 1941, the numbers of German troops required would be much reduced, to about sixty divisions, and only the amount of winter equipment necessary for those divisions was allowed for.

At first everything went well. Within a week, the first great encirclements took place, leading to the capture of 287,000 Red Army men, with 2,500 tanks and 1,500 guns in pockets around Bialystok and Minsk. On 3 July Halder, the German army Chief of Staff, wrote, 'the campaign against Russia has been won within the first fortnight'. His qualifications proved more accurate: 'This does not mean that it has ended. The size of the country and the stubborn resistance we encounter will keep our forces occupied for many more weeks.' Victory followed victory. On 15 July another pocket was formed by the envelopment of Smolensk and over 100,000 Red Army men, with 2,000 tanks and 1,900 guns were cut off. Far to the rear, 12,000 Russian prisoners, the remnants of three divisions, were taken at Mogilev, which held out until 26 July. Early in August, 54,000 Russians were captured around Roslavl. By then, however, it was evident that BARBAROSSA had failed: its objectives could not be secured before the autumn rains.

The Red Army, though terribly mauled, did not collapse; indeed, the determination and tenacity of its men steadily grew. The encirclements and forward thrusts of German mobile forces had to be followed up by the infantry, trudging ahead on foot, before rear areas could be made secure. The Soviet regime did not fall apart, and, on the contrary, popular nationalist response to alien invasion, strengthened by the ruthlessly brutal aspects of German occupation policies, increased support for it. Moreover, steady Russian resistance aggravated German supply problems through partisan warfare, which was organized and led by Red Army officers and men who had been left in the rear by speedy German advances. The slowing down of the triple-pronged offensive meant that a single objective of the original plan for BARBAROSSA had to be selected and given priority. The High Command of the army and the staff of Army Group Centre wanted to concentrate German mobile forces against Moscow. The assumption was that prestige and its importance as a centre of communications would compel Stalin to commit every available resource to defend the capital, and so offer the chance of a decisive defeat of the main Soviet forces.

Hitler disagreed. He believed that German control of the Baltic should be made secure in the north and that Army Group South should be strengthened in order to seize the Crimea, to prevent air attacks from

NORWAY

SWEDEN

BALTIC SEA

Murmansk

Archangel

Helsinki

Leningrad

Riga

U S S R

Vyazma

Smolensk

Mogilev

Moscow

Roslavl

Minsk

Berlin

Warsaw

Bialystok

Bryansk

Orel

R. Oder

Voronezh

R. Volga

Prague

Gomel

Vienna

R. Dniester

R. Dnieper

Kiev

Kharkov

Izyum

R. Donets

Stalingrad

URAL MOUNTAINS

Budapest

UKRAINE

GERMAN-DOMINATED
EUROPE

Rostov

Belgrade

Bucharest

CRIMEA

CASPIAN
SEA

Sofia

BLACK SEA

Batum

CAUCASUS
MOUNTAINS

Baku

T U R K E Y

IRAN

M E D I T E R R A N E A N   S E A

N

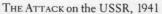

Start line for the attack on
the USSR 22 June 1941

Line reached 5 Dec 1941

0   200   400   600 km

0   200   400 miles

THE ATTACK on the USSR, 1941

bases there on the Romanian oil fields, to seize Ukrainian food supplies, and to capture Russian industries in the Donets basin. If the eastern war could not be won in 1941, Hitler was probably correct. Since 1945, he has been blamed for missing what has been alleged to have been a chance of victory in 1941, but in fact, by August, Russian resistance had ended that prospect. The advance of Army Group South had been slower than on the central front, even though its encirclement of more than sixteen Soviet divisions near Uman, with 103,000 prisoners, opened the way to the Dnieper early in August. Partly as a result, the Russians were left holding a large salient at Kiev. In consequence, Hitler's order to Army Group Centre to detach its right wing southwards, including Guderian's panzer group, produced first the capture of about 80,000 Russians near Gomel, and then one of the two greatest victories of the war, indeed of the whole of military history. Five Russian armies were trapped, 665,000 prisoners, 884 tanks and 3,700 guns were taken. Then Rundstedt's Army Group South was able to take Kharkov and advance to Rostov and to occupy the Crimea. While the Kiev pocket was being mopped up by the infantry of Army Group South, the strength of the mobile forces in Army Group Centre was being restored. At the beginning of September 1941, the 3rd Panzer Group was down to 41 per cent of tank strength and 4th Panzer Group to 70 per cent, but by the end of the month they were at 75 per cent and 100 per cent. In the first week of October the advance towards Moscow was resumed and these mobile groups created an enormous pocket around Vyazma, while Guderian's 2nd Panzer Group, though only at half-strength after the Kiev battles, made yet another around Briansk. As usual these pockets required time and hard fighting to clear but in the end the results rivalled the Kiev encirclement, with 660,000 prisoners, 1,242 tanks and 5,412 guns captured.

Looking back on it, the Germans should now have gone on to the defensive until the early summer of 1942. It is not surprising, however, that Hitler, the High Command of the army, and Army Group Centre all thought it worthwhile to renew the effort to take Moscow, for it seemed that the Soviet Union must be near collapse. The German army in the east had lost about 560,000 men, killed and wounded, one-sixth of their total original force (but a much higher proportion of the combat infantry). On the other hand, at least four million Soviet troops had been killed or captured. On 14 October the German Army Command ordered Moscow to be encircled. Soon alarm, and even panic, developed in the Russian capital. Apart from Stalin and the military headquarters, the government left. Army Group Centre, however, faced frightful supply problems. Rain and heavy use turned Russian roads into mud. Railheads were still well behind the forward troops, and the capacity of the railways was reduced by demolitions and by increasing partisan activity.

On the Russian side, on the other hand, undamaged railways converged on Moscow, now only a very short distance behind the front. When General Zhukov took over the defence of Moscow on 10 October 1941, he had 90,000 men at his disposal. Militia units were created from the workers of Moscow and women mobilized to dig trenches and build defensive obstacles. Stalin's spy, Richard Sorge, reported at the end of September that there was no immediate danger of a Japanese attack on the Soviet Far Eastern Territories. In October and November 1941, at least eight divisions, with about 1,000 tanks and 1,000 aircraft, were moved from the Far East.

Early in November the German attack had halted. On 7 November frost set in and, at first, movement became easier so that the attack was resumed on 15 November. By then the German infantry divisions were down to about 65 per cent combat efficiency and the panzer divisions down to 35 per cent. Only 30 per cent of German lorries were serviceable. No fresh units joined Army Group Centre, while the Red Army steadily reinforced Moscow with fresh troops from the east, including well-equipped and experienced winter fighters. Towards the end of November, extremely cold weather set in, interfering with machinery and reducing mobility and effectiveness for combat. On 5 December 1941 the German offensive ended; on the same day the Russian counter-offensive began. On 7 December 353 Japanese aircraft attacked the United States Pacific Fleet at Pearl Harbor. Soviet resistance had defeated Hitler's attempt to seize secure control of continental Europe before the United States went to war.

5

The United States enters the war:
the origins of the Japanese attack

THE Japanese home islands offered few natural resources for manufacturing industry and inadequate land to feed a rapidly rising population. Between 1920 and 1940 population rose from 55 million to 71 million. Increased foreign trade or emigration, or both, were essential. To finance imports of food and raw materials exports must grow and industry expand. Emigration would reduce pressure on the land. There were two methods of securing those objects: one was by co-operation with the great trading countries of the world, by fostering free trade and the international flow of capital, and by helping to maintain the peace of the world. The other was to use force to impose on the outside world the political and economic conditions of Japanese well-being. Japanese power might conquer areas for overseas settlement and privileged opportunities for trade and investment. The supply of raw materials, including fuel, might forcibly be made secure. Japan could then flourish and perhaps bring increasing benefits to its involuntary associates in a 'Greater East Asia Co-Prosperity Sphere'. The first policy was applied in the 1920s, the second in the 1930s: the second policy brought war in China in 1937 and world war in 1941. Japan went to war because of the failure of policies of peace and the consequent rise in influence of the armed services, especially the army.

In the 1920s the Japanese economy was growing on average by about 3.3 per cent per annum. This was a respectable performance by any standards except those of Japan—in the period 1890–1920, the figure was about 5.7 per cent while in the 1930s about 7.2 per cent was attained. Growth in manufacturing was more impressive in the 1920s, at 7 per cent per annum, but it was not enough to take up surplus population. Industry absorbed only 11 per cent of the increase in the labour force in that decade. Several factors combined to turn this respectable, if insufficient, economic growth into disaster. Government policy played its part. It was believed that trade would be furthered by a stable currency, fixed in value in relation to gold and therefore to other currencies similarly fixed. More damagingly, the Japanese authorities took the fashionable view that it was desirable to restore the pre-1914 foreign exchange value of the yen.

Japanese prices had to be forced down to raise the value of the yen to this level, and this was done by cutting government spending. There were two effects: economic activity was checked so that unemployment increased, and the armed services were annoyed by reduced military spending, which fell by nearly 15 per cent between 1928 and 1930. The trend was dramatized by Japanese participation in the Naval Disarmament Treaty of London of 1930, which aroused fierce opposition in the Japanese services and among nationalists.

The yen returned to the gold standard, at just under two to the dollar, on 11 January 1930. It was not a good moment. The world slump exacerbated the effect of domestic deflation. The Japanese economy was hit immediately by the depression in the United States. Forty per cent of Japanese farmers had some reliance on silk culture, and the collapse of United States demand led to a fall in the value of raw silk exports in 1931 to less than half the level of 1929. Japanese farmers were already suffering from low food prices, from which they were not protected by governments who were more concerned to foster modern industry. Imports, especially from Formosa (Taiwan) and Korea, then part of the Japanese overseas empire, caused the price of rice to fall by 1931 to less than half of that of 1925. After 1928, the rising value of the yen increased the burden of debt on agriculturalists.

From 1925 to 1930 the average real income of agricultural households, never very high, fell by about one-third. Rents moved down, too, so that the effects of the agricultural crisis hit both landlords and tenants and did not set off ill-feeling between rural classes. On the contrary, all sections of rural society resented the economically more successful minorities: skilled industrial workers and employees of modern businesses, especially the Zaibatsu, the great conglomerates headed by Mitsui and Mitsubishi. In 1930 half the Japanese population still depended on agriculture. The army drew most of its personnel from rural Japan: it was concerned about agricultural hardships, and they enabled it to find support for more forceful and expansionist foreign policies.

Two events marked the change in policy: the Mukden incident in September 1931 and the abandonment of the gold standard in December. In Manchuria, Japan had valuable political and economic rights, but the territory was part of China. The central government of China had little control over provincial Chinese potentates but it encouraged, and reflected, the development of Chinese nationalism hostile to foreign privileges. The Japanese government, headed by Wakatsuki, in which the internationalist Shidehara was Foreign Minister, favoured concessions to Chinese demands for the abolition of privileges seized from China. The local Japanese military commanders did not. On 18 September 1931 a bomb exploded near Mukden on the Japanese-owned South Manchurian railway. The Japanese Kwantung army, which guarded the railway, immediately put plans into effect for securing control of the whole of Manchuria. The government's wish for peace was defied by the local army command with the encouragement of a section of the general staff in Tokyo, and the central government could only accept the consequences. The United States administration and the League of Nations, under very hesitant British leadership, condemned the action in Manchuria and refused to recognize the new Japanese-sponsored state of Manchukuo. The United States would do nothing to enforce its views, however, and alone, the League could not, but its condemnations caused Japan to withdraw from the League in March 1933. The fragile Chinese government thus found international support and also the backing of much of the Chinese intelligentsia. To keep this support the Chinese government refused formal recognition of Japanese dominance in Manchuria and north China.

Japanese advance in Manchuria led, therefore, to the isolation of Japan in face of the hostility of Britain and the United States and of increasing Chinese nationalism. In consequence, Japanese xenophobia grew stronger and the old nationalist grievances—American and Australian restraints on Japanese immigration and the Washington and London treaty provisions for naval disarmament, agreed to by inter-nationalist-minded Japanese governments—were aggravated. Meanwhile, the exchange rate fixed when the yen returned to gold clearly overvalued the Japanese currency. More than half the gold and foreign exchange reserves held in Japan in January 1930 were lost in supporting the yen in 1930 and 1931. When the gold standard was abandoned in December 1931, the yen fell by about 40 per cent. In consequence Japanese exports became cheap in other currencies, and they quickly recovered and then boomed. The abandonment of a high exchange rate meant that it was no longer necessary to hold down Japanese prices. Government spending increased, financed by borrowing, with military spending as its main component. By 1938 government spending was three times the level of 1931 and military spending more than twelve times higher. The result was vigorous economic growth and increased employment with, of course, special emphasis on military needs: spending on the armed services in 1938 had five times the share of national output that it had had of a lower national output in 1931.

This transformation in Japanese economic and political policies was carried out, and the dominance of the military was secured, without a change in regime and without seizure of power in an armed *coup*. There were innumerable patriotic, militaristic societies and organizations, some of which had special appeal to junior officers. Some of them readily turned to violence or murder. One Prime Minister, two Finance Ministers, and a Lord Privy Seal were among those murdered; army *coups* were planned, and at least two actually attempted. These events were extreme symptoms of the mounting influence of the views of the military rather than the cause of that influence, however. The cause lay in the failure of the liberal internationalists, partly due to bad luck, partly to over-confidence, partly to the insensitivity to their problems shown by those who should have been their friends in Europe and America.

Thus, Japanese opinion moved towards acquiescence in the military approach, an attitude facilitated by the predilection of Japanese education and culture for co-operation and conformity as against competitive individualism. It would be wrong to suppose that liberal attitudes became extinct: they survived, notably in the westernized upper class, among some senior officers both in the army and navy, in the person of the Emperor, and in that of the most senior statesman, Saionji, who died in 1940 at the age of 92, preaching caution and good sense to the end. However, the dissidents of the 1920s, like Konoe, who was Prime Minister from June 1937 to January 1939 and July 1940 to October 1941, and who wrote as early as 1918, 'Anglo-American pacifism has nothing to do with justice or humanity . . . our international position ought to make people call for breaking up the *status quo* . . . the League of Nations . . . should be seen as the noxious thing it is', now represented the consensus even among civilians.

In 1932 the Japanese army was unsuccessful in an attempt to extend Japanese control in Shanghai but in 1933 was able to conquer the Chinese province of Jehol and add it to the puppet state of Manchukuo. For a few years a loosely negotiated truce supervened while the Japanese army continued to look for Chinese leaders who would accept and safeguard Japanese mercantile interests. One reason the truce continued was that Chiang Kai-shek, the leader of the Kuomintang, or Chinese Nationalist Party, was concerned to check the Chinese Communists rather than to challenge the Japanese. In December 1936, the danger of this attitude was sharply demonstrated to Chiang when some of his own officers revolted against him and declared in favour of collaboration with the Communists against the Japanese. Chiang recognized that he must at least pose as an anti-Japanese nationalist and evade Japanese attempts to win his collaboration. Meanwhile the Japanese army and navy agreed between themselves in May 1936 that the defence of Japan required preparations against the United States, the Soviet Union, Britain and China. There was, however, much disagreement among the Japanese on timing and priorities: how far existing resources should first be developed, how far and to where they should be extended, which threats should first be countered and when. Circumstances dictated the choices which eventually led to war and defeat.

The main problem was to increase economic resources and make them secure. Probably about one-third of Japanese manufactures were sold abroad; between the wars Japan was even more dependent on exports than Britain. In the 1930s tariff barriers were raised, especially against Japanese textile exports. Their impact and the fear of further barriers to trade generated a desire to make markets secure by political or military action. By 1936 Manchuria and the other Japanese-controlled overseas territories assured Japanese food imports, but only about 15 per cent of Japanese imports of industrial materials came from those territories. Seventy per cent of Japanese consumption of zinc and tin came from foreign sources, 90 per cent of lead, and all raw cotton and wool, aluminium, and rubber. In the 1930s the main source of foreign exchange was a trading surplus with China; in 1936 a favourable balance of 318 million yen on trade with China (including Manchuria) contrasted with a current deficit of 425 million yen with Europe, the United States and the British Dominions. This essential trade with China was threatened by Chinese nationalism. Between 1931 and 1933 Manchuria was made secure for Japan. The result was further Chinese resentment and boycott: in the 1920s, 25 per cent of Chinese imports came from Japan while in 1932 the figure fell to 14 per cent. In 1937 the Japanese began extended action against China.

In July fighting broke out at the Marco Polo bridge near Peking. This time the Japanese civilian authorities in Tokyo were more belligerent than the army and, on the Chinese side, Chiang was ready to force a conflict in north China: only as a leader of anti-Japanese nationalism could Chiang survive and retain Moscow's support in keeping the Chinese Communists in temporary alliance with him. Chiang's military forces proved disappointing. By the end of 1938 Japan was in control of all important Chinese ports, including Canton in the south, and Chiang had retired to Chungking in Szechuan. However, repeated efforts failed to persuade Chiang to work with the Japanese, and in 1940 they set up

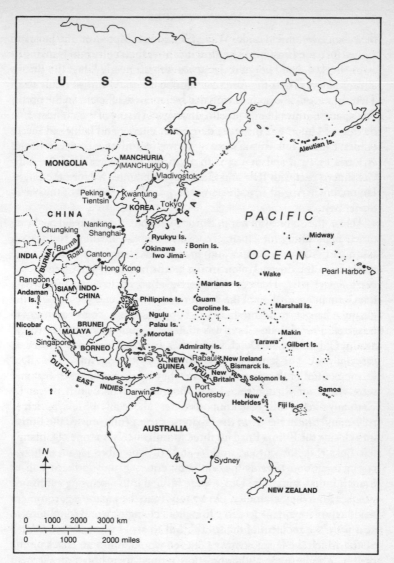

THE JAPANESE WAR, 1941–5

their own government under Wang Ching-wei. Moreover, the Japanese
earned increased hostility. The atrocities after their entry into Nanking in
1937 shocked world opinion. Japanese aircraft nearly killed the British
ambassador and sank the American gunboat *Panay*. British residents in
Tientsin were deliberately humiliated by Japanese officials. In the north,
the Japanese army put into practice the view of many of their officers that
the Soviet Union was the most dangerous enemy and launched severe
border battles, but Russia's strength was confirmed by clear Soviet
victories in 1938 and in 1939. In 1936 the Japanese signed the anti-
Comintern pact with Italy and Germany to counter-balance the Soviet
Union, but in August 1939 they were surprised and shocked by the Nazi–
Soviet pact.

At first, the outbreak of war in Europe in September 1939 did not bring
much opportunity for Japan. To expand southwards and risk war in
south-east Asia with Britain and France was dangerous now that the
threat from the Soviet Union in the north had been increased by the
Nazi–Soviet pact. However, the scene changed in May–June 1940:
the German occupation of the Netherlands and France presented to the
Japanese dangers to be forestalled and opportunities of easy conquests to
be seized. French Indo-China was strategically important in the struggle
against China, and the Dutch East Indies were rich in natural resources,
especially oil. The Japanese feared that the British or Americans might
secure control of these territories, but they could try to get in first and
seize them for themselves. Then the prospect of British defeat by
Germany offered still greater opportunities, above all in Malaya, rich in
rubber and tin. In July 1940 the Japanese successfully pressed the British
into closing the Burma Road for three months—this was one of Chiang's
few links with the outside world—and in September Japanese troops
began expansion towards the south by entering the northern half of
French Indo-China. The Dutch were bullied into promising continued
supplies from the East Indies. On 27 July 1940 the Japanese government
made a most important decision: to exploit 'changing world conditions' to
deal with 'the problem of the south', but to avoid war with the United
States, which the Japanese navy believed would follow an attack on the
British. The Japanese authorities thus pinned their hopes on German
victory over Britain. Then they could expect to expand Japanese control,
or occupation, southwards towards Malaya and the East Indies without
conflict. In signing the Tripartite Pact with Germany and Italy in
September 1940, the Japanese staked their claim to a share in the spoils,
at the eventual expense of the British Empire, in return for helping

Germany by discouraging United States entry into the European war.

Within a year the outlook had completely changed. Britain was no longer in imminent danger of defeat and Germany had invaded the Soviet Union. Japan had a choice: either to join in the destruction of the Soviet Union or, freed from the Russian threat in the north, to advance southwards. Increasingly, action seemed urgent as the United States began to use economic pressure to weaken and check Japan and encouraged the British and Dutch governments (the latter now in exile in London) to do the same in their eastern possessions. In July 1941 those in power in Japan—essentially the Prime Minister, the War, Navy, Home, and Finance ministers, and the general and supply staffs of the army and navy, with the Emperor and the court officials in the role of gloomy commentators—were uncertain what line of action to choose. They made preparations for both the northern and the southern options. They reinforced the Kwantung army for possible action against the Soviet Union and bullied the Vichy French government into allowing Japanese forces to enter southern Indo-China to set up advanced air and naval bases. To prevent this move, which threatened Malaya and the Philippines as well as the East Indies, President Roosevelt offered to arrange for a guaranteed neutralization of Indo-China; his offer reached Tokyo only after Japanese forces had moved in. The result of this action was an event fraught with the most dire consequences: the United States froze Japanese assets and imposed an embargo on the export of oil to Japan. The British and, to the surprise and dismay of the Japanese, the Dutch followed. Roosevelt had not intended a complete embargo. He had ordered that licences for the export of oil could be applied for on a peacetime scale and for petrol of lower than aviation quality. Having made this decision Roosevelt went to meet Churchill off Newfoundland while Secretary of State Hull happened to fall ill. Left to itself, the committee controlling the release of frozen Japanese funds made Japanese purchases impossible. When the President discovered what had happened, he thought it would weaken the impact on Japan to revert to his original intention. Consequently the Japanese were cornered: without oil they must either withdraw from China and renounce their 'Greater East Asia Co-Prosperity Sphere' or go to war.

For Roosevelt the Far East mattered principally because what happened there could affect the outcome of the struggle for Europe. Most Americans, too, were not greatly preoccupied by the condition of China, but those who were, were overwhelmingly hostile to Japanese ambitions. The reasons were not usually economic: in China, British and Japanese investment was dominant, with over one-third each, compared with only 6 per cent of total foreign investment in China from the United States. American exports to Japan were considerably larger than those to China, and in spite of the depreciation of the yen, the dollar value of American exports to Japan doubled between 1932 and 1937. Indeed, American firms were providing some of the equipment for aggressive Japanese expansion. Anti-Japanese opinion in the United States arose less from economic self-interest than from moral disapproval of violence and international lawlessness and from sympathy towards the Chiang Kai-shek regime as a government struggling for national independence and even for democracy. In the late 1930s Chiang was remarkably successful in winning sympathy abroad, helped, especially in the United States, by the work of his wife's family, which was headed by the financier T. V. Soong. Thus support existed for the long-sustained attitude of the Roosevelt administration towards the Japanese search for domination in China: repeated expression of disapproval of violence, of economic discrimination, of attacks on the territorial integrity of China, and of limitations on Chinese sovereignty. The door to trade with and invest-ment in China, the Americans insisted, should be open to all nations on equal terms.

After 1937 Japanese actions, which ran counter to all those principles and which interfered with the rights, and even safety, of Americans in China, reinforced anti-Japanese sentiment. Embargoes on exports to Japan began, in June 1938, with a State Department request to exporters not to send equipment that could be used for bombing civilians, and in December 1939 this was extended to metals needed for aircraft manufac-ture. In January 1940 the United States government caused the treaty of commerce with Japan to lapse so that legally enforceable embargoes could be ordered. The object was to help Chiang to check the Japanese advance in China. In June 1940 another urgent reason for checking Japan appeared. The British Empire was now alone in resistance to Hitler and the Japanese advance threatened British interests in China itself, in Hong Kong, Malaya, Singapore, Borneo, and ultimately in Burma and India. The Dominions of Australia and New Zealand, who were voluntarily engaged in the fight against Hitler, were also possible victims of Japanese ambitions.

In theory Britain could choose between two policies towards Japan. The policy actually carried out was to oppose Japanese advance, to help Chiang, and to prepare to defend the British economic and political stake in east Asia. Apart from British trade and investment in China, Malaya produced several essential raw materials, especially tin and rubber, North Borneo and Brunei produced oil, while it was axiomatic that India, Australia, and New Zealand must be preserved from foreign encroachment. An alternative British policy was to work with Japan, which shared a common interest in an orderly China in which xenophobic nationalism should be curbed. This might be done by arranging spheres of interest. Japan would be given a free hand in Manchuria and northern China in return for Japanese acceptance of British interests in Shanghai, the Yangtze valley, and the south. Such a prudent course was impossible. British internationalist opinion was opposed to Japanese armed expansion and noisily proclaimed the iniquity of collaboration with aggressors. Above all, the German threat made United States support indispensable to Britain in case of war. To make it possible for the American administration and Congress to give this support, the British had to stand for the virtuous causes of international order and democracy. Since, surprisingly, Chiang Kai-shek was supposed to believe in these causes, the British were compelled to oppose the Japanese rather than compromise with them.

British strategy in the Far East rested on the naval base at Singapore, completed in 1938. In case of war with Japan, Singapore island would be held against Japanese attack during the period required, of about three months, for the British main fleet to arrive and drive off the Japanese navy. The building of a hostile German navy in the 1930s made this strategy increasingly difficult; in 1940 the loss of the French fleet and the addition to the enemy of the Italian fleet made it wholly impracticable to dispatch a fleet sufficient to deal with the Japanese. Without American help, the British eastern empire was indefensible. British policy followed a consistent and predictable pattern of opposition to Japan in the hope that United States power would make it effective.

After May 1940 the British could not follow an independent policy at all, and were compelled to leave it to the United States government to determine what should happen in the East. Neither the President, nor his advisers, nor the American public wanted war with Japan. If America stopped Japanese expansion without war, then international order would be strengthened, Chiang and 'democracy' encouraged, and British resistance to Hitler facilitated. Japan's alliance with Germany and Italy in the Tripartite Pact in the autumn of 1940 showed that the Japanese leaders regarded the war as an opportunity and that they would join in if the United States became involved in war with Germany, which was possible, even probable, as a result of the increasingly energetic

American provision of 'all aid short of war' to the British Empire and then to the Soviet Union.

Hence the entry of Japanese forces into northern Indo-China in the summer of 1941 met a firm reply from the United States in the form of the oil embargo. Neither the United States nor Japan wanted war, but the conditions they required sharply diverged. Japan wanted Chiang to accept Japanese-imposed economic and political arrangements in China and wanted the United States to allow Japan to make secure the resources needed to impose such a solution of the 'China incident'. The United States administration insisted that supplies of the sinews of power to Japan would continue to be embargoed until Japan agreed to restore Chinese independence. The United States government preferred, in the end, to risk Japanese attack rather than award them a free hand in east Asia and the south-west Pacific, though until nearly the last minute it assumed that the Japanese would not risk war. General Tojo, the Japanese ex-War Minister who had just become Prime Minister, put the situation quite clearly during the review of policy demanded by Emperor Hirohito. The Americans, Tojo explained, were trying to

force upon Japan the Four Principles: (1) respect of territorial integrity and sovereignty, (2) non-interference in internal affairs, (3) non-discriminatory trade and (4) disapproval of changing the *status quo* by force . . . The United States demands that we accept these principles. We cannot do so, because we carried out the Manchurian Incident and the China Incident to get rid of the yoke based on those principles . . . They insist upon Japan's acceptance of the principle of the withdrawal of troops . . . We sent a large force of 1,000,000 men, and it has cost us well over 100,000 dead and wounded, their bereaved families, hardship for four years . . . China would become worse than she was before the Incident. She would even attempt to rule Manchuria, Korea, and Formosa. We can expect an expansion of our country only by stationing troops.

The Japanese army concluded as early as August that Germany was unlikely completely to destroy the Soviet Union in 1941. In the winter military operations would be impossible in the north. Therefore there should be time to secure Japanese resources by diplomacy or by conquest in rapid campaigns and still be ready to exploit any decisive German victory in Russia in the summer of 1942. The navy asserted that the use of force against British or Dutch possessions would involve war with the United States. Accordingly, the Japanese government agreed that an attempt should be made by diplomacy to secure the relaxation of the oil embargo but that, if this attempt failed, Japan should go to war with

Britain, America, and the Dutch empire. War should begin early in December 1941 for there was no time to lose: in a document setting out the case for war the Japanese civilian and military authorities explained

oil is the weak point of our Empire's national strength and fighting power . . . We are now gradually consuming oil that has been stockpiled . . . We will be self-sufficient for two years at most. This will be less if we carry out larger-scale military operations . . . our Empire will become powerless militarily. Meanwhile the naval and air forces of the United States will improve remarkably as time goes on . . . the United States navy will surpass the naval power of our Empire after next autumn . . . it is necessary to prepare for war in the shortest possible time so that we can conclude the main operations in the South quickly during this season and preserve our freedom of military action in the North [i.e. against the Soviet Union] after the spring of next year.

The Japanese authorities did not imagine that Japan could destroy the strength of the United States. They expected that Germany would knock the British out of the war and that Japan could conquer the resources needed for a protracted defence. Then the United States would see reason and decline the efforts required to smash the 'Greater East Asian Co-Prosperity Sphere'. As Tojo put it, on 12 November 1941 'America may be enraged for a while, but later she will come to understand.' This was a very odd view indeed, especially since the war was to begin with a surprise attack on the United States Pacific Fleet moored at Pearl Harbor. At 7.55 a.m. on Sunday, 7 December 1941, local time, the first bombs fell (3.25 a.m., 8 Dec. in Tokyo; 1.25 p.m., 7 Dec. in Washington; 6 p.m. 7 Dec. GMT). As a result of unintended delays, Cordell Hull, the American Secretary of State, was given the declaration of war one hour later.

In Japan the best-informed were worried. The Emperor and some of his circle, a few naval officers, especially among the most senior, many diplomatists, and representatives of banks and the large business concerns contemplated war with Britain and the United States with dismay. The voices of such people had been increasingly muted in the 1930s. Opposition, even within the government, to aggressive actions involved risk of assassination by nationalist extremists. The armed services, especially the army, gained in influence and, within the army, middle-rank staff officers, majors or colonels, tended to dominate their sometimes more cautious seniors. The navy, in order to maintain its influence and its budgetary allocations, had to compete in combativity with the army and, in particular, to assert the possibility of war with

America. Even those who were uneasy often resented the apparently high-handed attitude of the United States administration and the American assumption that Chiang Kai-shek's government was superior to that sponsored by the Japanese. Among the public, patriotism, encouraged by organizations such as the Reservists' Association, helped to induce conformity. By 1941 the Press was controlled and the parties in the never very powerful Diet had been merged into one—the 'Imperial Rule Assistance Association'. In December 1941 Tojo claimed that 'the people in general are aware that our nation, in view of the present world situation, stands at a crossroads, one road leading to glory and the other to decline'. However, controls had been 'strengthened' over 'those who are anti-war and anti-military, such as Communists, rebellious Koreans, certain religious leaders . . . in some cases we might have to subject some of them to preventive arrest'.

On 11 December 1941 Hitler and Mussolini also declared war on the United States. Now the main alignment of the Second World War was complete: the British Empire, the Soviet Union, and the United States against Germany, Italy, and Japan, though the Soviet Union did not declare war on Japan until 1945. Without the German declaration of war Roosevelt might not have been able to bring America into open war with Germany and so carry out the agreed Anglo-American strategic principle that the defeat of Germany should have priority over the defeat of Japan. We do not know why Hitler did it. In April 1941 he had assured the Japanese foreign minister Matsuoka that Germany would join in if Japan became involved in war with the United States. It was obviously valuable for Germany that Japanese aggression should distract her enemies and restrain the United States from all-out support for Britain and Russia. Hitler had also to try and prevent any Japanese–American settlement which would free American power for the Atlantic and Europe. Thus, though he seems to have hesitated, when faced, at the end of November 1941, with the prospect of imminent Japanese attack, there was nothing he could do except to repeat his pledge. In any case, the events of 1941 showed that war with the United States was possible in the near future, however much Hitler wished to postpone it. It was all the more necessary to make sure of Japan and to present the appearance of solidarity among the Axis allies. No doubt, too, if war were to come with the United States, Hitler thought it better to make it seem his own decision.

In 1941 Roosevelt had given as much aid to the enemies of Germany as American public opinion would tolerate. The President was a uniquely successful politician. Elected four times, he relied on careful and sensitive perception of electoral attitudes, keeping himself as representative, or even more representative, of those attitudes as Congress itself and leading opinion only when he was confident of the response. That he wished to do more than he thought public opinion would allow is shown by the eagerness with which he exploited, and even exaggerated, provocations offered by Germany. In April 1941 American air and naval patrols began to operate in the Atlantic west of 25 degrees west, with instructions to report to British warships any sightings of German vessels. In July 1941 American forces began to reinforce (and eventually to replace) the British garrison in Iceland, there since May 1940. On 4 September 1941 a German submarine attacked the USS *Greer*. On 6 September Roosevelt announced that American forces would attack any German or Italian submarine they found in the western Atlantic. Later that month Roosevelt secured from Congress the right to extend Lend-Lease aid to Russia. In October, Congress, with much hesitation, legislated to permit the arming of American merchant ships and to make them free to sail to the ports of belligerent countries. Though Roosevelt exploited new submarine attacks—on the USS *Kearny* and the *Reuben James*—the majorities for revision of neutrality legislation were small. Obviously congressmen thought Americans reluctant to risk getting the United States involved in the war. Now, after Pearl Harbor and Hitler's declaration of war, however, public support for fighting for victory became vigorous even among the small minority which blamed Roosevelt for having provoked the Japanese attack.

6

Japanese victories and disappointments: December 1941 to August 1942

TOGETHER, the United States, the British Empire, and the Soviet Union were certain to defeat Germany provided all of them went on fighting long enough. The defeat of Japan would be a lesser problem once they had disposed of Germany, especially if the Soviet Union then joined the British and Americans against Japan. The allies must win if they stayed together. The effort and length of time needed for victory was fixed principally by the proportion of the world that Germany and Japan could conquer before they were halted. Three great campaigns determined the result: the amphibious operations of Japan in the Pacific and south Asia, the German land offensive against Russia, and the submarine campaign against Britain.

In December 1941 the Japanese navy had in service ten battleships to which one very powerful ship, far bigger than any vessel in the United States or British navies, was added in that month (the *Yamato*, with 18.1-inch main armament), ten aircraft-carriers, of which four carried less than thirty-five aircraft and six up to seventy-two, eight heavy cruisers and eighteen light cruisers, 113 destroyers, and sixty-three submarines. The army had fifty-one divisions (the establishment of which was generally about 18,000 men). Most of them were in the home islands, or in Manchuria or China, and only eleven divisions were used for the attack against the Americans, British, and Dutch. The Japanese navy had about 1,000 first-line combat aircraft, of which half were land-based, and about 600 reconnaissance machines. The Japanese army had about 1,500 first-line aircraft, rather less than half of which were made available for the new war. The United States army had about 35,000 men in the Philippines, supported by 100,000 Filipinos, with about 250 aircraft, and 45,000 men in Hawaii with about 130 aircraft. In Malaya and Singapore the British had three divisions. In Burma there was one division of locally raised troops supported by a few Indian army units. At Hong Kong there was a combat strength of about 12,000 men. Elsewhere there were tiny garrisons such as the one Indian battalion in British

Borneo. The Royal Air Force had 246 aircraft in Malaya, mostly out-of-date.

The Japanese intended to seize a large, economically self-sufficient area and establish a defensive perimeter around it. Attacks on this defended area, the Japanese expected, would be so difficult that the enemy's will to fight would diminish until the American and British accepted the Japanese New Order in East Asia. Hong Kong, Malaya, and Singapore, the Philippines, the Dutch East Indies, Siam, Burma, the Nicobar and Andaman islands, Australian New Guinea, the Bismarck islands (with Rabaul), the Gilbert islands, Guam, and Wake islands were all to be captured within the opening months of the war. These conquests needed Japanese command of the sea to make invasions possible. The British and Dutch were weak at sea and the most formidable threat to Japanese ambitions came from the US Pacific Fleet based at Pearl Harbor, Hawaii. It had eight battleships, three aircraft-carriers, twelve heavy cruisers, nine light cruisers, and sixty-seven destroyers. Originally the Japanese intended, in case of war, to wait for the Pacific Fleet to move into Japanese waters, meanwhile weakening it by destroyer and submarine attack, and then to fight a decisive fleet action at a time and place chosen by the Japanese admiral. The snag was that Japanese conquests must be rapid, to forestall reinforcements of threatened points by Britain and the United States, but invasion fleets could not go to sea before the US Pacific Fleet was out of action. Admiral Yamamoto proposed a quicker method: a surprise air attack, launched from aircraft-carriers, on the American battle-fleet moored in Pearl Harbor. This was an extraordinarily risky scheme, for surprise was essential to success. Scrupulously, the Japanese authorities tried to get their declaration of war delivered in Washington 25 minutes before the attack began, but delays in decoding caused it to be delivered after the attack. However, if the commanders at Pearl Harbor had set up routine long-range air-reconnaissance patrols, the Japanese might have been detected well in advance. As it was, an unidentified midget submarine was detected four hours before the air strike, and effectively handled army radar provided 50 minutes' advance warning of the approach of aircraft. The midget submarine was sunk, an event reported to the naval Commander-in-Chief at least 30 minutes before the air attack; the radar report never reached him. The extreme daring of the Japanese attack brought its own reward. It was so totally unexpected that evidence that it was imminent was disregarded. Within half-an-hour the US battle-fleet had been put out of action and the Japanese were masters of the western Pacific. It was a complete victory but its full impact was temporary. Three damaged battleships were soon repaired (and three others eventually rejoined the fleet), the three aircraft-carriers were away from Pearl Harbor as were one battleship, nine heavy cruisers, three light cruisers, and eighteen destroyers, while two heavy cruisers, four light cruisers, and thirty-seven destroyers survived unscathed or lightly damaged.

The opening of the war in the Far East found the Royal Navy with only six out of fifteen capital ships immediately serviceable. The threat from the new German battleship *Tirpitz* and Italian battleship strength meant that the constitution of a substantial fleet for the Far East could not be considered until repairs and refitting of the others were completed. Meanwhile two capital ships, the *Prince of Wales* and *Repulse*, had been dispatched to Singapore. The new aircraft-carrier *Indomitable* was intended to join them but was accidentally damaged before setting off. The British admiral was well aware of the dangers of Japanese air attack, but sailed to intercept Japanese ships invading Malaya. Having been spotted by Japanese aircraft, he was withdrawing to the south when he paused to track down a non-existent landing force, of which he had received a false report. The wireless silence, customary among ships close to an enemy, meant that liaison with shore-based British aircraft was inadequate, and by the time fighters came to help the British ships against Japanese aerial torpedo and bomb attack, it was all over and both the *Prince of Wales* and the *Repulse* had been sunk.

At sea there was now no disputing Japanese mastery; on land, the most effective resistance seemed likely to come from British Empire forces defending Malaya and Singapore. There were three divisions (one Australian and two Indian), two Indian brigades, and two further brigades in Singapore, plus local volunteer forces. During the campaign another British division and two brigades arrived, plus about 9,000 men as replacements. The Japanese employed three divisions and a tank group, with over 150 tanks. The British had no tanks. British infantry divisions were made up of 13,700 officers and men. The Japanese divisions in Malaya had respectively 15,342 men (5th Division, mechanized), 12,649 (Imperial Guards Division, mechanized) and 22,206 (18th Division, horse transport).

In spite of numerical inferiority, the Japanese conquered Malaya and Singapore more rapidly than they expected: in ten weeks rather than fifteen. Myths surround this disaster to the British Empire. Singapore is said to have been a 'fortress' which could have been defended as readily as Sebastopol. In fact, its only fortress-like quality was that the island possessed very powerful fixed gun-batteries to counter sea-borne attack. A linked legend is that British military authorities had never contemplated enemy attack on Singapore island from the north—from Malaya—but it was always obvious that the naval base, which was on the north of the island, on the straits of Johore, would already have been rendered useless by a Japanese conquest of the Malayan mainland, and the British therefore assumed that they must hold Japanese ground forces well to the north of the straits. A more imprecise and tenacious belief is that Malaya and Singapore was a lotus land which sapped the military qualities of its defenders. General Wavell, who acted for a short time as the first of the inter-allied theatre commanders, and so briefly visited the scene, and who had some literary sensibility, got in first: 'The trouble goes a long way back: climate, the atmosphere of the country—the whole of Malaya has been asleep for at least 200 years.'

The reasons for defeat were less mysterious. Japanese dominance in the air and at sea made it impossible for the British to interfere with the invasion of Siam and northern Malaya, and this also enabled the Japanese army to carry out outflanking movements by sea. British strategy for the defence of Malaya relied increasingly on the air, but amidst the other British preoccupations of 1941, Singapore and Malaya never came at the top of the list of priorities. Though war with Japan seemed possible, the British still thought, as late as the end of November, that an attack on Malaya was unlikely before the spring of 1942. British resources were still meagre in relation to commitments, especially as long as it seemed possible that Germany would defeat the Soviet Union. British strategy was difficult to work out. The safety of the Singapore base from air attack required that the Japanese be held as far north as possible, yet ground forces had to be kept in and near Singapore in case of Japanese landings. The greatest factor in the British defeat was, however, the disparity between the military effectiveness of the Japanese compared with the defending troops. It was not a question of any tactical innovations nor of any special Japanese skill in jungles: in general, the Japanese advanced along roads and tracks and neither side attempted to move through jungles, except in short outflanking movements. Tanks greatly helped the attackers, but they came straight down the roads without any of the sweeping manoeuvres possible in Europe. The critical superiority of the Japanese was that they employed well-trained, experienced, battle-hardened infantry against troops most of whom lacked all those advantages. Japanese made good soldiers: their educational levels were high and they had a strong sense of obligation towards groups of which they became members, as well as an unusually firm belief that combat was honourable. The Japanese units in Malaya were among the best.

On the other side, the British Commonwealth forces lost about 140,000 men, including non-combatant troops, most of them taken prisoner. Of these 67,000 were Indians, 38,500 British, 18,500 Australians, and 14,000 local volunteers. The majority of the fighting soldiers were Indian. The British-organized and controlled Indian army was in peacetime entirely made up of volunteers—the word always used by the British to describe what sceptics might have called mercenaries. Junior officers were either British or Indian, but mostly British, while senior officers were invariably British: in 1939 there were 396 Indian officers and 4,028 British officers in the combatant arms of the Indian army. Indian brigades contained one purely British battalion from the British army, with two Indian army battalions (though brigades might consist entirely of British-officered Gurkha battalions). The Indian army was drawn from a highly complex society: within regiments were men of different religions, customs, and languages, and from various sections of an unhomogeneous population. The army had to create loyalty to an artificial community and could not rely on the national feelings that helped to cement European armies.

The war brought new stresses: accelerated modernization and rapid expansion. The peacetime Indian army relied on British artillery and technical services, and most of its cavalry was horsed. Now officers and NCOs, Indian and British, had to be found who could learn new skills and organize and train others. In consequence the old peacetime units were often deprived of their best men while new units had to rely on hastily trained leaders, often officers from Britain who were totally ignorant of India and who could not even speak the language of command. Recruits, often illiterate, could be fully trained and integrated into the army only by slow processes, which were discarded under the pressures of wartime expansion. In January 1940 the Indian army had 220,000 soldiers, in January 1941, 430,000, in January 1942 856,000. (A year later it had doubled again, to 1,565,000, and though the pace slackened in 1943, there were 2,024,000 by the end of that year and 2,210,000 by the beginning of 1945.) New weaponry made the task still more arduous. At the start of the war the Indian army had few artillery batteries; at the end there were 217. Deficiencies of training were very evident in the Malayan battles. Two of the Indian brigades sent to reinforce the army there had a high proportion of men who had been in their battalions for less than three months and most of their experienced officers and NCOs had been removed to train still newer contingents. On 11 December 1941 Japanese medium tanks burst upon the 1/14th Punjab Battalion, firing as they came. The Punjabis were understandably dismayed since for most of them this was their first sight of a tank.

British units faced fewer problems. However, their training was sometimes skimped: on 13 January 1942 the 53rd Brigade arrived at Singapore after eleven weeks bottled up in crowded troopships, and on 17 January it was in action in Johore. The best troops among the defenders were in the Australian 8th Division. Its units had trained together in Malaya or Australia for at least a year before the Japanese invasion began. They proved able to withstand the Japanese and even at the last moment, two days before the surrender, the Japanese shifted the spearhead of their attack to avoid them. By contrast, 1,900 Australian replacements arrived in mid-January. Some of them had no training at all, having been in the army for less than a month. Their military quality was even less than that of the 7,000 young and partially trained Indian reinforcements who came at the same time. Deficiencies among ordinary soldiers were supplemented by the usual, or worse than usual, failures of the British to develop clear and orderly chains of command and to establish rapid and effective liaison between neighbouring units. British relations with the Australian commander, Gordon Bennett, were not good; the latter disliked the public-school affectations of British senior officers. British other ranks commended themselves much more easily to Australians whose country, indeed, the British servicemen fortunate enough to go there during the war came to regard as an earthly paradise. In spite of these grave weaknesses, front-line troops never succumbed to panic and a coherent line was always held. At the end, with the notoriously ferocious Japanese closing in on the overcrowded town of Singapore, from which escape was possible only for a few, there were scenes of disorder and riot from deserters, often armed, mostly servicemen who had seen no combat. On 15 January 1942, with the Japanese 3 miles from the town centre and with the water supply broken, the British commander, General Percival, surrendered. Numerically this was the largest capitulation in British history.

Once the Japanese had defeated the American and British navies and overwhelmed British land and air forces in Malaya, there were no adequate forces to prevent them from seizing the most important item in their programme of grasping economic self-sufficiency by conquest: the Dutch East Indies.

The conquest of Malaya and the Dutch East Indies gave Japan three-quarters of the world's natural rubber, two-thirds of the tin, and, above all, enough oil for Japan's entire needs—provided it could be transported. The final Japanese object was to secure enough territory and outlying bases to guard Japan's economic sphere against all but the most determined, sustained, and costly attacks. In the Philippines, superior Japanese forces soon isolated the Americans in the Bataan peninsula, which held out until 9 April, and in Corregidor, a genuine fortress island, until 6 May. Two Japanese divisions, reinforced by another two after the capture of Rangoon, cleared the British out of Burma. In May 1942 the British seized Madagascar from the Vichy French in order to prevent the Japanese setting up a base on that side of the Indian Ocean. In the Pacific, the Japanese endeavoured to create a perimeter of defended island bases, adding Guam, which was seized at the outbreak of war, to Iwo Jima and the other Marianas, and adding Wake Island, taken on 22 December after fierce American resistance, to the Carolinas and Marshalls which had been Japanese mandates before the war. In the Gilbert Islands, Makin and Tarawa were occupied. In January and February, New Ireland and New Britain, including the important base at Rabaul, were occupied.

So successful was all this that the Japanese High Command became more ambitious: it decided to push the Japanese perimeter further outwards and to cut communications between the United States and Australia by the seizure of bases in Papua and the Solomon Islands, and eventually to take the New Hebrides, the Fiji Islands, and Samoa. Early in 1942 bases in northern Papua were taken, and in late March Bougainville and other islands in the Solomons. The Japanese then planned expeditions to Tulagi, further south in the Solomons, and a sea-borne attack on Port Moresby in southern Papua, within striking distance of Australia. Tulagi was no problem, but the attack on Port Moresby brought the first serious setback to the Japanese.

Already allied resistance was reviving: the Japanese fleet, the same that had assaulted Pearl Harbour, appeared in the Indian Ocean and inflicted serious losses on British ships but its carrier aircraft suffered grave losses at the hands of the Royal Air Force in Ceylon. The US Navy and Army Air Force had contrived to bomb Tokyo, and General MacArthur had gone to Australia to take command and encourage Australian self-defence by the promise of American reinforcement, on which, after the defeat of the British at Singapore, Australia and New Zealand now had to rely.

Before 17 April 1942 American intelligence, using decoded Japanese signals, learned that a Japanese landing was planned early in May in the Coral Sea, and soon afterwards discovered that Port Moresby was to be attacked. An allied task force, including two aircraft-carriers, was assembled on 6 and 7 May 1942. The Battle of the Coral Sea inaugurated a new type of naval battle, in which the ships involved never saw enemy ships or exchanged gunfire. The battle was entirely conducted by aircraft. One US fleet aircraft-carrier was lost but the Japanese lost an escort carrier. Above all, they were compelled to postpone the sea-borne attack on Port Moresby until the American Pacific Fleet was further weakened, an event which never took place.

Next came a decisive American victory, the Battle of Midway. Early in May, American intelligence intercepted and decoded Japanese radio signals giving news of a forthcoming naval offensive in the central Pacific, and by the middle of the month it became clear that they intended to send an expeditionary force to capture Midway Island. A powerful covering fleet hoped to engage a naval battle on Japanese terms. A diversionary attack was to seize strategic points in the Aleutian Islands. All this became known before the Japanese brought new naval codes into use on 1 June and interrupted the flow of information. The Japanese combined fleet put to sea under Admiral Yamamoto, flying his flag in the mighty *Yamato*. The whole Japanese battle fleet, of eleven battleships, ten cruisers, forty-four destroyers, and four fleet aircraft-carriers, with one light carrier, supported the assault forces. The US Pacific fleet assembled three fleet carriers, eight cruisers, and fifteen destroyers. The six American battleships in the Pacific were left at San Francisco since none of them could maintain the speed of the aircraft-carriers, so that either the latter would be impeded or the battleships lack air cover. On 19 May Admiral King, the US Chief of Naval Operations, asked the British for an aircraft-carrier but none was within range. Heavily outnumbered, the American ships were in position on 2 June 1942. Early on 4 June Japanese carrier planes attacked Midway. The American commander successfully timed his carrier plane counter-strike to coincide with Japanese refuelling and rearming. By mid-morning three of the four Japanese carriers were out of action and all sank that day; the fourth was knocked out in the afternoon and sank next morning. The American carrier *Yorktown* was lost, but the Midway section of the Japanese fleet was left without air cover against two surviving American carriers, and this compelled Yamamoto to withdraw his ships in spite of their overwhelming gun-power: Midway was safe, naval warfare transformed, and the limit of Japanese power reached.

The Japanese, whatever their later tactical successes, were now thrown on to the defensive. They proved more formidable in defence than any other participants in the war and many grim battles were to come, but the tide had turned. On 11 July 1942 they cancelled their plans to seize New Caledonia, Fiji, and Samoa. In Papua the Japanese gave up the plan to take Port Moresby from the sea, and an attempt by land was halted by Australian troops. On 7 August 1942 United States forces landed on Tulagi and Guadalcanal in the Solomons—the reconquest had begun, and it continued, with fierce fighting in areas where the climate provided continuous hardships as background to the horrors of ferocious campaigning.

7

The end of German expansion: the Atlantic, North Africa, and Russia, 1942–1943

THE main contestants in the submarine war on merchant shipping in 1942 and 1943, the British Admiralty and the German U-boat Command, both thought that it would decide who won the war, or at least whether or not Britain would be beaten. Grand Admiral Dönitz, the Commander-in-Chief of the German submarine force and, after January 1943, the head of the German navy, believed that the sinking of 700,000 tons a month of merchant shipping would defeat the British. When the Admiralty asked in November 1942 for more work on breaking the German submarine code, it declared that it was the only campaign 'in which the war can be lost'. In that month, the worst of the whole war for sinkings of allied merchant ships by enemy submarines, over 725,000 gross tons were lost. Moreover, the number of U-boats in action was growing: new boats exceeded losses by between five and ten every month.

Prospects looked grim for 1943, yet in a sense the battle of that year against German submarines was decided before it began. Shipbuilding in the United States grew so rapidly that construction of dry cargo ships on the allied side began to exceed losses in August 1942 and continued to do so in every month thereafter, with the one exception of November 1942. (Tankers were a different matter, but new ships exceeded losses after February 1943.) In 1941 US shipbuilding output had been 1,160,000 gross tons, in 1943 it reached over 13,500,000 tons. Dönitz had no chance of increasing sinkings at that rate, though the unintentional but persistent exaggeration of their successes by U-boat commanders may have misled him. On the other hand, Britain was being weakened because losses of ships under British control greatly exceeded new construction. In 1942 the British built 1.3 million tons while losses to British-controlled ships were nearly 4 million. Moreover, British output did not grow. In 1943 it was 1.2 million tons and in 1944 only just over 1 million. Survival, therefore, came to depend on ships built in the United States. So long as enough of these were allocated to British imports and so long as the Red Army fought the bulk of the German army and thereby prevented a German invasion, Britain was safe and the outline of allied strategy, based on an eventual landing in France or the Low Countries, could be maintained. What Dönitz was able to do, however, as well as increasing British dependence on the United States, was to delay the allied victory. In 1942, with an average of about 140 U-boats available for patrols, he made an allied invasion of France in 1943 very difficult, and with over 200 available early in 1943 he might reasonably hope to prevent an invasion in 1944.

After the British had broken the relevant code, the second half of 1941 was a comparatively unsuccessful period for U-boats. At the end of 1941, however, several factors helped the Germans: they began to break the British naval cipher 3, used by the American, British, and Canadian navies for organizing North Atlantic convoys; they complicated their own map references; and, in February 1942, they added a fourth wheel for the Enigma machines used for submarine work. Their own codes became indecipherable while in the same month their naval intelligence service finally mastered naval cipher 3. The outbreak of war with the United States provided new opportunities for U-boats—ships sailing off the western American seaboard, silhouetted against illuminated towns on the coast, with navigation marks in service and sometimes with the ships showing lights themselves. The US Navy Board was slow to introduce convoys, believing, contrary to British experience, that no convoy was better than a weak convoy. More and more U-boats attacked shipping off the American coast in the first six months of 1942, until the belated introduction of convoys caused them to return their attention to transatlantic convoys. The Germans could read allied radio signals; until the end of 1942, the allies could not read theirs. The Germans could direct U-boats to convoys; the allies could not direct convoys away from U-boats except by the comparatively uncertain method of direction-finding (of submarines' radio transmissions) by shore stations.

Looking back on 1942, and with nearly twice as many submarines to deploy in 1943, Dönitz could anticipate impressive results. In March 1943 forty U-boats attacked two convoys sailing close together from New York to Britain. Convoy SC 122 was made up of fifty-two ships escorted by two destroyers, five corvettes, and a frigate: ten ships were lost. Convoy HX 229 comprised forty ships escorted by four destroyers and one corvette: thirteen ships were lost. Only one U-boat was sunk. But this was to be the peak of U-boat success. At the beginning of May, the U-boat Command had about sixty submarines in several groups ready to attack convoys in the North Atlantic. In the next two weeks there were 525 merchant ships in convoy in the danger zone. Of these twenty were sunk but no less than twenty-two German submarines were lost. Dönitz was appalled. On 17 May 1943 he signalled to the defeated commanders, 'We can see no explanation for this failure'. On 22 May he sent the angry message, 'Anyone who thinks that combating convoys is no longer possible . . . is a weakling. The battle of the Atlantic is getting harder, but it is the determining element in the waging of the war', a signal which was followed next day by another ordering withdrawal from the North Atlantic: it was to be 'temporary' but U-boats never prevailed again in that most important piece of ocean.

In contrast to earlier British defeats of the U-boat, the victory this time was gained more by tactical superiority than by better signals intelligence. From 13 December 1942 British cryptanalysts began to read the German code used for U-boats, though not always quickly enough to be useful. After temporary failure in January and February 1943 following an allied procedural modification the Germans again broke naval cipher 3 and went on doing so until it was superseded in June 1943. At the critical time, in May 1943, the British were almost immediately decoding German orders to U-boats but German Naval Intelligence was similarly deciphering allied orders to convoys and their escorts. Thus, the allies changed convoy routings to avoid U-boat packs but the U-boat packs changed their dispositions to intercept along the new routes.

In any case, by the spring of 1943 the Atlantic, as the First Sea Lord put it, was 'so saturated by U-boats that the practice of evasion is rapidly becoming impossible'. The British had to fight their way through, relying on tenacity and technical innovations. 'Very Long-range Aircraft', which could patrol for four hours at a distance of 1,000 miles from their base, were helped at night by searchlights fixed beneath them. The development of centimetric (short-wave) radar enabled them to locate U-boats both night and day. From October 1942 centimetric radar began to be installed in escort vessels so that they could locate U-boats on the surface, as well as underwater by use of their existing Asdic (sonar) equipment (submarines when submerged had short range and very low speeds, so operated as much as possible on the surface). Another innovation was high-frequency direction finding (HF/DF, colloquially 'Huff-Duff') which began to be installed in escort vessels in July 1942 and which was standard by 1943. This enabled warships to locate U-boats when they made signals to shore headquarters or to each other and, if they were close, immediately to make full speed towards them. Furthermore, escorts' weapons were made more effective—depth-charges rolled over the side were increased in weight and their settings made more accurate, while the new 'hedgehog' enabled the use of depth charges to be speeded up by throwing them ahead of attacking vessels. Another new weapon was the escort carrier, a small aircraft-carrier working with escort support groups, which reinforced threatened convoys and carried out close-range search-and-attack operations against U-boats.

The defeat of the U-boats on the North Atlantic convoy routes was carried out by the Royal Navy, the Royal Air Force and the Royal Canadian Navy, with some help from the Royal Australian Air Force. In May 1943 six German submarines were sunk by US forces, of which one was in the North Atlantic, while thirty-three were sunk by British Commonwealth forces. When the U-boats moved further south in the Atlantic into areas of American responsibility (Admiral King had, sensibly, insisted that forces grouped by nationality were more effective than mixed forces), the US Navy showed its effectiveness. In particular it displayed its usual talent in co-operation between aircraft and warships: in July 1943 twenty-two U-boats were sunk by the Americans, half of them by aircraft. Four more were destroyed by combined British and American attack. In the same month the tonnage of allied merchant ships constructed since September 1939 exceeded the total tonnage of ships sunk since then. Accelerating production was more and more outdistancing declining losses. German technical advances came too late to undo the allied victory. After July 1943 submarines operating in the Atlantic sank much less than 100,000 tons each month—the highest figure was 73,000 in April 1945, when Germany was on the edge of defeat.

It was British forces, too, that first compelled a definitive German retreat in a land campaign. In Egypt, early in July 1942, the 8th Army, under General Auchinleck, held the Germans and Italians at El Alamein, 60 miles west of Alexandria, and they never got any further. It was the penultimate phase in a struggle which had begun when the Italian army advanced 65 miles into Egypt in September 1940. At the end of 1940 and early in 1941, the British drove the Italians westward for 340 miles, then in March to April the Italians, with the decisive support of German troops under Rommel, drove the British 370 miles to the east. At the end of 1941 a British offensive forced the Axis forces 340 miles back again but in two stages, from January to February 1942, and, in June, Rommel reached Alamein after an eastward advance of 570 miles. In October 1942 General Montgomery began a British advance of 1,500 miles which drove the Germans and Italians right out of Egypt and Libya.

There were constant factors in these campaigns. General von Ravenstein described the desert as 'a tactician's paradise and a quartermaster's hell'. Victorious advances made lines of communication grow longer while retreats moved back towards sources of supply: thus counter-offensives were facilitated. The Germans in the desert, as elsewhere, used better tactics than their opponents. Above all, their artillery, tanks, and infantry worked together in a manner the British found difficult to accomplish; indeed, mutual resentment sometimes developed between British infantry and armour. The German staff in Africa commented on the winter battles of 1941 to 1942, 'never anywhere at any time during the fighting in Libya did the British High Command concentrate all its available forces at the decisive point'.

Rommel himself was another constant advantage for the Axis side, not only for his energetic leadership and quick reactions but for the almost magical qualities attributed to him, especially, perhaps, by the British. Churchill made a flattering reference to him in the House of Commons: 'We have a very daring and skilful opponent against us, and, may I say across the havoc of war, a great general', while Auchinleck felt it necessary to write to his commanders that to speak of Rommel as a superman was bad for morale and must be forbidden.

Another disparity was in the quality of equipment. German tanks were superior until the arrival of the American-built Shermans in September 1942. (In June the British intercepted a message in which Hitler was reported to have described British tanks as 'tin'). British tank guns were inadequate and the main cruiser tank, the Crusader, was under-gunned, thin-skinned, and unreliable. Early in 1942 the American-built Grant produced some improvement but its comparatively effective gun had only limited traverse. In 1942 Auchlinleck insisted that he would need a superiority of three to two in tank numbers to balance the technical and tactical superiority of the Germans, though he thought equality in numbers with Italian tanks was sufficient. Only in 1942 did the 8th Army begin to receive the 6-pounder anti-tank gun to replace the ineffective 2-pounder, and nothing the allies produced ever challenged the supremacy of the dreaded German 88 mm anti-aircraft gun, used as a devastating anti-tank weapon. In the air, the German Me-109F easily outclassed all British fighters until the arrival of the Spitfire V in the spring and summer of 1942.

There was, however, a variable factor, and that was decisive: supply. The British had a comparatively safe line of supply from Britain, the

United States, and India. Provided sufficient shipping was allotted by the allies to cargoes for the Middle East, the delays of the Cape route to Egypt were manageable. The need to hold the Middle East in order to protect the supply route to Russia through Iran, and the need to defend the oilfields to help maintain India as a base for the containment of Japan and the support of China, were new motives which encouraged American support for the British defence. In 1942 it seemed possible that German forces from Africa and Russia might meet in Iraq or Iran and even that they might link up with a Japanese invasion of India. Such fears gave even higher priority to allied allocation of shipping and supplies to the British army in the Middle East.

On the Italo-German side supply could come only across the Mediterranean, and could be interfered with by submarines, surface ships, and aircraft. Effective interference needed good intelligence, and after July 1941 intercepted Italian radio signals gave the British advance notice of virtually every ship carrying troops or supplies across the Mediterranean for the Axis forces in North Africa, but the timing and course of enemy convoys or individual ships were sometimes changed after the original intention was signalled, often in response to British operations. The British, too, had to arrange for aerial sightings of ships they intended to attack, in order to conceal their success in code-breaking. Nevertheless, they carried out effective operations by aircraft, submarines, and surface ships ('Force K') from Malta and from bases in North Africa. The shift of much of the Luftwaffe to Russia in the summer of 1941 made things easier. In July and October 1941, the Germans and Italians lost one-fifth of the cargoes destined for North Africa; about 72,000 tons got through each month. In November 1941 no less than 62 per cent of the cargo was lost; only 30,000 tons arrived. The Axis units at the front needed 30,000 tons a month for regular consumption of fuel, ammunition, rations, and so on in addition to supplies for line of communication and base troops and for the Italian and German air forces in Africa. In December less was sent, heavily convoyed, and though losses were reduced to 18 per cent, it was only 39,000 tons that got through.

This was the period of the British buildup for the CRUSADER offensive in November 1941, successfully launched with substantial numerical superiority in tanks on the British side, against a straitened Rommel. The Germans replied by strengthening their supply lines. In November 1941, the Luftwaffe *Fliegerkorps II* began to arrive in Sicily from eastern Europe and German submarines were ordered to the Mediterranean. In Sicily, German air strength grew to 425 aircraft, though the Germans did not reach the planned total of 650 because of the Russian winter offensive. The prime importance of the Russian front was shown when these aircraft withdrew again, in June 1942, to the Balkans to replace air forces transferred to Russia to support the 1942 summer offensive. Before then, they had, with the U-boats—twenty-one German submarines were in the Mediterranean by the end of December 1941—and the Italian navy and air force, reversed the British success and restored superiority in North Africa to Rommel.

In November and December 1941, the aircraft-carrier *Ark Royal*, the battleship *Barham*, and three cruisers were sunk, while two battleships, the *Valiant* and the *Queen Elizabeth*, were put out of action by Italian midget submarines in Alexandria harbour. As a result, British surface ships could do little against heavily escorted Italian convoys, while British air and submarine operations from Malta against Rommel's supplies were steadily reduced by increasing bombing of the island and by successful attacks on British convoys supplying Malta. In late 1941 a single oil-tanker got through to Malta, and another early in January 1942. Later that month three out of a convoy of four ships arrived, and another tanker. In February, however, no ships reached Malta, in March one convoy with only about one-fifth of its supplies intact, and in April and May no convoys at all. In February, German and Italian bombers dropped 750 tons of bombs on the island, in March 2,000, and in April 5,500 tons (for comparison, the Germans dropped 520 tons in the raid on Coventry in November 1940). On concentrated and easily identified targets, such as the dockyard and towns around Grand Harbour, this bombing struck effectively. Malta continued to be a staging point for aircraft flying to the Middle East, but it ceased to be a base for striking at Axis shipping. Even the submarine flotilla was withdrawn in April 1942. In February and March 1942 the Germans and Italians lost only 9 per cent of cargoes to North Africa, and 107,000 tons arrived. In April they lost less than 1 per cent and 150,000 tons arrived, and in May under 7 per cent was lost and 86,000 tons reached Axis ports.

On 20 December 1941, Rommel's two panzer divisions had less than twenty-three serviceable tanks between them while the Italians had fifteen. But the day before, convoys had reached Benghazi and Tripoli, and their forty-four new tanks made possible Rommel's counter-attack at the end of December. On 5 January, fifty-four tanks were landed at Tripoli and another seventy-one on 24 January. British intelligence knew of these convoys but was not yet able to identify their cargoes. Hence Rommel's strength surprised the 8th Army and he was able to sustain an offensive which compelled the British to withdraw to the Gazala line. German reinforcement continued as more Axis ships moved safely across the Mediterranean. On 1 May 1942 Hitler and Mussolini agreed that the attack in the desert should be resumed at the end of May, but that the invasion of Malta should precede the eventual occupation of Egypt. Rommel opened his attack with 510 tanks, of which 282 were Italian. The German tanks included nineteen up-gunned Panzer III specials. The British had 499 battle tanks of which 242 were Grants and 257 the unreliable Crusaders, plus 287 infantry tanks, the latter unsuitable for tank-to-tank combat and mostly obsolete. By 15 June the British had been defeated in a series of battles and were reduced to fifty cruiser and twenty infantry tanks, and on 20 June Tobruk surrendered to the Germans, who captured 30,000 British and South African troops.

At this stage two important decisions were made. Hitler, having promoted Rommel to Field Marshal, accepted his proposal to conquer Egypt at once before the British could recover, and secured Mussolini's agreement to the postponement of the seizure of Malta. In Washington, President Roosevelt ordered the immediate despatch to the Middle East of 300 Sherman tanks, 100 self-propelled guns, and a large number of aircraft. Thus, the balance of strength began to shift back to the British side. In February 1942 the German battle-cruisers *Scharnhorst* and *Gneisenau*, having survived repeated bombing at Brest, dashed home up the Channel. This German success distressed the British public, but it helped the British Naval Command to spare warships from the Atlantic to escort aircraft-carriers from which to fly off fighters to Malta. In March thirty-one Spitfires flew to Malta from aircraft-carriers. In April another forty-six arrived, but most were quickly put out of action on the ground. In May more precautions were taken and seventy-seven Spitfires were safely delivered. Air supremacy over Malta began to return to the Royal Air Force. In June, however, one convoy to Malta turned back and another lost four out of six ships, but in July, fifty-nine more Spitfires flew in, while fuel and ammunition came in by submarine. That month a British submarine flotilla returned to Malta, and in August 1942 a large convoy reached the island. It had fourteen merchant ships, of which nine were sunk along with the aircraft-carrier *Eagle*, but it brought the largest cargo since September 1941. This was the last convoy to Malta that the Germans and Italians were able seriously to oppose. At the same time another fifty-six Spitfires flew in. By autumn 1942, therefore, Malta had been restored as a threat to Axis supplies to North Africa.

Rommel's gamble, his dash into Egypt, brought his forward echelons

THE WESTERN MEDITERRANEAN

to the British defensive position at El Alamein, 45 miles from Alexandria, on 29 June 1942. He attacked on 1 July. At this stage intelligence supplied the British commanders, as the official history puts it, 'with more information about more aspects of the enemy's operations than any forces enjoyed during any important campaign of the Second World War'. Every Enigma key used by the Germans in the North African fighting was being deciphered, usually within hours of being sent, Italian shipping codes continued to be read, and, in the field, tactical signals were efficiently intercepted. The value of signals intelligence' was immense, but can be exaggerated: the intentions of enemy commanders were seldom confided to radio signals, and tactical situations in land fighting often developed too rapidly for intelligence to keep up. Nor did the British have a monopoly of success. The Germans deciphered the main 8th Army code until January 1942 and then made up for its loss by breaking the cipher used for the ample reports to Washington of the United States military attaché in Cairo. The Germans fully exploited the characteristic carelessness in signals security of British formations in the field. But the British, on balance, did better than the Germans. Their code-breaking provided information about enemy shipping movements and about the strength in men and weapons and the dispositions of Rommel's forces. Operational intentions were sometimes revealed. One such occasion was before Rommel's attack on 1 July: an Enigma decrypt early on 30 June showed that he then proposed to attack that afternoon at 3 p.m. and would feint in the north before making his main assault. In the afternoon it was learned that the attack had been postponed until 1 July and that the 15th Panzer Division would attack in the centre of the line. This knowledge, though incomplete, helped Auchinleck to check Rommel. Two days later the latter broke off the attempt to drive the British back.

At the end of August 1942, when Rommel tried again, the British position had further improved. The substitution of new British commanders, Alexander as Commander-in-Chief, Middle East, and Montgomery in command of the 8th Army, was good for morale, largely because of Montgomery's skill in self-advertisement. British intelligence gathered even more material. From the beginning of August 1942, returns of the strength of the Axis forces in Africa were regularly made by radio and regularly deciphered. On 17 August, moreover, the British code-breakers at Bletchley in England passed on an appreciation made by Rommel's command on 15 August. Reinforcements had given his forces a temporary superiority, except in the air. Provided supplies arrived on time, he would attack on 26 August, having regrouped during the preceding moonlit nights. Rommel hoped to break through the British at the southern end of the front. It was at this point that intelligence and the re-creation of Malta's fighting forces enabled the British decisively to curtail the supplies reaching Rommel. On 15 and 17 August the British sank two cargo ships on the way to north Africa and, on 21 August a tanker. On 24 August and again on 27 August Rommel postponed the attack. On 29 August, after two more fuel ships had been sunk, Rommel concluded that he could attempt no more than a local operation to defeat the 8th Army at El Alamein. At 4 p.m. on 30 August Rommel decided to attack that night, with fuel for only four-and-a-half days' fighting and ammunition for a maximum of six days. That day another tanker was sunk and the Germans were forced to move fuel by air from Italy to the front. No sea-borne fuel reached the army until 4 September. On 1 September Rommel called off the battle of Alam Halfa, and on 2 September ordered a withdrawal to his original positions.

Rommel had been halted by the dispositions of a well-informed General Montgomery and by the interference with his supplies by well-informed British naval and air forces, using the resupplied Malta base. In

August, September, and October 1942 Axis forces lost about one-third of their supplies and, since the British could identify the most critical ships, the impact was even greater than that figure suggests.

Although they sent reinforcements by air, the relative strength of the Germans and Italians in Africa compared with the British continued to decline. Montgomery commanded overwhelming numbers when the 8th Army attacked at El Alamein in the evening of 23 October 1942. On 1 August there had been 34,000 German combat troops in the western desert. On 20 October there were 49,000 Germans and 54,000 Italians. The 8th Army by then had a fighting strength of 195,000: more than half of these were from Britain, the rest from India, Australia, New Zealand and South Africa, together with smaller contingents of the Fighting French (whose troops had distinguished themselves at a crisis in the earlier desert campaign) and from exiled Greek troops. Supplies from the United States equipped many of these: in the first nine months of 1942 there arrived in the Middle East 1,235 tanks from Britain and 1,218 from America, including the 300 Shermans, and about 24,000 British-made motor vehicles plus nearly 44,000 from America. For the Battle of El Alamein the British had ready for action 1,029 tanks, of which 252 were Shermans. Only 211 German tanks were immediately ready, of which eighty-eight were Pz III specials and thirty Pz IV specials, with 278 Italian tanks. The British were superior in artillery: over 900 medium and field guns against about 500; 1,451 anti-tank guns, 849 of which were the new 6-pounders, against about 800, only 86 of which were the formidable 88 mm. guns. In June to September, 2,141 aircraft had arrived in the Middle East: 1,381 from Britain and 760 from the United States. At the time of El Alamein the allies had over 900 fully operational aircraft in the Middle East, of which about 200 were South African and 130 part of the US Army Air Force. The Germans and Italians, for whom maintenance and fuel were difficult to provide, had probably only about 300 aircraft ready for the battle.

As a result of British superiority in the air and the German shortage of fuel, Rommel made dispositions quite different from those he would normally have adopted. Before going on sick leave, he split up his armoured units so that they could counter-attack at once any penetration of Axis defensive positions, rather than keeping them together to use in a battle of manœuvre. Movement brought attack from the air, and in any case was inhibited by lack of fuel. Rommel, returning to the desert after Montgomery's attack began on 23 October 1942, was therefore compelled to fight a static defensive battle in which his enemy could fully exploit superior strength in a struggle of attrition and where Montgomery's tenacity showed to advantage. After eleven days of intense fighting, Rommel, delayed for a few hours by one of Hitler's 'stand fast' signals, ordered a retreat which continued for 1,500 miles. Four days later, on 7 November 1942, British and American troops came ashore at the other end of north Africa, in French Morocco and Algeria. And on 20 November, the Russian offensive opened in the Stalingrad sector.

The great Russo-German land battle determined the whole course of the war. Without the long involvement of the bulk of the German army in Russia, the western allies could not have returned to continental Europe, even if, which is far from certain, Britain could still have been defended. Russian defeat must have brought either a war lasting for decades or a frail peace based on a provisional partition of the world. In 1940, helped by the sea, the British enabled the western end of a two-front war eventually to be restored. In 1941, 1942, and 1943 the Soviet Union maintained the eastern end against the bulk of German power and skill, which the English Channel had made it impossible to bring into action against Britain. In these years the eastern front saw the decisive battles of the war, which determined its character and the outlines of its eventual consequences. It is not surprising that Anglo-American policies and strategy were dominated by the need to keep Russia fighting: only so could they win in the foreseeable future.

In 1941 the West was able to do little to distract the German army from the Russian front. In June 1941 all German armoured divisions, motorized infantry divisions, Waffen SS divisions, and all the best infantry divisions were on the Russian front, except for the two panzer divisions in Africa. The other fifty-four divisions outside Russia were not mobile units or of the highest quality, and apart from Rommel's two divisions in Africa, the 150 divisions in the east included all the most effective formations. In the summer of 1942 the British kept nine German units away from the eastern front: the motorized 90th Light Division had gone to Africa and three panzer divisions (and five ordinary infantry divisions) were sent to the west from the eastern front between April and June 1942, and there followed two motorized infantry SS divisions in July. However, only one of those mobile units remained in the west after the crisis caused by the Russian encirclement of Stalingrad: the 10th Panzer Division, which was sent to north Africa after the Anglo-American landings in November 1942. The Hermann Goering mobile division was also dispatched to Tunisia (this was technically an air-force unit, hence its name). Thus at the time of the crisis in southern Russia in the winter of 1942/3, although Hitler was able to send some reinforcements to the east, the British and Americans were actively engaging five first-class German mobile divisions—the 10th, 15th, and 21st Panzer Divisions together with the motorized divisions 'Hermann Goering' and the 90th Light, in addition to smaller mobile formations. This made up a powerful panzer army. The western allies were keeping occupied a comparatively small number of German troops, but their fighting power made their removal from the eastern front an important help to the Red Army. North Africa was thus an authentic 'second front'.

Another contribution to German embarrassments in Russia was the diversion of transport aircraft to ferry men and supplies to north Africa because of British success in sinking ships in the Mediterranean. Then allied supplies for Russia, often shipped against tenacious opposition in arctic conditions, were of significant value in 1942. Before July 1942 over 2,500 aircraft and 3,500 tanks, and supplies such as 380,000 miles of telephone wire, had been despatched by the British and Americans.

Nevertheless, the bulk of the German army was on the Russian front and it was stopped by the Red army. In December 1941 numerous Soviet divisions, mostly badly under-strength, ill-equipped, short of transport, many of them inadequately trained, and often tactically mishandled by officers incapable of any manœuvre more complicated than frontal massed infantry attack, were launched at the German Army Group Centre, now, after its failure to take Moscow, at the end of drastically over-extended lines of communication, short of supplies, often ill-clad, and lacking proper shelter. The military 'genius' of Stalin and Hitler took over the battle. Stalin, greatly exaggerating German enfeeblement, insisted on a grand offensive on a wide front; Hitler rejected sensible suggestions for German withdrawal to prepared winter quarters.

In spite of the losses of 1941, the Red Army was numerically superior, with perhaps about four million men in the field armies against nearly three million on the German side, but in guns and tanks the Germans were numerically and qualitatively superior. The Soviet counter-attack was well-timed and secured immediate success. Zhukov, in command of the 'western front'—the Soviet army group in front of Moscow—wished to use all available resources, especially of transport, to concentrate against the salient created by the German advance towards Moscow. Brauchitsch, the Commander-in-Chief of the German army, wanted to withdraw Army Group Centre and, by shortening the line, make it possible to rest tired troops. Hitler, perhaps fearing that retreat might turn into rout and always disliking the damage to civilian morale caused by any retreat, forbade such a withdrawal. After bitter fighting and struggles with logistic problems, the Germans were forced back about as far as the line Brauchitsch had suggested in the first place. During January 1942 advancing Soviet forces threatened encirclement of two German armies. Zhukov claims that Stalin imposed his plan for a general offensive, against his protests, on 5 January 1942; two weeks later Stalin took two armies away from Zhukov into Supreme Command Reserve in order to reinforce other offensives.

The Russian winter offensive of early 1942 forced German withdrawals, but nowhere secured an annihilating victory—that had to wait another year. As yet Russian forces were not strong enough in tanks or transport to fight large-scale mobile battles. German battle casualties during the winter offensive were smaller than the Russian, and they suffered more from disease, including frostbite (German losses in battle were about 100,000 killed and 265,000 wounded, plus another 500,000 or so casualties through sickness).

In the spring, mud checked movement on both sides: the summer was the period of opportunity for the Germans when communications were at their best and superior skill had its full impact. Hitler intended a decisive campaign for 1942. Army Group South, brought up to full strength, would encircle and destroy Russian forces west of the River Don and, in the process, conquer the main pre-war industrial area of the Soviet Union. Then Stalingrad would be taken to cut the Volga supply route and protect the flank of a German advance to seize the Caucasus and the main Russian oil-producing region. The 4th and 1st Panzer armies would provide the mobile spearheads. Before the main offensive began, the Crimea would be cleared and a pincer movement carried out against a salient left over from the Russian winter offensive, at Izyum on the Donets river.

Manstein, commanding the German 11th Army, successfully directed hard-fought operations in the Crimea and inflicted about 250,000 casualties, while the Izyum salient was cut off and another 250,000 Russians killed, wounded, or captured. The German success was helped by Stalin's continued refusal to allow timely retreats. However, his education as a soldier seems to have been advanced by these events and orders to hold ground regardless of consequences ceased to flow from Supreme Headquarters. At last the Red Army was allowed to trade space for time. Encirclements were to be avoided by retreat. The German summer offensive, therefore, conquered enormous tracts of territory but destroyed comparatively few Soviet units. Slowly the Russians regrouped their forces and reinforced threatened sectors until the German armies became so extended that a counter-strike was possible.

The main German offensive began on 28 June at the northern end of Army Group South with a double envelopment and the capture of Voronezh on 6 July. Only 30,000 prisoners were taken, since most Russian forces had withdrawn in time across the River Don. In the next few weeks much of the area west of the Don was overrun in a series of fast-moving encirclements. Again only about 50,000 prisoners were taken as the main Russian armies withdrew. Though Stalin had a 'no retreat' order read out to troops at the end of July, withdrawal was no longer totally prohibited in the manner of 1941. Hitler reduced the effectiveness of the offensive by starting the southward move to the Caucasus before the objectives in the Don area had been secured. Army Group South was split into two army groups, 'A' to capture the Caucasus, 'B' to clear the Don bend and advance to Stalingrad. By the end of July there were thus two distinct lines of attack, each with two German armies. In August, Army Group A moved forward about 300 miles into the Caucasus and Army Group B, against stronger opposition, to the Volga and into Stalingrad itself, which stretched along the western bank of the river. At this stage German forces seemed triumphant. Many British and American observers felt that the Soviet Union might be forced into negotiation or even surrender.

In September, however, German advance reached its limits. Of the three objectives of the German offensive, only one had been achieved and that temporarily: Stalingrad was out of action as an industrial and communications centre and Volga river traffic was interrupted. But the Caucasus oilfields had not been captured, and a secure hold had not been gained on the newly conquered territories. And the spectacular advances concealed growing weaknesses. The lines of communication stretching back to one railway bridge over the Dnieper were inadequate to sustain the impetus of advance without interruptions and to maintain the strength of the forward echelons. Army Group A (of which Hitler himself took direct command for a time, exercised from his distant personal headquarters) and Army Group B were no longer mutually supporting. On its side the Soviet Supreme Command concentrated more and more forces against the German 6th Army and 4th Panzer Army at Stalingrad. For nearly three months a continuous and ferocious battle was fought there. In street-fighting the Germans lost most of the benefit of superior tactical skill and organization. Slowly and agonizingly the German 6th

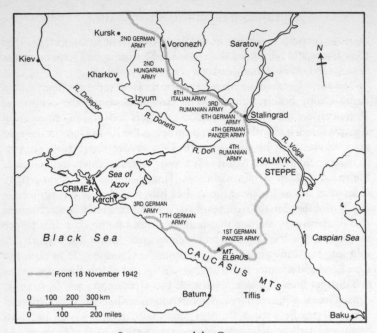

STALINGRAD and the CAUCASUS

Army set about clearing the town, street by street and house by house. From Stalingrad there stretched westward a long flank, guarded by Italian and Romanian troops.

Hitler had been aware from the beginning of the need to guard this flank. His original order of April 1942 noted that the Don front would become longer and longer. Defensive positions were to be prepared and the allied armies holding them were to be supported by German divisions in reserve. However, these German divisions were drawn into the fight for Stalingrad. As the risks involved in the weakly held salient of the Don bend became clearer, Hitler still refused any strategic withdrawal, insisting that the ground secured in 1942, with Stalingrad, must be retained as the starting line for the campaign of 1943. By mid-November one flank of the German salient, whose tip was at Stalingrad, was protected by a Romanian army with only the deceptively formidable-sounding 48th Panzer Corps in reserve, which consisted of one Romanian armoured division (with obsolete Czech tanks) and the German 22nd Panzer Division, which was under-strength and in process of re-equipment. Between them they had about eighty-five tanks, mostly light. On 19 November, after a prolonged artillery barrage, the Russians attacked—there descended the 5th Tank Army, with at least 300 tanks, most of them T-34s, to which the Romanians had no counter, and the 1st Guards Army. The other flank was guarded by the Romanian 4th Army and the German 4th Panzer Army. The latter had lost its mobile elements, detached either for the Don flank or for the fighting around Stalingrad itself. Under General Hoth's headquarters there were left only two Romanian and two German infantry divisions. On these forces there fell, on 20 November, the Soviet 51st and 57th armies, the former including the powerfully equipped 4th Mechanized Corps with 20,000 men, 2,000 lorries, and 220 tanks. On 23 November some of its units met forward units of 5th Tank Army and so cut off over 200,000 German troops at Stalingrad.

Hitler rejected the idea of an immediate attempt at break-out by the trapped 6th Army. Instead he chose to rely on supply by air to maintain it until relief could come from outside. The tonnage that could be sent by air proved inadequate, and the force assembled by Manstein to relieve General Paulus in Stalingrad could not get far enough. After weeks of hardship and savage combat Paulus ordered surrender on 1 February 1943. Of the 100,000 Germans taken prisoner, few ever returned to Germany. While Stalingrad fought on, its resistance helped to save the German army in the Caucasus from being cut off in its turn by a Russian attack on Rostov, but even so they were forced to give up this final attempt to seize the main Russian source of oil. With mobile reinforcements rushed from the west, Manstein was able, in his turn, to threaten Russian communications and, counter-attacking against heavy odds, to re-create a line in southern Russia close to that of early 1942. One more great German offensive was still to come, but the German invasion of Russia had reached its limit in the autumn of 1942: Stalin and the Soviet Union would survive. During that year Hitler himself said that Germany could not win the war unless the German army held the Caucasus and the Donets basin; this it had now failed to do.

How were the Germans contained? It was not the result of overwhelming numerical superiority on the part of the Red Army. What mattered were well-trained and well-equipped forces. In the summer of 1942 German ground forces in the east numbered 2,600,000. The Red Army probably fielded 3,000,000 to 3,500,000 men. More important was the improvement in the quality and equipment of Russian soldiers. From late 1941, 'Guards' units had been selected and given priority in equipment and manpower. Moreover, and this was perhaps the essential German disappointment, the loss of a high proportion of the industrial area of European Russia only temporarily halted the growth in Russian war production. In the second half of 1942 almost twice as many T-34 tanks were turned out as in the first half: 8,100 compared with 4,400. The inadequacy of German lines of communication was a major factor. On the Russian side better lateral communications enabled the Red Army more readily to reinforce critical sectors by drawing on others. Improving organization, too, increased Russian mobility, though there were instances of retreats that turned into disorderly flights in the summer of 1942. Supplies of lorries from the western allies began to contribute: by July 1942 the United States had dispatched to Russia more than 35,000 trucks and 6,000 jeeps. In July to October 1942 German forces on the southern front lost at least 150,000 more men than they could replace while Russian strength increased. In the Stalingrad sector German and Soviet forces were about equal in strength in July 1942, while by November the Russians outnumbered the Germans at least three to one, with Romanians, Hungarians, and Italians as an inadequate makeweight. The disparity facing Manstein's army group after the surrender at Stalingrad was even greater.

After Stalingrad, the balance of force on the eastern front ruled out a third attempt at a great German offensive to win the war at a stroke. Germany was on the strategic defensive, and from now on Hitler's hope was to separate the allies. To do this he tried to demonstrate that the destruction of the German invaders would need unacceptable efforts and that Stalin should seek some compromise. Then Hitler could once more play off east against west. In February 1943 Manstein suggested to Hitler that the Germans should leave the Red Army to take the initiative in attack against a flexible German defence so that German commanders could exploit their remaining superiority in mobility, organization, and tactics in fluid battles. Hitler preferred to launch another offensive: once again he chose a great encirclement, this time of the powerful Soviet forces poised in the Kursk salient. The German Command fixed a date for early May. However, Hitler delayed the attack for two months to assemble more new tanks, the mark V, or 'Panther', and the mark VI, or 'Tiger', and the 'Ferdinand' armoured self-propelled gun. The Panther had a 75 mm gun and effective frontal armour but was vulnerable from the sides; the Tiger was invulnerable from the front except at close range and mounted the formidable 88 mm gun. The Ferdinand (named after Ferdinand Porsche), was a long 88 mm gun on a Tiger chassis. Its total lack of secondary armament made it vulnerable to infantry. Even by July, tests of these weapons had not been completed. Through their excellent intelligence, some drived from information passed on by the British, some, perhaps, from signals intelligence developed by Soviet experts, the Russians knew German strength and intentions. The Germans, on their side, observed the increasing Russian concentration in the threatened sector. His advisers persuaded Stalin to wait for the German attack. The Russians constructed carefully planned defences in great depth. Both sides brought units up to strength, provided them with fresh equipment, and stockpiled supplies.

On 4 July 1943 the German attack began from the south and the next day the northern attack followed. The German commanders intended their two thrusts to meet around Kursk, a road- and rail-junction, and so to cut off at least five Russian armies. The long delay, however, had permitted enormous concentrations of troops. The whole Red Army numbered rather over 6 million officers and men, with about 4½ million in the field armies; the Germans had about 3 million on the eastern front. In the Kursk salient, and in the reserve assembled by the Soviet High Command, there were about 1,300,000 men, including nearly all the Russian armoured units. In attacks concentrated on limited sectors the Germans employed about 600,000 men, with eighteen panzer or panzer-grenadier divisions (the new name for motorized infantry divisions) and fifteen infantry divisions all brought up to full strength for the pincer-attacks from north and south. The Germans used over 2,500 tanks and assault guns, the Russians 3,000 or more, including some of the new heavy KV-85s. In the air the Russians had more than the 1,800 or so aircraft available to the Germans, and their quality had improved. Trucks sent by the western allies contributed, perhaps decisively, to Russian mobility: well over 100,000 lorries reached the Russians before Kursk. Reliable and sturdy American trucks suited Russian conditions, and with them the Red Army could field larger mobile forces and operate with more flexibility. That the entire German production of trucks in 1943 amounted to only 82,000 shows the importance of allied aid.

The German encirclement failed; the pincers did not close. The attacks from north and south were slowed down, and the intended annihilation turned into large-scale mutual attrition. On 12 July four Russian armies opened a diversionary offensive towards Briansk and Orel, north of the Kursk salient. On 13 July Hitler summoned the two German Army Group commanders to his headquarters and directed them to break off the offensive and release divisions for the west, including some of the top-quality mobile SS divisions. On 10 July the British and Americans had landed in Sicily and Hitler feared that the

Italians might soon leave the war and expose Italy and, worse still, the Balkans, to allied invasion. By that time the struggle at Kursk was already decided. At the time of the battle there were two-and-a-half times as many German troops on the Russian front as there were facing the western allies. Low-grade units or troops resting after service against the Russians predominated in the west. But the western allies had caused two panzer-grenadier divisions to be kept in Italy, another in France, and a panzer division in the Balkans. However, the western allies were not in actual combat with any German troops when Kursk began and they were containing no more German forces than at the time of Stalingrad. It was a Russian victory over the last great German offensive in the east.

8

Anglo-American strategies
for victory

THE strategy of the Soviet Union was simple: to expel German troops from its territory. Until that was done Stalin did not join with Britain and America in the war against Japan. The western allies faced more complicated choices. Three of their decisions settled the shape of the Second World War: they decided to defeat Germany first; to begin by evicting the Germans and their allies from north Africa and the Mediterranean; and to bombard German and Japanese factories and homes from the air.

Naturally the British gave priority to the war against Germany because Britain would be safe from attack only when Germany was beaten. American soldiers and politicians might think differently. As early as June 1939, the American army and navy Joint Planning Committee presented five outline plans for a war against Japan and Germany. The planners gave priority to 'Rainbow 2', in which the United States 'does not provide maximum participation in continental Europe' but put its main effort against Japan. In May 1940, when the German armies broke through on the western front, the heads of the US army and navy, General Marshall and Admiral Stark, alarmed by this sensational display of German strength and skill, brought out 'Rainbow 4' which planned for all resources to be used to defend the western hemisphere. At this moment, both Marshall and Stark took French and British defeat for granted and argued that the defence of the United States itself needed every ounce of available American strength.

On 13 June this plan reached President Roosevelt. In France the Germans had just overwhelmed the last French line of defence. Would Roosevelt support Churchill's defiance and order help to Britain or follow the gloomy forebodings of his professional advisers? At once, the President asked the Joint Planners to make a study on the assumption that Britain and the British Empire might fight on in spite of the defeat of France. Until his death, Roosevelt decided what Anglo-American strategy should be, putting his theoretical powers as Commander-in-Chief into practical effect. He never boasted of it, indeed apparently preferred to conceal it, no doubt to avoid the political hostility that civilian interference with the military might provoke. Now he acted by collecting evidence on the prospects for British survival; notably he sent Colonel Donovan (the later founder of of OSS–CIA) to Britain as his personal investigator. Donovan reported to Roosevelt in August that the British had a good chance of preventing a successful invasion. After he returned, two American generals and an admiral came over and con-cluded that the British should be helped in order to 'retain intact geographical positions from which successful land action can later be launched'. In consequence, Stark and Marshall reversed their earlier views and agreed that in case of war the United States should prepare for great land operations across the Atlantic and remain on 'a strict defensive' in the Pacific. Stark proposed, and Marshall agreed, that conversations with the British should be undertaken to work out a joint strategy if the United States came into the war.

Secret American–British talks took place in Washington in the first three months of 1941. A document entitled ABC-1 set out the resulting agreement. In case of war with Japan as well as Germany, strategy in the Far East would be defensive and 'the Atlantic and European area is considered to be the decisive theater'. Economic blockade, air attack, coastal raids, European resistance movements, and the early elimination of Italy, together with the buildup of forces for an eventual offensive against Germany, would win the war. The British inspired this strategy, but American military experts accepted it because their main concern at that stage was to keep the British fighting.

American soldiers developed a more independent approach as the danger to Britain became less urgent. After the German attack on Russia, British and American service chiefs met in Argentia harbour at the time of the 'Atlantic Conference' between Churchill and Roosevelt. Now American generals and admirals showed their unease about British strategy: in particular, they worried about the British inclination to hope for victory by propaganda, subversion, blockade, and bombing. 'We give to the heavy bomber first priority in production', the British told the Americans, and 'it may be that the methods described above will by themselves be enough to make Germany sue for peace'. The US service chiefs, though, insisted on 'the almost invariable rule that wars cannot be finally won without the use of land armies'. In November 1941 the British Chiefs of Staff felt it prudent to reassure Washington of their 'ultimate intention to land forces on [the] continent'. Already we can see the fundamental Anglo-American strategic disagreement. The chiefs of the American army wanted to concentrate forces as quickly as possible for a decisive encounter with the German army; the British wished to postpone this great land battle or even to avoid it altogether.

The United States military authorities could not try to impose their strategic ideas when they were not even in the war. Pearl Harbor and the coming of war with Germany, Italy, and Japan changed that. The Japanese onslaught proved much more difficult to stop than anyone had expected. Many Americans demanded speedy action to punish the aggressive treachery of Japan, so that American priority for war in Europe came into question. Churchill invited himself and his entourage to Washington as soon as the United States was forced into war. With some reluctance, Roosevelt agreed in spite of the obvious intention of the British to tell the Americans how to make war. The British brushed aside a request to avoid detailed discussions on strategy, for which the Americans consequently felt unprepared. British proposals dominated this ARCADIA conference. US planners did not know yet what even a purely defensive strategy in the Pacific would need. With deceptive ease the British and Americans approved a British-inspired strategy of clearing north Africa and opening the Mediterranean in 1942, and, for 1943, they tentatively outlined landings into continental Europe 'across the Mediterranean, from Turkey into the Balkans, or by landings in Western Europe'. There was to be 'ever-increasing air bombardment by British and American forces'.

British and American soldiers and statesmen agreed on three important points. They continued to give priority to the European war for, once Germany was beaten, Japanese defeat would inevitably follow, and the European war could be won if the Soviet Union was kept fighting. Secondly, British emphasis on strategic air attack on Germany now found a warm response from the United States Army Air Force. The existence of the Royal Air Force as a separate service brought about an increase in the status of the USAAF: the American Joint Chiefs of Staff, a body newly created to parallel the British Chiefs of Staff, included General Arnold as a quasi-equal air-force representative, even though that force was technically a mere part of the army and Arnold was nominally deputy to Marshall. Thus, in the Combined Chiefs of Staff, composed of the two sets of chiefs or their representatives, the body which directed the Anglo-American war, the concept of an independent strategic air force was fully represented, and British and American airmen supported each other's desire to attempt a war-winning bombing campaign. General Eaker, commander of the US bomber force in Britain, wrote down in April 1942 the credo of the 'bomber barons', that 'the destruction of the German war effort by air action alone was feasible and sound, and more economical than any other available'. Roosevelt and Churchill agreed on a third critical point: that Anglo-American ground forces should begin a new campaign against Germany before the end of 1942. They felt that they must be seen to be striving to help the Soviet Union, and that early American involvement in the European war was needed to prevent American attention becoming monopolized by the struggle in the Pacific. As a result, the British acquired a temporary veto on Anglo-American strategic plans, since any operation involving a risk of conflict with powerful German forces in 1942 must be combined with the British who, for the time being, had many more trained troops.

There followed the first conflict between Sir Alan Brooke and Marshall, the Chiefs of Staff of the British and American armies, about where to fight. Without difficulty, Churchill persuaded Roosevelt that the allies should seize French north Africa: 'to hold French north Africa against possible German attacks through Spain and Italy and to open the Mediterranean route', the latter objective implying a successful British advance from Egypt into Tripolitania. Consequently, in February 1942, US army GHQ in Washington unwillingly produced a plan for this Operation GYMNAST, subsequently renamed TORCH. It did not enjoy doing so. General McNair, its Chief of Staff, thought GYMNAST represented 'the ineffectual bleeding away of Army strength in British-sponsored projects'. The American staff passionately believed that forces should at once begin to be concentrated in England to launch the earliest possible challenge to the German army in northern France and Belgium. As it soon turned out, crises in the war against Japan, shortage of shipping, and British failure in Libya caused GYMNAST to be shelved.

Now the US army planners, chief of whom was General Eisenhower, head of the plans and operations staff, worked out their own solution. On 28 February 1942, Eisenhower presented a formal study to Marshall. He started with a military axiom: that the commander should first attack and defeat the weaker force of a divided enemy. Though this seemed not to fit the argument that Germany should be defeated first, Eisenhower pointed out that Germany had greater combat power than Japan yet was 'relatively' weaker since it was at war with the Soviet Union, it was accessible to attack from Britain, and it took three to four times as many ships to transport and maintain an American force in the Pacific as in the Atlantic theatre of war. Moreover, Britain had base facilities of a standard unequalled elsewhere. Hence, the paper argued, the essential tasks of American strategy were to maintain Britain and therefore to safeguard

Atlantic sea lanes, to keep Russia in the war, and to prevent the junction of Germany and Japan. The U-boat must be defeated and the allies should aim for 'the early initiation of operations that will draw off from the Russian front sizeable portions of the German army, both air and ground'. Eisenhower's conclusion was that

We should at once develop, in conjunction with the British, a definite plan for the operations against Northwest Europe . . . it should be sufficiently extensive in scale as to engage, from the middle of May onward, an increasing portion of the German Air Force, and by late summer an increasing amount of his ground forces.

American army planners worked out that 600,000 ground troops were needed for a 1942 invasion. First estimates of shipping space suggested that only 190,000 American troops could be sent to Britain by the end of September, and later estimates brought down the figures for infantry to 105,000, or 60,000 men in armoured units. For an invasion in 1943, the planners thought about one million troops were needed for an invasion in April and that probably not more than 400,000 could be transported in American ships. The British would therefore provide the overwhelming bulk of the forces for an emergency invasion in 1942 to take German units away from the Russian front, and even in spring 1943 an invasion would be preponderantly British. Marshall and his advisers concluded that absolute priority should be given to cross-Channel attack: the British and Americans should direct all 'production, special construction, training, troop movements, and allocation' to 'an attack, by combined forces of approximately 5,700 combat planes and 48 divisions against western Europe as soon as the necessary means can be accumulated in England—estimated at April 1, 1943'. The allies were to invade France in 1942 either if the Soviet Union were close to defeat or if, alternatively, the Germans were sufficiently weakened and demoralized. Roosevelt ordered a distinguished delegation to take these plans to England: on 8 April 1942 Marshall himself, together with Harry Hopkins, Roosevelt's closest collaborator, arrived there. In less than a week both the British Chiefs of Staff and the Prime Minister accepted the plan, and Churchill pronounced that 'the two nations would march ahead together in a noble brotherhood of arms'.

Later events make this ready British acquiescence seem to have been deceitful humbug. At the time Marshall correctly thought that many of those involved had 'reservations'. In fact only two days after Churchill's proclamation of assent, Brooke noted that 'the plans were fraught with the greatest dangers'. Brooke recognized what lay behind Marshall's proposals.

He has found that King, the American Naval Chief of Staff, is proving more and more of a drain on his military resources, continually calling for land-forces to capture and hold land-bases in the Pacific . . . MacArthur in Australia constitutes another threat by asking for forces to develop an offensive from Australia. To counter these moves Marshall has started the European offensive plan and is going one hundred per cent all out on it. It is a clever move which fits in with present political opinion and the desire to help Russia.

Since the end of 1941, when Churchill and Roosevelt met in Washington, things had gone very badly in the Pacific war. Japan seemed irresistible. Japanese forces took Malaya, then Singapore. They took Rangoon, cutting the land supply route to China, and threatened to invade India from Burma. Ceylon was vulnerable. Borneo had gone, and the Japanese had occupied the Dutch East Indies. Now they might be able to cut off Australia from outside help and launch an invasion. Their main aircraft carrier striking force attacked Darwin, in northern Australia, on 19 February. A few Japanese naval shells even struck Californian soil. Admiral King and General MacArthur wanted to throw back the Japanese before they could consolidate their immense conquests. Meanwhile, to stop the Japanese required urgent reinforcement. At the end of March 1942, twice as much of the shipping controlled by the US army was in the Pacific as in the Atlantic. In the first four months after Pearl Harbor 150,000 American troops were sent to take part in the war against Japan compared with less than 25,000 sent against Germany. Understandably, the British welcomed Marshall's continued commitment to Europe and felt it wise to support it and suppress, for the moment, their scepticism about the details. The British military regarded any cross-Channel invasion in 1942 or 1943 as too hazardous an operation, unless, unexpectedly, the Red Army had already destroyed the bulk of the German army. The British feared that the German defenders, by using the excellent European transport networks, could bring forward forces against an invasion more quickly and in greater numbers by land than the invader could do by sea. Invasion, they thought, was doomed to defeat unless German reinforcement routes could be destroyed or the German army kept occupied elsewhere. Brooke worked out a formula: there must be no more than twelve German mobile divisions in France at the time of any invasion.

The problem then arose: what should be done if invasion of France were impossible in 1942? Towards the end of May 1942, Molotov, second to Stalin in the Moscow hierarchy, visited London and Washington. He pressed for a second front in 1942. The Germans were assembling for a great summer offensive and Molotov asked the western allies to draw off at least forty German divisions. Churchill replied, explaining the difficulties, and then, as he reported his conversation to Roosevelt, added the remark, 'We must never let GYMNAST pass from our minds'. He still hankered after an invasion of French north Africa in 1942. However, Roosevelt allowed a public statement, after his talks with Molotov, which implied that a second front was planned for 1942. When Molotov returned to London, Churchill warned him in writing that the British could make no promise that there would be a landing in France in 1942. The British Cabinet agreed on 11 June that SLEDGEHAMMER, the 1942 landing, should be launched 'only in conditions which held out a good prospect of success', and the British Chiefs of Staff asserted that the feared collapse of Russian resistance would not bring the conditions of success. Meanwhile, Admiral Mountbatten went to Washington to explain the difficulties to the President. His report that Roosevelt was still interested in the invasion of French north Africa delighted Churchill, who hurried to Washington to clinch it, taking the British Chiefs of Staff with him. What Marshall resented was that the British, having agreed to give absolute priority to an invasion of France at the earliest possible time, now used Roosevelt's wish to act in the European theatre in 1942 to win his assent to an operation which would necessarily delay that invasion.

On 20 June 1942, Marshall, Brooke, and the Combined Chiefs of Staff agreed in Washington that the invasion of France 'at the earliest possible moment should be the principal offensive effort'. On the same day, in the President's house at Hyde Park, Churchill was urging something quite different: GYMNAST. Next day there was a compromise: the allies were to press on with plans and preparations for both GYMNAST and SLEDGEHAMMER. They would decide later which operation to carry out. This indecision did not last long: the British became more and more openly hostile to SLEDGEHAMMER and favourable to GYMNAST, while Marshall forcibly expressed distaste for anything that might distract from BOLERO, the code-name for the buildup for cross-Channel invasion, and was ready even to demand priority for the Pacific if the British insisted on the invasion of north-west Africa. On 8 July 1942 the British government conveyed to Washington its final rejection of SLEDGEHAMMER and its hope that the US would agree to GYMNAST. To the American argument that the invasion of north Africa would delay preparations for an invasion of France, Churchill presented a denial while Brooke argued that delay was worthwhile if it finally ruled out SLEDGEHAMMER. On 10 July the US Joint Chiefs of Staff compelled President Roosevelt to choose by objecting to any deviation from BOLERO. Marshall told the President that he wanted 'to force the British into acceptance of a concentrated effort against Germany, and if this proves impossible, to turn immediately to the Pacific with strong forces and drive for a decision against Japan'. Only with Roosevelt's support could he 'force' the British.

Marshall did not get it. The President asserted his powers as Commander-in-Chief and so dictated the subsequent course of the war against Germany. On 14 July he rejected the Pacific plan. He ordered Marshall, King, and Harry Hopkins to go to London. In formal instructions, Roosevelt set out his case that 'the defeat of Japan does not defeat Germany and that American concentration against Japan this year as in 1943 increases the chance of complete German domination of Europe and Africa . . . Defeat of Germany means the defeat of Japan probably', he added hopefully, 'without firing a shot or losing a life'. Roosevelt directed his emissaries to reach agreement with the British, 'within one week of your arrival', on offensive action against Germany involving American troops.

When the British finally rejected SLEDGEHAMMER, Roosevelt ordered Hopkins, Marshall, and King to settle on one of four solutions among which he gave preference to a British–American operation against French North Africa. The British and American Combined Chiefs of Staff (CCS) obeyed orders and drafted an elaborate agreement. Invasion of north-western Europe in 1943 (ROUNDUP) was to be assumed until 15 September 1942. If at that date the Red Army had been so weakened, freeing so many Germans, as to make ROUNDUP difficult for 1943, then the invasion of north-west Africa (GYMNAST) should take place before the end of 1942. The CCS agreed that ROUNDUP could then certainly be ruled out for 1943, and in that event the western allies would go on to the defensive in Europe. Churchill and Roosevelt brushed aside this careful military compromise, however. Prompted by a telegram from Churchill, the President, as US Commander-in-Chief, told the American Chiefs of Staff that TORCH (the new code name for the invasion of north-west Africa) was to be carried out at the earliest possible date and to have priority over all other operations.

Militarily Marshall was correct in wishing to give cross-Channel invasion total priority, but politically it would have been impossible to build up strength in Britain and remain inactive until British conditions for an invasion were secured—that is until allied bombing and the Red Army had sufficiently weakened the Germans. British and American public opinion would not have tolerated it because of sympathy for the Russians and because of the American desire to strike back at Japan. Both Churchill and Roosevelt were afraid, too, that Stalin might find it to his advantage to make peace and leave the 'imperialists' to fight it out. They insisted on immediate action rather than doing nothing, while making careful preparations for a decisive encounter later on. Moreover, in 1942 Roosevelt wanted to attract American attention to the European war; Churchill, after a long series of British disasters, needed victorious action to maintain both British morale and his own political position. Their decision also in the end brought a military advantage: the presence of British and American troops in the Mediterranean reduced German ability to concentrate against an invasion of northern France. This was an argument which appealed to Brooke much more than to Marshall, since it could also mean delaying the main invasion. Nevertheless, Brooke was right in his insistence that the invasion should take place only if no more than twelve German mobile divisions were in northern France when the assault began.

For the rest of 1942 the Pacific theatre attracted US ground forces as the Joint Chiefs adopted a policy of limited offensives to prevent the Japanese from settling into their defensive perimeter. Meanwhile, they put into effect the Roosevelt–Churchill strategy, while Marshall and his subordinates grumbled and muttered imprecations about diversions and dispersions. As Marshall predicted, 'subsidiary' operations in North Africa and the Mediterranean developed a life of their own, nourished by the strategy of the British Chiefs of Staff, 'which does not envisage large-scale land operations against the Axis until German morale and powers of resistance have cracked'. The British looked for more diversions in the Mediterranean to follow, or even accompany, the anticipated victory in Tunisia, and started thinking about operations against Sardinia, Sicily, or Crete several weeks before the invasion of Morocco and Algeria. It was Roosevelt, however, who took the initiative on 11 November 1942, when the invasion had just begun, and suggested that the British and American staffs should study 'the possibilities including forward movements directed against Sardinia, Sicily, Italy, Greece, and other Balkan areas, and including the possibility of obtaining Turkish support for an attack through the Black Sea against Germany's flank'. Churchill quickly responded: 'everything you say . . . is in absolute harmony with our views.' Strangely, Churchill apparently did not understand that these movements would delay an invasion of northern France, probably until 1944, and thus would displease Stalin. Here was matter for another conference. Roosevelt wanted to talk to Stalin, too, but the latter claimed that the war kept him too busy. Perhaps he suspected that the Anglo-Americans were going to evade his demands and preferred not to listen to their excuses.

The outcome was another Anglo-American colloquy, in January 1943 near Casablanca, within reach of Eisenhower, now in command of the allied forces in north-west Africa, and of British and American fighting troops for the political leaders to visit. Roosevelt alone looked forward to the conference with every sign of confidence and pleasure. The British feared that the Americans would want more resources for the Pacific war, while Marshall and his planners in the US War Department feared that the British would somehow drag the US army further into the Mediterranean. That is what happened, because Roosevelt wished it and once again it was Roosevelt's strategy that prevailed. To bring this about all he needed was to do nothing to impose unity on an American delegation divided amongst themselves, and to leave them to encounter the well-prepared unanimity of the British. Conveniently for Roosevelt, American soldiers blamed the British for their defeat. At the Casablanca conference, General Wedemeyer, Marshall's principal adviser there, thought the British 'super negotiators . . . We were confronted by generations and generations of experience in committee work and in rationalizing points of view. They had us on the defensive practically all the time.' Marshall struggled once again to get a full-scale cross-Channel invasion of France in 1943. The British argued that by autumn 1943 only twenty-three divisions could be made ready, which would not be enough unless Germany were weakened in advance. Moreover, British and American operations would then give no support to the Soviet Union during the summer of 1943. Churchill and Brooke wished to threaten Germany in the Mediterranean, especially by knocking Italy out of the war and bringing Turkey into it. The Turks settled one of these issues by requiring help on an impossibly large scale. Over Italy, the other US Chiefs of Staff, Admiral King and General Arnold, did not fully support Marshall. King understood that shipping would be freed if the Mediterranean were secured, while Arnold coveted air bases in Italy. Most important was that Roosevelt still wanted to keep Americans in action against Germans, in order to help, and to be seen to be helping, the Red Army. He shared the British view that nothing more than a SLEDGEHAM-

MER could be launched across the Channel in 1943, an invasion only to rescue the Russians or finish off the Germans if either reached the point of collapse. The British and American leaders, therefore, agreed to attack Sicily. At Casablanca however, they did not decide what should happen after they had captured the island. It did not seem urgent to do so for, when the allies decided to invade Sicily, the British 8th Army had not yet reached Tripoli, while the Germans had decided to defend Tunisia and were beginning to launch local counter-attacks.

In any case, German submarines ruled out a 1943 invasion of France strong enough to win a secure beachhead. By the end of June 1943 only 1,600,000 US army troops had gone to all overseas theatres. In the first quarter of 1943 the number of troops shipped abroad was well behind schedule. Moreover, at that moment there came to the surface an amazing Anglo-American misunderstanding. At the end of November 1942, Roosevelt assured Churchill that he could count on American shipping to make sure that British imports would be at least 27 million tons in 1943. The President did not tell the army, nor did he make clear what was meant by his remark that 'nearly 300,000 tons each month of carrying capacity' would have to be added by the Americans to the ships already used for British imports. When General Somerville, of the US Army Services of Supply, declared at Casablanca that more than one million American troops could be assembled and maintained in Britain by the end of 1943, that figure did not justify a full-scale invasion of France that year. But even that figure was based on a series of false assumptions: first, that the United States would not cede to the British the use of more than an extra 300,000 tons of carrying capacity in any one month, whereas the British imports needed monthly cumulative additions of that amount; secondly, that the British would be able to assist troop-carrying with their own ships; thirdly, that sinkings by U-boats would decline from the beginning of 1943. Taken together, these false assumptions meant an overestimate of allied shipping available in 1943 of approximately 6 million tons of carrying capacity.

The misunderstanding of Casablanca emerged in March 1943 when the British set out their current needs for shipping. To their anger and dismay, the Americans found their entire overseas deployment schedules wrecked. In spite of complaints from the American military, Roosevelt insisted on the maintenance of the British war effort as the first priority for American resources. Consequently, to invade France in 1943 became even more difficult. Meanwhile good news came from north Africa. At the end of March the British 8th Army arrived in Tunisia and began to co-operate with the British, French, and American forces in French north Africa to destroy the German and Italian armies in Tunisia and so clear the southern side of the Mediterranean. In order to decide what to do after the coming invasion of Sicily, Churchill and Roosevelt with their military advisers met in Washington at the TRIDENT conference in the second half of May 1943.

This time the American side was able to draw up a plan in advance, because Roosevelt agreed with his strategic advisers. They wanted the cross-Channel invasion to be fixed for the spring of 1944, and meanwhile they would tolerate operations in the Mediterranean designed to get Italy out of the war. How this was to be done was not specified, but in any case, the Americans insisted, no more forces would go to the Mediterranean. The fact that Eisenhower, even so, could use twenty-seven divisions for his planning of operations in the Mediterranean showed that the British, because of Roosevelt's support, had succeeded in turning the Mediterranean into a major Anglo-American theatre. Only twenty-nine divisions would be in Britain for the cross-Channel invasion in May 1944. Even that required a concession from the British. They agreed that the allies would move seven divisions from the Mediterranean to Britain after November 1943.

At TRIDENT, British and American soldiers apparently resolved the differences between them. The new agreements did not, however, remove fundamental differences of outlook. Marshall and the American army planners wanted to subordinate everything to preparations for the cross-Channel attack; the British wanted allied troops to fight Germans somewhere in the meantime. Only so, the British argued, could help be brought to the Soviet Union before the main operation could be launched, while, on the other hand, the Americans thought such diversions likely to delay the main operations and so delay really effective help to the Soviet Union. Both wanted to help Russia, because they knew that the defeat of Hitler would be almost impossible without the Red Army. Both believed that cross-Channel landings must take place. But they put different emphasis on different aspects of shared objectives, and as a result some Americans sometimes suspected, wrongly, that the British were insincere in their support of an invasion of France. Some American soldiers thought the British irresponsibly ready to sacrifice long-term plans to present opportunities, while some British soldiers thought the Americans naïvely rigid in their attachment to their plans.

By the time the next conference, QUADRANT, met in Quebec in mid-August 1943, Eisenhower and the allied commanders in the Mediterranean had successfully recommended that the capture of Sicily should lead on to the invasion of Italy. The early stages of the invasion showed how low Italian morale had become and how easily Italy could be separated from the Axis alliance, especially when, on 25 July, Mussolini was overthrown in a *coup* by Marshal Badoglio and other senior officers and by Mussolini's former supporters in the Fascist Grand Council. The decision to invade Italy confirmed Marshall's view that one operation in the Mediterranean led to another, but the British view that Italy was a comparatively easy target was also confirmed. The temptation of Italy seemed to Marshall dangerously seductive. By 1 July the United States had 520,000 troops in the Mediterranean compared with only 109,000 in Britain. British troops invaded the Italian mainland on 3 September followed by a larger British and American landing on 9 September. On 8 September the Italian surrender was announced.

At Quebec, as usual, Brooke emphasized the need for strength in the Mediterranean to weaken German opposition to the invasion of France, while Marshall emphasized the need to concentrate all resources on the invasion. Churchill, Roosevelt, and their Chiefs of Staff finally agreed on an Anglo-American strategy for the defeat of Germany. It rested on the assumption that the Soviet Union would remain in the war and continue to engage the bulk of the German army, though the intentions of the Soviet leadership were still enigmatic. Roosevelt hoped for a private conversation with Stalin, but once again could not persuade him to leave Russia. The British and Americans worked together in increasing mutual confidence, cordiality, and frankness, though Marshall and Stimson, the US Secretary for War, suspected Churchill and Brooke of dangerous excitement over the collapse of Italy. However, the British reassuringly came to Quebec with a definite plan for the invasion of France and accepted, at least for the moment, that no more allied forces could go to the Mediterranean and that American units would take no part in operations east of Italy. The British had got their diversion; the Americans had set limits to its size. The invasion of France was fixed for the spring of 1944.

Marshall asserted that allied strategy in the Far East was linked with planning for European victory. Marshall and Roosevelt at first believed that Chiang Kai-shek, the Chinese 'Generalissimo', and the Chinese forces they assumed he commanded, could fulfil a role in the war against Japan almost equivalent to that of Russia against Germany. The Americans should help to train and equip the Chinese and encourage them to take on the bulk of the Japanese ground forces and eventually to provide and defend air bases for long-range American bombers to attack Japan. This strategy went with Roosevelt's estimate of Chiang Kai-shek and his belief that Kuomintang China was a great power, one of the 'Big Four'. Churchill disagreed, saw little merit in Chiang's regime, and deeply resented Chiang's expression of views on, for instance, Indian nationalism. This disagreement extended to strategy. Chiang's role in the war depended on supplies reaching him either by air from Assam across the Himalayas, or by the difficult construction of a new 'Ledo road' to join India to the old 'Burma road' in northern Burma, or by the recapture of Rangoon and the reopening of the whole of the Burma road from there to China. To build the new Ledo road, the allies needed to conquer north Burma, while to bring back the Burma road into use required the reconquest of the whole of Burma. Until 1944 Marshall and Roosevelt pressed the British to join with Chiang to clear north Burma and to carry out a British amphibious attack to isolate Rangoon. The Americans argued that if the British refused, more American resources would have to go to the Pacific to make up for the loss of Chinese support which would be the consequence of British failure to open lines of supply to Chiang. The British, sceptical of the value of Chiang's support, thought landing-craft for amphibious operations better used in the Mediterranean and advocated reliance on American air supply to China.

Later in the war American enthusiasm for Chiang diminished. As an ally Chiang proved a disappointment, and methods of defeating Japan without him came to seem more promising. Disillusion among American planners appeared in 1943. In May the US Joint Staff planners suggested the recapture of Burma to supply China. Then Hong Kong would be seized, possibly by Chinese troops. With this new supply route, the Chinese, with British and American help, would clear Japanese-occupied territory for allied air bases. Thence would come an 'overwhelming bombing offensive against Japan' in which the Chinese would join, as they would in the final invasion of Japan if that were still needed. At Quebec, however, the American planners agreed that allied plans should be flexible in case 'China should drop out of the war or prove less effective than we now hope'. In November 1943 Churchill persuaded the Americans to agree to abandon the British amphibious operation against the Andaman Islands which had been intended to cut Japanese sea communication to Rangoon. Chiang had insisted on this attack as a condition of his co-operation in north Burma. Now Chiang was overruled and the landing-craft switched to Mediterranean operations, though not, as Churchill wished, to the eastern Mediterranean. Chiang's troops, as it turned out, so far from reconquering Japanese-held territory for allied air bases, were incapable of defending existing airfields. In April 1944 the Japanese began a series of advances in China, conquering immense new territories, establishing their control of effective north–south lines of communication, and overrunning most of the American airbases there. Not merely did the Japanese thus make it unsafe to set up air bases in China, but their seizure of Chinese ports finally ruled out any idea of invading Japan from China.

Climate made the Aleutian Islands in the north Pacific unpromising as a line of approach towards Japan. That left two possible strategies. The most melodramatically glamorous American soldier, General Douglas MacArthur, who combined real military skill with histrionic ability, vigorously supported capturing or bypassing the Solomon Islands, advancing from base to base along the coast of northern New Guinea using sea-borne attacks covered by land-based aircraft, and thence recapturing the Philippines and finishing off Japan from Luzon, the northernmost island of the Philippines. To do this he thought that maximum resources should be concentrated in the south-west Pacific, and put under his command. The US navy on the other hand, represented on the Joint Chiefs of Staff by a formidable personality, Admiral Ernest J. King, advocated amphibious operations, supported by naval guns and carrier-borne aircraft, against central Pacific islands. He proposed to advance towards Japan by way of the Marshall, Caroline, and Marianas islands. Marshall, as Chief of Staff of the US army, tried to prevent those two from shifting the main American effort away from Europe, though he frightened the British with the threat of his acquiescence. Everyone compromised. In theory the war against Japan should have been postponed until after the defeat of Germany, but in practice the United States fought both wars simultaneously. For the strategy of the Pacific war both MacArthur's and the American admirals' line of approach was carried out, until they came together in the assault on Leyte in the Philippines in October 1944, before separating once more to secure bases for the anticipated invasion of Japan: MacArthur in Luzon, Admiral Nimitz and the Pacific fleet in Iwo Jima and Okinawa.

At the beginning of 1944 the number of US fighting men in the Pacific was about equal to those waging the war against Germany, about 1,800,000 in each theatre, though there were more seamen and marines in the Pacific and more army and air force in Britain and the Mediterranean. Landing-craft dominated Anglo-American strategy. They were the essential means of putting ground forces ashore on enemy-held coastlines. By June 1944 the peak moment of strategic concentration in Europe, the allies assembled in Britain and the Mediterranean ready for action against Germany 1,609 landing-craft of the main larger types, which carried troops or tanks or trucks from the shore base to the enemy-held coast, compared with 376 in the Pacific. Of the main types of smaller landing-craft, those launched in the water from bigger vessels close to the objective, there were 3,029 ready for use in Europe compared with 3,609 available in the Pacific. Shortly after the first day of the Normandy invasion, when 150,000 allied troops were landed in France, an almost equally impressive troop lift took place in the Pacific. About 125,000 troops were carried 1,000 miles from the Marshalls to invade the Marianas. Decisive battles followed in both theatres. The approximate equality of American effort derived partly from Marshall's failure to persuade Roosevelt and Churchill to accept a strategy which he could successfully defend and justify to the advocates of priority for the Pacific, and perhaps even more from what the Americans called 'opportunism' when they disapproved of it, and 'flexibility' when they approved. At first, reinforcement in the Pacific was forced by emergencies there, and later on success encouraged exploitation. American strategy in the Pacific was flexible in another sense: the Joint Chiefs of Staff never decided whether General MacArthur or Admiral Nimitz should have priority. The US army and navy competed, in a more or less friendly manner, in speed of advance towards bases for the final assault on Japan.

Created partly by foresight, partly by the perils or opportunities of the moment, Anglo-American strategy succeeded. It is difficult convincingly to argue that the allies could more rapidly have forced German and Japanese surrender.

9

Economies at war

SUPERIOR resources won the war: the victors had greater numbers of men and women and made more weapons. In population and in industrial capacity, the allies, even after losing France, were stronger than the axis powers:

	Population in 1939	Steel output in tons (highest figure in the 1930s)
UK	47,961,000	13,192,000
France	41,600,000	6,221,000
USSR	190,000,000	18,800,000
USA	132,122,000	51,380,000
Germany (including Austria)	76,008,000	23,329,000
Italy	44,223,000	2,323,000
Japan	71,400,000	5,811,000

The populations in the British and French empires swelled allied totals: more than 500 million in the British Empire, more than 100 million in the French. Most were ill-nourished, unhealthy illiterates, but among them soldiers could be found, especially in French north Africa and India. The British Commonwealth and Empire possessed further resources for war. Canada and Australia had significant industries, and their populations, like those of New Zealand and white South Africa, were well-educated and physically and mentally capable of providing high-quality recruits. All these four self-governing 'dominions' followed the British lead and declared war in 1939. In India the British found troops for a large army, men of sufficient basic intelligence and physique to be employed as infantry, but less easily in technical and specialized arms or as effective NCOs and officers, because many educated middle-class Indians were reluctant to fight for a discriminatory imperial regime, even against enemies which most of them greatly disliked. Canada was an industrially advanced country, with engineering plants capable of mass-production. Canadians manufactured 4 per cent of the combat aircraft, 7 per cent of the tanks, and 32 per cent of the motor vehicles used by

British Empire forces, and they fielded an army corps for the invasion of Normandy in 1944.

	Population	Steel production (1939) in tons
Canada	11,682,000	1,407,000
South Africa (white population)	2,161,000	250,000
Australia	6,807,000	1,189,000
New Zealand	1,585,000	—
India	374,200,000	1,035,000

The Second World War was a war of mass armies. Governments balanced the demand for men from the armed services with the need for labour in agriculture and expanded industry. Maximum mobilized strengths are shown in the table.

UK	5,000,000	USA	11,700,000	Germany	9,500,000
		USSR	11,500,000	(at least 4 million more	
India	2,150,000	(at least 6 million		served before becoming	
		more served before		casualties)	
		becoming casualties)		Italy	4,000,000
		France	5,000,000	Japan	4,000,000

Education facilitates both industrial production and the effective use of modern weapons. Americans did best: about 15 per cent of those who were between 25 and 44 years old in 1940 had had some higher education, while of those who were then between 14 and 16 about 70 per cent were still at school. Britain lagged behind. Before 1939 only about 15 per cent stayed at school after the age of 14 and ten times fewer enjoyed any form of education after the age of 18 compared with the United States. Japan ranked high: nearly 8 per cent of Japanese males aged 25–44 in 1940 had undergone higher education, slightly more than in Canada. In the Soviet Union high levels of education among a minority still stood in sharp contrast to dominant but retreating backwardness; in 1926 over half the population was illiterate (in 1959 the official figure was 1.6 per cent). Germany in the later 1930s fell back educationally, but the Nazi regime inherited a long tradition of high standards. In 1930 a considerably higher proportion of German boys went to secondary schools than in Britain and France, though by 1940 this was no longer true.

Preparing for the allied invasion: Field Marshal Rommel and a staff officer, Major i. G. Behr, Normandy, April 1944

Montgomery at his headquarters in Normandy, 6 July 1944, with his puppies 'Hitler' and 'Rommel'

General de Gaulle back in France,
14 June 1944, after four years

Stalin, Truman, and Churchill, Potsdam, 17 July 1945

A sensitive measure of comparative standards of health, education, administrative efficiency, and technical competence is the infant mortality rate recording the deaths within their first year among each thousand babies born alive. For the five years before the war the following figures show average infant mortality rates.

USA	53.2	Italy	102.7
UK	58.2	Japan	110.4
Germany	66.3	British India	155.6
France	71.1		

In the United States non-white infants experienced a mortality rate of 83, while Italy contained two societies—in the south, towns showed nearly double the mortality of those in central Italy.

Production of aircraft provides the best single measure of industrial achievement in the war.

Numbers of aircraft

	1939	1940	1941	1942	1943	1944
USA	5,856	12,804	26,277	47,836	85,898	96,318
USSR	10,382	10,565	15,735	25,436	34,845	40,246
UK	7,940	15,049	20,094	23,672	26,263	26,461
Germany	8,295	10,826	11,424	15,288	25,094	39,275
Japan	4,467	4,768	5,088	8,861	16,393	28,180
Italy	n.a.	3,257	3,503	2,818	967 (8 months)	—

British and American aircraft factories produced even more than the numbers suggest. A high proportion of heavy bombers meant the British produced more aircraft in structure weight than the Germans, even in 1944, while the United States produced three times the weight of the combined output of Germany and Japan.

Modern large-scale land operations needed tanks, or their specialized derivative the self-propelled gun, and artillery and trucks. Warfare across the oceans needed cargo ships and warships to protect them or to sink enemy cargo carriers.

The Italians and Japanese made few tanks, only about 3,500 each during the war, and neither built tanks equal even to the medium tanks of

ECONOMIES AT WAR

Tank and self-propelled artillery production (including German assault guns)

	1940	1941	1942	1943	1944
UK	1,399	4,841	8,611	7,476	4,600
USSR	2,794	6,590	24,446	24,089	28,963
USA	331	4,052	34,000	42,497	20,565
Germany	2,200	5,200	9,300	19,800	27,300

other armies. American and Russian designers produced successful medium tanks, the Sherman and the T-34, but only the Russians produced heavy tanks which could successfully confront the German mark V (the 'Panther') and mark VI (the 'Tiger'). (The British also manufactured large numbers of armoured personnel carriers.) The Red Army gave priority to artillery: the table below shows production of guns of 75 mm calibre and above in the years 1940–4.

Production of guns

UK	41,000	Germany	128,000
USA	145,000	Japan	10,500
USSR	211,000	Italy	3,400

The strength of the American motor industry ensured superior mobility for all the allied armies.

Production of medium and heavy trucks

	1941	1942	1943	1944
USA	145,689	443,713	628,574	465,821
USSR	n.a.	30,900	45,500	52,600
UK	88,022	87,939	88,356	61,917
Germany	62,400	78,200	81,900	89,069
Japan	16,000	12,500	11,500	7,600

American trucks were unequalled for sturdiness and reliability. Moreover, the United States also produced nearly one million light trucks, mostly 'jeeps'. Another American industry expanded to a war-winning scale: shipbuilding.

Tonnage, gross, of merchant ships built

	1940	1941	1942	1943	1944	1945
UK	810,000	1,156,000	1,310,000	1,204,000	1,014,000	683,000
USA	n.a.	1,427,000	6,228,000	12,920,000	12,383,000	6,396,000
Japan	280,000	225,000	260,000	769,000	1,699,000	523,000

After 1941 Canadian yards produced another 2,250,000 tons of merchant ships. Warship building showed similar disproportion between the allies and the Axis, with one exception: submarines.

Numbers of surface warships built

	Battle-ships and battle-cruisers	Fleet aircraft carriers	Light aircraft carriers	Cruisers	Destroyers
UK					
1939–45	5	6	6	31	233
USA					
1941–5	10	18	116	46	288
Japan					
1941–5	2	6	14	6	70
Germany					
1939–45	2	—	—	3	18
Italy					
1940–3	3	—	—	3	5

Numbers of submarines at the outbreak of war and wartime building

		Outbreak	Built during war
Germany	(1.9.39)	57	1,111
Italy	(1.6.40)	115	4
Japan	(1.12.41)	63	125
UK	(1.9.39)	57	178
USA	(1.12.41)	111	177

Analysis of individual economies must begin with the German, the powerhouse of aggressive war. Few Germans were out of work when the war began. Consequently the Wehrmacht could get more weapons than were already being produced in only four ways. Productivity might increase: workers work harder and managers manage better. Men and women from sections of society that had not yet looked for work could be persuaded or compelled to take jobs in industry. The authorities might divert resources from civilian products. There remained the fourth option of armed conquest of labour and raw materials. Recruiting for the forces made industrial production more difficult: by May 1940, 4 million German men were removed from the labour force, and by September 1944 11 million had gone. German munitions production did increase: 75 per cent more than in 1939 in each of the two years 1940 and 1941, two-and-a-half times as much in 1942, four times the 1939 level in 1943, and five times in 1944. How were these increases achieved and why was maximum output reached only late in the war?

Many writers believe that Hitler and his advisers did not try before 1942 to bring German war production to its peak; before then, they say, Hitler preferred to maintain German civilian standards of living. They attribute to Hitler a theory of 'Blitzkrieg', lightning war, and deny that he wanted to prepare for a long war or ever contemplated a great war. Hitler's pursuit of self-sufficiency and his repeated demands for increased output of weapons make it hard to believe in his acceptance of any such 'theory'. It is more likely that events determined the chronology and scale of German weapons procurement. The weapons available in 1939, 1940, and 1941 were adequate for the conquest of Poland, Denmark, Norway, the Netherlands, Belgium, Luxemburg, France, Yugoslavia, Greece, and much of European Russia. When more weapons became necessary they were demanded with greater urgency than in those earlier years during which Hitler tolerated constraints which he tried later to overcome or circumvent. The most serious of these was the position of Goering, who had not enough power to insist on his own priorities yet could block attempts by other people to impose theirs. Only after Hitler transferred most of Goering's functions first to Todt and then to his architect and confidant, Speer, and gave them powers of direction, was co-ordination imposed. When he became Minister for War Production in February 1942, Speer followed Todt's innovation of getting manufacturers into discussions on priorities and resource allocations, reduced the power of the military customers, and curbed their ignorant interference in production procedures.

Until 1942, the army, air force, navy, and the civilian sector competed for resources. Orders overlapped, emphasis shifted from one item to another, scarce materials leaked into inessential uses, different services did not agree on interchangeable parts; after 1942, by contrast, competing orders, each for more than could be produced in many years, were reduced and balanced with the available labour and materials. As a result, less was ordered but far more was received.

At least until the end of 1941, Germany had seemed certain to win the war; thereafter it needed new efforts to prevent defeat. To accelerate production the government tried to get more Germans to work. In January 1943 all men between 60 and 65 and all women between 17 and 45 were told to register. Three and a half million did so but only one-fifth were placed in work. The Nazis believed that domestic discontent had defeated Germany in the First World War; this time they would make the war more comfortable for civilians. It is true that, in spite of the Nazis' theoretical objection to women at work, as high a proportion of women worked in Germany as in Britain. However, the Nazis failed to force women to change jobs and did not compel a high proportion of non-employed women to take jobs. It was partly because many women were needed on small farms or had young children, and partly because women whose husbands were in the forces received allowances so generous that the incentive to work was blunted, but it was also to avoid unpopularity. Thus, in contrast to Britain where nearly all women in domestic service moved into war work, the number of German women in domestic service was as high at the end of the war as at the beginning.

The regime increased extra war production by shifting from civilian to military production: in 1939, 58 per cent of the non-agricultural labour force was working for the home market, in 1941 the figure was 51 per cent and in 1944 it was down to 41 per cent. Working hours lengthened and productivity grew. German strength in machine tools helped: in Germany in 1943 there was one machine tool to 2.35 workers in the relevant industries, compared with one to 5.7 in the United Kingdom. For extra labour in war industry Germany increasingly relied on foreigners. By December 1944 no less than 38 per cent of the workforce was foreign, some of it voluntary, more of it consisting of prisoners of war, deportees, or slaves, some very well treated, some suffering or dying through overwork and malnutrition. This was, after all, what the Third Reich was for—to exploit or to murder non-Germans. At the end of 1944, 1,600,000 prisoners of war were working in Germany and 6 million other foreigners, about 2 million of whom were women. In 1943 more than

750,000 workers came from France, Belgium, and the Netherlands, many of them conscripted. These countries provided the most important new sources of skilled and semi-skilled labour for German industry, while from Poland, Russia, and the other eastern countries there came mostly unskilled workers, including women. More than 2,750,000 men and women were carried off from Russia. The people of the occupied countries also helped to feed Germany. They provided about one-third of German bread, meat, and fat. Their own consumption was depressed— standard rations in the occupied areas in 1943 gave about 1,500 calories per day, compared with 2,000 in Germany, while in Poland and German-occupied Russia standard rations were 800–850 calories per day. In 1943 the Germans took about 40 per cent of French industrial production. In 1942 to 1943 French factories produced over 50,000 trucks for the Germans, who also bought 15,000 used trucks. More advanced industrial production, such as aircraft, the German authorities preferred to keep within the Reich itself, and French industry mostly turned out non-military stores for the Wehrmacht or articles for German civilians. Thus, the German air force got only 2,500 aircraft from France, mainly transports or trainers, while French engineering workers turned out German combat aircraft in German factories.

Germany lacked natural resources, especially metals and minerals. Stockpiling, imports from neighbouring countries, seizures in occupied areas, and blockade-running prevented crippling shortages. Moreover, Goering's four-year plan organization sponsored whole new industries to cope with three difficulties: steelworks able to use low-grade home-produced iron-ore, and, even more adventurously, with the help of the I. G. Farben chemical group, synthetic oil and rubber factories. In 1938 5 per cent of rubber used in Germany was synthetic, in 1943 94 per cent. Sixteen per cent of German oil consumption was synthetic in 1938; by early 1944 the figure was 56 per cent. Synthetic oil production quadrupled between 1938 and 1944. It was not enough. Except for its armoured and motorized divisions, the pre-war German army relied, beyond its railheads, on horse-drawn transport. This remained true throughout the war, so that the Red Army, with lend-lease trucks and ample supplies of fuel, became more mobile than the Germans and eroded the original German superiority even in summer campaigns. As early as 1942 the Luftwaffe cut the training of pilots because of shortage of aviation fuel; this weakness enabled the allies decisively to reduce German mobility in the west in 1944. To fight a two-front war Hitler needed larger stocks and much longer preparation. However, he could not delay because, after

1938, France, Britain, and Russia were rapidly gaining strength. As a result he set off a challenge to the great powers of the world which shortage of German economic resources doomed to failure unless rapid conquest brought speedy amelioration. Russian resistance exposed the essential German weakness: lack of natural resources and, in the end, of people, which caused the German armed forces to run short of the skilled, intelligent, fit young men needed to fight a war against the rising superpowers. By 1944 the average age in the whole German army was $31\frac{1}{2}$ years, which was six years older than in the US army.

Russian fighting strength was based on an economy stronger than the Germans, or anyone else, had grasped. Crisis engulfed the Soviet Union in 1941. Stalin rejected what was militarily the most effective strategy for defence: to allow much of European Russia to be overrun by the Germans and to keep Soviet forces intact for eventual counter-strokes when German supply lines became over-extended. This strategy, however, would have allowed temptingly easy German access to the economic riches of western Russia, and its apparent acceptance of defeat might have destroyed confidence in the regime. The strategy Stalin adopted, of forward defence, led to even worse disasters: by November 1941 the Germans had seized more than half the entire Soviet productive capacity of coal and steel and more than one-third of Soviet grain-producing land. In the same period Soviet forces lost three times as many aircraft as Soviet industry could produce and more than twice as many tanks. Yet Russian factories made more weapons and munitions in 1942 than before the invasion began and the Soviet Union stopped the German conquest of Europe. As the Germans advanced, in 1941 and 1942, Russian machines and workers went east, beyond the Volga river and the Ural mountains. The government did not plan industrial evacuation in advance; to do so did not fit the strategy of forward defence. Managers sometimes quietly made their own plans, but most of them improvised, as the central authorities did, after the invasion. Before the war, Soviet economic planners expanded basic industry in the east, and by 1940 about one-third of Soviet coal and steel came from there, but it was only after the invasion that the bulk of arms production shifted to the eastern Soviet Union. At the time of the German attack, the armed services obtained less than one-fifth of their weapons from the east; in 1942 they received about three-quarters. One-and-a-half million truck-loads of industrial equipment rolled east, amidst great confusion, when workers often lost their machines and never caught up, but also with great successes as, for instance, the move of a tank works from Kharkov, which left at the last minute in October 1941, and which began on 8 December to turn out T-34s beyond the Urals. In the evacuation, 1,523 factories went east with about one-third of their original workers.

In 1942 armament production rose; total industrial production fell. In consequence, civilian consumption abruptly contracted. In 1942 civilians obtained 40 per cent less than in 1940. Since Russians consumed much less than westerners before the war, the cut was disproportionately severe. Food production collapsed. Meat and fat production per head of the population living outside German-occupied areas fell to about one-half and grain production to about one-third of the 1940 figure. In 1942 this meant hunger and starvation for those who did not have priority. To get more food, the government increased the number of labour days on collective farms from 254 to 352 per annum while 're-education' punished absenteeism. Women bore the brunt: in 1943 over three-quarters of the able-bodied collective farm population was female. In the machine tractor stations, the heart of the collective farm system, women replaced skilled men taken by the armed forces. In 1940 only one out of twenty-five tractor drivers was a woman but, by 1942, nearly one-half were.

The absence of men of military age brought a partial reversal of the regime's agrarian policy of the 1930s, when Stalin and his henchmen relied on coercion and close supervision to force the collectivized peasantry to produce food at prices fixed by the state, in order to feed the growing number of industrial workers. During the war, efforts to extract still more from the peasantry went with new incentives: the state increased its demands but permitted peasants to sell what they could produce on their own small plots at whatever prices they could get, sometimes as much as thirty times those paid for state procurements. Meanwhile town-dwellers eagerly cultivated urban plots of land and tripled the production of home-grown vegetables. Industry, as well as agriculture, absorbed more women. The Soviet Union had a relatively high proportion of women in industry before the war, 41 per cent in 1940, but that rose to 52 per cent, and women often filled the place of skilled workers in the expanding war industries. Training courses, according to Russian figures, turned out 13,000,000 newly skilled factory workers between 1941 and 1943. The authorities were able to direct workers to take any work anywhere. Incentives stimulated the efforts of the industrial work-force, both piece-rates and bonuses, with extra food rations for those who fulfilled or overfulfilled their productive norms.

Members of the Communist Party provided a directing élite marshalling the Soviet laity. Party members were ambitious and active men, whose interests were linked with those of the regime, and who were accustomed to high-handed leadership, backed by powerful sanctions. The decisive victory secured by the Soviet economy, which halted German conquest, was one of active leadership of a population, much of it unskilled, unschooled, and uncomprehending, by an educated minority which the hectic modernization of the 1930s had fostered. At the same time the regime developed a basic industrial capacity east of the Urals. As a result the Soviet Union held the German attack in 1941 by its own efforts; thereafter aid from its allies, especially from the United States, provided supplies equal to about one-tenth of all Soviet production. Nearly 3 million tons of high-quality steel, more than half a million tons of non-ferrous metals, four million tons of food and no less than 385,000 trucks plus 51,000 jeeps came from the United States. From 1942, the Red Army owed much of its food and most of its mobility to American supplies.

In the west, the second front depended on British survival and, after 1940, the British economy rested on American support. In 1943 and 1944 the United States provided more than one-quarter of the munitions supply of the British Empire: under lend-lease they gave nearly all of this without payment. In addition lend-lease supplied raw materials and tools for British industries and food for the people. As a result Britain reduced exports to a level, about one-third of pre-war volume, far lower than would have been possible if imports had been paid for. Thus, by 1944, 55 per cent of the British labour force was either in the forces or in civilian war work. Without loans or gifts from overseas, British imports, of food, war supplies, and materials for the manufacture of war supplies, could have been financed only by exports or by reserves of gold and foreign currency, reserves which were exhausted by the end of 1940.

The size of population limited the size of the British war effort: overseas aid, from Canada and the United States, in gifts and loans, and from the Empire, in the accumulation of sterling balances, raised the proportion of the British population that made war. By the time war broke out, the engineering industry employed all available skilled labourers; during the war it increased production by rearranging processes to make skilled workmen unnecessary, or by hastily training unskilled men and women. War lessened the objections of trade unions. Registered unemployed numbered 1,270,000 in June 1939; in 1944 the figure fell to 54,000. Otherwise the growth in the labour force came from women: 2 million began to work or moved from domestic service between 1939 and 1943.

In one respect these accretions did not make up for losses to the armed forces. A shortage developed of healthy men for very heavy and arduous work. Eventually the Ministry of Labour compelled young men, chosen by ballot among those due for military service, to enter coal mining. (It is a significant comment on the sources of morale that this was far more unpopular than compulsory military service. Mineworkers lacked the prestige of men in uniform and among the 22,000 so chosen, no less than 40 per cent of these 'Bevin boys' questioned their direction and 143 recalcitrants were imprisoned.) At the end of 1943 the British economy reached its limit. From then on more sailors, soldiers, and airmen meant less war production and more weapons meant fewer servicemen. Further reduction of living standards seemed impossible. The British could not employ the German solution of using the forced labour of foreigners— they employed no more than about a quarter of a million prisoners of war, mostly Italians. At the end of 1944 the army had to break up some units in France to provide replacements for others.

The British economic war involved allocation of labour between different uses: military, war manufacture, and production of goods and services for civilians. On 22 May 1940 an act of Parliament gave the Minister of Labour, Ernest Bevin, authority to require anyone over 16 to register and to direct them to any work on conditions laid down by the Minister. The government could also give instructions to managements. In spite of Bevin's reluctance to use compulsory powers the ministry issued over 1 million directions, but most workers moved to war work without formal compulsion. Building and construction received most of those directed: camps and airfields, in particular, often urgently needed workers in isolated areas. Workers in essential war industries could not leave their jobs nor could employers dismiss them without official permission.

The British government mobilized the population for war work more effectively than any other. The German authorities allotted to the armed forces and war work about the same proportion of the population—rather over half—but they eased the task by using foreigners for civilian production so making more Germans available. Compared with Germany, however, British productivity, production per worker, was lower. In 1944, with US productivity at 100 these figures result for the main industrial countries (from R. W. Goldsmith, in *Military Affairs*, 1946).

US	100	UK	41
Canada	57	USSR	39
Germany	48	Japan	17

High labour productivity, of course, had very little to do with 'hard work', more to do with effective management, but above all it came from the use of capital equipment. Hours of work tended to be longer in Britain, where, indeed, long hours sometimes led to absenteeism, than in Germany, and in the United States they were lower still. There is no evidence that the low productivity of Japanese workers came from exceptional laziness. Fashionable historians who suggest a particular penchant for idle self-indulgence among British workers have misread, or ignored, the evidence.

High productivity helps to explain the triumphant success of the American war economy. Mass production, based on designing and engineering skills, made as many weapons as the allies could use. Two examples stand out: at Willow Run, near Detroit, Ford Motors set up a completely new factory. Its main building covered 67 acres, it employed over 42,000 workers, and produced 8,685 B-24 'Liberator' bombers, reaching a rate of one per hour. Henry Kaiser developed yards building 'Liberty' ships, where prefabricated parts were welded. By the end of 1942, it took only 56 days, on average, to deliver a new ship, and one shipyard produced one in 14 days. While weapons poured out, the average standard of living of Americans rose. By 1944 the United States produced about 40 per cent of all weapons made everywhere by friend and foe.

Yet total civilian consumption in the war years grew by about 12 per cent. Government demand, financed by a huge deficit, of $57 billion in 1943, of which about half came from the banking system, compared with $22 billion raised in taxes in the same year, brought unemployed resources into use and stimulated increased productivity. The war years saw the depression of the 1930s overcome at last. Unemployment almost disappeared. At 9 million in July 1940, it fell to 780,000 in 1943. In the same period the number of women employed rose from 13.8 million to 18.7 million and average hours worked per week in industry rose from 37.3 to 45.3. Industrial production of civilian goods fell, by about one-third compared with 1940, and civilians could not find articles such as new radios, cars, and washing-machines. After 1941 the Japanese conquest of Malaya cut off most of the world's supply of natural rubber. As in Germany, a new synthetic rubber industry filled the gap and by 1944 produced 800,000 tons, 50 per cent more than the entire US consumption of rubber in 1939. In order to save rubber the government restricted motoring for pleasure and rationed petrol: each car on average travelled one-third fewer miles in 1943 than in 1941. In spite of restrictions and shortages customers of retail shops spent one-third more in 1944, in real terms, than between 1935 and 1939. The rich spent less, the poor more.

After Pearl Harbor the armed services issued lavish orders for weapons. In the first half of 1942 they placed contracts for $100 billion worth of weapons, more than the total value of American production hitherto attained even in the most prosperous year. This disorganized scramble caused stoppages when factories ran out of raw materials for particular contracts. From the end of 1942, the War Production Board, which had already forbidden non-essential use of scarce materials, organized priorities by giving to the procurement agencies (army, navy, and so on) quotas of scarce materials, such as steel, aluminium, and copper, to be allocated to producers, who could plan their output accordingly. In the United States as a whole, shortage of labour never became critical. To deal with scarcity of skilled workmen, employers broke down and simplified skilled jobs, trained workers, and promoted partly trained workers. In some areas, especially on the west coast, labour became scarce in 1942 and 1943. Direction of labour, after the British model, though suggested in Congress, was not adopted. On the west coast, area production committees arranged priority in recruitment to firms doing essential work through the employment service. The Office of War Mobilization, set up under James F. Byrnes in May 1943, determined overall production priorities.

The United States easily met the demands of war because the Red Army engaged most of the German army. In autumn 1941, on the assumption that the Germans would knock the Soviet Union out of the war, the War Department planned to create an American army of 213 divisions. In September 1942, when the German summer offensive seemed irresistible, the US General Staff estimated that 350 American divisions were needed to win the war. Thereafter the figure grew smaller. In June 1943, the military authorities suggested that the US Army might expand only to 100 divisions. By early 1944 the final figure was settled of a 90-division army. In May, General Marshall explained that the American military 'have staked our success on our air superiority, on Soviet numerical preponderance, and on the high quality of our ground combat units', fresh and well-equipped as they were; now he believed that the Russians would go on until the defeat of Germany.

Combined boards secured Anglo-American co-operation just as the Combined-Chiefs of Staff arranged military integration. They advised on the allocation of the joint resources of munitions, shipping, raw materials, and food among the allies, while the combined production and resources board rationalized production. Canada joined in the food and raw materials boards: only the British and Americans made up the others. The Soviet Union presented lists of its needs and did not discuss them, just as its military command did not discuss strategy and operations. The acknowledged skill and knowledge of the British members of these boards maintained equality in influence even when United States capacities more and more outstripped the British. Using their political and economic power, especially their near monopoly of the world's shipping, the British and Americans together ruled the non-Axis world, leading and directing the 'United Nations'.

Governments paid businessmen or managers for arms and the latter paid workers. Production expanded to meet demand. Unemployment disappeared in war economies and incentives increased wages. Workers had more money but there was less for them to buy. Rising prices bring demands for higher wages which make prices rise again. Acceleration of this inflationary cycle destroys confidence in the currency, brings social conflict, and eventually checks or stops production. The obvious solution, of raising taxation to cover military spending, may lead only to irrepressible demands for higher wages to pay those taxes. Governments at war raised taxation as high as they dared. They encouraged the relatively poor, who collectively held the main spending power, to accept high taxation by appeals to fairness based on 'equality of sacrifice'. In Britain, the Treasury lubricated a tax of 50 per cent on incomes, for single persons with above £400 a year, by removing $97\frac{1}{2}$ per cent of income above £20,000. Equally, indirect taxation at $16\frac{2}{3}$ per cent on many consumer goods was justified by taxing 'luxuries' at 100 per cent. However, taxation only financed half of British government expenditure in 1943. Savings or inflationary credit creation financed the rest. Saving became a 'duty' of the citizen, a duty repeatedly and eloquently drawn to his attention. To many sheltered civilians, exhortations to save dominated the cultural and artistic impact of the war and provided them with opportunities for 'patriotic' expressions of public solidarity with their neighbours in 'savings weeks' and the like. Governments took direct action to hold down prices by fixing maximum prices and sometimes paying subsidies to make those prices profitable to producers. Artificially low prices brought scarcity and therefore rationing, another familiar part of the civilian experience of war.

German measures against inflation proved the most effective. Between 1939 and 1943 the British working-class cost of living rose by 25 per cent, the German by only 10 per cent. Yet direct taxation during the war took a smaller proportion of personal incomes in Germany than in Britain and taxes met only about one-third of government spending. Conquest helped, for the Germans could impose their terms for purchases in occupied countries and so hold down the price of German imports from them. Moreover, in Germany an effective administration, with a formidable coercive apparatus, controlled prices, enforced rationing, and held wages down. The German authorities drained off purchasing power by compulsory lending to the state, thinly disguised. They put the funds of banks, savings banks and insurance companies at the government's disposal and compelled individuals and corporations to maintain accounts there. In Britain, Keynes advocated the same device of compulsory saving, but the Treasury applied it more timidly: in Germany, compulsory savings raised as much as did taxation while in Britain it was only about $3\frac{1}{2}$ per cent of total taxation. The German Economic Minister, Funk, claimed that plundering conquered territories would make easy eventual repayment of compulsory savings so that the government in effect forced Germans to gamble on victory.

In the Soviet Union, although in theory the government directed the economy, inflation was high. The authorities gave priority to incentives for the economically useful, and amidst catastrophic shortages the state could not protect the economically inessential by forcing equality of sacrifice. The war accentuated the tendency for the Soviet Union to break away from the egalitarianism of the early revolutionaries. The regime cared more about winning the support of those sections of the population who could contribute most to the war effort than about doctrinal purity. Official figures put the wartime increase in retail prices at 325 per cent.

In Italy the government adopted a relaxed attitude towards war finance. It assumed, wrongly, that an increased money supply would generate a corresponding increase in savings provided the state controlled wages, prices, and private investment, and rationed civilian construction. Arms production required extra imports because Italy needed imported raw materials and fuel, and exports fell because of concentration on production of war supplies, and because of the British blockade. On the free market at Geneva, Italian currency sold in June 1943 at less than one-seventh of its 1938 value and import prices rose sharply. Inflation followed. The official cost of living index rose three-and-a-half times between 1938 and 1943, while black-market prices rose much higher. Meanwhile, inhibited by shortages of imported materials, armaments production either did not grow or actually fell. Of coal, over $2\frac{1}{2}$ million tons less than was required each year came in during the war, only one-third of necessary raw materials for steel-making, and less than one-seventh of the oil required. The Germans preferred to take surplus Italian labour to Germany rather than allot raw materials to Italian war industry. Ill-equipped Italian armies met defeat in Africa, Russia, and south-eastern Europe. At home, industrial towns endured inflation, food shortages, and eventually allied bombing.

In March 1943 illegal strikes broke out: protests against falling living standards, which soon became demands for an end to the war and for political liberty. Mussolini and the Fascists had come to power to bring order at home and greatness abroad. Now Mussolini's only chance of survival was to persuade Hitler to seek peace or to detach Italy from the Axis alliance. He hardly dared to try, and a series of stressful interviews with Hitler led only to an exacerbation of the Duce's stomach cramps. Hence, as soon as the allied landings in Sicily showed Hitler's inability or unwillingness to defend Italian territory, Mussolini's former collaborators, the army, the Church, the business classes, and the royal family, ordered him out, acting through the hesitant voice of the king. Mussolini went quietly, even with relief, only to be 'rescued' later by his tenacious 'friend', Hitler, and restored to limited power in the German-sponsored Salo republic. Economic failures as well as the pointlessness of the war made active the enemies of the Fascist state and destroyed its will to fight.

Japanese war production also relied on imports. Steel production in Japan depended on imported iron ore and coking coal, its aircraft production on imported bauxite. Imports made up nine-tenths of its oil supply, and an essential proportion, about one-fifth, of its food. To make war, therefore, Japan needed ships. At the beginning of the war Japanese merchant ships totalled about 6 million tons; at the end the figure was below 2 million.

	Japanese merchant ships, gross tons	
	Built	Sunk
1942	260,059	971,855
1943	769,085	1,661,791
1944	1,699,203	5,557,976
1945 (to Aug.)	559,563	1,537,484

Shortage of ships caused shortage of the materials needed to make steel. As a result, Japanese steel plants produced much less than they could have done if supplies of iron ore and coke had been secure. Capacity rose between 1941 and 1944 from 11½ million tons to 15 million tons but actual output of ingot steel started to fall at the end of 1943, and stockpiles began to run out. In 1943 nearly 9 million tons was produced; in 1944 only 6½ million tons. In consequence, shipbuilding was curtailed, both of merchant ships and of escorting warships to protect them from American submarines. Shortage of ships meant shortage of oil. In 1940 Japan imported 37 million barrels; in 1944, 7 million. In April 1941 Japanese stocks of crude oil amounted to 20 million barrels; in April 1945, only 195,000. Shortages of steel and oil ruined Japanese air power. Aircraft engine production fell every month after August 1944 because lack of imported alloys made impossible a sufficient output of high-grade steel. Meanwhile, pilots missed training for lack of fuel. In 1944 trainees received only 70 hours and in 1945 as little as 50 hours. Ill-trained pilots, given fuel only for a one-way trip, carried out the 'Kamikaze' or suicide attacks on allied shipping in 1945. During the American assault on Okinawa in 1945 only about 20 per cent of suicide flights got through to their target. Figures for all first-line combat aircraft in the Pacific war summarize the operational outcome of the weakness of the Japanese economy.

	US aircraft	Japanese aircraft
Jan. 1943	3,537	3,200
Jan. 1944	11,442	4,050
Jan. 1945	17,976	4,600
July 1945	21,908	4,100

The Japanese military never expected the war to last so long since they made two assumptions when they began it. One was that Germany would win the war in Europe, the second that the United States would not persist in challenging the consequent reordering of the world by the victorious Axis. Their confidence, boosted by great victories, survived intact until the Guadalcanal campaign demonstrated American tenacity. From the end of 1942 they tried to increase war production to a level they had thought unnecessary when the war began a year before, and settled down to defend their conquests as long as necessary to wear down American resolve. They would have done better and been able to keep the war going even longer, if they had started this increase sooner and shown more competence in managing the economy. The army, in particular, never gave up its insistence on calling up men of military age, regardless of their industrial skills. Both the army and navy used their long-established industrial connections to assert their priority, and to demand careful attention to every shift in design required by the users of weapons regardless of any effect on production. The government tried to impose priorities in the use of manpower and the allocation of materials by establishing a Munitions Ministry in November 1943. The armed services, however, were too powerful to accept direction and the Munitions Minister found himself acting only as a mediator between army and navy. The problem for Japan, however, was less administrative incompetence than military vulnerability.

American attacks on Japanese shipping crippled Japan's economy, and industrial activity was coming to a halt when the war ended in August 1945. The war-winning weapon, which first arrested and then reversed Japanese efforts to produce more weapons, was the American submarine. This was a surprise. Before the war US navy submarines were trained only to attack enemy warships, especially battleships and aircraft-carriers. Indeed, the United States expected to observe the treaty provision which forbade attack on merchant ships unless their crews' safety was first assured—a clause making impossible war on cargo ships. The President demonstrated yet again the fragility of such restrictions by allowing the navy to respond to the surprise of Pearl Harbor with immediate resort to 'unrestricted submarine and air warfare'. American submarines started badly, with inaccurate torpedoes and crews trained to operate against battle fleets and showing undue caution against unarmed ships. Things improved, however, in time to exploit two decisive advantages which came in early 1943. American signals intelligence broke the code employed to direct Japanese merchant ships and the Japanese naval authorities introduced convoys, whose management created many readable signals. In consequence, with never more than fifty boats in operation, the United States submarine force contributed more than 70 per cent of the sinkings of Japanese cargo ships before August 1944, by which time the Japanese economy was in irreversible decline. Only in the last year of the war did American air attacks and air-laid mines overtake the success rate of submarine attack, mainly because, by then, nearly all remaining Japanese ships stuck to home waters, close inshore, seeking harbour at night. Those that ventured into the open sea rarely escaped submarines. Japanese escort vessels, weak in numbers, in radar, and signals intelligence, compared badly with those of the allies: they sank only just over forty American submarines, 18 per cent of those used in the Pacific. In the less one-sided U-boat war, the Germans lost 781 boats, about 71 per cent of those they put into service, and their casualties reached 80 per cent. Economic defeat laid open the Japanese people to the terrible climax of stategic bombing described in the next chapter.

10

Strategic bombing

IN the Second World War British and American leaders devoted much material and skill to 'strategic bombing' to destroy the economy and the will to fight of the enemy. In the summer of 1941, at the Atlantic meeting, the British staffs told the Americans that they hoped to defeat Germany by bombing alone. Yet one of the three great strategic air assaults of the war had already failed: the German 'blitz' on Britain. British experts expected 600,000 deaths and 1,200,000 serious injuries in two months of German attack. Respectable psychiatrists suggested there might be 3 to 4 million cases of neurotic disorder and panic hysteria. Understandably, the authorities had feared complete social collapse followed by an irresistible demand for peace. Nothing of the sort took place. Moreover, British counter-attack on German targets had also failed. A British inquiry concluded that in night raids on the Ruhr in June and July 1941, only about six aircraft out of every hundred got within 5 miles of their targets. Losses of bomber crews often exceeded the numbers of Germans killed as, for instance, in ten raids on Berlin in June to November 1941 when 133 Germans were killed compared with losses of about three times that number of British aircrew. At first sight it is surprising that the subsequent British and American bombing campaigns against Germany took place at all. On the other hand, the Royal Air Force originally came into existence as a separate force purely to bomb.

Well before the war, the RAF had successfully asked for a bombing force to be ready in 1942. In 1941, moreover, to abandon strategic bombing would be to waste resources already assembled, at a time when Britain needed some weapon to strike at Germany: to give a prospect of eventual victory when Britain was fighting alone, and later, to give active support to the Soviet Union. The navy could win the war only by blockade—a hope weakened first by Soviet help to Germany, then by German conquest of Russian resources; the army could never defeat the German army; and only the RAF remained. It had a friend at Churchill's court—the 'Prof', Lindemann, later Lord Cherwell. For instance, he set in train the inquiry which showed the inability of Bomber Command to hit its targets, but he merely concluded that it must improve its navigation.

Another advantage lay in the self-confidence of its leaders. They argued that the German bombing of Britain showed what could be done with a much larger force. Though the Luftwaffe had failed to drive the British population into hysterical panic, it had destroyed many buildings; people were less vulnerable than had been expected, houses much more. The German raid on Coventry, it was calculated, had dropped one ton of bombs for every 800 persons in the town. The morning after, the 'index of activity', so the air staff claimed, was down to 37 per cent of normal and it took over a month to recover. If enough bombers were available to drop that weight of bombs five or six times within six months, towns should effectively be destroyed. If RAF Bomber Command had a first-line force of 4,000 heavy bombers, that is 4,000 aircraft with fully trained crews and reserves of men and machines for replacement, rest, and repair, it could wipe out forty-three selected German towns and break Germany in six months.

In October 1941, however, Churchill refused to place 'unbounded confidence' in this 'means of attack . . . he is an unwise man who thinks there is any *certain* method of winning the war'. Production problems helped to restrain Churchill's enthusiasm. The RAF wanted 22,000 bombers to be made by July 1943 but, by then, British factories had produced only 11,500, of which less than half were the heavy bombers on which the RAF relied for concentrated weight of attack. Other parts of the RAF competed for some of these aircraft with Bomber Command. The United States authorities were not willing, once they came into the war, simply to place their bombers at the disposal of the RAF. By February 1943 the first-line strength of Bomber Command was only just over 1,000, and even in March 1945 it was under 2,000, though by then more than 1,000 were highly efficient 'Lancaster' bombers.

RAF Bomber Command alone never dropped the weight of bombs called for by the air staff in 1941, though, together with the US 8th Air Force, more than that amount was regularly delivered after June 1944. In March 1942 Lord Cherwell produced a prediction of the effects of bombing Germany with the aircraft he expected to be available, as distinct from the number Bomber Command would have liked. Assuming more accuracy than the air staff had done, he argued that in about fifteen months the great majority of the inhabitants of fifty-eight German towns would be

turned out of house and home. Investigation seems to show that having one's house demolished is most damaging to morale. People seem to mind it more than having their friends or even relatives killed. At Hull signs of strain were evident, though only one-tenth of the houses were demolished . . . we should be able to do ten times as much harm to each of the 58 principal German towns. There seems little doubt that this would break the spirit of the people.

An Air Ministry directive of 14 February 1942 told the Commander-in-Chief, Bomber Command, 'that the primary object of your operations should now be focused on the morale of the enemy civil population and in particular of the industrial workers'. Towns suggested for attack had specific industrial importance, but 'the aiming points are to be the built-up areas, not, for instance, the dockyards or aircraft factories'. Before the war the RAF expected to make daylight attacks on precise military objectives. Experience soon showed the British, as it showed the Luftwaffe, that bombers, flying unescorted in daylight, suffered excessive losses. Both air forces also discovered that, at night, targets smaller than large towns were hard to find, let alone to hit. German use of incendiary bombs impressed the British, who concluded that fire did more damage than high explosive. British tactics, therefore, developed night attacks, beginning with fire-raising which illuminated targets for a concentrated high explosive attack to disrupt the attempts of the victims to check the fires. The purpose was not directly to stop industry, for machinery had proved to be more difficult to destroy than buildings, but to disorganize towns and render the inhabitants incapable of, or unwilling to do, productive work. German propaganda accurately called it 'terror bombing'. In October 1942 the Air Ministry circulated a bombing code of conduct over German-occupied territories. Attacks must be confined to military objectives. Crews must take care to avoid loss of life to civilians near the target, and in case of doubt an attack should not be made. These rules, the code emphasized, did *not* apply to German, Italian, or Japanese territory. In Germany, 'area bombing' became normal British tactics. Attempts to hit precise targets were not given up, nor was daylight bombing, but until June 1944 the proportion of RAF attacks by day was very small. From 1942 to 1945 RAF Bomber Command destroyed an average of about half the built-up area of seventy German towns.

In 1942 Harris, the new Commander-in-Chief of Bomber Command, looked for spectacular successes to justify his claims. In March and April, British bombers made concentrated incendiary attacks on Lübeck and Rostock. Their centres were medieval, densely packed, and inflammable, 'more like a fire-lighter than a human habitation', as Harris wrote of Lübeck. In May Harris got together 1,046 aircraft to attack Cologne. This, and the two following 'thousand-bomber raids' on Essen and

Bremen, secured immense publicity. In 1942 the RAF dropped on Germany a somewhat smaller weight of bombs than the Luftwaffe carried to Britain in 1940 and 1941. In November 1942 Portal, the British Chief of Air Staff, proposed a greatly increased attack in 1943 and 1944. He now asked for a force growing to 6,000 first-line bombers, and gave the thousand-bomber raid on Cologne as an example of what could be done. In ninety minutes, he claimed, one-third of the inner zone of the town was completely destroyed, 20,000 houses were destroyed and many others were damaged, while 200,000 persons had to be evacuated. (In fact, 3,000 houses were destroyed and 45,000 people made homeless, though many only for a short period.) Portal promised ten attacks of 'Cologne' intensity on every industrial town in Germany with a population larger than 50,000: he predicted 6,000,000 houses destroyed, 25,000,000 Germans made homeless, and about 900,000 killed. Portal's plan presented the difficulty that it needed American aircraft and crews. The United States Army Air Force, however, disapproved of British tactics. It favoured precision bombing, aimed attacks on carefully selected targets of military importance carried out in daylight. Experience had taught the RAF that daylight attacks on defended targets were prohibitively costly and that large-scale night attacks could be aimed only against big towns. The Americans believed that it was better to cause a high degree of destruction in a few essential industries than to cause a small degree of destruction in many industries. The British thought the choice did not exist, and that the targets must be the entire German economy and German morale. American airmen thought this policy wasteful and believed that the British too readily assumed that enemy interceptor fighters must always defeat heavy bombers. They argued that disciplined formations of heavily-armed and well-armoured bombers could fend off defending fighters even in daylight combats. Portal asserted that bombers needed fighter escorts if they were to make daylight intrusions deep into Germany and claimed that an effective fighter was impossible to design with long enough range.

Churchill still doubted the success of plans to defeat Germany by aerial bombardment alone, and therefore thought it imprudent to encourage American concentration on bombing, especially since he also doubted American ability to bomb German territory. On the other hand, the USAAF leaders could be relied on to put the European war first in allied strategy provided their plans for an American bombing campaign were accepted. They would help to counter the US navy's dangerous inclination to put the main American effort in the Pacific. Moreover, an

American daylight bombing campaign, which implied the winning of daylight air superiority, would cause Marshall, the head of the US army, to view a great bombing campaign as a desirable, or even essential, preliminary to the invasion of north-western Europe. In this way he might come round to agree with Brooke and the British General Staff on the need to reduce German strength before the main invasion of Europe. So the makers of Anglo-American strategy agreed on the 'Combined Bomber Offensive'.

On 21 January 1943, at the Casablanca conference, the Combined Chiefs of Staff issued a directive to govern the operation of British and United States bomber commands in Britain. It incorporated both nations' doctrines. In British airmen's language it called for the 'progressive destruction and dislocation of the German military, industrial, and economic system and the undermining of the morale of the German people to a point where their capacity for armed resistance is fatally weakened', and then moved into American language and set out precise target systems. But attacks on the latter 'were subject to the exigencies of weather and tactical feasibility'. The way remained open for the British to persuade the Americans of the value of night as against day bombing and the Americans to persuade the British of the reverse. Soon General Eaker, the commander of the US 8th Air Force, worked out his plan for winning the war by destroying six selected target systems. His optimism, as so often in the Second World War, was strengthened by the grotesquely inflated claims of numbers of German aircraft destroyed that his bomber crews put forward after their opening attacks on France and the Low Countries. In the last six months of 1942, they claimed to have shot down 223 German aircraft, while the true figure was less than eight.

On 27 January 1943 American bombers attacked Germany itself for the first time, when ninety-one aircraft, B-17 'Flying Fortresses' and B-24 'Liberators', set off for Wilhelmshaven. Now began the Anglo-American bombing competition of 1943. The British won: in weight of bombs dropped, in length of sustained attack, and by making one of the most horrifyingly successful of all air raids. On the night of 24 July, 791 British bombers set out for Hamburg. Next day 181 American aircraft aimed at submarine yards there, and fifty-four more flew in on 26 July. On 27 July Bomber Command despatched 787 heavy bombers to Hamburg. Two nights later Bomber Command sent another 777 aircraft there, and yet another blow came on 2 August when 740 bombers were sent. WINDOW, a radar-jamming mass of reflecting strips, confused the German defences, and the British were able to make concentrated and quickly repeated attacks. Rather over one-third of the British bombers dropped their bombs within three miles of the aiming point in the centre of the city. Early on 27 July a shower of incendiary bombs set off fires in central Hamburg which merged into a mighty furnace of destruction. Temperatures reached 1,000 degrees Centigrade. This man-made inferno sucked in winds of hurricane force which united individual fires into a fire-storm covering more than six square miles. Lack of oxygen suffocated the occupants of shelters before fire cremated them. Forty to fifty thousand people were killed in Hamburg in these few days. As the police president of Hamburg described it,

amidst the howling of the fire-storm, the cries and groans of the dying, and the constant crash of bombs . . . children were torn away from their parents' hands by the force of the hurricane and hurled into the fire. People who thought they had escaped fell down, overcome by the devouring force of the heat and died in an instant. Refugees had to make their way over the dead and dying. The sick and infirm had to be left behind by rescuers as they themselves were in danger of burning . . . No flight of imagination will ever succeed in measuring and describing the gruesome scenes of horror in the many buried air-raid shelters. Posterity can only bow its head in honour of the fate of these innocents, sacrificed by the murderous lust of a sadistic enemy.

The Commander of RAF Bomber Command, Harris, sprinkled 1943 with prophecies of victory. On 15 May the bombing campaign 'cannot fail to be lethal within a period of time which in my view will be surprisingly short'; on 3 November, 'we can wreck Berlin from end to end if the USAAF will come in on it. It will cost between 400–500 aircraft. It will cost Germany the war'; on 7 December, 'the Lancaster force alone should be sufficient, but only just sufficient, to produce in Germany by April 1st 1944 a state of devastation in which surrender is inevitable'. Air Marshal Bottomley, the Deputy Chief of Air Staff, became sceptical. He cited Hitler himself to Harris: 'Whereas the German people feared the night attacks, Hitler and the German High Command feared the daylight precision attacks on individual factories. Hitler openly boasted that he could . . . control the morale of the population for some considerable time.' Harris's chief, Portal, still hesitantly hoped. He told the Combined Chiefs of Staff in December 1943 that the RAF had devastated one quarter of the built-up area of thirty-eight German towns, and that 'perhaps 6,000,000 people or more have been made homeless and have spread alarm and despondency in the areas to which they have gone'. German morale was 'at an extremely low ebb' and industrial devastation might be 'at least halfway . . . towards the point where Germany will become unable to continue the war'. Evidently Portal supposed that area bombing was having a serious impact on production as well as on morale, and his comment helps to explain the feebleness of his attempts to get Harris to conform with the Anglo-American agreement that the bomber offensive should aim, as its first priority, directly to weaken the Luftwaffe rather than attack the urban populations in general.

When nights were long Harris had his chance. Between 18 November 1943 and 24 March 1944 RAF bombers raided Berlin sixteen times, making more than 9,000 sorties. Meanwhile, Bomber Command struck other targets with more than 11,000 sorties in nineteen area attacks. Berlin suffered great damage but the British bombing did not 'wreck Berlin from end to end'. Bomber Command was not justified in its claim, in February 1944, that 'the administrative machine of the Nazis, their military and industrial organization, and, above all, their morale have by these attacks suffered a deadly wound from which they cannot recover'. Explosions or fires destroyed at least one-fifth of Berlin housing and killed more than 5,000 civilians, yet the victory went to the German defenders. Attacks deep inside Germany gave them their chance: in the thirty-five big raids of the 'Battle of Berlin', British losses averaged 5.2 per cent. At that rate bomber crews had a less than 50 per cent chance of surviving their first tour of duty of thirty sorties, and the chance of survival of a full aircrew career, with the normal second tour of twenty more operations, was even smaller. Worse still, the rate of loss increased at the beginning of 1944. In the four attacks on Berlin of December 1943, the bomber force lost on average 4.8 per cent of its strength in each operation, but in January 1944, six attacks on Berlin had average losses of 6.1 per cent while three elsewhere lost 7.2 per cent. In February one raid on Berlin lost 4.8 per cent but an attack on Leipzig lost 9.2 per cent of the attackers. Thereafter, Bomber Command switched to other targets and split its forces to avoid the concentrations of German night fighters. A return to Berlin in strength on 24 March 1944 led to losses of 9.1 per cent. On 30 March an attempt at concentrated bombing of Nuremberg brought disaster when 11.8 per cent of the attackers did not return. Five hundred and forty-five British aircrew were killed; 129 Germans, mostly civilians. Harris could no longer attempt concentrated and repeated attacks of the sort that had brought disaster to Hamburg. Early in April he wrote that, 'the strength of German defences would in time reach a point at which night bombing attacks by existing methods and types of heavy bombers would involve percentage casualty rates that could not in the long run be sustained'. The British took to night bombing to avoid German fighters. Now more and more German fighters were flying by night. The Luftwaffe was winning.

Meanwhile, it had also defeated the US 8th Air Force, but the Americans struck back. The British failed, as often in the Second World War, to persuade American commanders that experience had given them greater wisdom. The US air force insisted on precision bombing by daylight. In 1943 the North African campaign and American diversions to the Far East held down the strength of the 8th Air Force in Britain. However, their attacking forces rose in strength from about sixty heavy bombers to about 250 by the end of May. During that time American bombers concentrated on the German-occupied countries and made few attacks on the more heavily defended targets inside Germany itself, particularly since the Combined Chiefs of Staff gave priority to attacks on U-boat bases and building yards. Even so, they suffered losses of about 5.6 per cent. The German fighter force inflicted most harm.

In the second half of 1943 the US 8th Air Force gave battle. It set out to attack aircraft factories and installations supporting the Luftwaffe in Germany itself, well beyond the range of protecting fighter escort. The new phase began in July with attacks on Kassel and Oschersleben in which 9 per cent of the planes dispatched were lost, a number equal to no less than 19 per cent of the bombers that actually reached the target. In August 12 per cent of bombers dispatched to the Ruhr, Schweinfurt, and Regensburg did not return. General Eaker sent his bombers deep into Germany again in October. Attacks on Frankfurt, Wiesbaden, and the Saar endured only 4.5 per cent loss. On 10 October, however, the German defenders brought down nearly 10 per cent of bombers dispatched to Munster, and on 14 October, the 8th Air Force suffered a terrible blow at Schweinfurt, centre of German ball-bearing production. Two hundred and ninety-one bombers, all Flying Fortresses, so-called because of their alleged capacity for self-defence, attempted to reach Schweinfurt. Two hundred and twenty-nine did so. Sixty of them were destroyed. Yet on the very day of the Schweinfurt disaster, General Arnold, the USAAF Chief of Staff, declared the Luftwaffe to be near collapse. American commanders had been misled, once again, by the wildly, though honestly, exaggerated claims made by their bomber crews. Slowly it sank in that, in fact, German fighter strength was growing, and that the American attempt to win air supremacy had failed. Portal felt confirmed in his belief that long-range daylight bombing of Germany was impossible 'beyond escorting fighter range'. By contrast,

General Spaatz, the newly-made commander of all US strategic bombing in Europe, noted in January that fighter ranges would soon be extended 'as P-51s come more into the picture'.

The P-51 or Mustang had first been produced in the United States to British specifications. The RAF was disappointed when the first Mustangs were delivered at the end of 1941 and did not use it as a fighter. Neither did the USAAF then take any interest in it. Luckily the Rolls-Royce company thought it worth substituting for the original American engine a version of their Merlin engine, which powered the Spitfire fighter and the Lancaster bomber. With the Packard-Merlin engine, built in the United States under licence from Rolls-Royce, appeared the P-51B Mustang. It combined long range with performance that excelled any fighter in the world. Production began in June 1943, but only after the Schweinfurt disaster did General Arnold order that it should be produced in quantity and reserved for use as a fighter. By May 1945, 14,000 Mustangs had been turned out. In February 1944, General Spaatz renewed the battle with the Luftwaffe. On 20 February, clear weather came to Europe, and the US air force opened its 'Big Week' of precision daylight bombing. The 8th Air Force from Britain and the 15th Air Force from southern Italy attacked aircraft factories in Germany on 20, 21, 22, 24, and 25 February. American bombers made nearly 4,000 sorties, mostly from Britain, and about 3,500 sorties were made by escorting American fighters together with a contribution from RAF Spitfires. In association with 'Big Week', RAF Bomber Command put on about 2,000 sorties at night. What was new was that American bombers, flying across Germany, were escorted throughout, except where the rendezvous failed between fighters and bombers. Fiercer combats confronted defending German fighters. The Germans shot down about 6 per cent of the American bombers but lost about 450 single-seater fighters. In March 1944 the 8th Air Force again challenged German fighters to combat by making four heavy attacks on Berlin in addition to six other towns. (In only two of these attacks could the aimers see their targets, and in the others they bombed by radar observation, which produced area bombing as indiscriminate as British night bombing.) In this month the Germans lost another 450 day fighters. The German fighter force never recovered from the losses of February and March 1944. In April, as the Combined Chiefs of Staff had agreed, immediate preparations for the invasion of north-west Europe became the principal task of both RAF Bomber Command and the US air force.

This order followed great controversy among allied leaders. The chief 'bomber barons', Spaatz and Harris, believed that their forces, if left to themselves, could win the war, though they disagreed on how to do it. Spaatz wanted to attack German synthetic oil production. Then American aircraft would do further battle with German day fighters, which would be obliged to defend their own source of fuel, and within three months loss of fuel would halt the entire German war machine. Harris urged the continued obliteration of German towns. The British Air Marshal Tedder, backed by General Eisenhower, the commander of the coming invasion, demanded the destruction of the German transport system by attacks on its focal points, especially marshalling-yards. The RAF commander of the allied tactical air forces, backed by the armies, urged the need to cut German railways and roads leading to the immediate area of invasion. In reply, Harris emphasized and exaggerated the inaccuracy of his bombers, predicted the killing of tens of thousands of French civilians, and got Churchill to object to attacks on French and Belgian roads and railways. In the end, everyone had some of their own way, and even Harris and Spaatz recognized that they must contribute direct help to the coming invasion. German preparations to launch their new missiles forced allied heavy bombers to attack even more targets. They continued strategic bombing, however, and the US 8th Air Force exploited lengthening daylight to go for oil. The US 15th Air Force started, on 5 May, a series of raids on the oil wells at Ploesti in Romania, and on 12, 28, and 29 May the 8th Air Force attacked oil refineries and synthetic oil plants in Germany. The Germans shot down nearly 7 per cent of the attacking bombers but they lost more fighter aircraft, with their pilots, and were compelled to keep some of their diminishing fighter strength in Germany.

In consequence of the air battles over Germany, the Germans had ready in northern France only 170 single-seat fighters against the 10,000 combat aircraft the allies used to support the invasion of Normandy. Within a few days 300 more came from Germany, but the transfer itself brought losses, since pilots had to go into action from unfamiliar bases. This emphasized the fundamental weakness of the Luftwaffe: its lack of thoroughly trained pilots and crews. Goering and his staff neglected training until it was too late, and after mid-1944, German industry made many more aircraft than the Luftwaffe could use. Shortage of fuel, particularly aviation spirit, chronically afflicted German planners after the invasion of Russia, and the air force High Command failed to give sufficient allocations of petrol to training. Moreover, for much of the war, active air fleet commanders controlled training and, in any operational crisis, raided training schools for machines and experienced crews. The desperate need for pilots in 1944 caused hurried training. A good fighter pilot needed a year's training with at least 300 flying hours. British and American pilots got up to 400 flying hours or more; after July 1944 Germans made do with an average of 115, often completed without any chance to handle up-to-date combat machines. Skimped training caused a high rate of loss through accidents, and inexperience showed in combat. Moreover, inadequate training produced pilots unable to fly by instruments in bad weather. Once allied attacks began to make still more acute the shortage of fuel the quality of pilots declined further, and so the defence of oil production weakened even more. At the end, some of the world's first jet aircraft, which in performance outclassed all allied planes, were thrust into the hands of men who could not exploit them.

After June 1944, invasion month, the US 8th Air Force returned its principal effort to German targets, concentrating especially on oil; RAF Bomber Command, on the other hand, devoted its main attention to support of the armies in France until September. Thereafter, British bombers found attacks on German targets much less hazardous than in the spring as the Luftwaffe ran short of fuel. Moreover, it was now much harder for German night fighters to find their prey. The successes and failures of night bombing increasingly depended on electronics. When the British navigated their aircraft, and dropped their bombs, by uninterrupted electronic guidance, they struck hard even in cloudy weather; when the Luftwaffe detected British radar signals and used its own radar to find British bombers it inflicted serious losses. In the spring of 1944 German night fighters found British bombers in three ways: by using NAXOS to pick up signals from H2S, the British navigation aid; by using FLENSBURG to detect MONICA, which British bombers used to warn them of the presence of a German fighter behind them; and by using signals from IFF, the system for distinguishing between British and hostile aircraft, which British aircrews superstitiously, and incorrectly, believed spoiled the aim of German searchlights and anti-aircraft guns. To cap it all, German electronic engineers produced a short-wave radar, immune to existing British interference by WINDOW, which could detect British bombers at four miles' range: LICHTENSTEIN SN2. On 13 July 1944 the Germans lost their advantage when the pilot of one of the latest night-fighter versions of the Junkers 88, with the most recent electronic equipment, found, to his apparent dismay, that he had accidentally landed on a British airport. Soon Bomber Command crews began only briefly to turn on their H2S. MONICA was abandoned, and IFF sealed up.

From September, the British were able to jam LICHTENSTEIN SN2. Moreover, as a result of allied advances in France and Belgium, ground stations for the G-H system of navigation and bomb-aiming came closer to Germany, while German early-warning radar retreated.

Now Bomber Command and the US Strategic Air Force in Europe were ready to inflict catastrophic death and destruction. A few experienced German night-fighter pilots, if they had the fuel, and could find a target, still inflicted casualties, but though it remained numerically strong, the German night-fighter force no longer won large-scale victories. By the spring of 1945, British Bomber Command reached a combat strength of about 1,600, while the US 8th Air Force could fly into action over 2,000 bombers, though with smaller bomb-loads than the British. Between 1 September 1944 and the end of the war the RAF dropped nearly 400,000 tons of bombs on Germany, the USAAF about 350,000 tons, ten times as much as the Germans dispatched to Britain by bomber, flying-bomb, and rocket during the whole war. American bombers concentrated, by day, on oil and transport targets. The British returned, at last, to day bombing, but their main effort remained at night: against oil and transport, especially in the Ruhr region; and still, most powerfully, they carried out area bombing of cities. This culminated in the fourth great fire-storm. After Hamburg, Kassel, and Darmstadt, Dresden succumbed.

In January 1945 the Red Army launched its offensive towards East Germany and the western allies considered how to help, preferably in some visible and politically useful way, as a demonstration both of the western allies' power and of their loyalty to the alliance. Spaatz agreed with the British air staff, with Churchill's approval, that as a second priority to oil plants, bombing targets should be Berlin, Dresden, Leipzig, Chemnitz, and other cities 'where heavy attack will cause great confusion in civilian evacuation from the East and hamper movements of reinforcements from other fronts'. At Yalta on 4 February the Russian deputy Chief of Staff encouraged such attacks by asking that the Germans should be prevented from moving troops to the eastern front 'by air attacks against communications'. On the night of 13 February 1945 over 800 British bombers flew to Dresden and made one of the most devastating attacks of the war; next day, more than 400 American bombers followed, and 200 more on 15 February. Though no one knows exactly how many were killed, the British attack certainly caused more deaths than any other single European aerial bombardment, perhaps, indeed, more than any other air raid, including the atomic destruction of Hiroshima.

Since British and American civilians, more clearly than fighting soldiers, saw the end of the war approaching, and since Dresden had a name associated with art rather than war, the half-repressed moral unease aroused by bombing found new expression. Civilian casualties caused disquiet. Societies at war trained and equipped men to fight others similarly trained and equipped by hostile societies. To attack 'defence-less', 'innocent' civilians extended the impact of war to people some of whom were not capable of working, let alone fighting. A few critics also found distasteful the wanton destruction of beautiful buildings. Those directly involved in bombing campaigns, as well as those in whose name they were carried out, needed justifications they did not feel necessary for conventional armed combats. The authorities offered three lines of argument. Churchill put two of them in a speech of 30 June 1943, when he spoke of the Anglo-American bombers as the avenging angels of Jehovah (cf. Hosea 8:7):

Now those who sow the wind are reaping the whirlwind . . . This is a sombre prospect for the German people . . . but when we remind ourselves of the frightful cruelties and tyrannies with which the German armies, their gauleiters and subordinate tormentors, are now afflicting almost all Europe . . . we may feel sure that we bear the sword of justice and we are resolved to use that sword with the utmost severity to the full and to the end.

Thus, Churchill argued first, that the Germans started the bombing of civilians, so that bombing German civilians in their turn was legitimate, and secondly, that the Germans deserved punishment.

These arguments appeal less now than they did then: war is made against nations, and in wartime men find it particularly easy to believe that a nation whose policies are immoral is made up of immoral individuals. Germans were 'Huns': the only good German was a dead German. Even to those intellectually intoxicated by war, however, the third justification was the strongest: that bombing of towns helped to win the war more quickly. This invoked the only moral principle that sets limits to the horrors of war, that the sufferings imposed should be the smallest needed to secure its objects. It was comparatively easy to defend attempts to bomb 'military objectives': such as factories making military supplies, and the means of transporting them such as canals, railways, bridges, and tunnels, when the incidental killing of civilians was an unfortunate but inevitable concomitant. The US air forces in Europe, therefore, aroused less controversy than British Bomber Command. The Americans attempted precision bombing of targets individually selected for their military value; the British attacked residential areas to kill or frighten civilian workers. The effect was generally much the same: at least half of American bombs were dropped blind through cloud or haze, and, by 1944, American aiming at these invisible targets was less accurate than British; when the British tried precise bombing, their best performance (of their specialized squadrons) was better than anything American formations could attain.

Most people reconciled themselves to bombing of factories, oil refineries, and transport centres even if many civilians were incidentally killed or maimed or bombed out of house and home. Many, however, thought it wrong deliberately to attack civilians and their houses even for the purpose of weakening the enemy's war effort. Criticism of area bombing was expressed in both Houses of Parliament, especially by the Bishop of Chichester in the House of Lords, and, in the Commons, by members such as Hopkinson, a Liberal, who asked rhetorically: 'Because your enemy happens to be a nasty brute, is it really logical that you yourself should be a still more nasty brute?', and went on 'let it be the sort of war that all of us in our heart of hearts can go into with enthusiasm, in the sort of way that I do not think we can go with the bombing of open cities'. The government skilfully dissembled. On 31 March 1943 Stokes, a Labour MP, asked in the Commons whether 'instructions have been given to British airmen to engage in area bombing rather than limit their attention to purely military targets'. Sinclair, Secretary of State for Air, replied: 'The targets of Bomber Command are always military, but night bombing of military objectives necessarily involves bombing the area in which they are situated.' Harris worried that his bomber crews might resent orders that the government thus tried to conceal. He doubtless preferred Churchill's reply to the protests of the Bishop of Chichester and Lord Salisbury, when he defended RAF bombing in the House of Commons on 22 February 1944:

The idea that we should fetter or further restrict the use of this prime instrument for shortening the war will not be accepted by the Governments of the Allies. The proper course for German civilians and non-combatants is to quit the centres of munitions production and take refuge in the countryside. We intend to make war production in its widest sense impossible in all German cities, towns, and factory centres.

After Dresden, or rather, after the reaction to Dresden (the devastation of Würzburg on 16 March 1945 got less publicity), Churchill changed his mind. On 28 March he wrote: 'The destruction of Dresden remains a serious query against the conduct of allied bombing . . . I feel the need for more precise concentration upon military objectives, such as oil and communications behind the immediate battle-zone, rather than on mere acts of terror and wanton destruction, however impressive.' Harris replied with vigour:

I have always held and still maintain that . . . the progressive destruction and dislocation of the German military, industrial, and economic systems, could be carried out only by the elimination of German industrial cities and not merely by attacks on individual factories . . . attacks on cities like any other act of war are intolerable unless they are strategically justified.

By the latter phrase Harris meant 'saving the lives of allied soldiers . . . I do not personally regard the whole of the remaining cities of Germany as worth the bones of one British Grenadier'. Harris justified acts of war by results.

Subsequent analysts have not vindicated him. They have suggested that precision bombing of oil and communications weakened Germany more effectively than the area bombing favoured by Harris. The United States Strategic Bombing Survey, the most thorough enquiry, concluded that area bombing reduced German productive capacity by about 9 per cent in 1943 and about 17 per cent in 1944, but that the reduction in war production was lessened by German concentration on keeping up military output, so allowing losses in production to fall on inessential sectors. Heavy and successful area raids on towns reduced production by as much as 55 per cent in the following month, but most cities recovered to 80 per cent of normal within three months—which could mean complete restoration of output for war purposes. Concentration of resources, careful allocation of priorities, and dispersal of factories actually increased war production in 1943 and 1944, despite the bombing. RAF Bomber Command had one clear success, in the Ruhr: in the second half of 1944, steel production there fell by 80 per cent. Part of this success, which halved total German production, came from area bombing, part from precision attack on rail and water transport. Since the fall in production of high-grade steel was still greater, German war production carried on only by drawing on its ample stocks.

The US air force took the lead in attacking synthetic oil production, which fell from 316,000 tons per month in early 1944 to 107,000 in June, and to only 17,000 in September. Aviation fuel came from synthetic production, and the supply fell from 175,000 tons in April to 30,000 tons in July and to only 5,000 tons in September. Repeated attacks, on heavily defended plants, brought this victory—the largest plant, Leuna, was bombed twenty-two times. By the end of 1944, even with the most drastic economies, stocks were practically exhausted, and in the winter longer hours of darkness and bad weather permitted only a small recovery in production. Furthermore, the attack on synthetic oil plants turned out also to threaten production of the by-product, nitrates, and therefore production of fertilizers, explosives, and synthetic rubber. The bombing of another target, the German railway system, had measurable effects:

Number of freight-car loadings

Week ending	
19 Aug. 1944	900,000
31 Oct. 1944	700,000
23 Dec. 1944	550,000
3 Mar. 1945	214,000

Meanwhile, waterway traffic was impeded. Cuts in civilian transport delayed the impact on military production, but after December 1944 production in all industries fell steadily.

Moreover, allied bombing compelled the Germans to concentrate resources on defence. In the spring of 1944, as we have seen, the US air force gave battle to the German fighter force and made impossible any German challenge to allied air supremacy at the time of the invasion of Normandy. Also, German anti-aircraft artillery units diverted large numbers of men from the battle-fronts, though perhaps few of the highest quality, and diverted a substantial proportion of the production of 88 mm guns from use as field artillery, and, damagingly, from their use as the most effective anti-tank gun of the war. Clearly, strategic bombing weakened the German war economy. However, Harris greatly exaggerated when he claimed, in March 1945, that the bombing of German cities had given 'the armies a walkover . . . in France and Germany'. Indeed, it may have been the other way round: the successful invasion of France was perhaps a necessary pre-condition for the success of the strategic bomber in late 1944. The evidence suggests that his preference for area bombing of towns as against attacks on specific targets, 'panacea' targets, as he called them, was unsound. A decisive strategic attack needed bombers capable of precision attack in adverse conditions. A smaller number of even more highly-trained crews, aiming at specific targets would have had a greater impact on the German war economy at less cost in British, American, and German lives than was incurred by the campaign of the 8th Air Force and Bomber Command.

Bombing affected morale less than pre-war strategists had expected. They assumed that it would reduce or destroy civilian support for war and so lead to irresistible pressure on governments to make peace on any terms, or at least make civilians less willing or able to work productively to win the war. Loss of civilian morale, they imagined, would lead to erosion of the will of the enemy's armed forces to risk life and limb. In practice bombing sometimes raised morale. Of course, death and injury inevitably caused misery to those emotionally attached to the victim, and fear and sadness among many of those who witnessed them. Bombing, however, turned out to kill and injure many fewer people than had been expected. Buildings, especially relatively lightly-built ones, suffered more, but machinery often remained in good working order after the collapse or burning of factories. Bombing mainly brought homelessness, temporary or permanent. During the war the number of people left homeless after air attack was always greater than the number of casualties, until atomic bombs drastically increased the ratio of killing to destruction. In raids which cost Hamburg 3.3 per cent of its population, 48 per cent of dwellings became unusable; in Kobe the wrecking of over half of its dwellings went with the death of only 1 per cent of its population.

Effective bombing, then, left many homeless survivors. Complete mental collapse seldom followed: air raids produced transient and spasmodic symptoms of fear and stress much more than chronic mental disorders. Common depressive reactions, apathy, lethargy, gloomy attitudes, excessive docility, did not necessarily stop the carrying on of daily tasks. Minor coronary and stomach disorders and increases in, for example, peptic ulcers, which commonly followed air raids, were only intermittently disabling. British figures showed that the 'bombed out' returned to work on average six days after losing their homes. Destruction of housing led to higher levels of occupancy—more people per dwelling—though evacuation of mothers, children, and old people, who departed more readily after bombing attacks than people in employment, reduced the pressure in bombed towns. Even when fear impelled town-dwellers to trek each night into the surrounding countryside to seek safety, they turned up for work next day. After all, workers depended on their wages: hardship and stress did not reduce their need for regular pay. Apathy towards the war and public affairs, conviction of eventual defeat, even deep despair, did not necessarily reduce an individual's contribution to the war effort. A young mother who had worked in the kitchens at the Thyssen works in Duisberg until her baby was born in May 1944, and who stayed in the town until October 1944, told the US Strategic Bombing investigators after the war that she was 'not accustomed to stay away from work . . . it is one's duty to work. Also it was forbidden and furthermore I needed the money . . . we had to go ahead whether we wanted to or not. We couldn't simply say that we would not carry on any more . . . Often enough I was tired out with the war.'

Even if civilians wearied of war they could do little about it. Once governments had gained sufficient support to decide on war, they discouraged the expression of dissent by censorship and repression, and fostered the assumption that support for the war was normal and right. Moreover, bombing could improve the morale of those who lived through air raids without injury to themselves or to people close to them, or damage to their possessions. They often derived self-congratulatory pride from the experience and identified themselves more vigorously with the nation at war. How bombing affected morale was influenced by the energy and competence of local administration. Rapid response by emergency services: fire fighters, rescue workers, ambulance personnel, and hospital staff, effective food distribution, speedy removal of the dead, rehousing, the supply of clothing and bedding, helped to prevent resentment against the authorities, while their absence or breakdown caused anger to be diverted from the enemy to the government. In England, ineffective local government (in Coventry for instance), sometimes 'demoralized' the victims of attack, in the sense of generating uncooperative attitudes towards the authorities to an extent not experienced in London or in the effectively administered towns of Germany.

For most survivors, above all for the great majority who were neither wounded nor bombed-out but who suffered, at worst, fear, discomfort, and acute inconvenience, air raids produced psychological reassurance. Shared dangers brought people together. Urban agglomerations became communities. The shy and lonely found their neighbours approachable and a warm welcome for their helping hands. Suicides diminished as lonely men and women came to be needed and valued. Bombs broke down social barriers, and indiscriminate air attack diminished morale-lowering resentment of the wartime privileges of the relatively affluent—though in London, where the poorer districts were more accessible to the Luftwaffe, signs of such resentment occasionally appeared, which the government tried to counter by royal visits, ministerial tours, and by stressing evidence of shared dangers (for instance, by publicizing bombs dropped on Whitehall or close to Buckingham Palace). Where communal spirit grew and when its emotions could be directed, as in Britain and Germany, against an evidently ferocious enemy, bombing on balance strengthened morale. It was different in Japan.

In the Second World War, strategic bombing reached a climax with the American bombing of Japan in 1945. This campaign, which was made possible by the success of amphibious assaults on Pacific island bases by the US navy and marines, exploited and exacerbated the weaknesses created by submarine blockade and sapped Japanese civilian morale. As a result, influential civilians, headed by Emperor Hirohito, forced peace on those military men who thought that duty required them to prefer death (with that of millions of others) to surrender. At first American strategists hoped to bomb Japan from bases in China. The plan turned on the new B-29, 'very long range', bomber, the 'Superfortress', which came into service in June 1944. With four tons of bombs it had a range of 3,500 miles. However, the Chinese bases the American air force hoped to use were threatened by Japanese ground advances and, from the remote base at Chengtu which it had to use, even the B-29 could reach only Kyushu, the southernmost island of Japan. Moreover, supplies reached Chengtu by a difficult route and in limited amounts. In 1944 Army Air Force demands for better bases enabled the US Navy to get agreement that Admiral Nimitz should turn northwest to the Marianas, where Saipan, Tinian, and Guam offered good homes for the B-29s, as well as for submarines, rather than go on directly to join MacArthur in the recovery of the Philippines. On 24 November 1944, B-29s from Saipan took off for Tokyo, the first attack there since the raid from aircraft-carriers in April 1942.

The Army Air Force proceeded to re-enact, in a much shorter time-span, the original experiences of RAF Bomber Command over Germany. Until 9 March 1945 their bomber striking force concentrated on daylight, high-altitude, precision attacks, mainly against aircraft factories. Bomber crews ran into bad weather, found high winds at bombing altitudes, and saw their targets less than half the time in December 1944 and during less than one fifth of their bombing runs in February 1945. Most bombing was radar-guided and highly inaccurate. At best, 17 per cent of bombs fell nearer than 3,000 feet from the aiming-point. Moreover Japanese fighters, handled by what remained of their experienced airmen, inflicted heavy losses, which rose in January 1945 to

5.7 per cent. To secure airfields from which Mustangs could escort the Superfortresses, and prevent Japanese attacks on airfields in the Marianas, and to provide emergency landing grounds for stricken bombers, the American Chiefs of Staff ordered the seizure of Iwo Jima, only 650 miles from Japan. Before the end of the war about 2,400 B-29s made emergency landings there. By the time the Mustang fighter squadrons were ready for action, the B-29s had begun to follow new tactics, of low-level raids at night with a high proportion of incendiary bombs. Like the RAF attacks on Germany these raids set fire to houses, partly to reduce the productivity of industrial workers, partly to destroy morale by terror. On 9 March 1945, 334 B-29s set off for Tokyo and dropped incendiaries on a densely-populated area of dwellings, mostly made of wood and bamboo. Strong winds set off a fire-storm visible from 150 miles away. Sixteen square miles were burnt out. One quarter of Tokyo's buildings—267,000—were destroyed, 1,000,000 people lost their homes and about 80,000 people died. As a mechanism for slaughter, the American air force had caught up with the RAF some months before the atom bomb dropped on Hiroshima.

Until then Americans had shown distaste for area bombing, as an unpleasant British practice. General Kuter, assistant chief of the US Air Staff, thought it 'contrary to our national ideals to wage war against civilians'. Considerable excitement followed a statement by an RAF officer at Eisenhower's headquarters, after the Dresden bombing, which led to a press report that the allies had adopted 'deliberate terror bombing of the great German population centres'. Stimson, the US Secretary for War, publicly reaffirmed that 'our policy never has been to inflict terror bombing on civilian populations . . . our efforts still are confined to the attack of enemy military objectives'. Uneasily, however, he asked for an enquiry to get the 'facts'. The American air force Director of Intelligence, General McDonald, found them, complained that the Americans had been drawn into a policy of 'homicide and destruction', and suggested that ground forces might as well be told to 'kill all civilians and demolish all buildings in Germany'. Among the American public, moral inhibitions against the bombing of Japanese civilians were weaker than in the case of Germans because of the hostility inspired by the surprise attack on Pearl Harbor followed by the notorious Japanese ill-treatment of American prisoners, and reinforced by the general acceptance of racialist stereotypes. Even so, the authorities claimed they were attacking 'military objectives'. General Arnold, the head of the US Army Air Force, told Stimson that although small-scale Japanese war production was dispersed among individual houses in Japanese residential areas, the USAAF tried to minimize civilian casualties. Ignorance and eager self-deception came together in varying proportions to quiet worried consciences.

In the next four weeks after the Tokyo raid, five more cities lost 37 square miles of buildings. Then such raids ceased until late June, partly because stocks of incendiary bombs ran low, partly because attention shifted to the support of the invasion of Okinawa. Between late June and the end of the war on 14 August, fifty-five cities were attacked, with populations ranging from 30,000 to 325,000. On average about half of the built-up area was destroyed in each. On 27 July came an innovation: Le May, the commander of the B-29 offensive, arranged to have leaflets dropped on eleven cities giving warning that they were about to be attacked, and next night six of them were. He followed the same procedure twice more. By that time, American aircraft roamed safely over Japan, as the number of effectively trained Japanese pilots had dwindled during the Okinawa campaign. When weather permitted specific targets to be seen, precision bombing went on by day against economic objectives, while area bombing continued. In raids on big cities between 14 May and 15 June 1945 the loss rate was only 1.4 per cent; in the later attacks on smaller cities the Japanese brought down only one aircraft from over 8,000 American sorties. The raids struck effectively against civilian morale by making homeless about 22,000,000 people, one-third of the urban population of Japan.

Meanwhile the 509th Bombardment Group, of B-29s, was practising visual precision attacks by individual planes which sharply broke away immediately after bomb release. Certain cities, untouched or lightly bombed, were reserved for 509th Group. Two of its aircraft, each dropping a single bomb, brought strategic bombing to its climax. On 6 August at 8.15 a.m., one atomic bomb exploded above the centre of Hiroshima, and at 11.30 a.m. on 9 August a second exploded not quite over the centre of Nagasaki. Estimates of casualties vary: from 80,000 to 150,000 people were killed at Hiroshima and from 20,000 to 80,000 at Nagasaki, together with about 30,000 seriously injured in each place, mostly from terrible burns.

The B-29s weakened Japanese civilian morale. The American bombing campaign destroyed confidence in the army, which was held responsible for the failure to defend the people of Japan. The military command suffered in 1945 from its past reluctance to tell the truth about the way the war had been going: a suddenly disillusioned civilian population lost respect for the army. Moreover, the government had not made sufficient preparations to palliate the effects of bombing; air-raid precautions had not been thought necessary in a country expected to survive the war well out of range of the enemy air force. Rapid provision of care for the wounded and of food and shelter for the homeless is the most effective support for morale in bombed cities, and they were all defective. Under these circumstances victims' anger turns against the authorities and not the enemy. The population did not actually wish for an American victory—according to American investigators, most Japanese thought defeat would be followed by events such as 'brutalities, starvation, enslavement, or annihilation'—but had begun to expect it. Nor did the ordinary Japanese clamour for an end to the war. Not only was there no outlet or possible organization to enable people to make such a demand but, in any event, low morale in war shows itself in exclusive concern for individual self-preservation rather than for public issues. What made low morale in Japan significant was that members of the government shared it themselves and feared it, and began to try to curb the disastrous heroics of the leaders of the army.

11

Morale

'MORALE', the willingness to work harder, accept sacrifices, or take risks to help win the war, came mainly from two sources: a sense that the war was worth winning and a feeling of membership of a community, together with the desire to have the respect of others within it. Urgent and recognizable danger to a whole society strengthened morale, as in Britain in 1940, or Germany in 1944 and 1945, so long as there remained some hope of warding it off. Civilian morale and the morale of fighting men influenced each other, but their constituents differed between servicemen in active combat on the one side, and civilians and non-combatant servicemen on the other, though heavy aerial bombardment made them more alike. For civilians and inactive servicemen, a sense of long-term purpose mattered more than for men in combat, for whom short-term survival usually came first.

Civilians hoped the war would bring a better world. Conscious that the poorer sections of their societies were most vulnerable to the shortages and constraints of war, governments responded by demands for equality of sacrifice during the war and, often reluctantly, preached post-war social levelling. In Britain particularly, the managed wartime economy brought full employment and, even combined with rationing and its concomitant of regulated and subsidized prices, it seemed to many preferable to the 'free-for-all' economy supposedly associated with the depression of the 1930s. The war therefore encouraged acceptance of collectivist ideals and increased support for the Labour Party, whose ministers, notably Bevin and Morrison, seemed outstanding in their contributions to the direction of the civilian war-effort. One of the most successful of British publications in the war years proved to be an austere government publication, 'Social Insurance and Allied Services—Report by Sir William Beveridge', which sold over 100,000 copies when it appeared in December 1942. 'Now when the war is abolishing landmarks of every kind', the Beveridge report called for an attack on 'five giants': Want, Disease, Ignorance, Squalor, and Idleness. Beveridge's insurance scheme assumed a free National Health Service, reformed education and state-fostered full employment after the war. The Ministry of Information, responsible for the maintenance of civilian morale, recognized the importance of Beveridge and felt uneasy about the reticence of Churchill and some of his Conservative colleagues in supporting such post-war reform—a reticence which helps to explain Churchill's defeat in the election of 1945.

During the Second World War, the cinema flourished as a means of entertaining millions at minimum cost in labour. Every major belligerent produced inspiring films—well-disciplined documentaries or historical analogies—as well as tolerating 'escapism'. Tightly controlled economies allowed scope for other forms of self-indulgence. British and American cigarette smoking reached new levels, and even the abstentionist General Montgomery carried cigarettes in his vehicles to hand out to troops. Beer production was maintained in Britain at a lowered strength, although imported wine and home-produced spirits became scarce. European governments, by controlling scarce resources, could decide what painting, writing and music to encourage and what to inhibit. In Britain a further stage developed, of government subsidy: a means of maintaining morale which encouraged adventurous and non-commercial work. Otherwise the war tended to restrict the market for the arts and by lessening international contacts retarded artistic development. What further effects it had on the arts depended on its varied individual and personal impact on those who led artistic trends—attempted generalizations are futile and pretentious.

To win battles fighting men must voluntarily risk injury or death. Coercion by the state can put them on battlefields, but success in battle requires a controlled courage which cannot be compelled. All armies used conscription and combated desertion by seeking out and punishing offenders. Any Russian soldier caught in the rear areas by political police was liable to be shot. In the last days of the war SS units acted in the same way inside Germany, reinforcing a growing resort to capital punishment by the regular military authorities, who had executed perhaps 20,000 of the armed forces. From time to time British commanders asked for the death penalty to be restored for desertion. Such measures served principally to reassure the majority that endurance was what society expected; concern for the good opinion of others was the main motive for bravery and endurance. Their communities admired and cosseted soldiers, sailors, and airmen proportionately to the hazards they were assumed to face: aircrew, submariners, and parachute troops, for instance, could expect open adulation provided their society approved the war—here civilian morale powerfully affected that of the military. Carefully controlled publicity for military operations helped the morale of those engaged in them, as did unit and branch insignia, medals, and so forth.

However, easily the most important element in good morale in combat was for an individual to feel himself to be a valued member of a group. He must feel that his group cared for him, so that in return he would sacrifice himself to it and not let his comrades down. If such a group—a squad, platoon, bomber crew, or company, for example—inspired these deeply rewarding emotions of comradeship it became a formidable weapon. Provided its members, collectively and individually, found their commanders skilful, and provided remoter authority was seen to organize effective supply and training for the hazards of war, their morale became indestructible except under protracted and overwhelming stress. The Second World War, however, confirmed the lesson of the First: that everyone has a breaking point. When it came depended partly on an individual's morale, but more upon the nature and intensity of the stress of combat. In Normandy, from July to September 1944, for instance, one-fifth of all battle casualties in the 2nd British Army were psychiatric. Two American army psychiatrists concluded that among American soldiers in the Mediterranean theatre 'practically all men in rifle battalions who were not otherwise disabled ultimately became psychiatric casualties', and reckoned that an average soldier would be worn out by a year of fighting and that his efficiency would fall off much sooner. These American observers thought the British in Italy lasted longer because of their policy of pulling infantrymen out of the line for frequent short periods of rest, once every two weeks or less, in contrast to the American habit of keeping troops in line for up to two months or more. Many writers suppose ground combat in the Second World War somehow to have been less arduous than in the First. This illusion derives from the smaller proportion in the second war of troops who actively engaged the enemy and the greater number of specialist and rear-echelon troops. A normal British infantry division contained about 17,000 men, but only 4,000 carried a rifle and bayonet, and in the Pacific, one United States infantryman required an average of eighteen men in supply services to keep him firing. In Europe, the British and American armies suffered a higher rate of loss among front-line combat troops over comparable periods of time than in the First World War, and losses were worse still for the Germans and Russians.

Morale, therefore, was vital. The Japanese and Germans did better than their opponents. Both had cohesive societies whose members readily felt a sense of mutual solidarity and obligation, and possessed a comparatively much higher number of well-trained and intelligent officers and NCOs with long experience, than did the British and Americans. In particular, the German army contained many experienced and capable leaders, both officers and NCOs, drawn from a society where military service generally commanded high prestige, even in peacetime, and which possessed a powerful sense of national identity. British and American soldiers came from a society which, in peace, tended to despise a military career, and where class or ethnic factors lessened mutual confidence. Americans further weakened the morale of their infantry by a careful weeding-out of specialists and the intellectually gifted for branches of the service requiring technical knowledge or general intelligence. In the Soviet Union incompatibility of national origins and wide variation in educational attainments restricted the effective maintenance of morale to carefully chosen élite units. However morally superior their cause, the allies won the war by superiority in numbers and materials rather than by superiority in morale.

12

Driving back the Germans:
North Africa, Italy, and Russia

I T took more than two years of savage fighting after they had been halted, to drive the Germans back to Germany. Until the summer of 1943 Hitler could still reasonably hope to win: victory at Kursk would force the Soviet leadership to compromise, victory in the Atlantic would compel British surrender and keep the United States on the other side of the ocean. After the summer of 1943 he could only hope to delay defeat until the allies fell apart.

The European land campaigns from 1943 to 1945 followed a regular pattern. Hitler insisted on tenacious defence of German-held ground, even at the risk of encirclement. His generals wanted flexibility, including voluntary withdrawal, to preserve their forces and secure mobile battles in which superior German military skills had their greatest effects. On the allied side, Soviet commanders tried to use the growing mobility of their best units to exploit the rigidities imposed on their enemies and to bring together the locally overwhelming strength needed to outweigh German tactical prowess. British commanders, after the series of defeats from 1940 to 1942, viewed with alarm German agility in counter-attack and sought to keep 'balanced', that is, to avoid risky manœuvres. American commanders worried about the inexperience of their officers, NCOs, and men, and relied on material to compensate until experience had been gained, so that American forces needed an especially lavish scale of supply. With exceptions, such as Manstein's campaign in the Ukraine in 1943, the German attacks at Avranches and in the Ardennes, and Montgomery's attack at Arnhem, unimaginative battles of attrition marked the closing years of the war.

The first large-scale retreat forced on the Germans and their Italian allies followed Montgomery's victory at El Alamein and Eisenhower's landings in north-west Africa. Allied material superiority balanced a tactical caution inspired by respect for German military skill. Before the battle of El Alamein, Montgomery privately showed concern about the capacity of his 'somewhat untrained troops'. Afterwards, in pursuit of the Germans towards Tripoli and Tunisia, he avoided risks, intending to avoid the renewed blow to British morale which a successful strike by

Rommel against advanced or isolated British detachments would inflict. Rommel commented, 'the British command continued to observe its usual caution and showed little evidence of ability to make resolute decisions'. There was another reason for British delays: since the artillery was much the most effective part of the British army, pauses to bring up the guns made sense if the enemy should turn and fight. Rommel's retreat from Egypt began on 4 November 1942. Early in February 1943 his forces fell back into Tunisia. Late on 9 November 1942 American and British troops came ashore in French north-west Africa.[1]

British and American commanders preferred prudent tactics but, relying on superior navies and air forces, they applied daring strategies. Operation TORCH, the North African landings, included three descents on potentially hostile coasts—vessels of the first waves were loaded for immediate combat—after sailing through miles of U-boat-infested waters, for much of the time within range of German air reconnaissance. American forces landed on the Atlantic coast of Morocco, having come direct from the United States, while the forces destined for Oran and Algiers sailed from Britain. Anglo-American disagreement marked the planning stage. The British wished to land as far east as possible in order to reach Tunis and Bizerta before the Germans seized those ports. If they failed, Rommel would have a new supply line less vulnerable than that through Tripoli. They therefore urged a landing at Bone, about 140 miles from Tunis. United States planners insisted on a landing on the Atlantic coast of Morocco and opposed landings far into the Mediterranean: they feared Spanish co-operation in a German move to close the Straits of Gibraltar and to move into Spanish Morocco, thus cutting off any allied troops landed in the Mediterranean. An allied force landed on the Atlantic coast of Morocco could defend it against German or Spanish attacks on allied communications, while itself getting supplies through Casablanca. The Americans suggested Casablanca and Oran; the British Algiers and Bone. In the end enough landing-craft were found for three assaults: the furthest east on Algiers, further into the Mediterranean than the Americans wished, though not as near to Tunis as the British would have liked, the second on Oran, and the third in the area of Casablanca.

The attitude of the French preoccupied the allies. By Anglo-American agreement, the British took the lead in diplomacy in Spain, the Americans with Vichy France. The French authorities in Morocco, Algeria, and Tunisia obeyed Marshal Pétain's government at Vichy and applied

[1] See maps on pp. 56 and 103.

the Franco-German armistice. The Americans thought it possible to persuade the French not to resist allied invasion, especially if the dissident leader of Fighting France, General de Gaulle, and his followers were kept out and the supposedly provocative British put in the background. An intelligent French industrialist with enormous interests in north Africa, Jacques Lemaigre-Dubreuil, perceptive enough to recognize the winning side, assisted American emissaries in making contacts with the French authorities. The Americans concluded that French resistance would be nominal and quickly over. They believed that in a very right-wing, brave, French general, who had recently escaped from a German prisoner-of-war camp, they had someone who could secure the co-operation of senior French officers—this was General Giraud. Moreover, General Mast, Chief of Staff of the French 19th Army Corps, and General Béthouart, in command at Casablanca, agreed to seize control in their areas and arrange unopposed landings. In the event, the American and British forces landed at Algiers virtually unopposed. The Americans, however, had to overcome strong opposition from naval garrisons and batteries at Oran, while at Casablanca, Noguès, the shifty Resident-General of Morocco, got Béthouart arrested as a traitor. No one paid any attention to Giraud. Whether or not by chance, a much more important personage, Admiral Darlan, Marshal Pétain's deputy, was at Algiers. His first reaction was to order resistance to the allies everywhere. Only when he had realized the strength of the invasion did he order a general cease-fire on 10 November, when the allies had conquered Oran and were poised to attack the French at Casablanca.

The German response was facilitated by the French Resident-General at Tunis, Admiral Esteva, and the naval commander at Bizerta, Admiral Derrien, who made no attempt to resist the Germans. German troops began to fly in on 9 November and supply ships to arrive on 12 November, a rapid reaction which enabled the Germans and Italians, untroubled by the local French, to meet and check the advancing British and Americans some 40 miles west of Tunis and Bizerta about ten days after the invasion. British fears had proved correct: a battle for Tunisia had begun.

The Axis forces relied on short sea and air routes to Sicily and the Italian mainland. Allied supply lines were much longer and more complicated. German and Italian reinforcement of Tunisia was fast enough to maintain resistance there for six months. With what was left of their desert armies after their retreat from El Alamein, they assembled about 250,000 troops, three-fifths German. The allied side, after the arrival of the 8th Army, had about 650,000 troops in north-west Africa, rather over half of whom were British. Because of their logistic and administrative problems, the allied total included a much higher number, nearly two-thirds, of non-fighting soldiers in the lines of communication and the rear areas. In Tunisia the Germans showed their usual tactical skill while the Italian units fought more successfully in mountainous country where their lack of mobility handicapped them less than in the desert. Rommel's forces, having retreated into Tunisia behind the Mareth Line and so forced Montgomery to pause for a set-piece attack, had time to move north to launch a quick attack on the US 2nd Corps in central Tunisia. At the Kasserine Pass, the United States army now joined the long list of armies which failed when first attacked by German forces, but the Axis commanders had insufficient strength to exploit their success. The German–Italian High Command, indeed, had hoped for more, given what it called the 'low fighting value' of allied troops. General Montgomery finally pushed the Germans and Italians back into Tunisia in two victorious battles, Mareth and Wadi Akarit. In both battles, the Axis forces successfully disengaged, badly weakened, but capable of further tenacious defence.

In the end, the allies defeated the Germans and Italians in Tunisia by attacks on their sea-borne supplies, using submarines, surface ships, and aircraft. At first, use of the shorter route from Italy to Tunisia helped the Axis powers, and in November 1942, assisted by Hitler's reinforcement of German air strength in Sicily, they lost none of the supplies destined for Tunisia. In that month 95,000 tons of supplies and fuel reached Africa. In December, 65,000 tons arrived, in January 1943, 70,000 tons, and in February, 60,000. British and American attacks prevented nearly a quarter of cargoes from reaching their destination. These totals were well below what von Arnim and Rommel, the German commanders in Tunisia, thought necessary (150,000 tons), and their position became impossible when in March and April the allies stopped nearly half of Axis supplies from getting through. In March the German and Italian forces received 43,000 tons, in April only 30,000 tons. Early in May the allies stopped over three-quarters of the cargoes destined for Tunisia from reaching port. Intelligence contributed: British decoding of German and Italian maritime signals continued, but even more important was success in intercepting the signals controlling Axis air transport. Together with the establishment of allied airfields in eastern Algiers and Tripolitania, this led to the destruction in April of nearly two-thirds of the German transport aircraft in the Mediterranean. Moreover, it made possible attacks on escorting fighters and so facilitated attacks on sea-borne transport. Even so, the Germans at first halted allied advances on Tunisia and Bizerta, but it could not go on. By 4 May the Axis command had no longer enough fuel to ensure supplies of water, food, and ammunition for their troops. Hitler issued his usual orders to fight to the last man and the last round: Axis units, sensibly, fired off their ammunition, put their equipment out of action and surrendered; about 150,000 Germans and 90,000 Italians were captured. Allied casualties in north-west Africa, including the British 8th Army after it had reached Tunisia, were 11,000 killed and 40,000 wounded: rather more than half of whom were British, one-quarter American, and one-quarter French.

The American, British and German high commands were all content: the allies had won, they had cleared the southern seaboard of the Mediterranean, and they had diverted high-quality German troops and considerable air strength from the Russian front. Anglo-American co-operation, thanks above all to General Eisenhower, had worked surprisingly well. Especially at the higher levels, rivalries and ill feelings were now found as frequently between the allied services, army, air, and navy, as between nationalities. On his side, Hitler had managed to delay the outcome for six months and so had made still more unlikely an allied attack on France in 1943, had improved the chances of victory for the U-boats in the Atlantic, and shown, if anyone doubted it, that German morale and fighting capacity remained formidably high. Even the surviving troops got some rewards: the Germans were better off as prisoners of the British and Americans than of the Russians, and the allies in Tunis, at least from the French inhabitants, got a first taste of the welcome that friendly populations bestowed on their liberators.

At the Casablanca conference British and American political and military leaders had agreed that their forces should invade Sicily after conquering Tunisia. The invasion, Operation HUSKY, began on 10 July 1943 with the largest sea-borne assault of the entire war. A total of 2,590 vessels landed 180,000 men in the first wave. Troops reached Sicily from bases much more distant than in the Normandy landings in 1944, so that ships and landing-craft took longer to return to base. Most British troops came from Suez and Britain, as well as from Tunisia and Malta. American divisions came from Bizerta and Algiers, and one division came direct from the United States, with only a brief pause at Oran on the way. Reinforcements for the first troops ashore took longer to arrive, and the planners had to make sure that the initial assault was strengthened to survive the powerful and sustained opposition to be counted on from the German forces in Sicily, and possibly from the Italians, who on their side could rapidly be reinforced across the Messina Strait. Many things went wrong.

The structure of command increased British influence on Anglo-American operations. The British 8th Army had defeated and chased the Germans out of Egypt and Tripolitania, and its intervention had apparently turned the scales in Tunisia. Montgomery's record of success appeared almost to justify his extreme self-confidence. He thought he should be army commander in Sicily, with a United States corps under him. Militarily this was sound, but politically American and British status must be equal. Moreover, to elevate Montgomery to control of the armies would lose his incontestable skill in handling battles. Luckily, it seemed; Eisenhower's Tunisian expedient of putting General Alexander in command, under his own supreme authority, of both American and British armies could safely be repeated: Alexander, an elegant and well-mannered British officer, had shown himself a model of tact. Now Alexander followed his success as head of the team which had defeated Rommel, by relieving Eisenhower of the function of Army Group Commander, leaving him to deal with the administrative and political problems of north-western Africa. Unfortunately Montgomery, a stronger and more decisive personality, gave orders to Alexander rather than the other way round, so that Alexander, in effect, passed on Montgomery's wishes to the other part of his command—the American 7th Army under General Patton—rather than assessing the battle as a whole and adjudicating between conflicting needs and demands. Alexander gave way the more readily to Montgomery because they shared the common British prejudice that American soldiers were inferior, either because of lack of experience, or because they were 'soft': thus they both thought that Montgomery's 8th Army was the decisive weapon. The British also supplied the air and naval commanders, but both these men worked with their American colleagues more easily than with Montgomery, who, indeed, complained that Alexander failed to keep sufficiently close contact with their direction of operations.

The initial attacks, concentrated, as Montgomery had demanded, into a single zone in the south-east of Sicily, went well, with one big exception. The aircraft bringing in British and American airborne units by glider and parachute scattered the troops over wide areas of Sicily or dropped them into the sea. Many of the aircraft and their passengers battled through anti-aircraft fire from four armies, British, American, German, and Italian, and both British and American warships blazed away at any aircraft that came within range. On the ground, some found themselves attacked by American or British forces. The Axis command reacted to the allied invasion by blocking the British advance towards Catania and by powerful attacks on the American landings around Gela. Here two divisions, the Livorno, the best of the Italian units, and the Hermann Goering Panzer Division, attacked on the first and second days after the landing, the Germans using the new Tiger tank, heavily armoured and with the powerful 88 mm gun. The American 1st Division held its own, decisively helped by gunfire from warships offshore, and even succeeded in setting off a disorderly panic among a German battalion from the Hermann Goering Division.

By the third day after the landing, the American 46th Division, under Omar Bradley, had advanced inland and reached the main east–west road across the island towards which the 1st Division was also moving. At this stage Montgomery insisted that this road must be taken away from the Americans and given to the 8th Army. His original plan had been checked by German resistance before Catania, which prevented a British advance east of Etna towards Messina and the cutting off of the enemy's retreat. Now, therefore, he proposed to advance west of Etna. Though American troops were better placed to execute the new plan, Alexander carried out Montgomery's wishes and took the east–west road from them, giving the Germans more time to establish their defences and helping to delay the conquest of Sicily till mid-August, when the Germans, retreating in good order, successfully recrossed the Straits of Messina.

Bradley and Patton never forgot this display of Montgomery's self-centred conceit and harboured resentment and suspicion. Luckily for the alliance, Eisenhower's tact and Alexander's charm meant that such resentments were personal rather than national. While many Americans felt suspicion towards the British (or 'Limeys') and many British harboured condescension towards the Americans (or 'Yanks') most found sympathetic colleagues or even friends among the other nationality. Among subordinate members of inter-allied staffs such friendships came often from a shared dislike of higher authority. Thus, even the activities of domineering bullies like Montgomery and the posturing of many senior commanders like Patton, encouraged by the popular press with its liking for inter-allied competitiveness, did not prevent the development between British and Americans of the most closely-knit alliance ever known.

In May 1943 the Trident conference agreed to follow the conquest of Sicily with operations to force Italy out of the war. On 25 July Mussolini fell from power; next day the Combined Chiefs of Staff authorized Eisenhower to invade mainland Italy. The conference at Quebec received his proposals on 24 August. On 3 September Montgomery sent the 8th Army across the Messina Straits (Operation BAYTOWN) to distract German forces from the main attack (AVALANCHE), which took place a week later in the Bay of Salerno near Naples, roughly where the Germans expected an attack, since it was at the limit of single-seater fighter cover from the newly-occupied airfields in Sicily. On 8 September, the new Italian government announced an armistice. Early next morning the Anglo-American 5th Army, under General Mark Clark, began its landings near Salerno. The troops hoped to encounter friendly, unconditionally surrendering Italians; they met ferocious German counter-attacks. The 8th Army landings further south did not help much, even though Montgomery was reinforced by the 1st Airborne Division, sent by sea to Taranto: the terrain was perfect for defence and almost impossible for supply. The German defenders blocked Montgomery's advance by demolitions, mines, and booby traps, and concentrated their efforts against the Salerno landings. There two US divisions and two British divisions came ashore in the first twenty-four hours. Within three days the Germans had concentrated five divisions, all panzers or panzer-grenadiers, though greatly under strength. On 13 and 14 September German forces nearly broke through to the coast in the centre of the allied beach-head. On the 13th Clark ordered plans for separate evacuation of the British and American corps—perhaps for one to reinforce the other, perhaps for both to withdraw. By way of urgent reinforcement, two US parachute regiments made a night drop into the beach-head (this time without the disasters of the Sicilian drop), and 1,500 men were embarked on cruisers at Tripoli and dispatched to the British divisions at high speed. (Some of these British troops arrived in mutinous condition, fortunately after the height of the crisis.) On 16 September the German commander reported failure to crush the beach-head. He blamed allied naval bombardment and air attack. Ships' guns hit targets on land more accurately than expected, and techniques for observation, worked out in Sicily, proved themselves again. On 14 September the allied Mediterranean air force made over 2,000 sorties against tactical objectives. Ships and aircraft turned the scale, together with effective British and American field artillery. The German commanders cut their losses to preserve their strength and went over to the defensive.

The Battle of Salerno pleased the German commanders more than the victors. Kesselring, commanding, under Hitler, German armed forces in Italy, concluded that British and American troops were feeble in combat and that Italy could be held south of Rome. At the end of September,

Hitler changed his orders for slow retreat to northern Italy, and ordered that southern Italy should be defended as long as possible 'to block the enemy's bridge to the Balkans'. British and American commanders at Salerno viewed their own troops with unease and freely criticized their allies. British generals feared weak morale among their troops, American generals detected inadequate leadership among their junior officers. Some British officers therefore became even more cautious, while Americans became more inclined to force their troops into impossible tasks. The British increasingly complained of American rashness and carelessness, the Americans of British sluggishness. Both, however, carefully maintained conventional emollient attitudes of mutual con-gratulation, encouraged by General Alexander's tactful reticence.

Meanwhile Hitler could congratulate himself on containing allied forces in southern Italy. It is true that Marshall and Eisenhower could equally congratulate themselves on containing the Germans in Italy and keeping them away from France, but Churchill, who wanted the allies in Italy to pose a threat to fascist Europe, was angered by the successful defensive operations that Salerno encouraged the Germans to undertake. After Salerno the Germans carried out a retreat by stages to a naturally strong defensive belt strengthened by well-planned fortifications. They called it the Winter Line, of which the rivers Garigliano, Rapido, and Sangro, and Monte Cassino formed the main features. At first the allies expected to take Rome in October 1943; they did so on 5 June 1944. On 19 December 1943, Churchill, lying ill at Carthage, grumbled 'that the stagnation of the whole campaign on the Italian front is becoming scandalous'. This stagnation brought into question again the working out of allied grand strategy, and the narrative must climb back to that level.

Italy and the Mediterranean now became the centre of the most acrimonious strategic conflict of the war between the supreme British and American war leaders. At Quebec they had agreed how to win the war; now, in late 1943, the British showed new symptoms of 'opportunism' and of losing faith in OVERLORD, the cross-Channel attack. In 1942 and the first half of 1943 the British, with Roosevelt's help, got their way in Anglo-American strategic debates. Thereafter, Roosevelt assisted Mar-shall and the American Joint Chiefs to impose their will. It was not only that the United States had become more powerful than the British Empire; there was another cause—the erratic flippancy of British strate-gies. Churchill acted as the vociferous and pertinacious spokesman of views he usually, though not invariably, shared with the British Chiefs of Staff, led, in this context, by Brooke. Between October 1943 and August

1944 he bombarded Roosevelt and the American military, first with pleas for priority for various Mediterranean operations, including a landing in the south of France, even at the expense of delaying the invasion of north-western Europe; then for concentration, within the Mediterranean, on the Italian campaign, even at the expense of a landing in the south of France. The British constantly discovered 'new facts' to alter agreed plans. To the Americans the British appeared unreliable and shifty. Fortunately, Churchill's prestige and personality lessened the disruptive impact of his policies.

In October 1943 Churchill set on foot personal operations of his own, opposed by Brooke and the British planners: he wanted to occupy Rhodes and the Dodecanese islands and so, he hoped, bring Turkey into the war to start a campaign in the Balkans. The British had seized Kos, Leros, and some smaller islands a month before, when the Italians surrendered. Churchill high-handedly asked Roosevelt to send Marshall, the US army Chief of Staff, to Africa, so that he could convert him and the allied commanders in the Mediterranean to faith in Balkan operations. Roosevelt refused and the American Chiefs of Staff forbade any diversion of resources to the eastern Mediterranean. Molotov encouraged Churchill when he supported a suggestion put to him by Eden, the British Foreign Secretary, that Turkey should be brought into the war, and Churchill became correspondingly eager for the planned summit meeting with Stalin and Roosevelt once it seemed that Stalin might help the British to persuade the Americans to 'take full advantage of all opportunities' to attack 'in any and every area where we can do so with superiority', and not to 'attach vital importance to any particular date' for the invasion of France. What the British seem to have found difficult to grasp was the American determination to bring its full strength to bear on Germany.

At the end of July 1944 there would be thirty to forty divisions in the United States ready to fight the German army. They needed good ports, good bases, and effective rail and road networks to bring their strength into effect. Seaports like Antwerp and Marseilles and western European transport systems offered the chance of direct attack on Germany in a way that Trieste and 'the Ljubliana Gap' (much favoured by Churchill as opening a—notably exiguous—route to Austria), Istanbul, or Salonika did not. Perhaps the British did not really want to have American full strength deployed in Europe. Churchill made constant comparisons between British and American forces in the various theatres and asserted a British right to command whenever British forces outnumbered American. British strategy made sense only on the assumption that the allied strength deployed by late 1943 was near its zenith, as indeed for the British it was. Of course, the British did not put forward the argument that American forces should not be overwhelmingly greater than the British. They argued in favour of delaying the cross-Channel attack by pointing to the danger that the Germans could assemble more combat troops in France in the days and weeks following the invasion than the allies would be able to do, and insisted that German troops should be kept occupied elsewhere, away from northern France. The Americans feared that more allied troops than German would be kept occupied in the resulting 'side-shows' and that they would take away landing-craft from more important objectives.

Landing-craft dominated the worst Anglo-American disputes, especially the disposition of the largest craft, the LSTs, or Landing Ships, Tank. Marshall's failure, in 1942, to get overriding priority for the Cross-Channel attack enabled the US navy to give preference to surface-ship construction in 1943. The result was that there were too few landing-craft in 1944. They were essential not only to land troops and weapons for assaults on enemy-held coasts, but also to keep the invading troops supplied until they had captured seaports and brought them into use. Only landing-craft could bring in supplies across open beaches. The Americans thought that the diversionary operations favoured by the British would draw in more allied forces than originally intended, since unpredictable accidents of war could turn minor side-shows into major theatres, drawing in troops and landing-craft, and so delaying or preventing the main operations they were, in theory, supposed to help.

When the 'Big Three' met in Tehran, Stalin disappointed the British by insisting that OVERLORD should be carried out at the earliest possible date, and his military spokesman, Marshal Voroshilov, pressed the view that 'at the same time as the operation in northern France, operations should be undertaken in southern France. Operations in Italy and elsewhere in the Mediterranean must be considered as of secondary importance.' Stalin also produced unexpected good news: after the defeat of Germany, the Soviet Union would attack Japan.

This promise helped Churchill and the British Chiefs of Staff to reinforce their favourite theatre of war, the Mediterranean. They suggested that the prospect of eventual Russian intervention on land against Japan justified the abandonment of BUCCANEER, the amphibious operation, planned by Mountbatten's South-East Asia Command, which the Anglo-American Combined Chiefs of Staff had hoped would encourage Chiang Kai-Shek to attack the Japanese in China and north Burma. The

British exploited, too, the prospect of a landing in the south of France (ANVIL), which the Americans favoured, to justify sending to the Mediterranean the landing-craft freed by the abandonment of BUCCANEER. At the Anglo-American Cairo conference (SEXTANT) which followed Tehran, they persuaded Roosevelt to go back on his promise to Chiang Kai-Shek, and BUCCANEER was abandoned.

The British soon found other uses for the landing-craft once they were committed to the Mediterranean. In November 1943, planning began for a landing (SHINGLE) on the western Italian coast at Anzio, about 25 miles south of Rome. SHINGLE was designed to cut German lines of retreat from the Winter Line from which the forthcoming offensive of the 8th and 5th Armies, it was assumed, would be driving them and so accelerate the capture of Rome. The first date planned for SHINGLE was 20 December, and for that operation landing-craft needed for OVER-LORD would stay in the Mediterranean until after 5 January 1944 instead of leaving after 15 December. Soon these timings became impracticable because both the 8th and 5th Army offensives petered out, after hard-fought advances of a few miles in exceptionally rugged country. On 18 December SHINGLE was cancelled.

After the Cairo conference, Churchill fell ill. He was resting near Carthage when he heard the fate of SHINGLE, and as we have seen, he recovered his strength to complain bitterly of stagnation in the Italian campaign. He advocated a revived and enlarged SHINGLE. His idea was that the Anzio landing would threaten German communications with their Winter Line, so that the Germans would be compelled to withdraw from it without the need for a renewal of the costly allied attacks on their positions. Although this meant further delay in the departure of LSTs from the Mediterranean for Britain and OVERLORD, the American authorities agreed. In return they seized the opportunity to insist that operations in the Aegean must be 'side-tracked'.

On 22 January two allied divisions, reinforced by specialized units, landed at Anzio. The Germans acted fast: the High Command sent reinforcements from Germany and France, while Kesselring collected troops in Italy to oppose the new invasion. The allied commander, the American General Lucas, behaved cautiously, and after two days, instead of the allies threatening German communications, they were trapped in the beach-head. Churchill wrote: 'instead of hurling a wild cat on to the shore all we got was a stranded whale', complained of American lack of 'punch', and urged Alexander to give firm orders to his American subordinate commanders. (Unfortunately Alexander's amiability often led to lack of force and clarity.) The allied troops at Anzio found themselves besieged. Instead of their helping the main armies to break through the German lines, the main allied armies had to relieve the Anzio forces which by the end of January 1944, comprised the equivalent of three-and-a-half divisions facing five German divisions, and which, by mid-February, faced twice their strength on land.

Meanwhile, the main allied forces in southern Italy had reached the most formidable of the German winter positions, the Gustav Line on the Garigliano and Rapido rivers, incorporating the dominating massif of Monte Cassino. An attack, begun on 17 January, failed disastrously to get across the Rapido, and three attacks on Monte Cassino were beaten back, two in February and one in March: the first made by the Americans; the second, following protracted shelling and bombing, including the destruction of the abbey, by Indian, New Zealand, and American troops; the third by New Zealand and Indian forces, after a day in which over 700 aircraft and 890 guns bombed and shelled German positions. The British official historian draws attention to two points: first, 'the superb fighting of the German troops'; second, that 'there is very little evidence to suggest that [British and American] superior commanders . . . had acquainted themselves with the ground except by studying maps and air photographs and looking through binoculars from distant viewpoints. . . . It is very doubtful if these commanders really grasped the fearsome physical features of the ground or understood to what they were committing their troops.'

German defensive success at Cassino set off more Anglo-American bickering. It meant that LSTs had to supply the Anzio beachhead, and so they could not be made ready for the ANVIL landings in the south of France, a process which needed ten weeks. The British Chiefs of Staff and the British Mediterranean Commander-in-Chief, General Wilson, argued that ANVIL should be cancelled altogether and all resources in the Mediterranean concentrated on Italy to keep German troops busy there. The US Joint Chiefs of Staff insisted on ANVIL, and even promised to help it by moving LSTs from the Pacific to the Mediterranean. At the end of March the allies agreed to postpone ANVIL when General Wilson announced that Anzio would not be relieved by the main armies before mid-May, but the American Chiefs of Staff were then 'shocked and pained' by the British refusal to agree to a definite date for ANVIL. In order to frighten the British with their old bogey of giving first priority to the war against Japan, they withdrew their offer of landing-craft from the Pacific. At the end of April, however, the British Chiefs told the Americans that they favoured a landing in the south of France after OVERLORD had begun, and suggested that preparations for it should be made, in case it seemed preferable to further amphibious operations on the Italian coast. Mollified, the Americans set their landing-craft in motion for the Mediterranean. As we shall see, however, British support for ANVIL was far from reliable.

Late on 11 May 1944, the combat troops of the allied land forces in Italy, which by then included 254,000 British Empire troops (of whom about 45,000 were Canadian), 230,000 Americans, 72,000 French, and 46,000 Poles, launched their spring offensive (DIADEM). Five days later, the Germans withdrew from Cassino. Polish troops occupied the abbey ruins but it was the French Expeditionary Corps that distinguished itself, on the allied side, by a brilliant outflanking movement through the hills south of the Liri valley, which threatened the rear of the German position at Cassino. Juin, who had remained loyal to Vichy until November 1942, commanded the corps. Moroccans and Algerians provided much of the rank-and-file—regular soldiers from the old French army of North Africa. Their skill in mountain warfare freed them from the constraints forced on British and American units by their dependence on motor transport. Each British division possessed over three thousand vehicles and, while infantry divisions could temporarily do without many of their vehicles, armoured divisions could not. In column, a British armoured division took up 140 miles of road. In mountainous country, with narrow roads and many streams, such units advanced slowly and deployed with difficulty, while the French, ready to move on foot and bring supplies by mule, were quicker and manœuvred more freely. Juin's forces took a leading role in breaking through the German defensive line centred on Cassino, and then, in the next phase of the offensive, the attack on the Hitler Line, which began on 23 May, they repeated their success. As the Canadians attacked up the Liri valley from the Cassino area the French outflanked the German defenders by rapid advances in the Aurunci mountains. This compelled the Germans to begin a staged withdrawal to their last line south of Rome.

Meanwhile US forces in the Anzio beach-head struck north towards Valmontone to cut the German line of communication. The Anzio landings were about to carry out their initially planned purpose of intercepting the German retreat. It was wrecked, however, and Anzio made pointless when, on 25 May, General Mark Clark, the US Commander of the Anglo-American 5th Army, gave one of the silliest orders of the war. Disregarding the wishes of Alexander, the overall commander, he told Truscott, US Corps Commander, who expected to reach Valmontone in twenty-four hours, instead to shift the main effort of his forces towards a direct advance on Rome. Clark 'wanted his army to have the honour of capturing Rome', but that 'triumph' was soon forgotten and Clark is now remembered as the general who permitted the escape of the German 10th army. The German forces made an orderly withdrawal and Clark's troops entered Rome on 4 June 1944. Two days later the allies landed in Normandy.

The allied campaign in Italy helped the invasion of France by keeping German forces away from Normandy. On D-Day there were seven mobile divisions in Italy, compared with eleven in France and the Low Countries, and twenty-six on the eastern front. Of German combat divisions (of varying quality) there were 163 on the eastern front, twenty-seven in Italy, and fifty in France. The allied invasion of Normandy, limited in strength by availability of landing-craft, could take place only if German mobile forces in France were correspondingly limited in the period immediately following the attack. The Italian campaign helped also by threatening south-eastern Europe, where about forty German and German-controlled divisions, admittedly of inferior quality, were present on D-Day. The campaign was, therefore, a success.

Italy, however, provoked Anglo-American quarrels as heated, after the capture of Rome, as they had been in the months of stalemate. Until the allies linked up with the Anzio bridgehead, Churchill and Brooke had argued that the need for landing-craft to supply Anzio ruled out ANVIL, the landing in the south of France. Now, after the capture of Rome, they insisted that Alexander should be allowed to gather 'the full fruits of his victory' without being checked by losing troops for ANVIL. Alexander proposed to advance to the Po valley, and from there, by way of Trieste, to the 'Ljubliana Gap' which he would capture by the end of August. Thence the Ljubliana Gap would lead, across the eastern Alps, to Klagenfurt and into Austria. Later writers have promoted Churchill's emphatic support for Alexander's proposal into a critical episode in twentieth-century history. It is an example, it is claimed, of Churchill's prophetic wisdom. He had in mind, they assert, nothing less than to prevent, or limit, the spread of Soviet power in eastern Europe. Alexander's troops would forestall the Red Army and establish liberal democracy in countries otherwise doomed to fall into Communist hands. ANVIL, these commentators insist, was a futile substitute for this grand manœuvre. However, at the time Churchill stressed the help Alexander's move would offer to the advance of the Red Army and to the

Yugoslav partisans. According to him, the mere capture of Trieste would cause 'Hungary, Yugoslavia, Albania, Greece, the Aegean, Turkey, Bulgaria, and Romania' to be 'convulsed'.

The American Joint Chiefs of Staff believed that the British Chiefs had already agreed, when Marshall, King, and Arnold were in England just after the Normandy landings, that allied ground forces in Italy would go no further than the Pisa–Rimini line. Once again the British addiction to Mediterranean diversions roused American anger. Marshall and his colleagues were finding it impossible to keep the British more than fleetingly to one objective. Once again Churchill, Brooke, and Alexander, for their part, found the Americans rigid and unimaginative. To Churchill 'the Arnold, King, Marshall combination is one of the stupidest strategic teams ever seen'. On 26 June 1944 the British Chiefs suggested the cancellation of ANVIL. The Joint Chiefs replied at once with 'complete disagreement . . . the desire is to deploy as many United States divisions in France and as quickly as possible. A successful advance by Alexander's force in Italy does not promote this possibility.' Next day Churchill telegraphed to Roosevelt urging him 'to examine this matter in detail yourself . . . the tone of the United States Chiefs of Staff is arbitrary and certainly I see no prospect of agreement'. In reply Roosevelt telegraphed what were obviously Marshall's views, showing the futility of Churchill's arguments by pointing out that it would be impossible to maintain more than six divisions through the Ljubliana Gap.

The British Chiefs persuaded Churchill to give way but, he told Roosevelt, 'we are deeply grieved . . . His Majesty's Government, on the advice of their Chiefs of Staff, must enter a solemn protest'. His own first-draft reply to Roosevelt refused co-operation in ANVIL. His preoccupation with prestige came out in this unsent text:

We agreed that you will have the command in OVERLORD . . . we have to have command in the Mediterranean. But no one ever contemplated that everything that was hopeful in the Mediterranean should be flung on one side, like the rind of an orange, in order that some minor benefits might come to help the theatre of your command.

Churchill's words 'minor benefits' show lack of understanding of the purpose of the landing in the south of France, to secure Marseilles as a base. By the end of 1944 more supplies came through Marseilles than through any other port (18,000 tons a day, compared with 16,600 through Antwerp and 5 or 6,000 each through Cherbourg, Le Havre, and Rouen). At the last minute Churchill tried once more to block ANVIL, this time by suggesting a substitute landing on the north-western coast of France. Debate flared up again and, during four days, Churchill nagged the Americans and tried to secure Hopkins's support to overcome Marshall. On 8 August he finally gave way, only one week before the Americans and French carried out ANVIL (now renamed DRAGOON). In the short run the British were correct: powerful allied attacks in Italy would have distracted more Germans from the invasion areas in northern France, but the Americans were right in that the capture of Marseilles eventually permitted many more United States divisions to attack Germany.

The Italian campaign showed that the allies could successfully invade mainland Europe but also that the German defenders had a chance of defeating allied invasions, especially in the days immediately after an amphibious descent. The prospect of the 'Second Front', the British and American descent on north-western Europe, dominated and controlled the strategy of the year before D-Day. The first front, the Russo-German struggle, saw most of the fighting but the German side increasingly looked over its shoulder at the British and Americans. Justifying, to some extent, the British side in the Anglo-American strategic argument, Hitler feared invasion of the Balkans and Norway, as well as in France. By the end of 1943 there were 195 German divisions in Russia and eighty-four elsewhere outside the Reich. In Russia, though, German units fell more and more below their establishment, and while there were 2,850,000 German soldiers in Russia, there were 2,440,000 elsewhere. Moreover, the troops outside Russia were no longer only second-rate units or men from the east resting and refitting.

After Kursk the Red Army outmatched the Germans on the eastern front. By the end of 1943 it had more than 5,000,000 ground troops deployed against the Germans or in reserve. The Second World War, however, demonstrated that greater numbers alone did not bring victory. The German army remained, till the end, superior to all others in staff work and junior leadership. German units still reacted quickly and thought fast, but after 1943 the better Russian units, with new equipment, moved more rapidly than most German divisions could do. The Red Army's American-made trucks transformed its capacity for manœuvre. Their four-wheel or six-wheel drive made them serviceable in mud, the principal obstacle to military movement in the east. By 1943 Russian artillery, an élite service, became formidable in set-piece attacks, used as it was in concentrated mass at critical points.

From the summer of 1943, therefore, the German command lost the initiative on the eastern front and Soviet offensives succeeded each other, leaving only brief periods when the whole eastern front became stable. In the year between Kursk and June 1944, many local German counter-attacks took place and there were some substantial German victories, but the pattern was of Russian offensives, now on one sector of the front, now on another, which forced German mobile units to rush from crisis to crisis. The German commanders in the field would have preferred deliberate planned retreats to enable them to assemble reserves to restore strategic flexibility but Hitler repeatedly vetoed such proposals, and it was with difficulty that the Germans maintained a coherent defence during long and sometimes hurried unplanned retreats. Between 1943 and 1944 the Red Army advanced in some sectors as much as 600 miles, clearing the Ukraine of Germans, entering Romania, crossing the pre-war Polish frontier, and finally breaking the protracted siege of Leningrad. Hitler produced a rhetorical reply. He optimistically renamed the southern German army groups—Army Group South and Army Group A—and they became Army Groups North Ukraine and South Ukraine, areas from which the Germans had been driven out. Their only hope of justifying their new titles would come if the German defenders threw back the allied invasion of Normandy, and freed reinforcements for the eastern front.

13

D-Day and victory in Europe

FROM the first days of 1944 everyone, Germans and their enemies alike, knew that the Anglo-American invasion of north-western Europe was coming soon and that its success or failure would decide the outcome of the Second World War. Failure, followed by transfer of German strength to the east would change German prospects on both fronts and make stalemate and compromise much more likely.

Elaborate and visible preparations on both sides of the English channel preceded 'D-day', 6 June 1944. On the coasts of France and Belgium gangs of labourers, paid or coerced by the Todt organization, built concrete gun emplacements and sowed prickly obstacles on beaches and open fields, while, in Britain, masses of soldiers thronged the streets and equipment lay ready in the southern-English countryside. Jodl, one of Hitler's closest military advisers, anticipated 'the decisive struggle for the outcome of the war and our future'. Rommel, in command of the defending armies, expected 'the most decisive battle of the war which would determine the fate of the German people'. Hitler prepared in advance a message, given to the 'soldiers of the western front' at the 'historic hour' of the invasion, calling upon them to defend 'the national security, the existence and the future of our people'. In early 1944 he sent Rommel to accelerate the building of the 'Atlantic Wall', of steel and concrete gun positions and obstacles to assault-craft, tanks, and airborne landings. In five months, the army planted two-and-a-half-million mines. The strength of the German army in the west grew from fifty-three to fifty-eight divisions, and the additions were panzer divisions which helped to form a powerful armoured corps.

The German mobile divisions in France contained the best fighting troops in the world. They knew it, for after years of war they included survivors of successful encounters with Russian, British, and American troops, and their morale was high. Unaware of the weight of allied weaponry, they were confident of their mastery. Field Marshal von Rundstedt, in command in the west, General Geyr von Schweppenburg, commanding Panzer Group West, and Field Marshal Rommel disagreed on how to use these troops. Rundstedt and Geyr wanted to hold back the armour for an organized counter-attack in mass on the allied bridgehead, which, relying on mobility and superior staff work, would bring to bear, at the decisive points, more strength than the British and Americans could meanwhile assemble in their beach-heads. Rommel, who had experience of allied tactical bombing, which Rundstedt had not, believed that allied air attack would eliminate the advantage to the German side of road and rail communication, compared with allied dependence on sea-borne reinforcement, and therefore argued that the invasion must be defeated on the coast in the first days or even hours. He wanted to put the best German units close to the coast. Hitler imposed a compromise: he gave Rommel three panzer divisions and kept the rest in reserve. Since he did not know where the allies would land, German intelligence having failed to discover either the date or the place of the attack, Rommel kept one division close to the Normandy beaches, near to the eventual invasion area, one close to Amiens, near the area presumed most likely to be attacked, and the other in between. For coastal defence, Rommel had to rely on infantry divisions in quality ranging from low grade static divisions, containing a high proportion of 'Osttruppen', volunteers drawn from Red Army prisoners, intermingled with older German conscripts, to the first-class parachute divisions. Nineteen divisions in the west were good-quality infantry units.[1]

The allies tricked the Germans into the belief that they had about eighty divisions in Britain while in fact they had only thirty-seven available there, including four airborne and ten armoured. Eventually, once they took adequate ports, about forty more divisions could come in directly from the United States at a rate of four or five a month. British and American ground forces, then, were not overwhelmingly superior, but the allied air forces and navies transformed the balance of strength. On D-Day the allies had over 10,000 combat aircraft and more than 2,000 transport planes while the Germans could put into action just over 300 machines of all types. Reinforcements from Germany soon doubled their air strength, but in August the High Command restricted flying because of fuel shortage, and the consequent lack of training caused heavy losses. The allied navies bombarded the invasion coast and its hinterland with seven battleships, two monitors (with 15-inch guns), twenty-three cruisers, and seventy-seven destroyers, while in the North Sea, the British Home Fleet, with three battleships, three aircraft-

[1] By 1944 a full-strength German infantry division had 12,750 men, an army panzer division about 15,000 at full strength, and an SS panzer division about 20,000, while a full-strength panzer division had about 180 tanks, nearly all, in the west, late-model mark IVs or Vs. In all, the German armies in the west had about 1,800 tanks in June 1944.

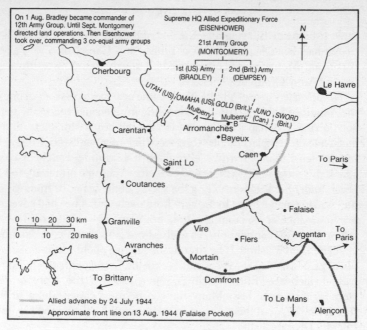

NORMANDY, 1944

carriers, seven cruisers, and ten destroyers was ready to hold off the few
large German surface vessels still seaworthy: three cruisers and a few
destroyers.

D-Day was cloudy and windy, but the weather was better than the day
before. Their forecast had been bad enough to persuade the German
defenders that they would not be disturbed on 6 June but the forecast
presented to Eisenhower, the allied Supreme Commander, had been just
good enough for him to order the attack.

Just after midnight on 5–6 June, soldiers rushed from six British gliders
and seized two bridges crossing the watercourses that formed the flank of
the eastern British invasion beach, SWORD. At 1.30 a.m., 13,000 American parachute troops began to drop behind the western, UTAH, beach.
Shortly after 3 a.m., German radar picked up the first echoes from the
2,727 vessels approaching the Normandy coast, which multiplied to
6,939 vessels, as smaller landing craft left their parent ships, but German
batteries waited to open fire until first light, about 5 a.m. One British
cruiser replied, then, at 5.36 a.m., the main allied naval bombardment
began. At 6.30 a.m. American soldiers waded ashore and an hour later
the British attacked their beaches. The allies sent in five infantry and

three airborne divisions and by the end of the day about 156,000 allied troops had been landed, 83,000 British and Canadian and 73,000 American. Montgomery commanded all allied ground forces through his 21st Army Group headquarters.

The defenders of the 'Atlantic Wall' came near to success only at one of the American beaches, OMAHA, where the invaders unexpectedly met a good-quality German infantry division behind beach obstacles, mines, and concrete emplacements corresponding more fully to Rommel's requirements than anywhere else along the 50-mile stretch of coast attacked. Troops waded ashore and crossed two or three hundred yards of beach under fire before reaching the shelter of the sea wall, from which they had to emerge to get to the exits from the beach. They had covering fire from tanks, some coming ashore from landing-craft, some floating ashore in canvas contraptions, as well as from guns mounted in landing-craft and from warships. The Americans suffered about 2,000 casualties out of 34,000 landed at OMAHA that day but the German infantry division, part of which faced British landings, suffered about 1,200, a proportionately higher rate of loss. Many more Americans came ashore in the succeeding days but there were no replacements for the 352nd German Infantry Division.

Once the British and Americans were established ashore, the outcome of the invasion depended on which side could more quickly get reinforcements to the area of the landings. In this race both sides were handicapped, the allies by lack of seaports and by bad weather, the Germans by allied air attacks on their reinforcement routes, by the French and Belgian Resistance, and by the needs of the eastern front. American troops captured Cherbourg on 29 June but only towards the end of July could the port begin to be used. Apart from two small harbours in the British sector, men and supplies came in over the beaches and allied planners had devised elaborate means of converting open beaches into improvised ports. One became famous, the MULBERRIES, artificial harbours whose main components were colossal concrete caissons towed afloat to OMAHA and GOLD beaches and sunk there, and then equipped with steel piers for unloading. The other main device, the GOOSEBERRIES, were breakwaters more traditionally made up of sunken blockships. It is not certain that the MULBERRIES were worth the effort. After the MULBERRY at OMAHA was destroyed in the great storm between 19 and 21 June, unloading tonnages there actually increased, from 9,000 tons on the last day before the storm, to 15,000 on 29 June. Immediately after the storm, however, the use of ammunition by troops in combat had to be restricted and the storm delayed a big British attack, west of Caen, for three days. By contrast the Luftwaffe, largely restricted to limited night bombing of the beaches, caused little delay, while fast German E-boats, though a dangerous nuisance, had no strategic effect and did less damage than minefields.

Before D-day, allied bombing of marshalling yards, locomotive repair shops, and rail bridges drastically reduced rail traffic in France. By giving priority to German military traffic its volume was kept up, but it suffered unpredictable and sometimes crippling delays. After D-day allied aircraft maintained and extended this 'interdiction' of movement towards the battle: now they smashed the Loire bridges as well as those over the Seine. In addition, they attacked road and rail junctions and crossroads, hunted soldiers and vehicles (even stalking individual trucks), and went for troop concentrations.

Once the allies had come ashore, Panzer Group West ordered two armoured divisions, the 12th SS, and Panzer Lehr, to join the 21st Panzer in a combined counter-attack. Both went by road and endured frequent allied bombing. Delays in moving these divisions meant that they were put in piecemeal to hold the line rather than concentrated for a full-scale riposte. From just south of the Loire, the 17th SS Panzer-Grenadier division took a week to reach the battlefield and launch an attack on Carentan, by which time the Americans were firmly established there; Montgomery, in his advance presentation, had expected it to be in action five days sooner. The 9th and 10th SS Panzer Divisions, transferred from the eastern front, took longer to get from Paris to Normandy than to get from Russia to France. The 2nd SS Panzer Division from south-western France was delayed first by units of the French Resistance (which evoked drastic reprisals: at Tulle, where the SS hanged 100 citizens, and at Oradour where part of the division slaughtered almost everyone there, about 600 men, women, and children), then by interference with railway traffic, and, finally, by British bombing of its fuel supplies, located with help from the Resistance, so that its first echelons arrived only on 28 June, to be put straight into battle, and the division did not come into action as a whole until early July.

Allied deception meant that the Germans, tricked into believing in non-existent divisions which could execute a second landing, kept their infantry tied down in the Pas de Calais and Belgium. On 7 June Rundstedt ordered two panzer divisions to move from there to Normandy, but the armour of 2nd Panzer came into action only on 24 June, while 1st SS Panzer, from Belgium, was so seriously delayed by air attack that the infantry joined in battle only on 28 June and the whole division on 9 July. Montgomery had feared that *all* these eight mobile divisions could move up and be in action by D+8, 14 June. By 16 June allied landings of troops were two days behind the planned dates, but 557,000 men, half of them British and half American, had come ashore, making up twenty full-strength divisions against fifteen German, some of them incomplete or under strength.

However, progress on land disappointed supreme headquarters (SHAEF). It took twenty-three days from D-Day to take Cherbourg instead of fifteen. The original plans expected the British to capture Caen on D-day in order to protect the flank of the Americans further to the west while the latter took Cherbourg, and secondly as a preliminary to exploitation beyond Caen to gain space for manœuvre and for airfields. In fact the British and Canadians took Caen on 9 July, more than a month later. On D-day congestion on the landing beaches and the immediate attack of 21st Panzer saved Caen for the Germans, and later the storm put allied buildup five or six days behind, while giving the Germans respite from air attack, enabling them to bring up reinforcements.

On 22 June the main Red Army summer offensive began on the eastern front, fulfilling Stalin's promise given at Tehran and ensuring that the Germans could not, in the end, match the allied buildup of strength. Meanwhile, the allies pressed the Germans so hard that they could never get together reserves for a full-scale counter-offensive, though for several weeks they frustrated allied attempts to enlarge their bridgehead as a preliminary to breaking out. At the eastern end of the bridgehead General Dempsey's British and Canadian 2nd Army made four large-scale attacks in June and July, two of them west of Caen, which gained little ground, one an attack on Caen itself which, on 9 July, 'liberated' what was left of the town after a preliminary attack by 470 heavy bombers, and another on both sides of Caen, soon brought to a halt. These attacks succeeded both in confirming the German assumption that the allies' priority was to take Caen and the open ground to the south before advancing eastwards to link up with the mythical second invasion, and in preventing the Germans from withdrawing their armoured divisions into reserve to prepare a counter-offensive.

Meanwhile the Americans, having taken Cherbourg, tried to break out of the bridgehead in order to clear Brittany and get its ports into use. British and Canadian attacks, though failing in their immediate objects, contributed to the success of the Americans. On 25 July the British and Canadians faced five armoured divisions and six infantry divisions, while against General Bradley's 1st US Army, the Germans had two armoured divisions, one panzer-grenadier division, two parachute divisions, two infantry divisions, and some battle-groups made up of remnants of divisions. The German formations on the British front were reasonably up to strength with 650 tanks, while against the 1st US Army was the equivalent in strength of only about five divisions with about 200 tanks. For some weeks the Americans slowly advanced through difficult *bocage* or 'hedgerow' country, to capture Saint-Lô on 18 July. One week later the breakout began. Operation COBRA, the attack southwards towards Avranches and Brittany, began with a 'carpet bombing' attack by over 2,000 aircraft on an area about 4 miles by 1½ miles immediately in front of the forward troops. Inaccurate aim killed or wounded 500 Americans, but the weight of explosive stunned the Panzer Lehr Division, already reduced by weeks of combat. Within two days American infantry cleared the way for combined columns of armour and infantry to break out. In fine weather, lavish air support hastened their advance. Relays of four fighter-bombers flew continuously, in half-hour shifts, over each column. Radio liaison enabled pilots to warn the leading tanks of enemy ahead and the ground commanders to call for immediate bomb or rocket strikes. It had taken the allies eight weeks to break the German ring; against overwhelming allied material superiority the German achievement commands respect.

At first, allied commanders intended to give priority after the breakthrough to the seizure of Breton ports. Montgomery, it is true, hoped for a simultaneous eastwards thrust towards Le Mans and Alençon, but it was Bradley's initiative that transformed the original allied strategy. On 1 August, Bradley became commander of 12th US Army Group but, for the time, remained under Montgomery's operational control. On 3 August, having secured the approval of Eisenhower and Montgomery, he directed that General Patton's newly created 3rd US Army should employ only minimum force in Brittany and that its main body should join 1st US Army in driving east into the open German flank. Recovering from the attempt on his life on 20 July, Hitler was also taking decisions. He had the choice of withdrawing from Normandy and re-creating a front much further east, or to counter-attack immediately and try once more to seal off the British and American landing, which, at last, the Germans had now recognized was going to be the only allied landing in northern France. He chose the more daring option and, on 2 August, he ordered Field Marshal von Kluge, who had taken over from both Rommel and Rundstedt, to assemble an armoured corps to attack from around Mortain to the sea at Avranches, so cutting off the American troops which had already moved south through that bottle-neck. Originally it was Kluge who put forward the idea as a delaying step, but the disastrous final decision was Hitler's. As a result, several panzer divisions moved west towards Mortain in the first week of August, while to the south of them American columns were moving east.

The German attack failed on the first day, 7 August. It began just after midnight and made progress at first, but when day came, with fine weather, the Germans had to dig in and try to conceal themselves from allied aircraft, notably ten squadrons of RAF Typhoons, and to protect themselves against American artillery 'operating', as the US army official historian writes, 'on the premise that it was better to waste shells than to miss a possible target'. Hitler, however, stuck to his plan and made Kluge prepare renewed attacks. As the British and Canadians attacked southwards from the original beach-head and as the Americans, advancing eastwards south of Kluge's spearheads, swung northward, the German armies between them, including the armoured divisions massed to fulfil Hitler's hope of clearing France of the allied intruders, found themselves in a closing trap. Only on 16 August did Hitler permit withdrawal westwards out of this pocket, and by that time only about 15 miles separated the Canadians, to the north in Falaise, from the Americans to the south in Argentan. Polish troops, attached to the Canadian army, met the Americans on 19 August, putting a thin cordon around the pocket. Within an area of about 7 miles by 6, about a dozen German divisions, once of high military quality, suffered continuous bombardment from artillery and the air. Probably between 20,000 and 40,000 troops escaped, but most of these were service troops not combat soldiers, of whom a high proportion were among the 50,000 taken prisoner and the 10,000 killed.

The utter failure of this attempt of Hitler's to restore a cordoned-off bridgehead as a preliminary to its eventual destruction, forced the attenuated formations in Army Group B into hasty retreat to avoid encirclement by allied divisions capable of much more rapid movement, as long as fuel reached them, than most German units. How far back the Germans had to go before trying to form a defensive line depended on two factors: the rate of the re-equipment and reinforcement of the German defenders and the difficulties of Anglo-American supply. Originally the allies planned to stop at the Seine and wait for their lines of communication to catch up; on 19 August, they determined to go beyond. Now the Germans began to withdraw from most of Belgium and Luxemburg, and from France except Alsace, Lorraine, and the Vosges. On 15 August the much-debated ANVIL (now renamed DRAGOON) landing took place in southern France and by the end of the month the newly landed American and French soldiers had taken Marseilles and were near Lyons.

On 24 and 25 August, French and American troops from Normandy reached the centre of Paris after some severe combats on the outskirts. SHAEF hoped to bypass Paris to avoid the delays and dangers of street-fighting and postpone the burden of feeding and supplying the town. De Gaulle and the French army objected. They feared that the fighting between the Resistance and the Germans, which broke out in mid-August, would lead to fire and massacre and perhaps to some kind of revolutionary takeover in Paris. General von Choltitz, the German governor, felt that central Paris should be kept peaceful in order to facilitate military transport, and therefore made a truce with Resistance leaders, in effect partitioning the city. Simultaneously he prepared strong points in the suburbs to check allied advances and to show loyalty to Hitler as long as necessary until the allies enabled him to surrender to overwhelming military force. On 25 August he surrendered an almost-undamaged Paris, which he had protected from Hitler's rhetorical orders to continue its defence until it was reduced to rubble. Next day de Gaulle marched through the city and took a parade of the French 2nd Armoured Division, which he stationed in Paris to keep order and support his authority.

It was not only French domestic problems that worried Eisenhower. Since D-day Anglo-American relations had changed. By the end of August 1944, 830,000 British troops had landed in north-western France compared with 1,220,000 Americans. Other US divisions were arriving from the south of France, and there were more to come across the Atlantic, while the British had to begin to break up existing divisions to find replacements for their casualties. An equal Anglo-American partnership descended on Normandy but as they approached Germany, American preponderance began to show. It was a bizarre accident that the extra contribution of skill and experience, with which the British hoped to balance the partnership, was now embodied in the strange figure of Field Marshal Montgomery, to use the rank he acquired on 1 September when he gave up overall command of allied land forces to Eisenhower. Contact between American and British senior officers sometimes provoked disharmony. In the British army between the wars there vigorously flourished stereotyped social attitudes moulded by upper-class or upper middle-class backgrounds, and codified by the routines of English public schools. The presence among very senior British officers of 'Brookie', 'Bimbo', 'Jumbo', and 'Simbo', for instance, suggests a milieu whose assumptions the intellectual attainments of British officers did not always enable them to question. The easy contact which a shared language made possible enabled the British to show their superficial self-confidence and so create resentment and suspicion among many Americans, but often enabled the Americans, in time, to discriminate and treat the British as individuals. Immediate acquaintance did not make Americans, as many British expected, confident in the professional superiority of British senior officers, but deeper knowledge sometimes generated relationships of mutual trust and respect as, for example, between Marshall and Dill, or Eisenhower and Admiral Cunningham. No such thing happened with 'Monty'.

Close acquaintance with 'Master', as his staff called him, evoked resentment except among his British courtiers and among some officers in clearly subordinate positions. He excelled in conceit, complacency, and arrogance of demeanour. Success at Alamein, and the praise that followed, exacerbated his belief that he was always right. Some commanders are admired for their flexibility; Montgomery insisted that 'his' battles (or 'parties' as he often called them) followed his prefabricated master plan. The British official historian, and Montgomery's approved biographer, afterwards followed his lead (and that of his staff) in rearranging facts to fit Monty's 'master plan', with confusing results. Thus, in Normandy events which were dangerous to the allies are made part of the plan, and all other generals become either more or less meritorious subordinate executants or uncomprehending and inexperienced obstructionists. The effect is to obscure Montgomery's merits as an observant manager of great battles who seemed never to succumb to fatigue or bewilderment, and whose decisiveness never faltered. His insistence that set-backs were, in fact, successes, provided for in his plan, aroused dismay when, for several weeks in June and July 1944, the allied bridgehead in Normandy was cordoned off by the Germans and restricted to an area so small and so lacking in logistical resources that allied buildup must eventually be overtaken by German, and in which the space needed for airfields could not be found. Montgomery's assumption that the eventual victory in Normandy was entirely his, together with the understandable emphasis British radio gave to British achievements, angered the Americans, who were engaged in winning the greatest American military victory ever seen. A more modest man than Montgomery would have got more credit for his achievements and not aroused the suspicion that his vanity dictated his strategy. Moreover, by July 1944, some American observers came to think that he was holding down British casualties and leaving the Americans to take the risks, in order to maintain the size and influence of his army group: a bad preliminary to Montgomery's repeated demands for Americans to be put under his command.

In the last two weeks of August 1944, allied commanders (and some Germans) began to believe that their forces could drive straight into Germany and surround the Ruhr region before going on to Berlin. On 18 August Montgomery urged that Bradley's 12th US and his own 21st British Army Groups should be kept together, that is to say all the British and American combat formations in France, except those coming from the south of France, in 'a solid mass of some forty divisions which would be so strong that it need fear nothing', to 'advance northwards, clear the coast as far as Antwerp, establish a powerful air force in Belgium and advance into the Ruhr'. Since he thought Eisenhower's 'ignorance as to how to run a war is absolute and complete', Montgomery 'must run the land battle for him'. Though it is true that he offered to serve under Bradley, Eisenhower never took that offer seriously, perhaps because of the implausibility of Montgomery's subordination to the much less self-assertive Bradley. To Montgomery, and his biographer, 23 August 1944, when he rejected this plan, was 'the day Eisenhower lost the chance of an early end to the war in the West'.

Obviously, Eisenhower had to take into account tensions in his team, though post-war ghost-writers and publishers encouraged writers of memoirs to give misleading prominence to outbursts of irritation and bad temper normal among people working under extreme stress. However, Eisenhower's reactions to Montgomery's suggestions (and they were far from outright rejection), derived from more material constraints than the fear of giving too much glory to Monty. The Supreme Commander was not only tactful and emollient, he was an intelligent soldier. At the end of August 1944 more than three-quarters of British and American supplies for the 12th and 21st Army Groups still came over the D-day beaches. The beaches, even the British MULBERRY, were bound to fail as autumn wore on and bad weather descended. Nearly all the rest came through Cherbourg. All supplies, therefore, had to come long distances to the armies as they approached Germany. In August the destruction of French railways brought dependence on road transport and by the end of the month American, and, even more frequently, British, trucks were breaking down for lack of maintenance. Three US divisions were immobilized so that their trucks could be taken away to form transport companies. Eisenhower turned down Montgomery's proposed forty division thrust because it could not be supplied. At the same time, however, he accepted his suggestions that the main allied effort should be north of the Ardennes, that this north-eastern advance should have priority, and that he should have power to carry out 'operational co-ordination' with the American 1st Army, though it should nominally remain in Bradley's 12th Army Group. Eisenhower rejected Patton's proposal for his 3rd Army to be given supply priority for an attack across the Rhine towards Frankfurt and beyond because Supreme Headquarters thought that it would then take longer to bring more ports into use and so make it impossible to keep supplied any sustained attack against serious opposition.

On 4 September, the day Antwerp docks (though not the approaches to them along the Scheldt) were captured intact, Montgomery's 21st Army Group presented a new proposal for a single thrust into Germany, this time by about eighteen divisions. This new project depended on certain assumptions: the British and American armies involved must have reached the Rhine, and have Antwerp in use, by 15 September, and the French rail network must be substantially restored. None of these assumptions were fulfilled, so Montgomery's proposal would have meant sending into Germany troops whose supplies might be interrupted by crises back in Normandy, notably storms in the Channel. The risk might have been worth taking if future German resistance would only be weak, and this was about to be tested by a third proposal for a smaller-scale single-thrust under Montgomery's direction. Eisenhower agreed to it and gave it overriding priority in supplies and the use of the allied strategic reserve—the airborne army.

On 17 September US parachute divisions were dropped to seize bridges over rivers and canals in and near Eindhoven and Nijmegen, including the Maas and the Waal, the southern branch of the Rhine, while British and Polish parachute troops flew in to seize bridges on the northern branch of the Rhine at Arnhem. The British 30th Corps, spearheaded by the Guards Armoured Division, was to advance about 60 miles to Arnhem up the main road from the Meuse-Escaut canal, and establish a bridgehead over the Rhine outflanking the West Wall, or 'Siegfried Line' as the allies called it, which the Germans had built in 1938 and were now energetically renewing. Montgomery's confidence appears to have encouraged him to ignore indications from ULTRA (intercepts of German signals coded by Enigma) that 9th and 10th SS

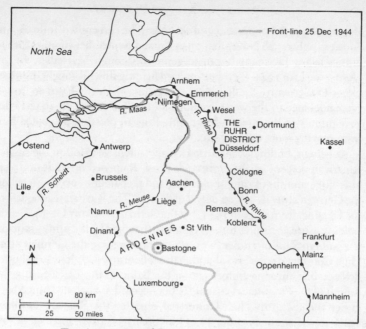

 shows a map with the following labels:

Front-line 25 Dec 1944

North Sea

Arnhem
Emmerich
Nijmegen
R. Maas
Wesel
R. Rhine
THE RUHR DISTRICT
Dortmund
Düsseldorf
Kassel
Ostend
Antwerp
Cologne
Brussels
Aachen
Bonn
Lille
R. Scheldt
R. Meuse
Liège
Remagen
R. Rhine
Namur
Koblenz
Dinant
ARDENNES
St Vith
Frankfurt
Bastogne
Mainz
Oppenheim
Luxembourg
Mannheim

N

0   40   80 km
0   25   50 miles

THE ARDENNES and RHINELAND CAMPAIGNS 1944–5

Panzer Divisions were re-equipping near Arnhem. Both the allied parachute divisions and the 30th Corps met strong opposition, while the British paratroops, isolated at Arnhem, suffered very heavily and their remnants had to escape to the south.

On 18 September Montgomery wrote to Eisenhower apparently assuming the success of this operation MARKET-GARDEN,

I consider that as *time* is so very important, we have got to decide what is necessary to go to Berlin and finish the war; the remainder must play a secondary role. It is my opinion that three Armies are enough, if you select the northern route, and I consider, from a maintenance point of view, it could be done.

Eisenhower replied with a reasoned rejection, or rather postponement: 'We must marshal our strength up along the western borders of Germany, to the Rhine if possible, ensure adequate maintenance by getting Antwerp working at full blast at the earliest possible moment and then carry out the drive you suggest.' The dispute concerned logistics—how much could be done without Antwerp? Arnhem showed the riskiness of Montgomery's adventurous suggestions. As it was, the main attention of his 21st Army Group turned at last to clearing the mouth of the Scheldt, a task which proved protracted and arduous. The first convoy unloaded in Antwerp only on 28 November 1944. In mid-September supplies for the armies facing Germany began to come in through Marseilles. In the closing weeks of 1944, therefore, as hard fighting slowly brought the allies closer to Germany, the logistical constraints lessened. Even so, allied preponderance in the west depended on the Red Army. In 1944 Hitler gave priority to the western front: only Russian pressure prevented him from moving more troops there.

At Tehran, Stalin had promised a Soviet offensive to follow the Anglo-American descent on the Normandy coast. It opened on 22 June 1944, after three months of careful planning and preparation, and inflicted on the German army its biggest defeat of the war. The Russian reconquest of the Ukraine, from 1943 to 1944, left the Germans in Army Group Centre holding a line 300 miles further east than that held by the army group on its southern flank. In order to create a central reserve the German army High Command wished to abandon this salient and withdraw to a shorter defence line running from Riga on the Baltic to the Black Sea at the mouth of the Dniester. As usual, Hitler opposed any retreat. Since both Hitler and the army High Command expected the Russians to attack again in the south in order to cut Germany off from supplies of raw materials and from Romanian oil, Army Group Centre was left with only two panzer divisions while to its south, Army Groups North- and South-Ukraine had eighteen panzer or panzer-grenadier divisions. The Red Army General Staff, in concert with the commanders of four 'Fronts' (Army Groups) which were co-ordinated by Vasilievski and Zhukov, worked out a battle involving deep penetrations followed by a series of double envelopments: the German army was to endure in 1944 what it had inflicted on the Polish army in 1939 and the Russian army itself in 1941. Breakthroughs by infantry, supported by huge artillery concentrations, were to be exploited by mobile armour.

Hitler's insistence on static defence, including the tenacious holding of 'fortress' towns supposed to disrupt enemy lines of communication, gave the Russians their opportunity. In contrast to 1941, 1942, and 1943, it was now the Russians who put on a mighty summer offensive, relying on the superior mobility of élite formations. Against Army Group Centre the Russians employed one-and-a-quarter million men, over 5,000 tanks, and 6,000 aircraft, a superiority of 5 or 6 to 1 in men, 7 or 8 to 1 in aircraft, and 9 or 10 to 1 in tanks. Within two weeks, three German armies were fragmented and, for the most part, encircled and destroyed, so that Army Group Centre was reduced to eight divisions and could not stop sweeping Russian advances. The Red Army reached the Vistula and the suburbs of Warsaw before extended supply lines and hastily assembled German reinforcements compelled a halt.

Elsewhere, too, the Russians crossed the pre-war frontiers of the Soviet Union. German Army Group South-Ukraine now defended Romania, which Germany had pulled into the war in 1941. By the spring of 1944, King Michael, and many senior officers and politicians, believed that Romania should abandon Germany, with or without the assent of the supposedly pro-German head of government, Antonescu. The latter had recently insisted on Romanian equality with the Germans in control of the forces defending his country, with the consequence that Romanian troops came under Romanian command. Their armies were able to make ready to abandon the Germans. The defence of Romania rested on about 800,000 soldiers, less than half of whom were German. Moreover, the German High Command was compelled to remove most of its mobile divisions from Army Group South-Ukraine to shore up Army Group Centre. By August it had one under-strength panzer and one panzer-grenadier division, with less than 200 tanks and assault guns between them.

On 20 August two Red Army Fronts, under Tolbukhin and Malinovski, co-ordinated by Timoshenko, attacked with about 900,000 men, including six tank and mechanized corps, with 1,400 tanks and assault guns. The Russians moved through Romanian units which either did not resist or themselves turned to attack the Germans. On 23 August King Michael ordered Antonescu's arrest and announced Romania's surrender. On 31 August the Red Army entered Bucharest, having surrounded and destroyed most of Army Group South-Ukraine. In turn, Bulgaria hastily affirmed its neutrality in the Soviet–German war and tried to get out of its nominal war with Britain and the United States. On 5 September Stalin accelerated the Bulgarian evolution by a Soviet declaration of war which soon led to the seizure of power in Sofia by a coalition, including Communists. This new government put the Bulgarian army under Soviet command. These changes threatened the supply lines to German forces in Greece and, early in October, Hitler reluctantly ordered their complete withdrawal.

From June to September 1944 the German army in the west lost 55,000 killed and 340,000 missing, and on the eastern front 215,000 killed and 625,000 missing, roughly one-and-a-quarter million men lost, two-thirds to the Red Army. Fleets of British and American bombers now roamed freely over the Reich. Why did Germany fight on until May 1945?

Hitler preferred death to unconditional surrender. He, and the more committed Nazis, had no choice since unconditional surrender meant trial and execution by the victors. Even in September 1944, however, Hitler thought he might prolong his life and that of the Third Reich. If the alliance against him broke up, all might still be well. His perceptions of foreign opinion were ill-informed and crude: he correctly grasped the anomalous nature of the alliance between the western powers and the Soviet Union, but failed to observe that neither side could risk separate negotiation with any German government until Hitler himself had been removed. If such negotiations had begun, the other partner in the alliance would be obliged to tempt the Germans with better terms. Then, selling his alliance to the highest bidder, Hitler would recover European dominance. German defeat was a prerequisite of conflict between Russia and the West. He also hoped to separate the British from the Americans, as well as those allies from the Soviet Union, but unfortunately for him Anglo-American tensions mainly involved competition in gaining prestige for the defeat of Hitler. It was victory that brought out inter-allied dissensions, which concerned the post-war world and were muted as long as Hitler survived. He hoped, however, that if the war could be kept going long enough, allied determination would weaken. Moreover, in spite of disasters on both fronts, he saw comforting prospects by sea, air and land.

Hitler hoped to re-enact the campaign of 1940 and 1941, but this time successfully to force Britain to compromise. He would attack London from the air, destroy British sea communications by submarine attack, and eject British ground forces from the Continent by a rapid armoured thrust through the Ardennes. New 'secret weapons' would make all the difference. 'Revenge weapon number 1', the V-1, was a pilotless aircraft with an explosive warhead, the 'flying bomb' as its English targets called it, or, more colloquially, the 'Doodlebug'. With a warhead of one ton, it had a range of about 200 miles and flew at about 400 miles per hour. The first arrived on 13 June 1944, the last on 29 March 1945, after the V-1 had killed over 6,000 British civilians. But British defence became increasingly effective as anti-aircraft guns employed new radar and the proximity fuse, conceived in Britain and developed in the United States, which exploded its shell without needing actually to hit its target. By the end they were knocking down three-quarters of the missiles that got across the coast. On 8 September, however, the first V-2 arrived. Against the V-2, there was no defence, but German supplies were limited. It was a missile, rocket-propelled to a height of 50 or 60 miles, and attaining a speed of 3,600 miles per hour, with a warhead similar to the V-1. In England these rockets killed 2,754 civilians. After September 1944, Antwerp suffered as heavily as London; but the inaccuracy of the V-weapons meant that civilian damage was far greater than to military targets. Greater Antwerp was hit by 1,214 V-weapons, but only 150 flying bombs and 152 rockets fell in the port area. Other transport centres were attacked, especially Liège, and 5,400 were killed in northern France and Belgium.

At sea, Dönitz looked forward to a new submarine offensive in British waters. He persuaded Hitler to give priority to the building of two new submarines—the type XXI and type XXIII. These had the 'schnorkel', which made it unnecessary to surface for air, and, with more powerful electric batteries and streamlined hulls, they could move much faster underwater and for longer periods, so that now whole cruises could take place submerged. Moreover, the new submarines had radar to detect hostile aircraft mounted on their 'schnorkel' tubes. Most methods of submarine detection became ineffective. In the end Dönitz was disappointed—production failed because of shortage of skilled labour and raw materials and because bombing disrupted transport of prefabricated U-boat sections as well as their assembly. In the autumn of 1944, the US navy anticipated that 300 new U-boats might soon be in operation, but by the end of the war only 180 had been built. Another new weapon also came too late. The Germans were ahead in the design and building of jet aircraft. Hitler, however, delayed the appearance of jet fighters by insisting on their adaptation as tactical bombers. It was not until 18 March 1945 that large formations of jet fighters attacked an allied bomber force. Twenty-four were lost out of 1,250 heavy bombers assaulting Berlin, in spite of about 500 defending fighters. In spite of delays the Germans led the way and British jets first joined in operations, with one squadron of Meteors, only at the end of April 1945.

Hitler's main hope was a big land offensive. On 16 September 1944, he told his daily situation conference that he intended to launch an attack from the Ardennes towards the Meuse to retake Antwerp and cut the supply lines to the British and American forces north of Antwerp. Hitler directed a reserve to be gathered from panzer divisions taken out of the line and refitted and rested, from new divisions formed from personnel transferred from air-force ground staff or from the navy, from men of military age combed out from civilian employment, and by extending the age of liability for military service. He chose Himmler, who embodied the coercive power of the Nazi state, to supervise this process. Priority in equipment went to the western front, to make 12 Panzer divisions ready for the attack. The army commanders involved wished to limit their objectives to the destruction of allied forces east of the Meuse; Hitler insisted that Antwerp must be taken.

The attack never even reached the Meuse, apart from a car-load of Germans disguised in American uniforms who were rounded up in Dinant. It began well: on 16 December thirty German divisions attacked on a 50-mile front against five American divisions and achieved complete surprise. Now, success needed speed. The armoured spearheads must quickly seize crossings over the Meuse and, to maintain momentum, they needed fuel and ammunition when and where they were required. Infantry must follow to secure lines of communication and to defend flanks in the rear of the leading armour. The attacks needed well-organized and unimpeded movement on the few, and often narrow, roads in the Ardennes. German staff officers could supply the organization, but their number was restricted by the need for secrecy, so that until the last minute advance planning was confined to a limited number in Model's Army Group B. The outcome of the 'Battle of the Bulge' followed from one simple fact: American forces moved faster than German. Much had changed since the German army roared through the Ardennes in 1940, seized crossings over the Meuse, and rushed to the sea. Then the French infantry were as slow as the German or slower, but the American units of 1944 were completely motorized: more than 48,000 vehicles of the US 1st Army moved into the battle zone in the critical period, from 17 to 26 December. German army trucks, many of them captured from exotic sources, broke down more often than American and blocked narrow roads. The German army lived in two worlds: the Tiger tank was the most formidable in the world, yet its infantry might have been in the First World War, indeed some German divisions had more horses than was normal in 1918. The mixture of motorized and horse-drawn transport led to frequent confusion. Worst of all, though, was the effect of allied air power.

German commanders hoped for bad weather to inhibit flying, even though the rain and mud of the first week of the offensive slowed their troops, but on 23 December the weather cleared. Allied air forces struck at once and next day dispatched nearly 6,000 sorties. On 26 December Model forbade any major movement by day. When, on 28 December, snow and blizzards descended, movement was no easier. At critical moments armoured spearheads were halted by lack of fuel. Though the Germans had accumulated sufficient stocks in the rear the problem was to get it to the forward troops. In 1940 the Germans had perfect weather and air superiority. The French could set out to reach their defensive line on the Meuse only after the German invasion of Belgium had begun, while in 1944 the British and Americans were established there, with supply dumps well forward. In 1940 the German attack had met only lightly armed French and Belgian cavalry before closing to the Meuse. The crucial difference in 1944 was that the resistance, generally tenacious, of American troops in prepared positions, gave time to the allied command to reinforce critical points. On the first day, Eisenhower ordered the 7th Armoured Division to St Vith; it reached there late on 17 December and held out until 21 December, obstructing one of the two main German supply lines. At Bastogne, the other important road junction, there arrived the 101st Airborne Division, in trucks collected together at short notice at Reims where it was resting. After a hundred-mile journey, it was ready for action on the morning of 19 December. The Germans did not take Bastogne, though it was surrounded from 21 to 26 December until relieved by Americans attacking from the south. General Patton was able to relieve Bastogne because the German 7th Army, to the south of the two panzer armies responsible for the breakout, was not strong enough to pin down his 3rd US Army.

The murderous proclivities of the 1st SS Panzer Division, which led the initial exploitation and, on 17 December, began a trail of killings by shooting more than a hundred disarmed American prisoners, stimulated the tenacious defence of the Americans. As early as 18 December, Model reported failure, but it was on 24 and 25 December that the offensive reached its limit. The 2nd Panzer Division got within 4 miles of the Meuse at Dinant. By that time strong British forces guarded the Meuse crossings and the German spearheads were halted by lack of fuel. On Christmas Day the American 2nd Armoured Division cut off the forward elements of the 2nd Panzer. The Germans got no further.

These varied demonstrations of the Wehrmacht's continued striking power, whose impact on allied confidence was immensely exaggerated by German propaganda (and it seems, by Hitler himself) strengthened Hitler's power inside Germany. The failure of the only serious attempt by Germans to overthrow his dictatorship, on 20 July 1944, had also increased his hold. The active conspirators came from the best-informed section of the German army, who knew that Germany was losing the war, were aware that Hitler's military direction was accelerating defeat, and understood that there was no hope of alleviating the disasters facing Germany while Hitler remained an obstacle to any hope of compromise with the allies. Some felt that, win or lose, Hitler's regime was morally intolerable. During the few hours between 12.40 p.m., the time of the explosion of the bomb that Colonel von Stauffenberg had left close to Hitler, and the time when it was announced that Hitler had survived, leading resisters in Berlin (and Paris) tried to take over. Knowledge of their identity made easier a savage repression. Thenceforward the army was closely supervised by Nazis and dissent became doubly perilous. The men of 20 July had no time to set out their case in public and their action only increased support for Hitler. The Führer's personal popularity had grown during the war. Many Germans distinguished Hitler from 'the Nazis' who were thought of as responsible for the unpopular aspects of the regime, while Hitler, in contrast to his self-seeking associates, was perceived as austerely sacrificing himself to secure the future of Germany. Until Germany was on the brink of total ruin, defeat increased support for Hitler among those who still had emotion to spare from the trials of daily existence. The bomb plot of 20 July seemed to betray the German nation in its fight to survive. As more and more of occupied Europe was lost, the war came increasingly to appear a matter of survival, rather than one fought for the luxury of conquest.

For some this view was confirmed by 'terror bombing' and by the allied insistence on 'unconditional surrender'. Anglo-American bombing in the last months exceeded everything that had come before. The reaction of most civilians was either apathetic concentration on daily problems, resentment towards the British and Americans, or, less commonly, hostility towards the German authorities, especially where they were felt to be deficient in their responses to air raids. Among front-line troops worry about those at home went with disappearance of the resentment often felt by fighting troops towards the privileges of those who do not share their dangers. Fear of what defeat would bring stiffened German resistance until, in the spring of 1945, concern for immediate self-preservation overwhelmed everything else. 'Unconditional surrender' caused alarm, exploited and encouraged by Goebbels' Propaganda Ministry. At the second Quebec Conference in September 1944, Roosevelt and Churchill supplied a welcome gift to Goebbels in the 'plan' put up by Morgenthau, Secretary to the US Treasury, demanding the post-war conversion of Germany 'into a country primarily agricultural and pastoral in its character', with the elimination of its metallurgical, chemical, and electrical industries. Allied headquarters, impressed by the continued ferocity of German resistance, urged Roosevelt to relent and offer some inducement to encourage German capitulation. Roosevelt suggested to Churchill a joint statement 'to help break down German morale promising that this war does not seek to devastate Germany or eliminate the German people'. Churchill replied, after consulting the British Cabinet and Chiefs of Staff, that to make any such statement would suggest weakness, and pointed out that what the Germans feared 'is a large proportion of their people being taken off to toil to death in Russia, or as they say, Siberia'. Moreover, U. J.[1] certainly contemplates demanding two or three million Nazi youth, Gestapo men, etc., doing prolonged reparation work. . . . We could not therefore give the Germans any assurances on this subject without consultation with U. J.' Nor was German surrender likely to be encouraged by knowledge of Stalin's proposals for the transfer of German territory to Poland and the expulsion of the German inhabitants. It was more important to postpone disagreement with Stalin than to reassure the enemy. Only vague reassurances were provided for the Germans, such as Churchill's message of 18 January 1945: 'We demand unconditional surrender, but you well know how strict are the moral limits within which our action is confined. We are no extirpators of nations, or butchers of peoples.'

German faith in the Führer apparently survived until a surprisingly late date. No doubt contemporary German police reports exaggerated it but its tenacity was confirmed by allied interrogations of prisoners of war. When it failed, a pretence could be forced: in East Prussia in July 1944, Gauleiter Greiser observed of 'individuals who lack political faith and strong hearts' that 'the Party and state know ways of rendering them harmless'.

Only on 9 January 1945 did Eisenhower learn that a new Russian offensive was about to begin, evidence of the weak liaison with Stalin's command. Churchill elicited this information with a message to Stalin which implied that the allies needed help in the west. In response, Stalin later claimed, he advanced the starting date of the attack, which began on 12 January. While on the central sector the Red Army had halted on the Vistula, Russian attacks had already struck towards the Baltic and in Hungary. Perhaps the Russian command hoped to secure the flanks of its central fronts before renewing the direct advance towards Germany. Since Hitler attached more importance to Hungary, as a source of oil, and to the Baltic, for training of U-boat crews, than to Poland, the defence of these areas drew forces away from the central sector. On

---

[1] 'Uncle Joe'=Joseph Stalin, who was very angry when Roosevelt told him of this harmless sobriquet.

14 September 1944, four Russian 'Fronts', with 133 rifle divisions, six tank, and one mechanized corps, about 900,000 men, attacked the thirty-two divisions in German Army Group North. Within ten days Estonia was cleared of German troops ('liberated', the conventional verb of this period, was sometimes ironic), then much of Latvia, including Riga. Then the Russians shifted their main effort towards the Baltic coast north of Memel. This move isolated most of Army Group North, with twenty-six divisions, which remained in north-west Latvia by Hitler's decision until the end of the war. The southern flank of this attack was covered by an invasion of east Prussia, meeting fierce resistance and a strong German counter-attack which reconquered ground occupied by Russians. There the Germans discovered and publicized the horrors of Russian conquest of German territory: another reason for a stiffening of resistance among German soldiers.

On 6 October 1944 two Russian 'Fronts' began a full-scale attack into Hungary. Hitler sent reinforcements and ordered that Budapest should be defended at all costs. The Germans foiled an attempt to get Hungary out of the war by arresting the Regent, Horthy, and imposing a puppet regime under Szalasi. General Antonov told Churchill and Roosevelt the effects of these Russian operations at Yalta on 4 February 1945.

Both of these attacks were for the Germans very painful and they quickly reacted to our attacks by a swift transfer of power onto the flanks at the expense of the central sector of our front; thus, of 24 tank divisions on our front [that is, on the whole eastern front], representing the principal German striking power, 11 tank divisions were drawn into the Budapest sector, 6 tank divisions into the East Prussian (3 tank divisions were located in Courland) and thus on the central part of the front there remained only 4 tank divisions. The aim of the High Command was accomplished.

Moreover, in mid-January, Hitler ordered the 6th SS Panzer Army to Hungary, after its failure in the Ardennes, in spite of Guderian's pleadings for it to be moved to the Polish front. After delays caused by the need to refit after the Ardennes, and by allied bombing of German railways, it arrived in Hungary, and launched an abortive offensive in early March to retake Budapest and the Hungarian oilfields.

The Russian staffs, directed by Zhukov and Antonov, began work in October 1944 on the offensive of January 1945. Originally it was timed for the third week of January; it began on 12 January. Historians lack direct evidence of the reasons and motives for Soviet actions and base their interpretations on inferences from those actions, inferences which can easily diverge when used in support of different writers' interpretations. A possible explanation of the date of attack lies in the weather. The Russian offensive began from the Vistula and Narew rivers and its objective was the Oder. It had to use Polish roads which in wet weather mostly turned into impassable mud. The Russian advance needed frost, yet the attack began in wet and misty conditions. Some historians have suggested, however, that forecasts already predicted frost after a few days and that this determined the date of the attack rather than the needs of allies, regardless of weather, which Stalin adduced to Air Marshal Tedder, Eisenhower's deputy, on 15 January: 'It would be foolish for me to stand aside and let the Germans annihilate you; they would only turn back on me when you were disposed of. Similarly it is to your interest to do everything possible to keep the Germans from annihilating me.' (Later, as we shall see, Stalin apparently came to believe that the western allies might be collaborating with the Germans.)

In January 1945 the overall balance of strength in men and weapons on the whole eastern front was about 3 to 1. In the central sector, Zhukov's 1st Belorussian Front and Konev's 1st Ukrainian Front had about 2,200,000 troops against about 400,000 German. At the bridgeheads over the Vistula, the principal points of attack, the Russians concentrated forces superior by 9 or 10 to 1 in men, tanks, and artillery. Big Russian attacks began with an immense artillery bombardment followed by infantry assaults on successive defence lines to secure breakthroughs. Armoured and motorized troops moved through the rifle divisions to carry out rapid advances. For this offensive, Russian troops were carefully indoctrinated with reminders of German devastations and brutality in occupied Russia. Now individual vengeance was promised. Hitler, more than ever opposed to any withdrawals, tried to veto the defending armies' counter to Russian artillery bombardments—retreat to prepared positions in the rear immediately before the barrage opened. Determined to fight on, he was ready to ensure that the killing and the smashing of human bodies continued: 'I have never in my life learned the meaning of the word capitulation . . . as far as I am concerned, my health could be destroyed by worry without its in the slightest changing my decision to fight until in the end the balance tips to our side.' His response to the offensive was to grasp tighter control by requiring that every German commander down to divisional level must report any operational order to his headquarters in time to give him the opportunity to countermand it.

By the beginning of February, the Russians had 'liberated' Warsaw and advanced beyond to the River Oder, with bridgeheads near Küstrin and

Frankfurt, well into Germany and about 40 miles from Berlin. The Russian advance stopped at the beginning of February. Supply problems accumulated in a forward move of up to 300 miles. An early thaw disrupted Russian supply routes and in Polish territory the Red Army could not count on eager help from the local population. Moreover, the Germans, on Hitler's insistence, held Poznań and Torun, until late in February, towns on the only direct all-weather road from Warsaw to Berlin. At Yalta, the British Chief of Staff, Brooke, asked Antonov when the next Russian offensive would begin. Antonov replied that 'the most difficult season' was still to come: 'the second part of March and the month of April. This was the period when roads became impassable' so that May was apparently the likely moment.

On the western front, the Germans accompanied their retreat from the Ardennes 'bulge' with an attack into Alsace, where American forces had been weakened by diversions from the Ardennes battle. To create a reserve there, Eisenhower proposed to shorten the line by withdrawing from Strasbourg. In one of the celebrated crises of the war de Gaulle intervened, and demonstrated the value to France of his high-handed firmness when Eisenhower abandoned this manœuvre. Four days later Eisenhower faced another crisis that caused him 'more distress and worry' than all the rest. In a press-conference on the Ardennes battle, on 7 January, Field Marshal Montgomery attempted tactfulness and caused enormous offence. He praised Eisenhower for putting him in command of the Americans north of the German breakthrough, and applauded the bravery of American soldiers. Assisted and supported by 'British troops fighting on both sides of American forces who have suffered a hard blow', the latter had earned Montgomery's 'public tribute': 'I salute the brave fighting men of America, I never want to fight alongside better soldiers.' Unfortunately he did not salute his American colleague, General Bradley, to whom he had recently explained that the German breakthrough 'was entirely our own fault'. 'Poor chap', he wrote to Brooke, 'he is such a decent fellow and the whole thing is a bitter pill for him.'

Montgomery had a cure for Bradley's problems in handling the 12th Army Group, and set it out in a letter to Eisenhower at the end of December:

I would like to refer to the matter of operational control of all forces engaged in the northern thrust towards the Ruhr . . . it will be necessary for you to be very firm . . . your directive should finish with this sentence: 'From now onwards full operational direction, control and co-ordination of these operations is vested in the C-in-C, 21 Army Group', that is, Bradley and his army commanders, Simpson, Hodges, and Patton, were to be subordinate to Montgomery. Montgomery knew how to win the war. A powerful thrust must be directed north of the Ruhr. First, crossings over the Rhine must be secured. Second, the Ruhr region should be cut off from the rest of Germany. Third, a single thrust should drive on Berlin. All necessary resources of troops and supplies should be assembled under Montgomery's direction and everything else halted. Unfortunately, Montgomery believed, Eisenhower knew nothing about war and he was weak. In consequence there was 'no grip', and American commanders were allowed to ignore Montgomery's master plan. Patton especially needed very firm restraint, which Bradley and Eisenhower did not apply, to prevent his trying to defeat the enemy on fallacious principles. Montgomery, consistently monomaniac, repeatedly deman-ded control of all ground forces in the theatre. Eisenhower refused, and Marshall prevented Churchill from getting Roosevelt's support.

In 1945, in consequence, Montgomery had to contemplate the unfolding of the strategy of Eisenhower's Supreme Allied Headquarters, nagging when it limited his scope, conducting some highly successful operations, and enjoying his role as 'Britain's greatest hero since Nelson'. This strategy involved closing on to the Rhine before establishing two bridgeheads followed by a double envelopment of the Ruhr. Sub-sequently the remaining German forces would be destroyed as circum-stances suggested. Montgomery, and most later British writers, complained that clearing all the left bank of the Rhine meant unnecess-ary delay. Eisenhower insisted that to win the secure and highly defensible line of the Rhine would make easier the eventual concentra-tion of resources for a northern thrust under Montgomery, a concentra-tion complained of by Patton and his admirers. Montgomery, and later British historians, also complained that it was wrong to attempt two lines of attack across the Rhine into Germany and that this must weaken the principal effort to be launched by Montgomery. Eisenhower's reply was that logistics limited the northern effort to thirty-six divisions (21st Army Group agreed), and that some of the other fifty American (or French) divisions could usefully be employed to weaken German concentration against Montgomery's effort and perhaps to take up the principal role if his attack faltered. In practice, the only weakness in Eisenhower's strategy proved to be that it deprived Montgomery of a monopoly of military success.

The destruction of German forces west of the Rhine took place in three stages. Montgomery used the 1st Canadian Army and the 9th US Army in clearing the Rhine from Emmerich to Düsseldorf. Floods delayed the 9th Army, so that the British and Canadians faced strong opposition from high-quality German parachute troops. The next stage was for Bradley's 12th Army group to reach the river between Düsseldorf and Koblenz. Then Patton, with the US 3rd Army, struck south to the Koblenz–Mannheim sector, while Patch and the 7th US Army, which had come through Marseilles and the south of France, moved north-eastwards, so that these two American armies trapped much of two German armies. The Rhineland campaign took from 8 February to 21 March because Hitler ordered his troops to stand west of the Rhine rather than to retire in good order behind the river. In consequence, about 250,000 Germans were captured, while allied casualties, except among the British and Canadians in the north, were comparatively light. Moreover, on 7 March advanced units of the American 1st Army found an intact bridge over the Rhine at Remagen, between Bonn and Koblenz, which had been kept for retreating Germans, and rushed it before it could be destroyed. Within two weeks six bridges had been built to support a twenty-mile bridgehead. On 22 March Patton secured a bridgehead for his army by a surprise assault at Oppenheim, south of Mainz. Now it was again Montgomery's turn, this time to launch the main offensive across the Rhine further to the north. His crossing was one of the great set-pieces of the whole war. Bomber Command obliterated Wesel, 3,500 guns laid down a preliminary bombardment along a thirty-five-mile front, and two airborne divisions flew in. Churchill, Brooke, and Eisenhower came to watch. Montgomery crossed on 23 and 24 March. By 26 March twelve bridges were in operation. Two days later British armour broke out. On 25 March the Americans broke through south of the Ruhr. Further south the US 1st and 3rd Armies joined up their bridgeheads and drove north-west towards Kassel.

On 28 March Montgomery, having put forward his scheme for the final offensive towards Berlin, was distressed to be told by Eisenhower that he was to return the 9th US Army to Bradley's command after the Ruhr had been encircled, that the 21st Army Group (Montgomery) should drive north-west towards Hamburg and Lübeck, and that the 12th Army Group (Bradley) was to carry out the principal allied thrust, not towards Berlin, but towards Leipzig and Dresden. Eisenhower also sent a message to Stalin to explain that his main effort would be on the axis Erfurt–Leipzig–Dresden. To Montgomery he added the justification that 'Berlin . . . has become only a geographical location; I have never been interested in those. My purpose is to destroy the enemy forces and his powers to resist.' Churchill protested to Roosevelt that to leave the Russians to take Berlin would make them feel they were the dominant contributor to the common victory.

May this not lead them into a mood which will raise grave and formidable difficulties in the future? I therefore consider that from a political standpoint we should march as far east into Germany as possible and that should Berlin be in our grasp we should certainly take it.

But Eisenhower, the US Chiefs of Staff, and Roosevelt all insisted that military needs must take priority over politics.

At this stage, Stalin seems to have been especially suspicious towards the western allies, probably because he suspected that they were indeed, as Churchill wished, intending to advance far to the east. He replied on 1 April to Eisenhower, agreeing that

Berlin has lost its previous strategic importance. In the Soviet High Command plans secondary forces will therefore be allotted in the direction of Berlin . . . The main blow by the Soviet forces will begin in approximately the second half of May.

This blow would also be aimed at the 'Erfurt, Leipzig, Dresden area'. About that time Stalin gave orders to prepare, with the greatest possible speed, an attack on Berlin in overwhelming strength! It was certainly a lie when Stalin told Harriman one day before the great onslaught, that it was directed at Dresden. The evidence suggests that Stalin believed the western allies to be preparing to collaborate with the defeated Germans against the Soviet Union. His, perhaps understandable, reaction to the exclusion of the Russians from discussions between Anglo-American representatives and Karl Wolff, an SS general, concerning the possible surrender of German forces in Italy seems conclusive. He sent a message to Roosevelt on 3 April: 'at the present moment the Germans on the Western front in fact have ceased the war against England and the United States. At the same time the Germans continue the war with Russia.' Stalin claimed an agreement had been made, 'on the basis of which the German commander on the Western Front—Marshal Kesselring has agreed to open the front and permit the Anglo-American troops to advance to the East, and the Anglo-Americans have promised in return to ease for the Germans the peace terms'. It is true that more and more German soldiers, especially after the Rhine crossings, showed eagerness to surrender to the British and Americans to avoid any risk of capture by the Russians.

GERMANY DIVIDED (1937 FRONTIERS)

Probably Stalin intended the Soviet attack which began on 16 April to make sure that Russia got the territories promised in February at the Yalta conference with Churchill and Roosevelt. Aimed at Berlin, it involved the usual intense concentration of artillery (up to one gun every 10 metres) in support of 193 divisions attacking forty-five weak German divisions plus middle-aged men, boys, and spare policemen collected together in the *Volkssturm*, whose most effective weapon was the anti-tank grenade launcher, the *Panzerfaust*. The Russians met savage resistance. From the west, the Americans were across the Elbe by 13 April; the Red Army surrounded Berlin only on 25 April. Even so it is not certain that the American forces could have got through to Berlin. In any event, there was no race—or rather the race had only one runner, the Red Army.

Similarly Eisenhower, at the request of the Russians, restrained Patton from a race to Prague, which he could almost certainly have won. In April, except in the Ruhr pocket, where Model held out until 21 April, when he shot himself, leaving over 300,000 German prisoners to be rounded up, the British and Americans met only sporadic, though sometimes determined, resistance, and their advance was principally restrained by traffic jams. By the end of the month even German troops facing the Russians were found fleeing to the west to surrender to the British or Americans.

On 30 April 1945, satisfied that there was no more death and destruction he could arrange, Hitler killed himself and left Admiral Dönitz to carry on. On 2 May the British reached the Baltic at Lübeck. This time Eisenhower had urged speed on Montgomery so that he should forestall the Russians. He wanted to make sure the Red Army should not occupy Denmark and that, if a campaign were needed to liberate Norway, it should be Anglo-American. Here Supreme Headquarters asserted western claims while accepting Stalin's elsewhere. Churchill's suggestion for advances on Berlin and Prague, if they had been possible, involved the risky process of challenging Russian claims that he and Roosevelt had already agreed.

Dönitz continued the attempt to split the alliance by seeking to surrender separately to the western allies. The end came raggedly. In Italy, German forces surrendered on 2 May. Montgomery, approached by emissaries of Dönitz, refused to accept the surrender of German forces facing the Red Army, except as individuals. On 4 May 1945, therefore, all German forces opposing the 21st Army Group in Holland, north-west Germany, and Denmark surrendered to him: there followed a series of local surrenders. At 2.41 a.m. on 7 May 1945, Jodl made a general surrender at Supreme Allied Headquarters in Reims to American, British, French, and Russian representatives. This was not good enough for the Soviet authorities who insisted on another surrender in Zhukov's headquarters in Berlin. After a long wrangle between Tedder and Vishinski about who should sign for the western allies, Keitel led a German delegation in surrendering shortly before midnight on 8 May.

14

The defeat of Japan and
the atom bomb

To defeat Japan, American strategists used blockade and bombing to reduce its war production and as a preliminary to an eventual invasion. The conquest of islands in the Pacific provided harbours for submarines nearer to their targets, airfields in striking distance of Japan, and finally bases for the invasion. Superiority at sea and in the air enabled the Americans to conquer these new bases. They advanced step by step, the size of the steps being determined by the limit of the range of land-based aircraft operating from their existing strong points or, in more adventurous operations, they relied on carrier-based air support. To those involved in the fighting the campaigns leading to American victory seemed less one-sided than they do in retrospect. Though the United States must win, if it tried, yet Japanese garrisons, scattered over their far-flung conquests of 1941 and early 1942, resisted with more obstinacy than any other troops have ever shown.

In September 1943, forced on to the defensive, Japanese Imperial Headquarters accepted the eventual loss of their easterly conquests and determined to hold a reduced perimeter on an imaginary line through the Bonins–Marianas–Carolines–Western New Guinea–Dutch East Indies to Burma. Beyond this line, in the Gilbert and Marshall Islands, in the Solomons, the Bismarck Archipelago, the Admiralty Islands and Western New Guinea, Japanese garrisons fought fierce delaying actions. When the Americans attacked the newly defined imperial perimeter, the Japanese navy came out in force on two occasions to challenge American dominance of the ocean. On the first occasion, in June 1944, at the Battle of the Philippine Sea, the Japanese attempted to prevent the capture of Saipan in the Marianas, part of Admiral Nimitz's advance across the central Pacific. On the second occasion, at Leyte Gulf in October 1944, the Japanese fleet tried to stop the recapture of the Philippines by the combined forces of General MacArthur's south-western Pacific advance and those of Admiral Nimitz from the central Pacific.

On 15 June 1944 two divisions of US marines began to land on Saipan. Immediately the Japanese Commander-in-Chief gave the order: 'The

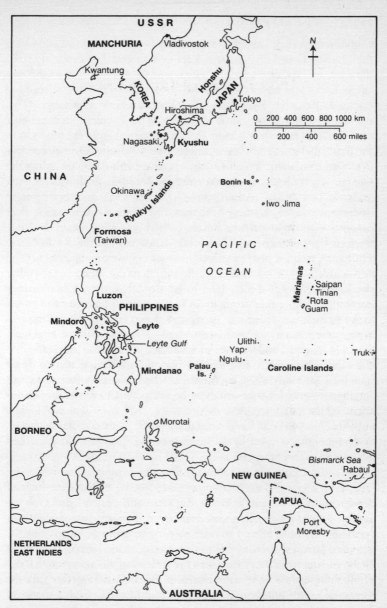

THE PACIFIC WAR, 1944–5

Combined Fleet will attack the enemy in the Marianas and annihilate the invasion force.' Five minutes later he repeated Togo's signal before the Battle of Tsushima in 1905, 'The fate of the Empire rests on this one battle. Every man is expected to do his utmost.' After three days' steaming eastwards from the Philippines, the Emperor sent a message, 'This operation has immense bearing on the fate of the Empire. It is hoped that the forces will exert their utmost and achieve as magnificent results as in the Battle of Tsushima.' The Japanese, under Admiral Ozawa, had five fleet aircraft-carriers, four light carriers, five battleships, including the two largest ever built, the *Yamato* and the *Musashi*, both with 18-inch guns, eleven heavy cruisers, two light cruisers, and twenty-eight destroyers. Under Admiral Spruance, off Saipan, were seven fleet carriers, eight light carriers, seven battleships, eight heavy cruisers, thirteen light cruisers, and sixty-nine destroyers. In the Battle of the Philippine Sea, air strikes replaced conflict between surface ships. The American fleet carried more aircraft (956) than the Japanese (473), but the Japanese expected their land-based aircraft, from the islands they controlled, to give them equality in numbers, and relied on the longer range of their planes (which, unarmoured and lacking self-sealing fuel tanks, were comparatively unencumbered), the accessibility of land bases for rapid resupply, and the tactical advantage of steaming into battle into the wind, which meant that their carriers did not have to turn to fly off and land their aircraft. The Americans had two advantages. Signals intelligence enabled submarines to be positioned to report any movement of the main Japanese carrier force, and they had ample fuel supplies. All American naval airmen, therefore, were elaborately trained and frequently exercised; by the summer of 1944 Japanese airmen lacked both training and practice.

On 19 June Japanese aircraft made four attacks on the American fleet. The result was the 'Great Marianas Turkey Shoot'. British techniques of fighter control, in securing defensive interceptions, practised and rehearsed by American carriers, were reinforced by the work of Japanese-speaking American officers who listened to the instructions given by the directing Japanese airborne officer and responded with appropriate orders to the defending fighters. The victory of American naval airmen that day rivalled those of the RAF in the Battle of Britain, and together with the victory at Leyte Gulf showed that invasion of Japan was only a matter of time. In the 'Turkey Shoot' the Japanese lost about 330 planes and 400 crew; the Americans 30 aircraft and 27 crew. The next day, 20 June, United States carriers counter-attacked the retreating Japanese. They did so dangerously late: they found the Japanese only when they were already 300 miles away, at maximum American range. Some American planes could not get back. To land those that did the carriers had to sail into the wind, which put them still further away. American planes returned after dark. The carriers plunged into the night, ablaze with lights to signal the way home, and searched the surrounding waters. Thirty aircraft were lost in action, eighty more crashed in the sea, but only forty-nine aircrew were lost, 160 having been pulled from the ocean, while the attack had sunk one Japanese carrier and destroyed two-thirds of what was left of Ozawa's aircraft. American submarines sank two more fleet aircraft carriers, making three in all. The Japanese carrier force, which had opened the war so dramatically, was reduced to a shadow.

The second attempt to overturn American naval supremacy, at the Battle of Leyte Gulf, followed the invasion of the Philippines, whose reconquest by the Americans threatened to break the remaining sea links between Japan and its southern conquests, with their vital raw materials. On 20 October 1944 US forces assaulted Leyte, an island well-suited to provide air and sea bases to support further conquests. Preliminary attacks by carrier-based American aircraft on Japanese airfields in Formosa showed how training and ample exercises gave them superiority over the Japanese air forces: about 500 Japanese aircraft were destroyed at the cost of ninety American planes. Thus the Americans reduced air support for the impending Japanese naval attack on the American beachheads at Leyte.

The Battle for Leyte Gulf was the biggest naval battle of the Second World War. These ships took part (with losses in brackets), to which should be added one Australian heavy cruiser:

	US Navy	Japanese
Fleet Aircraft Carriers	5 (1)	1 (1)
Battleship-carriers	—	2
Light Carriers	21 (3)	5 (3)
Battleships	12	7 (3)
Heavy cruisers	5	13 (6)
Light cruisers	11	4 (4)
Destroyers	80 (4)	37 (12)

The Japanese attacked in three groups. The first, far to the north of Leyte, included all available carriers (with a much reduced complement of aircraft) which the Japanese hoped would attract the fastest and strongest American ships away from Leyte Gulf. There, two Japanese forces coming independently, one from the south of Leyte and the other, a powerful fleet with the two super-battleships, coming from the north, were to meet in Leyte Gulf on X-Day, 25 October, and destroy the supply ships supporting the American landings. The Japanese plan worked well in outline, badly in detail. Admiral Halsey dashed off to the north with the fastest and most powerful American carriers and battleships in pursuit of the Japanese carriers, just as their commander had hoped he would do. The remaining American heavy warships moved south to confront the Japanese attack from the south, their American commander apparently imagining that Admiral Halsey had left behind sufficient strength to block the main Japanese attacking fleet in its approach to the northern end of Leyte Gulf through the Philippine archipelago.

Admiral Kurita therefore reached the decisive point in overwhelming strength. At sunrise on 25 September his four battleships, six heavy cruisers, and two light cruisers, with accompanying destroyers, emerged from the morning mist with nothing to stop them reaching the American beach-heads on Leyte except sixteen slow, lightly-gunned, unarmoured, escort carriers and their screen of destroyers. Three minutes after the Japanese opened fire the American Admiral Sprague broadcast, un-coded, asking all who could to send help.

Admiral Kurita, however, did not sense impending victory. The last two days had not been very happy for him. At dawn on 23 October, as his flagship, the heavy cruiser *Atago*, led his powerful fleet towards the Philippines, American submarines attacked. Four torpedoes struck *Atago* and Kurita and his staff found themselves swimming. Picked up by a destroyer, Kurita was in time to watch another torpedoed heavy cruiser explode. Next morning, transferred to the super-battleship *Yamato*, he encountered the first American air strike just after 8 a.m. Halsey's fleet launched 259 aircraft sorties against Kurita's force, using bombers and torpedo-carrying planes. In spite of the immense number of anti-aircraft guns that the Japanese ships possessed, only eighteen American planes were lost. *Yamato* was hit twice by bombs. *Musashi*, its sister ship, took seventeen bomb hits and nineteen torpedoes before sinking. Halsey concluded, relying on the customarily optimistic reports of his aircrews, that Kurita could be ignored during the time required for him to deal with the Japanese northern carrier fleet, and disappeared hundreds of miles to the north at high speed.

South of Leyte, the last classic naval battle took place in a night-action on 24 and 25 October. It opened when American torpedo-boats and destroyers, relying on high speed and manœuvrability, skirmished with the big ships of the first Japanese force steaming towards Leyte Gulf from the south and disrupted their formations by torpedo attack. They sank one battleship and one destroyer and disabled two more destroyers. Then, as the surviving Japanese vessels came on, they found, at right angles, 'crossing their T', six American battleships in line of battle. Battleship *Yamashiro* ran into fire from five battleships, after eight minutes turned away on fire, and sank twenty minutes later without having hit the enemy—the Americans had radar-controlled guns and the Japanese did not. The weaker second section of the Japanese southern fleet prudently turned back.

Before daybreak on 25 October, therefore, Kurita, trying to carry out Tokyo's order of the previous evening 'All forces will dash to the attack, trusting in divine guidance', learnt that the southern force he expected to meet him had been destroyed. The appearance on the horizon of American carriers caused him as much dismay as the sight of the masts of his battleships caused the Americans. The latter reacted by throwing up smoke screens and launching their aircraft for immediate attack. By now Kurita feared American aircraft and had lost confidence in Japanese land-based planes and in his own anti-aircraft fire. He finally decided it was time to go when he read an intercepted message from the American admiral in Leyte Gulf requesting 'despatch of fast battleships and a fast carrier air strike', implying to the worried Kurita that powerful ships were close at hand. For six hours a weak American force had kept him from sailing south into Leyte Gulf and then induced him to withdraw. During the same time Halsey, with the biggest and best American carriers and battleships, pursued the distant Japanese northern force. Before his battleships could get into range they were ordered back to the south in response to the appeals for help from Leyte Gulf, where they arrived too late to intercept Kurita. However, Halsey's carrier force struck from the air and sank no fewer than four Japanese carriers.

During the rest of the war what was left of the Imperial Japanese Navy was crippled by lack of fuel and condemned to demoralizing inactivity. Its final stroke was symbolic. When the Americans invaded Okinawa in April 1945, only the remaining super-battleship, *Yamato*, could be given fuel to sail there, with one cruiser and eight destroyers. Six American battleships, seven cruisers, and twenty-one destroyers prepared to intercept. American carrier aircraft got in first. The Japanese ships did not even complete one day out of harbour. *Yamato* sank after being hit by five bombs and ten torpedoes. Four damaged Japanese destroyers got back. The Americans employed 386 planes. Twelve men and ten planes were lost.

Japanese failure to defeat the Americans at sea and in the air made it impossible for them to prevent amphibious assaults on the garrisons of their scattered conquests and the advance of American forces to bases from which air attack and, if necessary, invasion could be unleashed on the Japanese home islands, first, as it was planned, on Kyushu and later on Honshu itself. However, Japanese ground troops, equipped at key points with ample stocks of food and munitions, imposed heavy losses. At Saipan in the Marianas, for instance, 30,000 Japanese inflicted 14,000 American casualties before they themselves were killed almost to a man. That represented about 20 per cent of the 70,000 American combat troops sent in. Japanese troops, with rare exceptions, preferred death to surrender. In Saipan, American troops saw a Japanese officer beheading his troops with his sword to spare them the dishonour of capture, and hundreds of civilian auxiliaries and their families leaping from the cliffs at the last moment of defeat. Japanese warrior tradition, carefully instilled in their soldiers, prescribed surrender to be dishonourable. Japanese soldiers were told that Americans would torture and kill their prisoners but, should they survive the enemy, Japanese army regulations laid down that their surrender was a crime punishable by death. The close-knit, homogeneous, nature of Japanese society made indoctrination easy, and its cultural isolation, together with the Japanese sense of racial superiority, protected such values from scepticism. Japanese soldiers, therefore, had to be given individual attention by their opponents, since they refused to recognize defeat and were not ready, when isolated, simply to lie low until they could be rounded up. Some Americans confirmed Japanese official propaganda and, inspired by their own racial contempt and by stories, often true, of Japanese ill-treatment of American prisoners, frequently killed Japanese who offered to surrender. Individual prisoners, or those in small groups, were not often taken. War crimes were not all on one side, though the 'justice' of the post-war victors made them seem so.

The Americans bypassed enemy islands and bases, unafraid of the consequences, once Japanese mobility was lost and Japanese air power curtailed. In the central Pacific, Nimitz moved from Makin and Tarawa in the Gilberts (November 1943) to Kwajalein and Eniwetok in the Marshalls (January–February 1944), to Saipan, Tinian, and Guam in the Marianas (June–July 1944), thence to the Palaus, Ulithi, and Ngulu

(September–October 1944), while MacArthur moved into the Bismarck Archipelago (January–March 1944), and then along the northern New Guinea coast in a series of amphibious landings, and so to Morotai in September. The two forces combined for the attack on Leyte in October, whence MacArthur attacked Mindoro and Luzon (December 1944–January 1945). Japanese troops held out in parts of Luzon until the end of the war, but MacArthur secured first-class rear bases there for the final attack on Japan. On 19 February 1945 marines landed on Iwo Jima to secure landing grounds for escorting fighter aircraft and for damaged B-29 bombers returning from attacks on the Japanese home islands. This island, about 5 miles long by 2½ miles wide, took six weeks to conquer, in spite of the heaviest naval bombardment of the Second World War. Japanese casualties were 20,700 killed and 216 prisoners, American 6,812 killed and 19,189 wounded, about 30 per cent of the entire force. (Wounded Japanese killed themselves or were finished off by their colleagues or, sometimes, by Americans.) In two US marine divisions, casualties in infantry regiments reached 75 per cent.

Next came the Ryukyu Islands, of which the largest is Okinawa, intended as the main forward base for the invasion of Honshu. Here took place the hardest fighting of the entire Pacific war. Japanese defenders totalled about 77,000; the United States navy landed 60,000 troops on the first day, building up to about 190,000. One novelty was the presence of the Royal Navy, operating in the Pacific war with a balanced self-supporting fleet (two battleships, four aircraft-carriers, five cruisers plus two from New Zealand and one from Canada, and destroyers). For the Okinawa invasion it joined an American fleet of eight battleships, eleven fleet carriers, six light carriers, five heavy cruisers, and thirteen light cruisers. Another feature of the Okinawa battle was the repeated Japanese use of kamikaze (Heavenly Wind) suicide tactics, especially in mass attacks, the so-called *Kikusui* (Floating Chrysanthemum) attacks. These began at Leyte on 25 October 1944. Now, between 6 April and 22 June 1945, 1,900 Japanese pilots aimed their explosives-laden aircraft at American and British ships (the steel flight decks of British aircraft carriers were an advantage compared with the wooden decks favoured by American naval architects). They sank twenty-five ships, scored 182 hits, and ninety-seven damaging near-misses. In addition, about 5,000 conventional sorties were flown by the Japanese—they had saved aircraft and hastily trained pilots for this decisive battle. Conventional planes sometimes launched another suicide weapon, a rocket-assisted, piloted glider bomb, the '*Baka*', a stand-off missile guided by a human suicide.

The kamikaze seemed, for a time, a serious danger, especially to the radar picket ships, generally destroyers, stationed to give warning to the main bodies. However, the kamikaze loss rate of slightly under 100 per cent (accounting for the few who turned back because of mechanical defects) meant that it was an ephemeral one. 355 took part in the first mass attack on 6 April: forty-five in the last on 22 June.

Fighting on Okinawa took nearly three months, from 1 April to 22 June, on a narrow island about 60 miles long and of irregular width, from 3 to 15 miles. It was more intense even than on Iwo Jima. By the end of May about 50,000 Japanese troops had been killed and exactly 227 prisoners taken. The Japanese fought in well-prepared deep-dug defensive positions, countering heavy American artillery and naval gunfire by keeping cover until the moment of assault and then using fire patterns carefully registered in advance. Their artillery was well concealed and protected. American dug-outs and trenches were necessarily comparatively improvised and shallow, and their infantry attacks could only be frontal, over ground providing scanty cover, with no chance of outflanking manœuvres. Japanese positions had to be broken by explosives and their defenders expelled by flame-throwers and individually killed. American killed came to 7,000, wounded to 32,000. More than two-thirds of two army divisions were killed or wounded. In addition the Americans suffered 26,000 'non-battle casualties', nearly all 'combat fatigue', neuro-psychiatric cases suffering breakdowns under the stress of battle. Early treatment, a sensible innovation of the Second World War, produced good results, however, and only about 20 per cent had to be reassigned to non-combatant roles.

Until the battles for Saipan, Iwo Jima, and Okinawa, combat in the Pacific had been less intense than against the Germans. Now, it seemed, the nearer Japan came to defeat the harder the Japanese fought. In eighteen months the Americans had advanced 3,000 miles; in the south of Okinawa it took three weeks to get less than 3 miles through the Machinato Line and another month to get another 3 miles through the Shuri Line, then two weeks for 6 miles (all these movements on a front of about 6 or 7 miles wide), and another week to kill the Japanese in the remaining 4 miles to the southern tip of the island. Though it is true that 7,000 were taken prisoner at the end, many of these were Okinawan conscripts.

The invasion of the Japanese home islands seemed likely to call forth even more suicidal desperation from their defenders. As soon as they lost Okinawa on 22 June 1945, the Japanese navy and army began to hoard fuel and aircraft and hurriedly train more pilots to attack the invaders. Moreover, most American intelligence exaggerated the remaining Japanese production capacity and reserves of raw materials. In June the US Joint Chiefs of Staff agreed on their strategy for the final defeat of Japan. In November 1945, thirteen or fourteen American divisions would invade Kyushu, and in March 1946, twenty-five divisions (with a small British Commonwealth force) would attack Honshu itself and impose unconditional surrender, perhaps amid the ruins of Tokyo. Stalin had promised that the Soviet Union would enter the war against Japan about three months after the German surrender. On 28 May he told Hopkins that he would be ready to attack on 8 August. Thus, the Red Army would keep busy the Japanese armies in Manchuria and China. The American air force declared that it could win the war alone by October 1945, with massed B-29s, but the American army and navy remained sceptical.

This strategy for the final defeat of Japan developed from the way the war had been fought, with two modifications: first, Nationalist China's part had become much smaller than originally expected, and as a result the largely British campaign in Burma did not contribute to the final victory over Japan and became a private British war for the restoration of the Empire in south-east Asia; secondly, the Soviet Union had come to matter more, though after Okinawa, when allied ships cruised freely around Japan, the defeat of the Kwantung army ceased to be a prior condition of invasion of the Japanese home islands, since allied sea and air forces could prevent it from reaching them. During the war with Japan, however, as this conventional strategy evolved, scientists, technologists, and engineers assembled the basis for an alternative strategy: the atom bomb.

In 1939, scientists in several countries warned governments of the theoretical possibility of atomic explosion. In the United States, Szilard drafted a communication to Roosevelt, with Einstein's signature to give added weight. In England, Thompson, of Imperial College, spoke to Sir Henry Tizard, the chief scientific adviser to the government, and got a message to Ismay, secretary of the Committee of Imperial Defence. Accordingly, in May 1939, the Air Ministry ordered one ton of uranium oxide. In the spring of 1939 Professor Hentsch, of Hamburg, wrote to the German War Ministry drawing attention to the possibility of a new explosive: 'the country to use it first will have a decisive advantage over the others.' The Reich Ministry of Economics began to look for uranium. Raoul Dautry, the French Minister for Armaments, started to take a close interest in nuclear research in 1939. French physicists concentrated on exploring the possibilities of a controlled chain reaction using uranium, with heavy water as a 'moderator' for slowing down neutrons. Early in 1940 a member of the French secret service bought the entire world stock of heavy water. It was transferred to England in June 1940. By that time the French team, most of whom came to Cambridge when France fell, were working on the isolation of a new fissionable element, plutonium. Simultaneously, two American physicists published an account of the process. There was, therefore, no 'secret' behind the atom bomb. The basic theoretical principles were public and the problem in exploiting atomic energy lay only in their application.

To make an atomic weapon needed the isolation of enough uranium-235 for a 'critical mass', that is, an amount of sufficient volume and density to prevent too high a proportion of freed neutrons from dispersing their energy without being 'captured' by further nuclei and causing the latter to split. Alternatively, 'piles' were needed to generate controlled chain-reactions to transmute uranium-238 into the fissile element plutonium. These operations required whole new industries operating completely novel equipment.

At first political leaders and the scientists who advised them assumed that atomic energy would not be relevant in the present war: they supposed that they should carefully observe the enemy's progress and keep up with it only as a defensive precaution. It was in Britain that atomic fission was first seen as a weapon to decide this war. In March 1940, O. R. Frisch and R. F. Peierls wrote a memorandum which went at once to those with direct influence on government. In a few lucid pages, these refugees from the Nazis set out why and how an atom bomb could be constructed from uranium-235 and outlined the lethal effects both from explosion and radiation. Helped by another refugee physicist, Simon, of the Clarendon Laboratory in Oxford, Peierls convinced Lindemann (later Lord Cherwell, Churchill's closest scientific adviser) and ensured the highest priority for nuclear research from the Churchill government. To supervise research the MAUD Committee was set up in April 1940. It reported in July 1941 that 'a uranium bomb is practicable and likely to lead to decisive results in the war'. Research had so far confirmed the arguments of Frisch and Peierls, and it was now time to build a factory: 'material for the first bomb could be ready by the end of 1943'. Since the outlines of the project 'are such as would be likely to suggest themselves to any capable physicist', it was urgent to get in first.

Even though the Nazis had forced the departure of many of the best German scientists and were about to murder some who had not escaped in time, 'capable physicists' remained in Germany, some, though not all, eager to use their skills for Nazi victory.

The British now moved fast. In the United States, still neutral, nuclear research proceeded slowly, concentrating on uranium as a source of peacetime power. E. O. Lawrence, of Berkeley, however, produced microscopic quantities of plutonium and found its potentially explosive qualities greater even than U-235. In August 1941 he heard of the research sponsored by the MAUD Committee in Britain and of its conclusions. He discussed the possibilities of a bomb with V. Bush and J. B. Conant, who independently received drafts of the MAUD report. The latter two scientists were especially important: Bush, with Conant as his deputy, was now at the head of an 'Office of Scientific Research and Development' with access to the President. In August, Bush and Conant suggested to the British a joint Anglo-American study of uranium, and in October 1941, Roosevelt approved complete exchange of information with the British and wrote to Churchill suggesting that 'any extended efforts may be co-ordinated or even jointly conducted'. The British neglected these approaches and preferred separate research and production. Probably the minds of Cherwell and Churchill were settled on a *post-war* need for British independent production, since, for a weapon to win this war, American co-operation could only be an advantage. The case produced by the British, that American security might be inadequate, sounds like an excuse rather than an explanation (the treachery of Dr Fuchs, of the British scientific team in America, makes it ironical).

By the summer of 1942, things had changed. American entry into the war removed all restraints on nuclear research and production, and in a few months the United States caught up almost completely on the theoretical side and moved well ahead of the British in experiment and production. The British, for their part, had discovered, as Sir John Anderson, the Minister in Charge, told Churchill at the end of July 1942, 'that the production plant will have to be on such a huge scale that its erection in this country will be out of the question during the war'. (It seems to have been this factor that explains the failure of the German scientists to try to make a bomb for use in the current war.) Now it was the British who sought co-operation and the Americans who were reluctant. Churchill pursued Roosevelt, who responded with amiable expressions of willingness, subsequently belied by his subordinate executives. The flow of information had dried up.

On both sides of the Atlantic post-war prospects aroused alarm. The Americans thought the British wanted to exploit access to American nuclear developments for post-war commercial advantage; the British feared a future world in which the Russians might have the bomb and the British would not. Sir John Anderson wrote, 'we cannot afford after the war to face the future without this weapon and rely entirely on America should Russia or some other power develop it'. Unless the Americans helped the British to keep up with the application of nuclear science, they would, therefore, have to do it almost alone despite the consequent hindrance to Britain's war effort. The American authorities involved (and all these transactions were known to very few), seem to have thought that when Congress came to inquire into the spending of enormous sums for secret purposes, the military strengthening of an American ally would be more acceptable than the commercial reinforcement of a possible competitor. While Bush and Conant, the directing American scientists, felt the United States could make nuclear weapons alone, they thought the help of British scientists, and that of refugees in Britain, might save perhaps a few weeks of valuable time, especially in devising plant for separating uranium-235 by gaseous diffusion (forcing uranium hexafluoride through membranes with perforations of .0001 mm diameter).

Once the British persuaded the Americans that they renounced commercial advantage from knowledge of the rapidly growing American nuclear know-how, agreement became possible. Roosevelt and Churchill signed a document at the first Quebec Conference in August 1943. They agreed that neither country would use nuclear weapons, nor pass on information on their manufacture to other countries, without the other's consent. Churchill formally disclaimed 'any interest' in 'industrial and commercial aspects beyond what may be considered by the President of the United States to be fair and just and in harmony with the economic welfare of the world'. Scientific exchange was to be 'full and effective', but interchange of information on 'design, construction and operation of large-scale plants' was to be restricted to what was needed to bring the project 'to fruition at the earliest moment'. The British had secured only a limited partnership, having missed their chance.

A year later, on 18 September 1944, Churchill and Roosevelt discussed atomic energy once more and initialled an agreed document. The bomb 'might perhaps, after mature consideration, be used against the Japanese' (at that moment Germany seemed on the point of collapse).

Apparently Morgenthau, the American Treasury Secretary, and Roosevelt were impressed by Britain's likely post-war economic problems: atomic power might make up for an expected shortage of coal. Roosevelt promised 'full collaboration' on atomic energy between Britain and the United States after the war 'for military and commercial purposes' in order, it seems, to strengthen America's most reliable ally. (This pledge, which Roosevelt kept to himself, proved worthless under his successor, President Truman.) Against the wishes of their scientific advisers, including Bush, Cherwell, and Anderson, Churchill and Roosevelt agreed on another matter of high policy. Scientists, British and American, knowing that the Soviet Union and eventually other countries could make nuclear weapons, feared a deadly arms race. They argued that if Stalin were told everything about the development and progress of nuclear research and production, he would be more likely to join in working out a scheme for international control of nuclear weapons, together with adequate inspection. Bush and Conant, the chief American scientists in the 'Manhattan Project' to develop the atomic bomb, objected to an exclusive Anglo-American exchange of information mainly because they feared Russian reaction (in contrast to General Groves, the military director of the project, who, correctly as it turned out, feared that British-sponsored scientists might be security risks). Churchill vehemently insisted that the British and Americans should tell no one, and managed to get Roosevelt's agreement. Perhaps Roosevelt, like other American non-scientists, felt that the uncooperative attitude appearing on Stalin's part, especially over Poland, compelled the retention of the British and American technical lead, at least as a possible bargaining counter. At any rate, the British and American governments gave no word to Stalin until Truman, with deliberate casualness, told him on 24 July 1945 that the United States had a new weapon of great destructive power. Stalin replied equally casually that he hoped the Americans would make 'good use of it against the Japanese'. We do not know how much Stalin already knew, but it is probable that he was well-informed and had already given high priority to research in the Soviet Union.

Vice-President Truman knew nothing of the bomb when Roosevelt died suddenly on 12 April 1945, yet he had to decide what to do with it. That evening, Stimson mentioned it to the new President, and James Byrnes who, as Director of the Office of War Mobilization, had learnt of it from Roosevelt, told him more the next day. Stimson had been, from the start, the Cabinet minister responsible for the development of the atom bomb, and as Secretary for War he was well acquainted with American strategy in the Pacific. One other made up the centre of the group on whom Truman relied for advice on this most serious of issues: General Marshall, the Chief of Staff of the United States army, who, by ability and personality, dominated American military counsels in the Second World War. A conscientious, humanely-inclined conservatism coloured the attitudes of Stimson and Marshall. Single-handed, and against strong disagreement from those who thought it a perfect target to demonstrate the effects of atomic bombing, Stimson saved the historic city of Kyoto from the fate of Hiroshima. As for Marshall, when Groves gave him the news of Hiroshima, he 'expressed his feelings that we should guard against too much gratification because it undoubtedly involved a large number of Japanese casualties'. Byrnes, the politician, worried more about relations with Russia than about defeating Japan, and thought of the bomb as a means of strengthening American post-war diplomacy rather than as a means of killing Japanese. None of these people thought of the bomb as an implement of retribution.

On 25 April 1945 Stimson and General Groves, the administrative head of the atomic programme, fully briefed the President, who agreed that a committee should be set up to consider the problem of the post-war use and control of atomic energy. In practice it also considered how to use the bomb to force Japan's surrender. A uranium-235 bomb would be ready about 1 August and could be used without prior test; a plutonium bomb would be ready for testing early in July, and one should be ready for use early in August. One influential American believed that the war with Japan could be ended at once: Joseph Grew, formerly ambassador in Tokyo and now acting Secretary of State, thought the Japanese should be told that 'unconditional surrender' would not lead to the ruin of their society and economy and that the Emperor could remain on his throne. Grew hoped to strengthen the conservatively minded Japanese civilian statesmen and the more cautious-minded among senior officers, serving and retired, especially in the navy, against the fanatically bellicose army, especially the younger and middle-grade staff officers. As Japan descended into disaster, conservatives there wished to reverse the violent foreign policies pursued since 1931 and to restore a world in which aggressive trading would replace armed conquest as the essential tool of Japanese aspirations. Kido, the Lord Privy Seal, whose access to the Emperor made him the key member of the peace party, and senior statesmen such as Shigemitsu, Konoe, and Togo wanted peace. They hardly dared say so. Wartime convention dictated noisy affirmation of belief in victory, and rational analysis was called 'defeatism' or 'treason'. Moreover, some army officers were ready to arrest or murder anyone inclined to peace. Army staff officers asserted that an honourable peace, by which they meant one maintaining the prestige of the army, was more likely *after* an invasion of the home islands. They expected to kill and wound a large number of Americans and to win tactical victories. Then a compromise peace might be made or, if not, Japan would be 'purified' by a suicidal defence and the restoration of civilian values would somehow be prevented. On their side, civilian conservatives feared that revolution might be the outcome of protracted and painful defeat. American bombing, food shortages, and what they thought to be the weakness of civilian morale exacerbated their fears. They wanted to prevent the radical army leaders from ruining the Japanese state in preference to accepting defeat. To check the army they looked to the Emperor for support.

Grew managed to get a presidential statement which Truman included in his declaration on Germany's defeat on 8 May 1945: he followed his insistence that 'Our blows will not cease until the Japanese military and naval forces lay down their arms in unconditional surrender', by a conciliatory explanation of 'unconditional surrender':

It means the termination of the influence of the military leaders who have brought Japan to the present brink of disaster. It means provision for the return of soldiers and sailors to their families, their farms, their jobs. It means not prolonging the present agony and suffering of the Japanese in the vain hope of victory. Unconditional surrender does not mean the extermination or enslavement of the Japanese people.

Grew hoped for an explicit statement that the Emperor could remain, and he urged the idea in the next weeks. At the end of May, Truman seemed sympathetic, but Marshall vetoed it because to make any concession to the Japanese during the savage fighting on Okinawa might strengthen their morale. He felt that a concession should be postponed until the Americans were strengthened by possession of the atom bomb.

Hence the Declaration of Potsdam, agreed on by Churchill, Stalin, and Chiang Kai-shek, came on 26 July after the trial of the plutonium bomb in New Mexico and after the U-235 bomb was ready for use. This threatened the employment of 'might . . . immeasurably greater than that which when applied to resisting Nazis, necessarily laid waste to the lands, the industry, and the method of life of the whole German people', and warned of 'prompt and utter destruction', but promised that after an allied occupation of Japan there would be established 'in accordance with the freely expressed will of the Japanese people a peacefully inclined and responsible government'. Too many dissenting voices prevented an explicit American promise to retain the Emperor. The whole system of government, including the Emperor, had been condemned with such violence that to suggest, with victory in sight, that the Emperor might not be too bad after all, risked suggesting the understandably unpopular thought that the war to that extent had been pointless.

On 28 July, Suzuki, the supposedly moderate Japanese Prime Minister, announced that the government would ignore the Potsdam Declaration. A gulf separated the peace desired by the Americans—occupation, loss of all Japanese territories outside the home islands, no absolute promise of retention of the throne—from what the Japanese government, even in July 1945, still hoped to hear. They looked for the help of the Soviet Union. In return for territorial concessions to Russia, the Japanese government apparently believed that Stalin might work with Japan to moderate American demands. This illusion, based on the perception of strains in the anti-German alliance which blinded Japanese diplomacy to the evident truth that Stalin could more securely make gains in the east with the United States than with Japan, kept Japanese diplomacy futilely occupied until the moment of the Russian declaration of war on Japan on 8 August 1945.

Suzuki's reply to the Potsdam warning confirmed Truman and his advisers in the belief that even a comparatively moderate Japanese government needed to be shocked into surrender. The Russian declaration of war, which Stalin, on 28 May, predicted for early August, was to be one shock. The other was the atom bomb. The committee approved by Truman to consider its use began a two-day meeting on 31 May 1945. The scientists pressed for disclosure to the Soviet Union to try to get co-operation in international control. General Marshall was sympathetic, though sceptical about Russian willingness to agree to inspection, and suggested inviting Russian observers to the plutonium bomb test. Byrnes opposed this, and wished to defend and exploit an American tactical monopoly, whose duration he overestimated. He already showed interest in the bomb as a weight in the Russo-American balance of power, and consequently was keen to show it off soon.

The committee considered a demonstration of the power of the bomb in some unpopulated spot. Two difficulties arose: that of finding an unpopulated area in which damage would be suitably impressive, and that of the slight risk of failure of the bomb, which would increase rather than destroy Japanese will to fight. The same argument applied to advance warning of the use of the bomb against a city. Moreover, the Japanese might shoot down the single aircraft carrying the bomb. The committee recommended, therefore, that the bomb should be used without warning against a military target in a densely populated area. The scientists, however, were encouraged to continue to study the possibility of an effective demonstration, sparing loss of life. Pressure came from scientists outside the committee to avoid direct use, but the scientific panel of the committee could still think of 'no technical demonstration likely to bring an end to the war'. Orders went out even before the Potsdam Declaration on 25 July, Marshall sent approval, from Potsdam, of a message to Spaatz: 'the 509th Composite Group, 20th Air Force, will deliver its first special bomb as soon as weather will permit visual bombing after about 3 August 1945 on one of the targets: Hiroshima, Kokura, Niigata and Nagasaki . . . additional bombs will be delivered on the above targets as soon as made ready.' Unless Japan surrendered soon, the explosive and fire-bombs raining on Japanese towns from the air and the shells thrown at the coast by American and British warships, now sailing at will off Japan, undisturbed by the suicide pilots whom the Japanese were hoarding for the final battle, would be reinforced by 'the basic power of the universe'. There was to be no pause in the terror. Meanwhile, the Japanese Foreign Minister instructed Sato, ambassador in Moscow, to persuade Stalin to receive a special envoy from Tokyo.

The weather was bad over Japan at the beginning of August, but the forecast on 5 August suggested clear weather for the next day. Early on 6 August, three B-29s set off from Tinian to Hiroshima. At 7 a.m. the sky there was reported mainly clear. At 8.15 a.m. the bomb was released at 32,000 feet. After 45 seconds it exploded about 2,000 feet above Hiroshima. In Washington, a presidential statement threatened the Japanese people with 'a rain of ruin from the air, the like of which has never been seen on this earth'. On 8 August, Togo and Emperor Hirohito agreed that the war must end, and the Potsdam terms be accepted. Later, news came that the Soviet Union had declared war.

Next day the Supreme Council assembled: Suzuki, the Prime Minister, Togo, Foreign Minister, Yonai, Navy Minister, Anami, War Minister, Umezu, Army Chief of Staff, and Toyoda, Navy Chief of Staff. Suzuki and Yonai supported Togo's proposal to surrender provided the Emperor's position was preserved; the other three wanted to reject American demands for military occupation and war-crimes trials and to fight on. At this stage news came of the destruction of Nagasaki by the second atomic bomb. At the end of protracted debate, Suzuki went to the Emperor and proposed that an imperial conference should be called. At midnight there was a peaceful *coup d'état*. Custom demanded that ministers should present the Emperor only agreed recommendations; now Suzuki asked the Emperor himself to decide. Hirohito read a prepared statement concluding that, 'we must bear the unbearable' and agree to Togo's suggestion. At 3 a.m. the full cabinet met and agreed to the imperial decision: the rules had been reversed for the Emperor's correct role was to approve cabinet decisions.

Early on 10 August, cables went via Berne and Stockholm to the allied capitals offering to accept the Potsdam Declaration provided the 'prerogatives' of the Emperor remained. Rapid deliberation in Washington, followed by quick discussion with the British, Chinese, and Soviet governments permitted the reply to reach Tokyo on 12 August. It insisted that the Emperor and the Japanese government would be subordinate to the allied command of occupation forces, but that the Japanese people would eventually decide on their form of government. Truman stopped strategic bombing. The Japanese army tried again. On 13 August, Anami, Umezu, and Toyoda demanded rejection of the Potsdam demands as newly interpreted. On the morning of 14 August the Emperor summoned an imperial conference. The delay caused the American air force to be unleashed again, and B-29s, without loss to themselves, destroyed half of one middle-sized Japanese town, one-fifth of another, and attacked five further targets. After listening to the three dissidents, the Emperor desired his ministers to accept the allied demands. Some middle-ranking officers attempted that night to seize power and 'rescue' the Emperor from 'treacherous counsels': they got no help from War Minister Anami, who led the way to acquiescence in the Emperor's will before his own ceremonial suicide, thus doing nothing to foil the long-matured exploitation of the Emperor's sympathies by the civilian advocates of peace. It is hard to decide whether it was the atom bomb or the Russian declaration of war that enabled the Emperor to act as he did. Probably it was the conventional bombing, followed by Hiroshima—the Emperor himself cited 'a new and most cruel bomb'. Next day, 15 August, the Emperor, in the third act of his temporary seizure of the reality of sovereign power that was theoretically his, broadcast to the nation. The Second World War was over.

15

From war to peace: Anglo-American relations

In the summer of 1944, for the last time, the Anglo-American partnership remained superficially equal. More British than American soldiers were fighting the Germans and Japanese. Against Germany, the RAF contributed as much as the USAAF and the Royal Navy still played the larger part. The same numbers of British and Americans made the initial landings in Normandy. By the time Germany was defeated things looked different. In the first half of 1944 the British people saw with awe, and sometimes envy, the signs of the national wealth of America in the equipment of their troops and their superior pay and comfort. In 1945 the self-dramatization of Field Marshal Montgomery could not hide the shrinkage of his command to a small sector of the front. In the war against Japan, the successes of British and Indian troops in Burma now belonged to a side-show, and the late contribution of the Royal Navy to the main attack, though significant, was clearly subordinate, while the RAF never joined in the obliteration of Japanese towns.

Yet the British people felt themselves citizens of a victorious great power, the centre of an Empire whose devotion to the mother country, or to the King-Emperor, had been shown in the past six years in many well-publicized ways. They felt the merit of their survival as the only undefeated country to have fought against Nazi Germany from the beginning and believed themselves, not without reason, to be admired by the western Europeans, eagerly reaching for leadership from so successful a democracy. The British military dominated allied affairs in the Mediterranean, Africa, Greece, the Near East, India, Burma, and at the end of the war, in much of France, Belgium, the Netherlands (together with the Canadians), Denmark, and Norway, and were poised to retake Malaya and Singapore and to receive the surrender of the Japanese in the Dutch East Indies and southern Indo-China. At Potsdam, Attlee and Bevin smoothly inherited the roles of Churchill and Eden as spokesmen for one of the Big Three. In 1945, most citizens of Britain, and many Cabinet ministers, exaggerated its ability to remain an independent world power. Past economic strength blinded them to the financial constraints which reflected the lack of the resources of a superpower. Keynes, who devoted the last two years of his life to financial negotiation with the United States, observed:

All our reflex actions are those of a rich man . . . The financial problems of war have been surmounted so easily and so silently that the average man sees no reason to suppose that the financial problems of the peace will be any more difficult.

In reality, lend-lease compromised British independence in wartime, and the end of the war, with the abrupt end of lend-lease, left Britain insolvent. In November 1944, for instance, an Anglo-American quarrel, typical of the disputes brought by the approach of peace, caused Roosevelt to show his teeth. The American civil air transport companies wanted deregulation of international air routes; the British wanted some degree of market-sharing, particularly because of the wartime agreement that British aircraft production should be entirely military, leaving transport aircraft to be developed in the United States. Roosevelt sent a message to Churchill:

We are doing our best to meet your lend-lease needs. We will face Congress on that subject in a few weeks and it will not be in a generous mood if it and the people feel that the United Kingdom has not agreed to a generally beneficial air agreement.

This threat came at the time of the worst Anglo-American discord of the war years. As victory seemed near, Americans thought Britain to be an obstacle to the creation of a world of harmonious international co-operation to secure peace, prosperity, and democracy. Churchill and the British they felt to be concerned with spheres of interest and balance of power, risking international co-operation and consensus, too preoccupied with the politics and economics of Empire, unduly ready to collaborate with reactionary conservative forces. They showed their feelings over a series of issues in 1944 and 1945: Argentina, Greece, Italy, and Palestine raised particularly vicious conflicts. On the broadest issues, United States policy detached itself from British. Before and during meetings of the 'Big Three' at Yalta and Potsdam, Roosevelt and Truman declined to join with the British in a shared position towards the Soviet Union: 'ganging up on the Russians', they argued, would forfeit Soviet sympathy, though they sometimes found themselves forced into it. At this time, they showed no sympathy for British imperial links. Roosevelt demeaned himself at Yalta by toadying towards Stalin. On 4 February 1945 he 'hoped that Marshal Stalin would again propose a toast to the execution of 50,000 officers of the German army', a grim *plaisanterie* which had already aroused Churchill's disgusted protest. A few days later Churchill reacted violently to the idea of international 'machinery' for dealing 'with territorial trusteeship and dependent areas'. The American record reads:

He said that under no circumstances would he ever consent to forty or fifty nations thrusting interfering fingers into the life's existence of the British Empire. As long as he was Minister, he would never yield one scrap of their heritage. He continued in this vein [the report goes on], for several minutes.

The State Department in Washington believed that British eagerness to make a long-term contract for meat supply with Argentina implied British support for an anti-American pro-Fascist regime in an area where American wishes should come first. United States producers could easily supply meat, but the British feared yet greater dependence on the United States and refused to risk the alienation of a reliable future customer. Once again Roosevelt allowed the whip to be cracked: a meat contract with Argentina 'would have repercussions in the press, in public discussion, and in Congress at a most unfortunate time' (that is, when lend-lease appropriations were considered). The fact that the British went ahead reduced the likelihood of generous handling of lend-lease after the end of the German war.

Italy led to a public American rebuke to the British. There the State Department objected to a private British veto on the possible appointment, as Foreign Minister, of Count Sforza, whom Churchill believed to be intriguing with left-wing forces. In Washington, the State Department announced 'We expect the Italians to work out their problems of government along democratic lines without influence from outside', and then extended its complaint to Greece, where the British had sent in the army to hold back armed Communist guerrillas: 'This policy would apply to an even more pronounced degree with regard to governments of the United Nations in their liberated territories.' An American observer at allied headquarters in the Mediterranean reported British reactions: they ask that Americans 'resist a temptation to lecture the British from a pulpit of moral superiority', and that they 'should not take this opportunity of abusing them as anti-democratic reactionaries up to old imperialist games, brutally suppressing the spontaneous and popular will of the Greek people'.

Palestine aroused still more emotion after the end of the German war, when surviving Jews wished to seek a new home there. The British authorities refused to allow unrestricted immigration, fearful of Arab reactions. The result was a Jewish campaign of terror against the British in Palestine, followed by British repression and American outrage. A New York representative voted against the post-war British loan, to deny 'money for the British that would be used to support soldiers to maim and strafe innocent people in Palestine'.

Lend-lease had been intended only to meet war-time needs, and the Americans restricted it after the German war to avoid its assisting Britain's post-war economic recovery. Then, to everyone's surprise, President Truman legalistically ordered its complete end only two days after the Japanese surrender. The British economy gasped for breath.

The war had caused three weaknesses: before lend-lease began, British foreign investments had had to be sold to pay for imported food and munitions from the United States; in order to meet military costs abroad, and to finance imports from sterling countries, huge debts had piled up from Britain to sterling area countries; and to increase British arms manufacture the volume of export production had gone down to 30 per cent of pre-war. Britain's liabilities increased and assets fell; foreign earnings diminished while expenses abroad swelled. At the end of the war, Britain was spending about £2,100 million per annum more than came in from foreign receipts; (1945 figures should be multiplied 20 to 25 times to give approximate equivalents at the end of the 1980s). The United States, if lend-lease had continued for the whole year, would have provided £1,100 million, Canada £250 million and loans from the sterling area (in increased sterling balances) £750 million. Even assuming a surge in exports and the end of the wartime need for weapons, and that the British people would live no better than they had done in the later years of the war, a deficit of about £1,000 million was expected in 1946. Keynes told the Cabinet, in August 1945, 'that there is no source from which we can raise sufficient funds to enable us to live and spend on the scale we contemplate except the United States'. Brand, the British Treasury representative in Washington, commented: 'We have to continue to pose . . . as equal partners with the US and USSR, but have to tell the former we can't pay our bills.'

The British faced two alternatives. One was drastically to reduce overseas spending, to withdraw British troops from abroad, to give up bases, to leave Greece, to run down the occupation of the British zone in Germany, that is to abandon great power pretensions, and at the same time to restrict British importers to purchases from those countries whose currency could most easily be secured, as well as restricting total imports by further reducing British standards of living. Keynes called this option 'starvation corner'. The other was to persuade the United States to cover the British external deficit until British exports had grown sufficiently. Keynes led the team sent to Washington to do this. He felt confident in the force of his two arguments. One, however, carried more conviction in London than in Washington: that for two years the Americans left the British to fight the Nazis and that the British had, throughout the war, contributed a proportionately greater effort than the Americans. Americans thought, on the other hand, that the United States had chivalrously come to the assistance of a friend in danger, that they had decisively contributed to victory in two world wars, and that they deserved grateful thanks rather than the presentation of a British account for British services rendered. The second argument, though, convinced knowledgeable Americans that a bankrupt Britain would inhibit the creation of the world they wished to see. They wanted a world free for trade and investment, without discrimination or monopoly. This would benefit the mature capitalist economy of the United States, advance peace, and bring greater prosperity for all. A bankrupt Britain, defensively distorting trade patterns to shelter its economic debility, would make the new world unattainable. A Britain strong enough to abate preferences for its imperial partners, and to allow free convertibility of its currency, was worth paying for; indeed, if necessary, American financial strength might be employed to force a Britain, refreshed by dollar credit, to follow the paths of economic rectitude. Hence, the American loan had conditions: 4,400 million dollars, with interest and with a British promise to make current British earnings from foreign trade convertible into dollars one year after the credit came into effect.

The British signed the agreement in December 1945, grumbling at the failure of the United States to recognize British wartime virtue and to make a free gift as an extension of the writing-off of lend-lease. Yet only in July 1946 did the loan get through Congress, amidst complaints of self-seeking British exploitation of American generosity. The loan passed, not as a generous gesture to the British, but on arguments of self-interest. One of the American negotiators explained to a Congressional committee, 'this loan is to increase international trade' and so 'open the markets of England and many other countries to our exporters'. Another argument increasingly influenced the well-informed: in March 1946, for instance, Admiral Leahy, the President's Chief of Staff, told Byrnes, Secretary of State, that the 'defeat or disintegration of the British Empire would eliminate from Eurasia the last bulwark of resistance between the

United States and Soviet expansion'. This argument did not yet appeal to many Americans: when Churchill that month spoke of 'an iron curtain' which had 'descended across the continent' of Europe, and accused the Soviet Union of seeking 'the indefinite expansion of their power and doctrines', he stirred up instant disapproval of his call for a 'special relationship between the British Commonwealth and Empire and the United States'. At this moment two phases overlapped in the evolving attitudes of Americans. The President, senior officials, and soldiers were in the second phase of post-war American attitudes to Britain; most of the public was still in the first. The former group already believed that the United States should sustain British influence, strength, and prosperity; the latter still perceived Britain and the British Empire as an obstacle to international understanding, free trade, and democracy. Soon, growing fear of the Soviet Union transformed Churchill into a revered prophet. American officials and senior soldiers changed their view first, mostly in 1945, as the hopes of Yalta became fainter; Congress and the public followed more slowly.

In the years between Germany's defeat and the growth of fear of Russia, the Anglo-American relationship seemed one of quarrels and of ill-feeling. In these years, however, the disputes were still the quarrels of intimacy. A significant number of Americans disliked and suspected the British; some in Britain remained supercilious, or resentfully envious, or both; yet at all levels of society friendship and trust remained to a degree unequalled between foreign nations. Indeed, it was difficult for British citizens, on whom various nationalities had impinged after 1939, to think of Americans as truly foreign. Generally, the two nations shared common purposes and differed only on means. Even American aspirations for free trade and universal self-determination were shared by most British, however drastically they might differ on the ways of reaching these goals. Officials and the military often came to treat their allied colleagues as if barriers of nationality did not exist, and British and Americans struggled together against other British or Americans. Even in the worst moments of the negotiations for the American loan, Keynes felt able to write of the Americans he dealt with:

We are working in an atmosphere of great friendliness and an intense desire to work something out to our advantage. The governing group, as I see it, with ready access to the White House, who can be pretty sure of influencing the President in the long run, very clearly intend to do their best for us.

Asked their opinions of the 'English' by army psychologists, three-quarters of representative samples of ordinary American soldiers consistently expressed favourable views, even in June 1944 when they had been disembarked in millions into a strained and underfed community. One of these new Anglophiles, an American bomber pilot, wrote home from East Anglia, 'In spite of the bad manners of the Americans, I have never heard a word of complaint from the English'. From the enforced co-operation of the war years emerged a surprising degree of mutual friendship. Congressional opinion, reflecting public opinion at home, was often much less favourable. Post-war American public-opinion polls consistently showed strong opposition to a loan to Britain. It seems that the Americans who knew the British best came to like them the most. The same applied to the British. In spite of the bickerings of politicians and generals, and the occasional brawls of soldiers, mutual good will and trust burgeoned in the war years and survived, amongst those who had worked together, for many years to come.

16

From alliance to Cold War: the Soviet Union and the West

THE Grand Alliance of the British Empire, the Soviet Union, and the United States, won the war. At times, the western allies and Soviet Russia feared that the other side might attempt an understanding with the Germans. Hitler's well-proven untrustworthiness ruled this out unless he and the Nazis were first removed from power, but even then each side could only have risked an alliance with a German regime completely committed to it, either a liberal democracy or a Communist state. Without such a regime, a break in the Grand Alliance would simply put Germany in a position to accept escalating bids for her support from both sides. In consequence, neither side could risk collaboration with Germany until the Nazis were overthrown; neither side could risk separate offers to potential successors of the Nazi regime before it had disappeared, for fear of prematurely destroying the coalition. No one in Germany, as it turned out, could overthrow the Nazis without such offers (and almost certainly not with any offers that either the western allies or the Soviet Union could make).

Hitler kept the alliance together: would it survive him? Continued co-operation between the wartime allies could secure world peace, and in Britain and the United States (and very likely in the Soviet Union too) most people hoped that the three powers would agree on the future organization of mankind throughout the world. The three powers would act together, perhaps with China and France, to keep the peace, and each one of the great powers would supervise the application of agreed principles in particular parts of the world. The unpopular alternative was the division of the world into spheres of interest within each of which the Big Three (or perhaps the five) would impose their untrammelled will, spheres which might be defined by agreement, or as the outcome of open or implied threats of war. The first unmistakable and public evidence that the last outcome threatened what was later known as the 'Cold War' came when the Red Army reached the outskirts of Warsaw in July 1944.

At the end of that month German civilians began to leave Warsaw. General calls to revolt, which the Russians, or their Polish supporters, regularly issued, became specifically addressed to Warsaw in a direct appeal to insurrection in the city made on 28 July 1944. On 1 August armed Polish resistance fighters seized control of parts of Warsaw and attacked the German occupying forces. The revolt was begun and led by Poles who did not support the Russians. They belonged to the Home Army, loyal to the Polish government in exile in London rather than to the Russian-sponsored Polish Committee of National Liberation set up in Lublin when the Red Army arrived. The Soviet government seemed indecisive. It must have been well aware that the object of the leaders of the revolt was to reduce Russian influence in liberated Poland by taking power ahead of the Red Army, and it knew that their views on the future territory and government of Poland were quite opposed to its own. Most Poles, especially among those influential in London, objected to losing Polish territory east of the Curzon Line, the draft frontier of 1919, and insisted on the frontier imposed after the Polish victory over the Red Army in 1920. They had no desire to see a Polish government amenable to Russian wishes, whereas Stalin insisted on a 'friendly' Polish government and the Curzon Line. On the other hand, the Home Army in Warsaw was fighting bravely against heavy odds and, at first, against some of the most barbaric and undisciplined of German-controlled forces. To abandon men and women engaged in fierce combat with the Germans would commend the Soviet government neither to Western opinion nor to Poles. At first Stalin promised air supply to the Poles, then refused all assistance, but later he relented and ordered supplies to be dropped from the air and even committed Polish ground forces, associated with the Lublin Poles, to attempt to relieve Warsaw.

Two things struck Western opinion: Soviet denunciations of the Polish insurgents as 'reckless and criminal adventurers', and the Russian refusal, until very late, to allow United States or British aircraft (including Polish squadrons serving with the RAF) to land on Soviet airfields after they had dropped supplies on Warsaw. Encouraged by the Polish government in London, many suspected, almost certainly wrongly, that Stalin had ordered the Red Army not to attack Warsaw so that German troops could crush the Home Army there.

The Warsaw rising succeeded in one respect, in advertising Russian policies towards Poland. Otherwise it was a total defeat for the Polish insurgents. Once the Germans had decided to hold Warsaw, the Home Army faced defeat whatever it did. If it remained passive and failed to fight the Germans, it would lose Polish support to the rival resistance movement, the Russian-sponsored People's Army, while if it rose in revolt it was foredoomed to be crushed or to be rescued by the Russians. If the Germans decided to stay, it could not seize Warsaw and then open the gates of a self-liberated Polish-run capital city to the Red Army. The Germans did decide to stay, and inflicted a crippling defeat on the Home Army which culminated in the surrender of the Poles on 4 October, after weeks of desperate struggle. Probably about one quarter of the total strength of the Home Army, of about 200,000, had been in Warsaw. Most of them had no weapons, and the loss of its 5,000 or so armed soldiers, together with the deaths of up to 200,000 inhabitants of Warsaw, drastically weakened the underground state and its ability to resist the Soviet-sponsored Lublin Committee.

The sufferings of Warsaw roused sympathy in the west, especially in Britain, where many people remembered that in 1939, too, Poland had received little support from her allies. It did so more effectively than the discovery, in 1943, that thousands of Polish army officers, missing since 1939, had been shot by the Russians at Katyn, for reasons still unknown, a discovery publicly brushed aside in Britain and America as a German propaganda trick. However, in spite of the Warsaw rising, Churchill, although he was more concerned than Roosevelt about what became of Poland, attempted to secure for the London Poles nothing more than the best terms of surrender to Russian wishes.

On 26 April 1943, complaining of Polish requests for an impartial inquiry into the Katyn murders, the Soviet government broke diplomatic relations with the London Polish government, and on 27 July 1944, Moscow recognized the Lublin Committee as the 'only lawful organ of executive power'. It was dominated by the Communists, Bierut and Gomulka, with Osobka-Morawski, a non-Communist socialist who provided a respectable front. Thus, the Soviet government claimed Poland for its post-war sphere of control. Churchill swallowed the resentment he felt at the embarrassing Russian refusal to help the Warsaw rising. He could do so because he blamed the intransigence of the London Poles for Russian hostility. The British government had repeatedly urged them to accept the Curzon Line as the new eastern frontier of Poland and cede vast tracts of pre-war Poland to the Soviet Union. Churchill and Eden thought that, if the Poles did this, there was then a good chance that the Russians would tolerate at least a semi-independent Poland. These two British ministers flew to Moscow on 9 October for a visit of ten days, during which Churchill summoned the Polish Prime Minister, Mikolajczyk, and the Foreign Minister, Romer, from London and violently bullied them ('a decent but feeble lot of fools' in his words) in an attempt to get them to accept the Curzon Line and

POLAND: POST-WAR FRONTIERS

agree to merge with the Lublin Poles, 'the greatest villains imaginable'. Churchill made everything clear to Mikolajczyk: he told him he would not 'wreck the peace of Europe because of quarrels between Poles'.

Understandably Churchill found Stalin very friendly during their meetings: evidently the British allotted Poland to the Russian sphere, and the United States (represented by Harriman as 'observer') apparently made no objection. Churchill and Stalin, without Harriman, also carved up much of south-eastern Europe. Bizarrely expressing themselves, on Churchill's initiative, in percentages of predominance, Stalin and Molotov secured '90' per cent in Romania and '80' per cent in Hungary and Bulgaria, while Britain 'in accord with USA' secured '90' per cent in Greece. 'Predominance' in Yugoslavia was '50–50': perhaps neither side cared enough, or perhaps they recognized that Tito and the Yugoslav partisans, who controlled substantial areas, might have a word to say. Mikolajczyk did not give in. He suggested to Churchill that Britain, America, and Russia should impose a settlement on the Poles but refused to ease the way by simulating voluntary acceptance. Churchill and Roosevelt had their public opinions to consider but so did Mikolajczyk. Back in London he resigned, and was succeeded by a London Polish government even more hostile than himself to compromise over the frontier and with the Lublin Poles. In January 1945, the Soviet Union recognized the latter as the provisional government of Poland and, as the Red Army resumed its advance, installed it in Warsaw. There followed armed attacks on the 'London' Polish Home Army in Poland by Russian troops and Communist-controlled Polish forces.

The fate of Poland loomed large in inter-allied debates at the two great meetings of 1945 which organized the post-war world: in February, when Stalin, Roosevelt, and Churchill met at Yalta in the Crimea; and in August, when Stalin, Truman, and Churchill (until he was replaced by Attlee) met at Potsdam. It indicated why three-power collaboration to rule the world was impossible, and how it was that the partition of Europe and Asia, though successfully accomplished in the end, went with strife, suspicion, and fears of war. In retrospect, it seems that the 'Big Three' could easily and amicably have arranged the spheres of influence that eventually grew from the military and political events of the war, except in Germany. The difficulty in organizing spheres of influence came from the Anglo-American side. Stalin appears to have postponed world revolution indefinitely and to have limited himself in the immediate future to the building and defence of 'socialism in one country'. A main object of the rulers of the Soviet Union, therefore, seems to have been to gain security from external threats by extending Russian influence over neighbouring countries. Their post-war ambitions were geographically limited. The Americans, and, with reservations, the British, insisted on the applicability everywhere of the principles of the 'Atlantic Charter'. This called for democracy, in the Western sense of universal suffrage, free elections of representative legislative assemblies with members drawn from competing political parties, freedom of expression for minorities, together with the removal of barriers to trade and investment, and respect for rights of property. In Poland the objectives of the Anglo-Americans and of the Soviet Union were incompatible. No genuinely democratic Polish government (in the Western sense) could be relied on to pursue foreign and defence policies acceptable to the Soviet Union. Since Poland mattered most of all to Russian security against future invasion, the Soviet rulers insisted in practice (whatever they said), that Russian wishes must override Polish aspirations and Poland be placed firmly in the Russian sphere.

A friendly partition would have recognized Russian control of Poland as a natural consequence of the Red Army's presence. Elsewhere, by the end of 1944, important pieces of the eventual unfriendly partition of

Europe were already in place. The British and Americans took care to exclude the Russians from any effective share in running the parts of Italy they conquered, while in Greece, British troops landed, after the Germans departed, and fought to keep the Communist-organized section of the Greek Resistance out of power. The western allies, however, could not repay Stalin's tolerance of those assertions of their own claims to dominance by demonstrating corresponding detachment from Polish affairs. Neither Roosevelt nor Truman could maintain American support for involvement in international affairs while bargaining for an old-fashioned balance of power. They had to insist on the universal application of the principles of 'democracy', a word whose meaning varied between Moscow and Washington. The British thought the Poles to be brave fighters against Germany, who had resisted when the Soviet government was in league with the Nazis, and whose true feelings, they believed, were represented by Polish spokesmen in London. At Yalta, Churchill supported Poland with his best oratory: 'The sovereign independence and freedom of Poland . . . is dear to the hearts of the nation of Britain . . . our most earnest desire which we care about as much as our lives is that Poland be mistress in her own house and in her own soul.' The 'London Poles' eloquently emphasized the unrepresentative character of the 'Lublin Poles'. British and American sympathy went out to the heroes of the Warsaw rising. At the end of the war, by contrast, the British and American governments calmly accepted, with hardly a grumble, the incorporation of Latvia, Estonia, and Lithuania in the Soviet Union following their forceful seizure in 1940. The British and American public cared about Poland but easily forgot the Baltic states.

At Yalta, at what Churchill called 'the crucial point of this great conference', the three powers agreed that the Russian Foreign Minister, Molotov, and the British and American ambassadors in Moscow should arrange for the reorganization of the 'Lublin' government on a 'broader democratic basis with the inclusion of democratic leaders from Poland itself and from Poles abroad'. The three agreed that the Curzon Line should be the new Polish frontier, and that Poland must gain substantial territory from Germany. The expanded Polish government would be pledged to the 'holding of free and unfettered elections as soon as possible on the basis of universal suffrage and secret ballot'. 'All democratic and anti-Nazi parties' were to have the right to put forward candidates. Churchill and Roosevelt promised to shift recognition from the Polish government in London to the afforced provisional government in

Warsaw. In Moscow things went very slowly. The Warsaw Poles and the Russians took a long time to swallow Mikolajczyk as the price of Western recognition. Presumably the Russian military command was seeking a substitute in their talks, late in March 1945, with fifteen Polish under-ground leaders, including the former chief of the Home Army. However, the talks failed and the Russians promptly imprisoned the Poles as a preliminary to trying them for 'treason'. In April, Stalin told Churchill he would use his influence to get his Warsaw Poles to approve Mikolajczyk, once the latter had accepted the Yalta conditions, that is, the Curzon Line. On 6 July 1945 formal British and American recognition was transferred from the London Polish government to the newly expanded government, which included Mikolajczyk and four of his supporters.

Soon afterwards the Big Three met at Potsdam. At lunch alone with President Truman on the second day, Churchill raised the question, 'Were all those States which had passed into Russian control to be free and independent, or not?' According to him, 'the President attached great importance to this, and evidently intends to press with severity the need of this true independence in accordance with free, full, and unfettered elections'. Stalin was reassuring: and told Churchill that:

in all the countries liberated by the Red Army the Russian policy was to see a strong, independent, sovereign state. He was against sovietization of any of those countries. They would have free elections, and all except Fascist parties would participate.

There was not much the western allies could do to make sure of it. The British Foreign Office thought the captured German fleet was their best card: 'we should only give the Russians part of the fleet in return for some comparable concession'. Stalin brushed this aside by asserting that Russia had a right to a share. Ernest Bevin did better, in the closing stage of the conference, as the new Labour Foreign Secretary. Without asking their allies, the Russians, having conquered that part of Germany between the old western Polish frontier and the Oder and western Neisse rivers, handed it all over to the Poles, who proceeded to expel the Germans that were left there and to settle Poles. Before giving British ratification Bevin confronted the Polish government, and on 31 July 1945 bullied out of Bierut, its Communist chairman, a promise of elections 'early in 1946 and possibly earlier'.

In fact, short of threatening a new war, it was hard to enforce such promises; on its side the US State Department hoped that Russian desire for post-war credits would give the United States power to influence

Soviet policy. In 1945, however, nothing came of this proposal, and the Soviet government proved unexpectedly ready to do without. US Secretary of State Byrnes's hope that the nuclear bomb would somehow make the Soviet Union more tractable proved equally false; no doubt the Russians knew that all-out war was not in question. In the end, the Polish 'elections' took place on 19 January 1947. It took time to prepare them. The Communists tried to get Mikolajczyk to accept a subordinate place for his party, the Polish Peasant Party, on a joint list. Mikolajczyk's demand for a fair share foiled these negotiations, and his insistence on standing as a separate party compelled the Communists to rig the election. They used the Polish army, so far as they could rely on it, their police force, and a newly recruited party militia to intimidate and bully, a process not altogether one-sided, since Resistance forces killed over 2,000 government officials in the year before the polling. On polling day, voting was rarely secret, the counting was generally carried out by the Communists, and the official 'result' was supplied by the Party. The 'democratic bloc' was allotted 80 per cent of the votes and Mikolajczyk's party 10 per cent. The best guess of the votes genuinely cast gives 20 per cent to the bloc and 70 per cent to Mikolajczyk's party. Mikolajczyk's hope that the Soviet Union would think it worthwhile, in pursuit of stability and good relations with the west, to tolerate freedom in Poland, had vanished, and he himself fled from Poland in October 1947.

Stalin told a Yugoslav delegation early in 1945: 'This war is not as in the past; whoever occupies the territory also imposes on it his own social system. Everyone imposes his own system as far as his army has power to do so.' In 1945, Bulgaria, Romania, Hungary, Poland, Albania, and the Baltic states were in the power of the Red Army, and the Soviet social system followed. Poland was the most striking victim: in the war from the first day, she had suffered terribly from the most murderous policies of the Nazis (and of the Soviet Union). Of all those countries, Poland fought hardest against the Germans but had most cause to dislike the Russians. There Stalin's proposition found its most dramatic application. In Yugoslavia, by contrast, Communist power rested on real local support derived from the most successful movement of resistance to Axis occupation of the war. Finland, the remaining state in the Russian sphere of influence in Europe, got off lightly and retained domestic independence at the price of international subservience and the cession of every strategic position desired by the Soviet Union. Czechoslovakia's wartime government in exile believed that it could retain a similar freedom: there, in the end, it was the strength of the domestic Communists that wrecked the calculation. Britain and the United States, on their side, were firm in their own application of Stalin's principle: France, Belgium, the Netherlands, Luxemburg, Italy, Norway, and Denmark (in Denmark the British made a special effort to arrive before the Red Army), were all set on the course of liberal democracy in 1945, and Greece was forcibly defended against Communism. Relations between east and west got worse partly because the western powers, though accepting it in practice, objected to partition in theory. The western allies said to the Soviet Union, in effect, 'where we conquer we control; where you conquer, you share control'.

Stalin and Molotov hit back by pointing to Italy, and to British action in Greece, but seem to have done so only to demonstrate how tolerant a good ally should be of the other allies' conduct in their spheres: at Yalta Stalin even made a joke of his own tolerance. When Roosevelt secured acceptance of the 'declaration on liberated Europe' under which the Big Three promised to set up authorities 'broadly representative of all democratic elements in the population', which would arrange for 'free elections of governments responsive to the will of the people', Molotov suggested the addition to the declaration that, 'support will be given to the political leaders of those countries who have taken an active part in the struggle against the German invaders'. Stalin teased Churchill by assuring him that this amendment did not apply to Greece, where British troops barred from political power the Communist leaders of the most active Greek resistance movement, and then reassured Churchill that on his side he respected spheres of influence: 'Marshal Stalin said he had complete confidence in British policy in Greece.' This was the same meeting at which the fate of Poland was settled and at which Molotov blocked the suggestion that the three ambassadors should observe and report on the 'free elections' there, 'since he felt certain this would be offensive to the Poles'.

Underneath the cynicism and humbug there lay a grave issue: the wartime allies were delimiting the influence of two ideologies. Verbal ambiguity facilitated agreement at Yalta and Potsdam and helps to explain the subsequent sense of betrayal. To a Marxist, 'free elections' conducted by 'democratic elements' to determine the 'will of the people' must necessarily produce Communist regimes. The 'masses', though perhaps deluded into subjective error, must 'objectively' wish for the brotherhood of mankind which the dictatorship of the proletariat, once it has brought the class struggle to its predestined end, will inevitably produce. True freedom lies in following the real will of mankind, advancing with the ineluctable tides of history, and therefore in following the leadership of those equipped to predict their movements, that is, members of soundly-constituted Communist parties. The economy would be organized by the state for the good of the people. Churchill, Attlee, Roosevelt, and Truman believed in government by parties or individuals, competing by means of unrestricted debate for votes, freely and secretly given by all male (and perhaps all female) adults. They believed in an economy actuated by market forces based on individual choice, restricted by greater or lesser state intervention to compensate for market imperfections and to help the unsuccessful and unlucky. During the war, western opinion was encouraged to think of the rulers of the Soviet Union as participants in a war for democracy and freedom against the right of the state to exact unquestioning obedience. It was a disquieting discovery, most dramatic in relation to Poland, that, to Soviet man, freedom meant unquestioning obedience.

However, western statesmen, having done their best, short of giving up any attempt to work with the Soviet Union, to secure the future of liberal democracy beyond the 'iron curtain' as Churchill described the frontier of the Soviet sphere of influence, put up with this frontier, accepted Soviet dominance beyond it, exchanged fulsome toasts with Stalin and his henchmen, clinked glasses, and went on negotiating. Alarmingly, Stalin sometimes showed symptoms of seeking even more and further extending his sphere. Two instances, strongly reminiscent of old-style Russian policies, upset British and American leaders in the closing months of the war. In northern Iran, Russian troops, there by agreement with Britain and the United States to organize and protect the supply lines used for the bulk of lend-lease aid to Russia, showed signs of settling in and of encouraging local dissidents, the Tudeh party, to help them to badger the Shah's government for oil concessions. From Turkey came news, in the spring of 1945, that Molotov had asked for Kars and Ardahan in the Caucasus, and worst of all, for a Russian base in the Straits. Nothing came of either: steady rejection by the British and Americans induced Russian retreat. British and American policy-makers drew two conclusions from 1945: that the Soviet Union would spread Communism and seize territory wherever possible, and that firmness was the best counter. More slowly than ministers and officials, sections of British and American public opinion also began to lose faith in Russian impeccability.

At the end of the war the problem of Germany held the Big Three together. They agreed that Germany should be kept whole and governed as a unity. Each of the three wanted this to make sure that the others pursued desirable objectives: this required three-power co-operation in governing a united Germany. Stalin wanted reparations for Russia to come from all Germany; the British and Americans wanted a modicum of economic revival in Germany to enable that payment of reparations to be made without causing Germany to become a financial and moral burden on the western powers. Both objects needed central planning. All three powers wished to maintain a single government of a united Germany; each wanted Germany to be run in different ways, dictated by their individual interests. The Cold War in Europe began, setting off the confrontation of the Berlin blockade, three years after the war, when the Soviet Union tried to force the western powers to continue the allied government of a united Germany to enable it to veto the priority the British and Americans gave to German economic revival. The Russian attempt to compel the maintenance of a united, but paralysed, central administration for Germany paradoxically brought about an enduring partition of it.

Representatives of the three powers had worked out a division of Germany (within its 1937 frontiers) into zones of military occupation, allotted to each of the three armies, with Berlin separately divided into three zones of occupation. The outline was evolved at the beginning of 1944, and proved, fortunately for east–west relations, to be close to the line the Russians and Anglo-American armies had reached when Germany surrendered. The Big Three ratified the arrangement at Yalta. The British, alarmed by the prospect of finding themselves alone with the Russians in Germany after the two years which Roosevelt announced at Yalta to be the limit of American occupation, successfully insisted on giving the French a fourth zone in West Germany and Berlin, both taken from the Anglo-American zones. The powers agreed to govern from Berlin, through an allied control commission headed by the military commanders of the four zones. Only at the Potsdam Conference, from which the French were excluded, did the three powers agree, with difficulty, on the objects of four-power government in Germany. The issues that soon shattered four-power government and led to the partition of Germany dominated the conference. The British and Americans pointed out that the transfer to the Poles by the Russians of part of their zone in East Germany would jeopardize the supply of food from the predominantly agricultural east to the industrialized west, and make unavailable coal from Upper Silesia. They feared, too, that the Russian demand for reparations (and, as everyone agreed, their reparations were to be in kind not in money) would make impossible the revival of industrial exporting from the western zones, especially from the Ruhr in the British zone, on a scale sufficient to finance necessary food imports. Moreover, most British economists thought it impossible for the European economy to recover if German economic activity were to be strangled by reparations. Byrnes, the American Secretary of State, worked out a compromise plan which formed the main result of the Potsdam Conference: Attlee and Truman agreed that the Poles should occupy the German territories they claimed, and in return, Stalin agreed to limit Russian demands for reparations from the western zones and to supply food and coal from the Russian and Polish zones to the west.

It was these issues that soon broke the hard-won consensus of 1945 between Russia and the British and Americans. Within three years the western powers had thrown off the Russian veto on their policies for economic recovery in their zones of Germany, and so rejected four-power control over a united Germany. The western powers insisted on reduced reparations, combined with higher levels of German industrial production than the Soviet Union wished to permit, and, to restore economic life in their zones, they created a new German currency which they introduced into the western zones without Russian consent. Stalin tried to reimpose four-power control and the Russian veto by the Berlin blockade. This time the tensions between east and west came from a Russian attempt to assert the right of the Soviet Union to intervene in the western sphere of influence. The outcome was, first to bring war into sight, and then to complete and make firm and lasting the partition of Europe into spheres of influence. The partition of Germany, which neither side wished for, but which both sides preferred to the other's conditions for unity, led to the erection of the most formidable frontier ever constructed. This section of the European line of partition split a national community. Movement between one part of Germany and the other, even sending letters and making telephone calls across the divide, became difficult or impossible. Families were split, lovers driven apart. The effects of the failure of the wartime allies to preserve the fragile Potsdam agreement and the joint rule of Europe hit Germans most drastically of all: one of the numerous dire consequences of the action of that minority of Germans who first put Hitler into power and destroyed the possibility of peaceful European evolution.

In the Far East, the defeat of Japan ended with a comfortably arranged partition between the United States and the Soviet Union, complicated by the immense problem of China. Roosevelt and the United States State Department committed themselves during the war to the notion that China was a great power, one of the Big Four. Indeed, both Roosevelt and Truman insisted that China should have a special place, as a great power, in the new world organization, the 'United Nations', which both of them believed to be the most effective device for forestalling a slide of the American people back to isolation and international irresponsibility: hence, with the British-sponsored addition of France, the appearance of the 'Big Five', each possessing a veto in the United Nations peace-keeping conciliabulum, the Security Council. The war cast doubt on the great power status of Kuomintang or 'Nationalist' China under 'General-issimo' Chiang Kai-shek. The KMT army showed itself, except for a few units trained and equipped by Americans, unable to fight the Japanese. In any case, the KMT leadership preferred to keep its army for a post-war confrontation with the Communists. Under the tactically shrewd leader-ship of Mao Tse-tung the prestige of the Communists steadily rose as the more effective fighting force. The KMT, deprived by the Japanese of the essential traditional sources of revenue from the traffic of seaports, and administratively too inefficient to develop effective alternative sources of revenue, relied on inflationary finance. The consequent dramatic rise of prices spread corruption among officers and officials as they defended their real incomes. At the top, large-scale corruption and misappropri-ation of American economic aid was commonplace. Even so, few observers expected the regime to crumble as rapidly as it did. At the end of the war, therefore, both the United States and the Soviet governments exhibited understandable uncertainty about the future of China. The Americans tried to avert civil war in China by persuading the Commun-ists, whose uncorrupt administration and careful search for support among poorer peasants slowly increased their power, to enter into some form of coalition government with the KMT. Stalin regarded with evident unease the independent, self-supporting Chinese Communist party whose subordination to Moscow could in no way be counted on. From the Soviet Union Mao got scant support, and American attempts to prop up the KMT failed in the years after the war because of the weakness of the Nationalists rather than as a result of Soviet intervention.

Elsewhere post-war partitioning went smoothly. As agreed at Yalta, the Soviet Union recovered what Russia had lost to the Japanese in 1905: South Sakhalin, the lease of Port Arthur, the running of the railways in Manchuria, as well as the Kurile Islands. The United States secured the Ryukus for military bases and the Navy Department insisted that they should be under exclusive American control. Surprisingly, the Russians accepted an undivided, American-dominated occupation of Japan. Apart from a claim to occupy Hokkaido and some objection to the American monopoly of control (through the viceregal figure of General MacArthur), both points apparently made by the Russians only to strengthen their negotiating positions elsewhere, they put little difficulty in the way of this far-reaching outcome of 1945. One section of the partition between Americans and Russians, however, proved a time-bomb. At the last moment, just before Japan's surrender, the American military recognized that they could not, except by agreement, take over any part of Korea before Russian troops arrived. They therefore proposed that the Russians should occupy north Korea down to the 38 degree parallel. The Russians accepted, and kept their pledge even though the whole of Korea was initially open to their advance. The two Franken-steins set up their own monsters in their respective zones—Syngman Rhee (free enterprise) in the south and Kim il Sung (socialism) in the north, and then lost control of them. Both the new states demanded a united Korea, and in 1950 Kim il Sung started the next big war to try to bring it about. The Korean War, perceived in the west as having been set off by Stalin, confirmed the belief that the partition of the world that followed the Second World War could be maintained only by armed strength, and so protracted and intensified the Cold War.

17

The impact of war: the murder of the European Jews

DURING the war the German government arranged to murder the Jews in the areas it controlled. No rulers of an advanced modern nation have ever attempted anything so far-reaching in its wickedness. Indiscriminate killing became familiar in the Second World War, but conventional or nuclear bombing, for example, was meant to win the war, not carried out as something desirable in itself. Some historians compare the Soviet labour camps of Stalin's time, but we have too little evidence of intention or outcome to sustain them: possibly the lamentable nature of the labour camps of the Soviet Union, like that of German prisoner-of-war camps in the east, was the outcome of incompetent carelessness, rather than of well-thought-out planning of the kind the Germans put into the extermination of the Jews. This is the only instance of a government-directed, bureaucratically organized attempt at the annihilation of an entire people. To ask how a handful of Nazis turned irrational theories into mass murder is to put a uniquely important historical question about the way human beings can behave in 'civilized' societies.

Hitler made known his views long before he came to power. *Mein Kampf* is full of the Jewish peril: 'the forces which now have the direction of affairs in their hands are Jews here and Jews there and Jews everywhere.' Both capitalism and socialism foster Jewish power: 'the Jew gained an increasing influence in all economic undertakings by means of his predominance in the stock exchange', while 'the shrewd Jew . . . gradually becomes the leader of the trade union movement' and Marxism 'systematically aims at delivering the world into the hands of the Jews'. Even so, hope remained of defeating this 'parasite', this 'pernicious bacillus':

as long as a people remain racially pure they can never be overcome by the Jew . . . that is why the Jew systematically endeavours to lower the racial quality of a people by permanently adulterating the blood of the individuals which make up that people. [But] The German Reich shall foster the most valuable section of our people [and] lead them slowly and surely to a dominant position in the world.

Awesome responsibility rests on those Germans—about one-third of the electorate—who, by voting Nazi in 1932, enabled Hitler to launch his murderous career. Two considerations lessen the guilt of most of them. One is that they regarded Hitler's anti-Jewish effusions as rant, not to be taken seriously. The second is essential in understanding how this entire horrifying episode could occur: resentment of allegedly unfair Jewish success and prosperity, somehow connected with Jewish cultural particularities, was common in European societies in the early twentieth century. In consequence, many thought Hitler's outbursts only to be over-emphatic denunciations of real, and more or less distasteful, phenomena. Medieval fears of Jews as the murderers of Christ, the slayers of Christian children for blood for ritual bread, and the practitioners of a usury forbidden to Christians, were revived in nineteenth-century Europe by conservative and nationalist opponents of rationalistic liberalism, who were often supported, against a common enemy, by the churches. In Russia, in 1882, following violent anti-Jewish riots (encouraged by the police), in the western part of the empire where Jews were allowed to live, the Tsar ordered the restriction of Jews to urban ghettos and the confiscation of their rural property. In consequence, impoverished Jews fled westwards from the over-populated western Russian provinces to the equally over-populated Polish provinces of the Tsarist empire and beyond. In western Europe, anti-Semites complained simultaneously of the success in the professions and finance of rich Jews, and of competition for employment and in petty trade of poor Jews from the east. In France, the Dreyfus affair brought anti-Semitism into the centre of politics. In Germany, Stöcker, a court preacher, started an anti-Jewish Christian Socialist party which combined hostility to liberalism and social democracy, both accused of cosmopolitan indifference to German interests. In Austria, Schönerer and Lueger enabled anti-semitic groups to win control of local government in Vienna and the surrounding provinces in the last years of the nineteenth century. In Britain and the United States, a genteel anti-Semitism tried to counter the alleged advantage of Jews in finance, trade, medicine, and the law by decorous discrimination. Thus, few British Jews became judges or ambassadors, and in both Britain and America non-Jewish bankers and stockbrokers congratulated themselves on more gentlemanly forms of greed than those they attributed to Jews.

So Hitler's regime came into a world where many believed there was a 'Jewish problem' requiring a solution. Even Roosevelt referred, at Casablanca in 1943, to the 'understandable complaints which the Germans bore towards the Jews in Germany, namely that . . . over fifty per cent [*sic*] of the lawyers, doctors, school teachers, college professors, etc., in Germany were Jews'. Before the war, apart from outbursts of violence in 1933 and 1934, and in November 1938, the Nazi government persecuted by legal decree. It excluded Jews from the civil service, from posts in universities and schools, from practising law or medicine, denied them German citizenship, and prohibited 'race-pollution'— sexual relations with non-Jews. In order to make Germany 'pure of Jews' the Nazis used more and more drastic means to force them to emigrate, while Hitler from time to time made vague but ominous remarks. In April 1937, he told party leaders that the 'Jewish problem' will 'be settled one way or another in due course', and on 30 January 1939, he made a public 'prophecy':

if the Jewish international financiers inside and outside Europe succeed in involving the nations in another war, the result will not be world bolshevism and therefore a victory for Judaism; it will be the annihilation of the Jews in Europe.

We do not know when the Germans decided to massacre the Jews of Europe, nor how the decision was made or who made it. There is controversy about Hitler's part in the origins of the 'final solution'. Some historians think that he had always intended to kill the Jews and that circumstances determined only his timing; others, that the march of events evoked the decision itself. Some believe that Hitler must have been the initiator; others, that the initiative came from subordinates zealously interpreting the well-known wish of the Führer that the German Reich should be made free of Jews. All serious historians, however, agree that at some stage Hitler approved.

Indiscriminate slaughter began with the Jews the Germans caught in the conquered areas of the Soviet Union in the summer of 1941. Behind the invading armies there came four SS Action Groups (*Einsatzgruppen*), less than 3,000 men in all, who worked in twelve 'Kommandos' to kill Red Army political commissars, civilian Communist officials, and as SS General Heydrich, the chief of the security police (SD), ordered in writing: 'Jews in Party and State employment, and other radical elements (saboteurs, propagandists, snipers, assassins, inciters etc.).' From Hitler's headquarters, Field Marshal Keitel ordered all army troops to be told that, 'the struggle against Bolshevism demands ruthless and energetic action, first of all against the Jews as the main bearers of Bolshevism'. It seems that such instructions suggested to the *Einsatzgruppen* that complete 'cleansing' was called for. With assistance from German police units, SS combat troops, sometimes from the army, and from local helpers, the *Einsatzgruppen* slaughtered 400–500,000 Jews, irrespective of age or sex, by the end of 1941.

Before the Russian campaign, the favoured 'solution' for the Jewish problem was enforced migration, and from 1939 to 1941 the 'experts' mulled over two plans. One was to move Jews to the Polish 'General Gouvernement', that is, the part of German-occupied Poland which was not added to Germany proper. Several hundred thousand Jews were moved from the Polish territories newly incorporated into Germany, and, in addition to Poles surplus to German needs for cheap labour, shifted into the 'General Gouvernement'. In the summer of 1940 a new scheme suggested the transportation of Jews to Madagascar, which would be taken from its French rulers and made into a Jewish national home run by the SS. British refusal to make peace spoiled the scheme. By early 1941, therefore, the General Gouvernement was crowded with Jews. Frank, the German Governor-General, objected to more, but in mid-October 1941, deportations of Jews began from inside Germany's pre-war frontiers, from which Hitler was impatient to drive all Jews. The first train-loads went to the ghetto in Lodz, now added to Germany (and renamed Litzmannstadt), but the next train-loads, from November 1941 to January 1942, went to Warsaw, in the General Gouvernement, and to Kaunas, Minsk, and Riga in the area of the killing squads. The latter applied their usual procedures and killed many on arrival; some soon after. The second phase of the 'final solution' had begun: in the first murder squads had rounded up Jews in lands conquered from the Red Army and killed them on the spot; now Jews from elsewhere in Europe were packed into trains and delivered for slaughter.

The Wannsee Conference in Berlin in January 1942 assembled senior civil servants, military officials, and police officers to work out efficient procedures for the capture and transportation of the victims. Soon Himmler and his men improved their methods of killing. Shooting proved slow and difficult to conceal. The Nazi authorities cared nothing about what Poles or Russians thought, but German soldiers were a different matter. In December 1941 an officer on the staff of Army Group Centre protested that 'the officer corps, almost to a man, is against the shooting of Jews, prisoners, and commissars', which they thought 'a stain on the honour of the German army', while the commander of an infantry regiment wrote that it went counter to 'our concepts of custom and decency that a mass slaughter of human beings should be carried out quite publicly'. The killers now found seclusion in human abattoirs. Instead of shooting, some commandos used vans with the exhaust fumes directed inside. Killing centres sprang up, equipped with such vehicles, or with fixed installations, using carbon monoxide from diesel engines, or gases compressed in cylinders. The more highly developed, however, used pellets of solidified prussic acid, hydrogen cyanide (trade name Zyklon), dropped into gas chambers, where they vaporized into lethal fumes. With crematoria attached, gas chambers could handle a rapid throughput. Individual centres gave 'special treatment' to up to 10,000 victims a day, though the crematoria sometimes lagged behind.

Within about six months, then, the SS and the SD expanded their original mission of killing committed Bolsheviks into that of killing all the Jews they could round up. The 'final solution' of the Jewish problem had begun. In less than four years they killed about five million men, women, and children. The table shows the probable number of Jews killed in various countries and the approximate proportion of that figure to the Jewish population in those countries at the beginning of the 'final solution':

Poland (1939 frontiers)	2,500,000	90%
Czech 'Protectorate'	75,000	90%
Austria	50,000	90%
Serbia	20,000	90%
Germany (1937 frontiers)	125,000	85%
Greece	60,000	80%
Croatia	28,000	80%
Luxemburg	800	80%
Baltic States	200,000	75%
Slovakia	65,000	75%
Western USSR (1939 frontiers)	1,000,000	70%
Hungary (1942 frontiers)	550,000	70%
Netherlands	100,000	70%
Belgium	25,000	45%
Norway	750	40%
France	75,000	25%
Romania (1942 frontiers)	120,000	20%
Bulgaria (1942 frontiers)	11,000	15%
Italy	6,800	15%
Denmark	50	1%

The 'final solution' succeeded best where German control was strongest, least inhibited by local laws, and least reliant on the help of local governments and administrators. Even in German-run areas the perpetrators used local helpers, recruited by inducement or threat, and relied on the co-operation of some of the victims, while elsewhere non-German bureaucrats and policemen were essential to identify Jews and assemble them for deportation. Many people share responsibility for mass murder: the small number of Nazi instigators, the killers, German and east European, some of the German military authorities, parts of the army, German police and officials, especially from the Foreign Office and from the Ministries of the Interior, of Justice, and of Finance, together with non-German police forces, bureaucrats, and politicians and, more widely still, all those who neglected opportunities to hinder the murderers or help the victims. At first, historians fixed the guilt of genocide on to Nazis and a handful of 'SS sadists and psychopaths'. Today some of them accuse both Europeans and the outside world: 'only because such a relatively small number of people were prepared to oppose the persecution and to provide aid and rescue were the Nazis able to execute their plans on such a large scale'; the number of victims 'reflects not only the genocidal single-mindedness of the Nazis and their collaborators, but also and perhaps above all, the indifference of the rest of the world'.

Who took part? Why did they take part? How far did they know what they were doing? Only a few at the centre of the Third Reich knew everything: Hitler, Himmler, Goering, Goebbels, Heydrich, Kaltenbrunner, and a few in the RSHA (the Reich Security Head Office), the organizing centre, including executives like Müller and Eichmann who arranged deportation, and the directors of its branch offices in occupied Europe. These people, having poisoned their minds with lunatic theories, thought they were devotedly steeling themselves to render a service to the German people and to humanity by destroying the Jewish 'bacillus' and countering the malevolent designs of a race striving for the domination of the world. Himmler, the best informed of all, told an audience of senior murderers at Poznań, in October 1943, of the 'extermination of the Jewish people . . . an unwritten and never-to-be-written page of glory in our history'. Most of his audience 'know what it is like to see 100 corpses side by side, or 500 or 1,000', but they had 'remained decent', and 'we have carried out the most difficult of tasks in a spirit of love for our own people and have suffered no harm to our inner being'. The SS, Himmler claimed in 1944, carried 'the burden of our people', a task capable of being carried out only by 'fanatical deeply-committed National Socialists'.

Nazism enabled killers to think of Jews as dangerous vermin. This was most difficult for those in direct contact with the victims: for those who shot mothers and children and tumbled their warm, and sometimes half-alive, bodies into freshly-dug ditches. Frequently intoxicated by drink, they were initiated by already-hardened colleagues who provided that feeling of membership in a small and select group which deadened individual moral inhibitions. They toughened themselves into professionals, doing an onerous job that someone had to undertake, and they separated this work from their private lives and attitudes. They were encouraged to make unquestioning obedience to orders the highest moral duty. Even so, the leaders of the SS tried to reduce the strain by improved, impersonal methods of killing, and by employing Jewish victims, or volunteer squads of Lithuanians, Latvians, Estonians, Ukrainians, or ethnic Germans (the *Volksdeutschen*). Volunteers were easily recruited from anti-Soviet resisters, who readily believed, as did nationalists throughout Europe, that Jews sided with their particular enemies, especially when, like the Jews of eastern Poland and the Baltic states, they were alien in culture and language and made up an envied lower middle-class in regions which were usually desperately poor. To these auxiliaries the SS tried to leave their most unpleasant tasks: in the Ukraine the German killing-squads left them to shoot women and children, and generally they did more than their share of the direct work of rounding up and shooting.

In the killing centres, Germans had the key posts: medically-qualified SS doctors selected prisoners for immediate death as against reprieve for labour, SS guards herded them to their separate fates, SS men dropped Zyklon pellets through the roof of the 'shower rooms' or started the motors whose exhaust fumes asphyxiated the victims; but the corpses were cleared and shovelled into crematoria, or into mass graves, by squads of Jews who then made everything tidy for the next consignment of 'pieces' of humanity. The six death camps, Auschwitz, Treblinka, Belzec, Sobibor, Kulmhof (Chelmno), and Lublin (Majdanek), needed few German personnel. Auschwitz became enlarged because there the SS increasingly employed Jews, and other prisoners, as cheap labour, sometimes as skilled workers (these had the best chance of survival) or as subjects in medical experiments. Fit and fortunate prisoners had a chance of life: out of 35,000 Auschwitz prisoners whose labour was hired by the SS to I. G. Farben, nearly 10,000 survived. To supervise labourers, the SS used other prisoners whom they rewarded with privileges, small payments, and hope of survival. The most privileged prisoners were non-Jewish Germans, political prisoners, who were often Communists, and ordinary criminals. Even Auschwitz, the largest and most complicated centre, needed only about 3,500 German SS guards. In all, probably less than 10,000 Germans were employed directly in mass shootings or in the guarding and running of killing centres. Some of these were racist fanatics, a few were psychopaths, but most obeyed orders and consoled themselves for the unpleasant work by its safety and comfort compared with the alternative of front-line combat. A government of a large state, if it is so inclined, can find that number of people prepared to undertake that sort of service; the distinctive feature of the Third Reich was not that Germans were specially murderous, but that they obeyed a government which was.

More disconcerting is the large number and variety of people inside and outside Germany who contributed to the rounding-up and delivery of Jews for slaughter, and the small number who objected or tried to hinder the process. How many were consciously accomplices in the murder of Jews? The instigators ordered the strictest secrecy, but could not completely maintain it. Mass executions by shooting were witnessed, and talked about, by ordinary German soldiers in Poland and Russia. The killing factories were better hidden, but news came from a few who escaped and from Polish observers. The Polish government in London got reliable information and made it public. From June 1942 the BBC and other allied radio stations broadcast the news over Europe and the RAF spread it in leaflets dropped from the air. In December 1942 the British, American, and Soviet governments, together with the allied European governments-in-exile in London, issued a formal, and accurate, denunciation of the mechanism of murder, promised to track down and punish the perpetrators, and used every means to disseminate this statement. Although the Nazis insisted that allied propaganda told lies and that Jews were, in fact, put to work before permanent resettlement 'in the east', the populations of Europe could have known the truth.

The evidence suggests that they did not. For one thing, it was, and is, hard to believe that so barbarous and pointless an event could be real. Rumours seemed exaggerated or absurd, the stories of eyewitnesses to represent isolated excesses, perhaps provoked by terrorist partisans. More important was that, for those who found themselves cogs in the machine of destruction, the truth was inconvenient or unacceptable. The truth might compel protest or resistance, with the risk of harsh German revenge on whole families or, at least, the loss of employment and a bleak future: better to refuse to think the unthinkable and to reject the truth as impossible, not to know too much or inquire too deeply. When Eden read the allied statement to the House of Commons and the question of who was responsible was raised, a member interrupted: 'the whole German nation.' Certainly there were some 'respectable' Germans in important positions, who secretly regarded Nazis with disdain, who could not avoid knowledge of much of the process and made no move: men like Weiszäcker, the official head of the German Foreign Office, or some of the directors of firms like Krupp, Siemens, or I. G. Farben, who employed Jewish slaves. When they were not themselves keen anti-Semites who approved what they knew, they persuaded themselves that individual resistance or protest was futile. Elements of the army, particularly staff officers in rear echelons, and units engaged in anti-partisan work, co-operated in mass shootings in eastern and south-eastern Europe, and tried to persuade themselves that killing Jews helped the repression of anti-German resistance. Even so, it is probable that Germans, on average, were more ignorant of the evil work of their government than the populations of the countries it oppressed. Listening to broadcasts from London was not as much practised in Germany as it was in, say, the Netherlands, Belgium, and France. Scepticism towards the allies and faith in the rectitude of German authorities ran higher in Germany than elsewhere.

Even in countries whose population hated the Germans, as allies or as occupiers (these became more and more the same), most people did not understand what was happening to the Jews of Europe. Among the victims themselves, most did not know, or refused to allow themselves to know. In August 1942, in the Warsaw ghetto, a historian faced with details of the extermination procedure at Treblinka explained how, in periods of stress in the past, collective fears had swept whole communities without any foundation in fact. In September 1943, in the Lodz ghetto, Jakub Poznański wrote in his diary, 'people are exaggerating as usual. Even if certain excesses have taken place in some cities, that still does not incline one to believe that Jews are being mass-murdered. At least I consider that out of the question.' As late as March 1944, Edith Klebinder, deported from Lyons to Auschwitz, thought 'that it was only a matter of going to work in Germany': she was selected for the work camp and survived: the children and old people she travelled with were gassed and cremated on arrival.

Especially in states which kept some degree of independence, the RSHA needed co-operation from local police and administrators: in Bulgaria, Romania, and France the Germans found it difficult to capture relatively long-settled or assimilated Jews because the local authorities would not help. In Hungary, where the last great round-ups took place, the destruction process was delayed until 1944 when, with the Red Army coming closer, the Germans seized control and bullied the Hungarians into acquiescence. In the Netherlands, Dutch administrators and police generally did what they were told; in Belgium recalcitrant officials saved many Jews, even though these were mostly foreign and vulnerable. In Italy and Italian-occupied areas, Jews were safe until the Germans took over or imposed a neo-Fascist regime under a puppet-Mussolini, with its own brutal squads. Were these non-German executants conscious accomplices in murder? A few high-up, fanatical, pro-Nazi collaborators like Darnand, head of the Vichy militia, which helped the Germans when the regular French police would not, probably got the news from their German friends; other non-Germans, especially those in high authority, did not try to know, and among their subordinates who carried out the deportations few believed they were sending the Jews to their death. Indigenous police often proved brutal; some of the French, many of the Hungarian, for instance. Some were natural bullies, others reacted viciously to Jewish reluctance or protest because it cast doubt on their own self-justificatory belief that no one intended gravely to harm those they turned out of their homes or bundled into wagons.

Few grasped the full horror of the 'final solution', but what *was* visible was appalling: swift and brutal actions, goods trains packed with the victims moving agonisingly to an unknown future at the mercy of hysterical persecutors. To this evil there were many fully conscious accomplices, but even as late as 1943 and 1944 they may have persuaded themselves that the Germans truthfully wanted Jews to work rather than to be killed, for by then they were combing Europe for workers to deport to Germany. Admiral Horthy, the Hungarian regent, assured a worried Hungarian bishop in April 1944 that

a large number of forced labourers were required of Hungary . . . A few hundred thousand Jews will leave in this way but not a single hair of their heads will be touched, just as is the case with the many hundreds of thousands of Hungarian workers who have been working in Germany.

Within the next three months the Germans gassed 400,000 Hungarian Jews. If policemen wondered why they should deport babies and old women 'for labour', they were reassured, for 'experience' had proved that 'the Jews' willingness to work diminishes when they are separated from their families'.

Most controversial of all are the Jewish accomplices in the final solution. The Nazis' talent for corruption brought Jews to spy on Jews, to denounce hidden Jews, to hunt Jews, by the offer, always unreliable, of privileged exemption from deportation. Critically for the smooth working of the final solution, the Nazis used Jews as leaders and wherever they went created Jewish 'councils' to list, assemble, organize, and tranquillize Jews. The Germans deferred deportation of these Jewish officials, allowed them to choose others for deferment, and encouraged them to hope for permanent exemption. Jewish 'councillors' or 'elders' also co-operated for unselfish reasons. They believed that disciplined conformity to German wishes presented the only hope of survival for their communities. Although these prominent Jews often had the best knowledge of the realities of the 'final solution', they saw no hope in resistance or evasion, only certain and immediate suffering instead of the postponement of a fate which might never be realized. The Germans encouraged these visions, so convenient for their plans, sometimes mouthing soft words of deceit. On 31 March 1944, Eichmann told the central Hungarian Jewish Council, which he had himself created as a by-product of the German military occupation of Hungary a few days before, that 'if Jews showed a proper attitude, no harm would befall them . . . After the war the Jews would be free to do whatever they wanted.' The Jewish councillors passed on this message to local communities who therefore disbelieved the warnings of a small number of Jewish resisters from other regions. The members of Jewish councils thought they acted for the best; in practice they helped the Germans. Adam Czerniaków, the head of the Jewish Council in the Warsaw ghetto, killed himself when he realized the truth. In Belgium, the anti-German resistance attacked the Jewish Council, setting fire to its register of Jews, and killed the Jewish official in charge of selecting Jews for 'labour' drafts. Both men were victims of Nazi techniques of corruption and deceit.

Most of those involved in the murder of the Jews were not conscious accomplices but knowingly participated or acquiesced in an often brutal, and always ruthless, uprooting of Jewish communities and families all over Europe. How many of those who were not involved tried to help the victims? The question arouses bitter disputes over the fate of the largest Jewish community, that of pre-war Poland. Some writers insist that non-Jewish Poles were generally anti-Semitic and disinclined to help the Jews, indeed that Poles helped the Germans to capture Jews in flight or in hiding. Others point to the extraordinary hazards Poles faced if they helped Jews since the Germans did not hesitate to execute whole families or even destroy entire villages found sheltering them, and point to the help provided by the Home Army and Zegota, the organization for help to the Jews, which was financed and sponsored by the Delegatura, the agency in Poland of the London Polish government, and to the work of the Delegatura in distributing relief from Jewish funds abroad. Probably about 12,000 Jews received aid. Most Polish Jews spoke Yiddish as their first language, so their persecutors could readily pick them out from non-Jews; escape offered greater hope to middle-class Polonized Jews. In the countryside, many peasants felt envious hostility towards petty Jewish traders and craftsmen, however poor the latter might be. Among Polish right-wing nationalists, anti-Semitism, reinforced by the belief that Jews supported Communist Russia, took extreme forms. The Polish Home Army tried to keep its military potential for the politically decisive moment of the German withdrawal and so showed reluctance prematurely to set off an armed resistance of the sort that helped Jews to escape in Serbia and Croatia and in the western Soviet Union.

Elsewhere there is less dispute about the facts. In some countries governments and populations showed concern to protect long-settled Jews who shared the native language and culture, but less readiness to obstruct German wishes towards newly-arrived Jews or those in newly occupied, or frontier, regions. Thus, the Romanian and Bulgarian governments deported Jews from newly occupied, or reoccupied, ter-ritories, but refused to hand over the Jews of their old kingdoms, while the Vichy French government helped the Germans to deport stateless or non-French Jews, but obstructed the deportation of French Jews. In Germany itself 'privileged Jews' (those married to non-Jewish Germans) were safer from harm than in areas where the SS took less trouble, and their connections sometimes helped hunted Jews, who were frequently indistinguishable from other Germans. Active resistance movements helped the Jews to survive. The Belgian Resistance was more effective in the decisive years than the Dutch (in the Netherlands successful German counter-intelligence weakened resistance), and organized shelter for Jews. Thus, in the Netherlands, though a generally sympathetic popula-tion found hiding-places for as many as 40,000 Jews, only about half of those survived till liberation. There, too, the local administration was more effectively under the thumb of Nazi rulers, compared with Belgium, where the German army ruled. The Belgian Resistance helped Jews to form their own resistance to the co-operative policies of the German-sponsored Jewish council. In France, too, active resistance movements helped Jews to escape capture by the SS or the Vichy militia in 1943 and 1944. In the Netherlands, Belgium, France, and Italy, ministers of religion, Catholic and Protestant, often contributed to rescue, by hiding Jews and by using their influence on governments. Pulpit denunciation of anti-Semitic brutality helps to explain the with-drawal of full co-operation with the Germans by the Vichy government in September 1942. In Slovakia and Hungary, intervention by Vatican representatives induced the heads of governments, very belatedly in both cases, to halt deportations. In general, Italians and Danes come out best. The Danish Resistance, with the connivance of the Danish police, saved nearly all the Jews in Denmark by shipping them to Sweden. The Italian government used its privileges, as the chief European ally of Germany, to limit persecution to expulsion from governmental positions and so on, and refused to deliver to the Germans any Jews from Italy or from its zones of military occupation; while the Italian army sometimes used force to prevent the SS from gaining access to its prey. After Italy left the war and the Germans installed a draconian military occupation, the SS and its collaborators from the Italian Fascists, who supported Mussolini's new German-sponsored puppet government, found the Italian police totally unreliable in obeying their anti-Jewish instructions. Most Italians, if they could choose, helped Jews rather than their hunters.

In Europe as a whole only a minority, sometimes a small minority, helped Jews, but even in Austria and Germany indifference to their fate was not complete. In this disaster few were heroic, few completely villainous: most men and women, amidst the shocks of war, looked after themselves and those close to them. Unfortunately, the Germans had given power to wicked men and given them control of the most effective armed forces ever known. They were able to demonstrate the evil an immoral government can contrive even in supposedly enlightened societies.

Historians have widened the debate on responsibility still further. Two scholars (B. Wasserstein and D. S. Wyman) have published well-documented and well-argued attacks on the behaviour towards the destruction of the European Jews of the British government and people, 'who passed by on the other side', and on the 'Abandonment of the Jews' by the United States. How much did the British and Americans know? How far do they share in guilty responsibility? After the summer of 1942 the information was there and in December 1942 it was formally proclaimed. From the summer of 1944 everyone could know full details of the Auschwitz extermination centre. Yet, as in occupied Europe, 'knowing' is an elusive idea. Many noticed these further German outrages and soon forgot them as their improbability caused renewed incredulity and as the war roared on with endless news of death and suffering, causing a brutalization necessary for mental endurance. Emotion concentrated on kith and kin, and for British and Americans the bloodbaths of eastern Europe were distant horrors, readily put out of mind. It was not a question of anti-Semitic indifference to Jews but of concentration on hazards and deaths of more personal relevance. The well-publicized Katyn massacre of Polish officers, the subject of sensational inter-allied wrangling, met no more and no less 'indifference' in the west towards the victims than did news of the discovery of rows of slaughtered Jews in Russia and Poland. The British and American authorities further lessened public awareness by refusal to follow the Nazi practice of distinguishing Jews as racially separate from the societies in which they lived, and so they obscured the uniqueness of the Jewish fate in German-occupied Europe. The inter-allied Moscow Declaration of 1943 threatened war criminals with judgement 'by the peoples they have outraged', and made no mention of Jews in their list of those peoples. Allied governments thus gave the impression to their peoples that the Germans were killing indiscriminately. Emphasis on this point obscured the single-minded German concentration on slaughtering Jews, which, except for gypsies, had no parallel even in the German treatment of non-Jewish Poles and Russians.

The British and American peoples supposed that they and their governments were doing their best to stop all German killings. Those people share no conscious responsibility at all for the fate of the European Jews. What they noted of German activities pushed pre-war British and American anti-Semitism out of fashion, and its vestigial survival did not cause indifference to mass murder. Perhaps, however, the British and American governments did less than they could have done. The two governments thought that they should destroy the Nazi regime as quickly as possible and thought it obvious that this was the best way to stop murder by Germans and their underlings. Could they have lessened the number of victims of the Nazis without prolonging the war? There were ways in which this might have been done. It is not likely that they could have rescued many of the murdered Jews but they might have rescued some of them. The Germans began the 'final solution' some time in the second half of 1941. It is certain that the reluctance of the governments and the peoples of the United States and of the British Empire to accept refugees from Germany, Poland, Austria, and Czechoslovakia in the 1930s and the early war years caused the eventual death of tens of thousands; but at that time the British and Americans thought they were, at worst, condemning them to systematic persecution but not to death. The Americans and British became possible accomplices to murder only in 1941. Thereafter, the seemingly most dramatic rescue projects were illusions.

At the end of 1942 Marshal Antonescu, the Romanian chief minister, proposed to allow up to 80,000 Jews to emigrate to Palestine on payment of a substantial fee for each of them. The plan helped to set off a new episode in a continuing Anglo-American dispute where each argued that the other could take more refugees. The British insisted that the United Kingdom was short of food and accommodation, and, much less plausibly, that the Empire was already overcrowded, but the worst fear of British officials in the Foreign and Colonial Offices was that the Americans would insist that Jews should go to British-controlled Palestine. Most British soldiers and administrators feared that this would provoke a renewal of the pre-war Arab rising against Jewish immigration, and feared for British influence in the Arab Middle East. On their side, American officials dreaded hostile reaction in Congress to any threat to the immigration laws. American and, more emphatically, British officials expressed fears that Hitler and the Axis powers were beginning to say, in effect, 'take these peoples off our hands or we shall kill them', and that the threat would extend to millions of civilians, Jewish and non-Jewish. Neither the British nor the Americans worked out a response. At the Bermuda Conference in the spring of 1943, they sympathised with each other's difficulties and agreed, correctly, that shipping was in short supply. Fortunately, the Romanian government had decided in any case to reject German pleas and to stop deportation of Jews, so that allied hesitation sacrificed no extra victims. In 1944 the 'offer' made by Admiral Horthy to permit the emigration of 7,800 Jews, an offer made at the same time as he ordered an end to Eichmann's deportations from Hungary, caused officials in London to worry about where they could put liberated Jews. Their delays damaged no one, for Hitler made his toleration of the offer conditional on Horthy's agreement to apply the final solution to the remaining Hungarian Jews. The most sensational proposal, passed to the western allies by Joel Brand, a Hungarian Jew used by the SS as their emissary, was empty. This was Eichmann's 'offer' to release one million Jews. Originally it may have been designed to tranquillize the Hungarian Jews whose deportation Eichmann was then preparing. It developed into a crude attempt to break the anti-German alliance by asking the British and Americans to supply scarce alloys and 10,000 trucks to be used only against the Red Army. The British squashed this attempt to snatch German victory from the closing jaws of defeat by splitting the alliance, and quickly informed the Soviet Union in order to forestall the Russian suspicions that an independent Soviet discovery would have aroused.

With one exception, greater efforts by the British and Americans (short of a successful invasion of France in 1943) could have had only a marginal effect, though a marginal saving of life was obviously worthwhile. Britain and the United States might have given more encouragement to neutrals, Spain, Sweden, Switzerland, and Turkey, to admit escaping Jews, especially by guaranteeing that they would not be left responsible for the permanent accommodation of refugees. First, of course, these countries had to feel safe from German invasion. By the time it became clear that the allies would win the war, late in 1943, most Jewish victims were already dead. An inter-allied pledge that they would help Jewish refugees to return to their countries of origin was prevented by the inability of the Soviet Union to agree with the Polish government on where Poland ended and the Soviet Union began, but in the later years of the war the British and Americans successfully worked on the neutrals to relax their frontier controls, and so enable some Jews to survive.

The missed opportunity most likely to have saved a large number of Jews seems, on present evidence, to have been the bombing of Auschwitz; not attacks on railways leading to the killing centre, which would have been futile, but an attack on the killing installations themselves. By the summer of 1944, the 15th US Air Force, based in Italy, could reach the target. It was not certain whether it could destroy the killing centres and, if so, whether or not the Germans would substitute other methods or other locations, but it was worth trying. The rejection by the US War Department showed how, in an intensely fought war, such a change in existing strategic policies could be brought about only by the direct involvement of the highest military authorities, the President and the Joint Chiefs of Staff. Churchill, who could have thrust the issue on them, instead handed it to his subordinates who, from Eden downwards, fitted it into their own established departmental policies and effectively stifled the suggestion. In the United States, Roosevelt had set up what he meant to be a powerful 'War Refugee Board' and, preoccupied in working out decisive operations in two hemispheres and arranging the future of the world, left it to deal with the rescue of Jews. In practice, the Board, without the direct intervention of the President, could get no more than cursory and dismissive replies from the planners of military operations. It is misleading to ascribe allied inaction to indifference: the men at the top necessarily made the winning of the war and the organizing of the peace their first concern, and their subordinates were left to themselves and therefore left to defend their departmental preoccupations. In doing so, it is true, they put on the record some pleas for the primary importance of their individual official concerns which now seem odious and sometimes anti-Semitic: their imagination was confined in blinkers left in place by those with wider vision of the course of events.

The fate of the European Jews has irrevocably eroded human self-esteem and self-confidence. Nazi murderers succeeded, by terror, fraud, bribery, or appeal to anti-Semitism, in gaining the co-operation or connivance of large sections of varied European societies, where few grasped the full savagery of Nazi actions but everyone knew that deportation meant at best ruined lives and broken homes and at worst enslavement and speedy death. The Nazis exposed human evasiveness, cowardice, and selfishness. Many Germans retain a sense of guilt because it was their society that gave power to the Nazis. Other western Europeans, including the British, know that their relative freedom from guilt rests on historical accident, not moral superiority. A small minority of individuals showed heroism; few nations can feel reassured of the moral worth of their individual members.

18

The impact of war: casualties, crisis and change

THE effects of the war spread far beyond the battlefields. The military machines of the great powers moved men and women away from their homes, some for good. As states organized materials and men for war, they inflicted hardships and death, or bestowed rewards and opportunities. Racial prejudice, applied by armed and ferocious police, shifted or destroyed whole communities. Not only physical violence but also economic requirements changed relationships between nations, societies, and individuals. The war brought ruin to many, to others, emancipation and hope. To some war gave the profound satisfactions of co-operative endeavour, to some the loneliness of fear and the self-absorption of misery. No other years have transformed so drastically the expectations of millions of men and women.

The struggle for eastern Europe accounted for most war deaths. Soviet sources give 20 million as the number of citizens of the Soviet Union killed during the war: 8–9 million servicemen (including 2 million prisoners who died in German hands) and the rest civilians. When premature death from hunger and exposure among those deported to Germany, sent off eastwards in the Soviet Union, or made homeless by military or punitive action is taken into account, this figure may well under-state the losses of war. The Soviet census of 1959 showed a deficit of about 50 million compared with the population predictable, in stable circumstances, from the 1939 population figures. That total, however, includes the births that failed to take place because of separations and because of the loss of men in battle: among those aged from 20 to 24 in 1943, there survived after the war only 6 men for every 10 women. Military deaths were almost exclusively male; civilian deaths, though they included many women and children, were preponderantly male. In Soviet labour camps a high death-rate prevailed, while forced labourers in German hands probably fared even worse. Great battles raged and homes were deliberately destroyed: in the German-occupied area more than half of all dwellings were damaged or destroyed. The Soviet authorities animated guerrillas against German supply lines and the Germans responded with savage repression. Villages suspected of harbouring any hostile elements the Germans routinely laid waste, then shot at least the entire adult male population. Many civilians became 'volunteer helpers' to the Germans, often ending up as '*Osttruppen*', soldiers in German uniforms, employed as static troops against the allied invaders in the West.

German police and occupation troops tried to keep order in Poland and Yugoslavia with equally unrestrained resort to intimidatory murder and slow death by overwork and starvation in or out of organized concentration camps. Polish losses are impossible to enumerate with confidence: post-war boundaries were radically different from pre-war, and Poles had been deported in huge numbers both by the German and the Soviet authorities. The Polish official figure is just over 6 million from the citizens of pre-war Poland, including about 3 million Jews. Military casualties in battle came to about 150,000. Of the remainder, many had been moved east into Russia or west to Germany, deported to the General Gouvernement and treated as expendable slave labour, or had died of hunger or by shooting, a fate common among intellectuals, priests, and upper and middle-class leaders of society, whether at the hands of the Soviet regime, as class enemies, or by the Germans, as opponents of the dominance of the master race. Acts of resistance, as in the Warsaw rising, together with Russian and German bombing and bombardment, led to the deaths of hundreds of thousands, while hunger allowed diseases to take hold and increased mortality in every age group. Poland was fought over twice, when the Germans went east and when the Russians drove them back to the west. German occupation, of the harshest kind, bringing famine, slave labour, and murder, brutalities justified by the doctrine that Poles had no right to live except for the benefit of Germans, lasted longer than any other country had to endure. From 1939 to 1941, the Soviet rulers carried out deportations and killings in their half of Poland in order to destroy the Polish spirit of independence, and returned in 1944 to finish the job. Even 6 million may not be an exaggerated total of Polish deaths, though Russian writers must include many of those, as Soviet citizens, in the Soviet Union's 20 million loss.

Figures for German war losses vary between 4 million, including 500,000 civilians and 125,000 Jews, and over 7 million including 3,200,000 civilian dead. For Germans coming from within the frontiers of 1937 the smaller figures are more accurate, though they may under-estimate loss of life among Germans who fled or were driven from the areas taken by Poland in 1945 which had been German before the war.

Casualties among the *Volksdeutschen*, those of German language and culture from outside 1937 Germany, cannot accurately be determined: some German post-war figures appear to maximize these losses, perhaps to emphasize the real sufferings of many east-European Germans, especially those from within the 1937 frontiers of Poland and Czechoslovakia, as the policies of deportation and resettlement inaugurated by the Nazis were turned against their intended beneficiaries. Large numbers, who had found it prudent to get themselves on the list of *Volksdeutschen* under German occupation, cast off this label with all speed when the Germans withdrew, and should not be counted among the dead.

In Greece and Yugoslavia, resistance movements attacked the German occupiers, who applied their normal repressive measures, with a basic tariff for reprisal actions of fifty locals to be killed for every German lost to 'terrorists' or 'bandits'. In some areas, resistance movements fought each other or, in Yugoslavia, fought the Fascist supporters of the Axis-sponsored Croatian regime, the Ustashi. In Yugoslavia, total deaths due to the war probably came to about 1½ million, most of them civilian. In Greece, 20,000 soldiers and about 80,000 civilians were killed, in addition to 60,000 Jews, and famine caused an estimated 140,000 additional deaths. Changing frontiers make uncertain the figures for Hungary, Romania, and Czechoslovakia; apart from Jewish victims, they lost about two to three hundred thousand each, with a high proportion of civilian loss of life in Czechoslovakia and Hungary. Bulgaria escaped comparatively lightly with about 10,000 soldiers killed and very few non-Jewish civilians. Norway and Denmark, both exempt from Nazi racial hostility, suffered few casualties: Norway about 10,000, Denmark even fewer. Finland's losses, in its wars with the Soviet Union, were almost entirely military, about 80,000.

In the west, the German occupiers behaved with comparative correctness and inflicted death and destruction proportionately much less than in their eastern 'living space'. Occupied and defeated France, however, lost more lives than victorious Britain: fewer French combatants died (about 250,000), but many more civilians, from three to four hundred thousand, were killed in air raids, as victims of German reprisals, or in deportation to concentration camps or forced labour in Germany. Belgium suffered rather over 10,000 military killed and about 50,000 civilians.

In the Netherlands, the Dutch administrative mechanism remained in working order throughout the war and maintained accurate records which effectively illustrate the hazards of war and German occupation. Military losses, in combat against the Japanese as well as against the Germans, were 7,900 but, in addition, 3,700 were killed fighting *for* the Germans, mostly in combat units of the Waffen SS, for which the Germans recruited widely and with special enthusiasm among those of 'aryan' stock, whom they encouraged to join in defending the 'new Europe' against the Bolsheviks. Among Dutch civilians, over 5,000 died as forced labourers in Germany, some in allied bombing raids, some through illness and hard conditions of work: over 300,000 Dutchmen were at work in Germany by the end of the war, only a few of whom went voluntarily. In the closing months of the war, press-gangs rounded men up in street-trawls and house searches, and put them to work to patch up railways which were now under increasing allied bombardment. Nearly 3,000 Dutchmen and a few women were executed by the Germans, usually in reprisal shootings: when the German police chief was wounded by resisters in April 1945, more than 250 Dutch hostages were executed. Another 20,000 civilians died as a result of military operations. At the time of the airborne operations against Nijmegen and Arnhem, the allies asked the Dutch railway workers to strike, and they paralysed most of the Dutch railway system for the rest of the war. Sadly, this strike did more material damage to the people of the western Netherlands than to the German military, who gave priority to their own traffic. Bad weather and shortage of petrol, combined with the effects of the strike, prevented supplies of food from the producers of the north-west from reaching the towns of Holland. There, rations fell to starvation level, at 500 calories daily, and, in spite of Swiss and Swedish Red Cross assistance, the old and poor suffered severely: an estimated 16,000 extra deaths resulted. To those Dutch dead we should add about 100,000 murdered Jews, to get a total civilian loss of life inflicted by German occupation of over 150,000. It is an instructive measure of the lethal nature of German occupation to compare this with the loss of life of a country of comparable population, Australia, which, participating in the war throughout its duration, sent troops to play a distinguished part in Europe against Italy and Germany as well as against Japan, lost about 19,000 lives in all, half in Europe, half in the East. Like France, Italy was intensely fought over and there too civilians split into pro- and anti-Germans in bitter internal struggles. Italian losses were about 400,000, half civilian and half military.

In the Far Eastern war, Chinese losses are too uncertain to allow even the most approximate figure to be suggested. The Japanese, from 1941 to

1945, lost in the army and navy 1,740,000 men, of whom only about one-third fell in combat, most dying through hunger and disease, and in addition the Japanese claim that of the 1.3 million civilians and soldiers who surrendered to the Russians in August 1945, about 300,000 never came back. Civilian deaths in the Japanese home islands amounted to about 300,000. Britain lost 264,000 servicemen and 90,000 civilians (two-thirds through bombing); the United States about 300,000 servicemen and 5,000 civilians. From the British Empire, Canada lost 35,000, Australia 19,000, New Zealand 11,000, South Africa 8,000, the British colonies 20,000, and India 32,000 soldiers, plus millions of dead in the famine of 1943 which was exacerbated by diversion of shipping to make up for allied shortages elsewhere.

Total population soon recovered. The horrors of war, with its separations and instabilities, brought longings for domesticity, marriage, and parenthood. In France the birth-rate, falling after 1930, began to rise again as early as 1942 and from 14.5 per thousand it bounded up in 1946 and 1947 to a peak of over 21. In England the birth-rate reached 20.5 in 1947, up by 50 per cent from 1941, a figure never recorded since. The generations which would bear the brunt of the war married in large numbers when war came: the wartime separation delayed a corresponding rise in births. Especially in Russia and Germany, shortage of men, as well as shortage of food checked the post-war 'baby boom'. In Germany the birth-rate reached a peak in 1939 at 20.4, a level never attained thereafter, though a comparatively small increase after the war culminated at 16.8 in 1949. After the war, among 20 to 40 year olds in Germany, there survived only about 6 men to every 10 women. In 1946 the birth-rate in the Soviet Union stood at 23.8, which, though high by western standards, was drastically below the 36.5 of 1939.

One benign consequence of the war helped population to recover by assisting in a big reduction in death-rates, especially among younger people: the discovery of penicillin and its derivatives, and their manufacture on a colossal scale. On 25 May 1940, at Oxford, Howard Florey and an assistant injected eight mice with virulent streptococci; four were treated with penicillin which had been isolated by the team led by Florey. Next morning the four untreated mice were dead, while only one of the others showed any sign of illness. Producing the amounts needed to treat human patients delayed its first use until February 1941, on an Oxford policeman, who died only because the available penicillin ran out before his complete recovery.

In July, Florey flew to the United States to try to persuade the

American drug industry to use its greater resources to produce penicillin. He got the support of the Committee on Medical Research of the Office of Scientific Research and Development. The head of OSRD, Vannevar Bush, later famous for his association with the atom bomb project, secured the financial support of the US government. At about the same time, Fleming, who first noticed the possibilities of penicillin in 1929 but failed to develop them, won the support of the British Ministry of Supply. In 1943, the US War Production Board itself took over the direction of penicillin production. In March 1943, descriptions of the treatment with penicillin of 187 cases in Britain were published, and in August, of 500 cases in the United States. These included 129 cases of gonorrhoea, all promptly cured. The enthusiasm of British and American military authorities knew no bounds: here was treatment for septic wounds and an immediate cure for most venereal disease, which had infected an alarming number of British and an even larger number of American troops, highly paid amidst the hygienic hazards of Europe and north Africa (German troops, with stricter discipline and organized and supervised brothels, had a significant advantage). By the spring of 1944, penicillin began to be available for civilian hospitals, and by June 1944 enough was available for all severe allied casualties following the assault on Normandy. For once the needs of war worked to the benefit of mankind. It is wrong to attribute the decline in death-rates that followed the war (some time after immediate post-war disruptions) entirely to the chemotherapeutic revolution in the treatment of infectious diseases but, principally because of the work of Florey and his associates, it accentuated an existing trend based on environmental and nutritional advance, itself reinforced by the unexpected prosperity of the post-war years.

The greatest number of wartime civilian deaths occurred in those areas where resistance movements were strongest: Russia, Poland, and Yugoslavia. In all those countries guerrilla war against the German occupiers escalated into sustained battles, and in the other occupied countries, including Italy after 1943, 'the Resistance' became a force to be reckoned with by the Germans, and by the allies, both militarily and politically, and an increasing influence on the pattern of life under German rule. In Poland, a clandestine state mechanism grew up, owing allegiance to the Polish government in exile, with military departments, weakly armed but highly effective in intelligence-gathering and in giving expression to Polish national feeling. From September 1939 until June 1941, the months of the Russo-German partition, both occupiers attempted to crush the Polish intelligentsia by deportation and killing.

Thereafter, when Russia was at war with Germany, attempts at co-operation between the Polish government in London, and the home army loyal to it in Poland, on the one side, and the Soviet government on the other, limped to a complete breakdown. Polish resistance- to the German occupiers lacked material support from outside, yet effectively sabotaged German-controlled roads and railways before its culmination in the disastrous Warsaw rising in 1944. Earlier that year, the German military command in the General Gouvernement reported that 'the railways and roads can no longer be considered safe when it is a question of directing resources to the east'. The Polish Resistance faced the problem of all non-Communist movements. Attacks on the enemy often led to frightful reprisals which the inconvenience inflicted on the Germans did not justify. Moreover, the Resistance leaders wished to preserve their forces for the decisive moment when they could co-ordinate action with their allies or, in Poland, forestall the Red Army and establish dominance at the moment of the German retreat.

For Communists, on the other hand, the decisive moment began on 22 June 1941, when Germany invaded the Soviet Union, and for them the slightest weakening of the Germans justified any price. Furthermore, they believed that German reprisals raised readiness for active resistance on the part of 'the masses'. In the German-occupied areas of the Soviet Union itself the Red Army put these principles into full effect. It organized and directed partisan groups behind the German front, relying on soldiers who had been encircled but not captured, and on officers, military and political, flown in or infiltrated into the German rear areas. Their task was to harry the lengthy German lines of communication, critically important in the eastern war, and to force the peasantry to reject collaboration with the invaders. Since murderous reprisals descended on those who showed recalcitrance to German orders, and since both sides tried to destroy crops and livestock that might benefit their enemies, life became exceptionally hazardous. Many tried to go with the winning side and were often caught out. As everywhere else in Europe, the Germans spurred resistance by their mounting demands for labour, carrying out arbitrary round-ups and deportations, to which joining the partisans could present a more attractive alternative. Famine and violent death stalked the rear areas where the German occupation, in the vast spaces of the Soviet Union, could exercise control only by occasional punitive expeditions in which as many as twenty German divisions took part.

In Yugoslavia, away from the main towns, railways, and roads, the Germans and the Croat nationalist satellite government could maintain only sporadic control, especially after the Italian forces changed sides in September 1943. Here Communist and non-Communist resistance movements conflicted in aims and tactics. The *Cetniks*, built up by officers of the Royal Yugoslav Army, socially and ethnically conservative, hoping to maintain Serb domination, tried to reserve their strength to assert the claims of pre-war legitimacy at the end of the war when Axis-sponsored Yugoslav collaborators would fade away. This attitude evolved into a tacit bargain with the occupiers: 'leave us alone and we shall do the same to you.' They, and the royal Yugoslav government in exile, watched with alarm the growth of a rival resistance movement which, in the mountains and forests, began to construct the basis of a rival state: 'Tito' and his Communist associates, accustomed to clandestine organization, formed a resistance network which disregarded, or even welcomed, enemy reprisals provoked by its own attacks, as the most effective means of recruitment. By 1943, Tito had a flexibly organized army of a quarter of a million men (and women) and the British led the way in bringing him assistance, impressed by the number of Germans he kept occupied and by the chance of strengthening the German belief in a forthcoming allied invasion of south-east Europe. In 1943 and 1944, the British and Americans brought 12,000 wounded partisans out to Italy for treatment, and in the autumn of 1944, the Yugoslav partisans were able to call for air support from Italy while they harassed the German retreat from Greece. In Yugoslavia, Tito ended the war poised to establish a Communist state, relying on non-Communist socialist support and on his own prestige as one of the victors over Nazism.

In Greece, a parallel situation led to a different outcome. Communist resistance fighters showed themselves more aggressive and readier to risk reprisals than more conservative groups, and the communist ELAS won support as effective opponents of the Nazis. In October 1944 the liberal Greek government in exile returned to Athens, following the German withdrawal, but ELAS refused to disarm and British troops intervened to keep order against strikes and demonstrations. Churchill visited Greece in December to impose a regency and left a civil war well under way, with a British-supported Greek government fighting ELAS.

In western Europe, German occupying troops behaved with comparative tact; indeed, the private conduct of individual German soldiers probably remained throughout the war, on average, more disciplined and less riotous than that of the eventual liberators. At first, few people joined in the resistance movements, which amounted to little more than muttering in corners, listening to BBC radio from London, and making modestly defiant gestures, such as chalking slogans on walls. Persecution of Jews sparked off some active resistance, notably in Holland during the strike of February 1941. After June 1941 the commitment of the Communists reinforced resistance, especially in France. In France, too, the disappearance of the unoccupied zone and the disbanding of the 100,000-man army which had been allowed under the Armistice of 1940, made resisters of regular soldiers. Above all, in 1943, the imposition of compulsory labour service in Germany faced active members of the population with a choice between disobedience or deportation, and recruited large numbers to the Resistance. Hence the growth of the Maquis, bands who took to the mountains of southern France. Some of these, forced to live by theft, terrorized the local populations as much, or more, than they did German garrisons. By 1944 certain areas in southern France turned into Maquis redoubts, fixed positions which sometimes attracted overwhelming German concentrations against them. In July 1944 disaster struck the Vercors redoubt, where Maquis forces had concentrated from a wide area. Misled by orders for general insurrection in France, issued by allied headquarters in England before the invasion, they expected speedy help from airborne troops and instead were crushed by strong German forces.

For the British and Americans, support for the resistance in western Europe was never a high priority: the commanders of both air forces insisted that their aircraft had more important things to do than drop supplies and weapons to irregular forces. Allied commanders thought of resistance activity as a possible, but unreliable, bonus to add to the efforts of their own forces. Even at the time of the invasion in 1944, the resistance movements were under-equipped: only about 10,000 of the French Resistance forces were armed for more than one day's serious fighting, plus about 40,000 more lightly armed, out of a far larger number eager to join in driving out the German occupiers.

The military success of western European resistance is hard to measure: sabotage, material or by calculated administrative delay, was more effective than armed attack. The Belgian and French Resistance effectively supplemented allied bombing in the disruption of the German-controlled railway network to hamper enemy counter-attack on the allied landings. Moreover, its clandestine escape routes for allied airmen returned valuable fully-trained pilots and crews to their squadrons: by mid-1944, British or American aircrew who baled out west of Germany had a fifty-fifty chance of avoiding German capture. In Italy, strong resistance movements grew up in the north after 1943, stimulated by the harsh German occupation which followed the Italian government's surrender to the allies and by opposition to the collaborationist Fascists of Mussolini's Salo republic. In May 1944, General Alexander publicly credited the Italian Resistance with keeping busy in Italy as many as a quarter of the German divisions there, though this sort of remark perhaps contained an element of morale-boosting exaggeration. There seem to have been about 80,000 effective combatants, with perhaps twice as many ready to fight if they could get weapons. In April 1945, in almost every town in northern Italy, the partisans seized control, accelerated the departure of the retreating armies, took revenge on those who had supported Mussolini's revived Fascist state, and ran affairs for up to two weeks before the allies arrived.

In both France and Italy, the Resistance frightened its friends as much, or perhaps more, than it frightened the Nazis and their helpers. In 1944, when General de Gaulle struggled to secure his independence of the United States and Britain and his control of France, he worried most about the Resistance. Control of France would give him independence from the allies, but the Resistance might prevent him from securing it. Resisters came from all sections of society and from every political shade: most, however, were young, adventurous, hostile to hierarchies, and opposed to the cautious conservatism that Vichy embodied, which, on its side, appealed to the propertied and those of established social position. Many men and women of the Resistance hoped, vaguely but intensely, for reform and renewal and for a democratic society somehow freed of obstacles to the emancipation and happiness of its citizens. The Communist-controlled section of the Resistance, the *Francs-Tireurs Partisans* or FTP, venturesome and well-organized, attracted support from non-Communists and, applying the Second World War Communist doctrine of 'unity at the base' among anti-Fascists, readily co-operated with other active movements whose members shared the general admiration for the wartime achievements of the Red Army and the Soviet Union. During the war, Communists, as always, tried to extend the influence of their party, a process which did not necessarily mean that every individual national party expected to take power in any immediately foreseeable future.

In France, de Gaulle feared that the Communists would try to seize power at the moment of liberation, exploiting the arms and prestige of the Resistance, whose leaders, as he explained in his memoirs, would cover him with honorific laurels and divert from him the levers of command. Paris riveted his attention: when the Resistance there won control from the weak grasp of the German governor, de Gaulle insisted that the French armoured division should be directed on Paris and kept there for long enough to enable the Resistance to be disarmed. De Gaulle felt safer with the few army officers who had joined him before 1942, or with those, more numerous, who had joined him after renouncing their previous obedience to Vichy. His style of liberation involved the nomination of carefully chosen individuals as prefects, or as super-prefects, the *'Commissaires de la République'*. The most difficult area was south-west France, where the German armies withdrew in August without immediate pursuit by the allies. There, for a while, the Resistance dominated, and Resistance heroes, self-promoted 'colonels', presided, sometimes unwillingly, over 'purification', the improvised trial and execution of collaborators, many genuinely guilty, some victims of vindictive and unjustified denunciation, some merely standing in the way of 'anti-Fascist' supremacy. Figures of ten to twenty thousand 'collaborators' killed at the time of liberation seem possible. De Gaulle exploited his prestige to restore the authority of the state machine. In visits to towns, he accepted the acclamation of the multitude, for whom he represented the defeat of Vichy and the Germans, while increasingly securing the support of those who had accepted Vichy and who now looked for an alternative defender of the established order. Not for the last time, de Gaulle simultaneously gained the support of the left against the right and of the right as a defender against the left. Repeatedly, de Gaulle appeared in a town, thanked the Resistance, sometimes perfunctorily, and ordered its members to disband, surrender their weapons and resume life as individual citizens, or join the army. At the cost of the bitter resentment of some of the Resistance, who found their reformism spurned and the old order returning, the French state returned to vigour.

In Italy, General Cadorna parachuted into Lombardy in August 1944 as military adviser to the Resistance. Later he reported that 'in this partisan warfare the Communist Party is predominant', and did not conceal 'its intention of seizing the reins and setting up a regime similar to the Russian'. This analysis was accepted by the British Foreign Office and by the allied military headquarters in Italy, although it was probably incorrect, for, on their side, the Communists were bent only on 'a struggle for a parliamentary democratic republic', a tactical ambition shared by the Resistance in general, including the powerful non-Communist 'Justice and Liberty'. Especially after events in Greece and Tito's political evolution confirmed British fears, allied headquarters tried to prevent the 'extreme communist elements taking control' in the

interval between the German retreat and allied occupation of northern
Italy. In April 1945, partisan revolt disorganized and hastened the final
German withdrawal, and killed ten thousand or so Fascists or suspected
Fascists, including Mussolini and his mistress, but after a few days allied
troops and allied military government took over. Where the Resistance
took control for brief periods, surprised allied authorities found them
good administrators; their leaders resented their rapid supersession by
allied-approved nominees of the more conservative Rome government,
however relieved local businessmen and conservatives may have been.

In the Far Eastern war, resistance, which asserted local nationalism,
was not necessarily more hostile to the Japanese than to the former
colonial masters, the British, Dutch, or French. In Burma and the
Dutch East Indies the Japanese encouraged local nationalists and even
helped them to build up patriotic militias, to their own cost in Burma,
where the militia changed sides to the allies at the end of the war. In
Malaya, however, a Communist-led Resistance, directed against the
Japanese, came into being among the Malayan Chinese whom the
Japanese occupiers ruthlessly persecuted. With them, the British in
South-East Asia Command, and in the 14th Army, formed an alliance
which brought arms to the resistance force of two to three thousand
guerrillas. In London it was calculated that their aid to the British
reconquest of Malaya outweighed the political risks, but the war ended
before the British invasion and, in 1948, the Chinese-dominated
Malayan Communist Party broke into a revolt which took the British six
years to defeat. The most successful resistance movement of all was that
led by the Chinese Communist Party. The war against Japan enabled it to
pose as the best embodiment of Chinese anti-Japanese, anti-European
nationalism, as well as of reform, compared with the increasingly
corrupt, inefficient Kuomintang, with its profiteering clique of leaders
and its alliances with war-lords and bandit chiefs. While it would be
incorrect to attribute its position solely to wartime developments, the war
pushed the KMT into a position in which it could not compromise with
Japan, while its internal weaknesses made it almost valueless as an anti-
Japanese force. The scene was set for the Chinese Civil War and the
emergence of the 'People's Republic'.

Fifty or sixty million human beings lost their lives because of the war;
about the same number were uprooted from their homes, temporarily or
permanently. Soldiers, sailors, and airmen of all the nations involved,
most of them pulled from civilian life, endured, or sometimes enjoyed,
temporary absences from home. Members of the American and British

Empire armed services travelled most widely and, apart from the Japanese, stayed away from home longest. German troops remained in Europe, except for an excursion to north Africa. They could be moved with comparative ease from one theatre of war to another, and home leave was easily available. It was not uncommon for wartime German soldiers to move from the Volga to the Loire or from Narvik to Tripoli. Even for German soldiers there were good times in the war as well as bad: administrative troops passing the war in France and leading the retreat in 1944 might find the war more than tolerable. British troops, away from home for years in uncomfortable surroundings in North Africa, sometimes found compensations later on in France and Italy where they were more likely to be welcome than Germans. For that majority of servicemen who had only distant contact with fighting, the war provided adventure without undue danger. Except for the minority of the millions of American soldiers overseas who found themselves at the sharp end of war, above all the combat infantry and bomber crews, the war was not hazardous. Many could enjoy unexpected and exotic experiences, even though some American soldiers seemed bored by the unfamiliar. In Britain, Americans, well-fed, well-paid, speaking the language, and most of them welcome for most of the time, found pleasures in their temporary migration. Black American soldiers encountered an unsegregated and, in the 1940s, non-racialist society. Though it is true that United States servicemen brought with them, and transplanted into extensive bases, reassuring reminders of home, yet they often made close contact with the natives. Over 60,000 American servicemen married British women.

Wartime separation, partly by encouraging hasty marriages, made families less stable: in the United States the divorce-rate doubled by 1945; in Britain it increased five times. Illegitimate births increased by 50 per cent in the United States and trebled in Britain. Bombing and the threat of bombing disrupted family life; especially in Britain and Germany, evacuation of children from threatened towns led to interrupted schooling and loss of parental care. In 1946, the British army found its intake of 19-year-olds seriously deficient in educational accomplishments compared with those who had left school before the war. Even so, the handicaps they faced were small compared with those endured by the inhabitants of German-occupied territories in the east of Europe or those inflicted by German conscription of young labour in the west as well as in the east. One measure of movement comes from Britain, where the British Post Office recorded 60 million changes of address from 1939 to

1945 among a population of about 40 million. Mobilization of labour, for food and weapons production, caused men and women to move and relationships between them to change.

Some historians think the war brought fundamental and permanent emancipation to women. Women became responsible for their own lives because men were away; they directed their families and their households; more received incomes of their own, from allowances for wives and young children of serving men, wages from industry, or pay from the women's services. They entered occupations hitherto reserved for men. Some women found opportunities for self-reliant independence and for more rewarding lives than before the war. It can be argued, however, that such gains were limited and transitory. Careers were not opened: women's jobs were wartime expedients rather than long-term vocations. Managerial or supervisory positions were conceded to women only with reluctance, and in industry women were only grudgingly allotted to skilled jobs. It is in Britain and the United States that the situation of women after the war needs particular scrutiny. In Germany and the Soviet Union, high levels of wartime casualties among men ensured, when their economies recovered, an increasing demand for working women. Elsewhere, among the inhabitants of German-occupied countries, war work was in no way liberating, while in Japan rigid patterns of male domination easily survived the war unshaken, to meet the more effectively reforming experience of the American occupation.

The dominant fact about the wartime liberation of women in Britain and the United States, so far as it took place, is that it was unwelcome to almost everyone concerned and thought to be a temporary anomaly. The men who went to war expected to return to enjoy their pre-war priority over women in employment, except in specifically 'women's work'. In Britain, pressure from the Minister of Labour, Ernest Bevin, won promises of day-care for small children, but it was provided only on a limited scale, and what there was disappeared after the war. It is true that the number of nursery schools was then greatly increased, but they, observing school hours (or less) and school holidays, did not fit the needs of a full-time working mother. In the United States, the government vigorously promoted day nurseries but only as a wartime expedient. The authorities both in Britain and the United States thought of the demand for the labour of working mothers as a wartime necessity, not as something desirable in itself, and most women seem to have agreed. The dangers and worries of war enhanced the retrospectively romanticized attractions of pre-war domesticity.

The war, moreover, added to the prestige of 'masculinity': the most admired roles in it were men's: dashing, decisive commanders, air-force pilots, submarine crews, parachute troops, commandos, tank captains. (Women distinguished themselves in secret work, especially in the Resistance—one reason why de Gaulle, in early 1944, at a time when he needed to confirm Resistance support for himself, decreed women's suffrage in France.) With some men risking their lives and all the millions of men in uniform in principle ready to do so, few women were greatly inclined to question their right to cosseting and privileges after the longed-for moment of their return. It was not a time when women thought of challenging men's dominance or were encouraged to do so: one scholar, for instance, points to wartime publicity with 'male-authored images that reified gender arrangements as rigidly as they had been demarcated in the Victorian period'. Immediately after the war women married earlier, married more often, and had more children than before the war. In 1931, in Britain, women were 29.8 per cent of the working population; in 1951 they were 30.8 per cent. In the United States, in the years before the war, 25.9 per cent of the working force were women, and in 1945, 36 per cent; but the figures were back to 27.9 per cent in 1947. The war interrupted a slowly developing twentieth-century evolution towards greater freedom for women; what caused its resumption was post-war prosperity rather than the transitory increases in opportunity during the war years.

Permanent, forced, migration struck parts of eastern Europe during and after the war. The pestilence of armed Germans, spreading over Europe in the years from 1939 to 1942, caused tens of millions of men, women, and children to be uprooted from their homes. To deportation for extermination and deportation for labour must be added deportation for resettlement. Hitler constantly wished to colonize and Germanize 'the East'. The process began during the war. Poland came first: in 1939 the Germans began to destroy the independent Polish nation. Two methods predominated, the removal of the leaders of Polish society (during the war about half of professionally-qualified Poles lost their lives), and the expulsion of Polish peasants and their replacement by German settlers. In 1939 large areas of pre-war Poland became new German provinces, 'Danzig-West Prussia' and the 'Wartheland': their pre-war population was 10 million, of whom nearly 9 million were Poles. More Germans were needed there and fewer Poles. In 1939 cattle trucks rolled: at an hour's notice or less, with at most 60 lb of belongings, hastily collected, Polish peasant families were beaten and kicked into trains, bolted and barred and dispatched into the General Gouvernement. Their families were often broken up: selected children removed to be 'Germanized', the men imprisoned in the dreaded work camps. In their place came German-speakers from eastern Europe, by arrangement with other governments before 1941, thereafter by the direct exercise of German power. At least three-quarters of a million Poles were moved in this way.

Two German agencies, the 'Reich Commission for the Strengthening of Germanism' and the 'Main Office for Race and Settlement Questions' collected together and shuffled about potential German settlers from Romania, Yugoslavia, the Baltic States, Eastern Poland, and the south Tyrol: about one and a quarter million Germans were uprooted, sometimes by vigorous compulsion. About half a million were settled in Poland, mainly in annexed Polish territory; the rest were shifted about in temporary camps. In May 1942 a grandiose scheme, the 'General Plan East', proposed the settlement of $3\frac{1}{2}$ million Germans in the next twenty-five years, with mobile garrisons to be scattered in European Russia to assist these German soldier-peasants to hold down the natives. The garrisons would go to the frontiers, as distinct from the areas to be annexed to the Greater Reich where more intensive settlement would be undertaken. Defeat prevented more than sporadic starts. In the General Gouvernement, 110,000 Poles were evicted from the area around Zamosc (renamed Himmlerstadt) to clear land for German settlement. Further east, in November 1942, seven villages in the Ukraine were cleared and ethnic Germans moved in. As late as spring 1944, 65,000 men and women, allegedly Finnish, were 'returned' to Finland from north Estonia to clear the way for German settlers. Eventually such 'Nordics' as Danes, Norwegians, Swedes, and even English, were to be encouraged to go east, and in the Netherlands, in 1942, a Dutch eastern company started operations to plan emigration to 'the East'.

To strengthen 'socialism', the government of the Soviet Union also packed humans into cattle trucks. In 1939 and 1940 their authorities deported up to a million of the Polish upper and middle classes and landed gentry from the half of Poland they occupied under the Nazi-Soviet Pact; indeed, at that time such persons found themselves safer in the German General Gouvernement. After the Soviet Union was forced into the war, some of the survivors of the process were released from the Siberian labour camps which were the normal destination of human freight. The newly occupied Baltic States received similar treatment, with over 100,000 'bourgeois', landowners, intellectuals, and clergy, packed off to Siberia in cattle-trucks. To prevent possible collaboration with the invaders, Stalin sent the nearly half a million German-speaking inhabitants of the Volga basin to Siberia. Muslim inhabitants of southern Russia suffered from one of Stalin's most vicious decrees. In response to their alleged collaboration with the German occupation, Stalin rounded up about 600,000 Crimean Tartars, Kalmycks, Chechens, and Karachai, who were despatched to Siberia from 1944 to 1946.

In the summer of 1943 the German retreat from Russia began, with fighting all the way, accompanied by the destruction of useful equipment, food stocks, the poisoning of wells, and the removal of workers who might be useful to the advancing Red Army. German and German-controlled humanity flowed westwards. Then, in 1944, the new German settlers in the east began to flee the wrath to come, followed by the older-established German dwellers in former Polish lands. In 1945 and 1946, Germans were turned out of Czechoslovakia and from the German territories newly seized by the Poles. Now it was the turn of the Poles to settle on land from which Germans had been deported, and Czechs moved into the Sudeten territories which the Munich Agreement had awarded to Hitler in 1938, and expelled the Germans. By 1947 10 million or more Germans moved west into post-1945 Germany, many of them into the British and American zones of occupation. It was the largest migration ever recorded, inflicting on Germans some of the iniquities the agents of 'Germanism' had earlier meted out. First the Red Army smashed into German homes, permitted, for a time, to indulge in indiscriminate revenge on Germans. Pillage, rape, and murder struck the victims. Then followed the Polish and Czech expulsions, sometimes carried out with a callous indifference, or with an active brutality induced by five years endurance of the German master race. There was much loss of life, especially among the very young and the very old. At Potsdam, during the frequent discussions on Poland, Churchill and Truman made repeated protests. In the end, the western allies secured agreement that transfer of populations should be 'orderly and humane' but, as the Russians said, even if the Polish and Czech governments tried, it was difficult for them to curb the bitterness of their peoples.

In 1945 yet another forcible deportation worried those who knew of it. Many Russians fell into British and American hands on the western front in 1944 and 1945. The allies expected no problem. They assumed that most of them had been coerced into service with the German military machine and that their 'liberation' would lead to their eager return to their victorious homeland. At Yalta the western allies promised to send back all Soviet citizens. In May to September 1945, over 2 million were sent back. Often allied troops had to use force; sometimes people to whom the Soviet Union had no claim, including émigrés from the civil war period, were returned, as well as citizens of territories annexed by the Soviet Union since 1939. It seems that the Soviet authorities generally shot those who had collaborated with the Germans and that a high proportion of the others ended in labour camps. American and British soldiers became increasingly reluctant to force these men (and, sometimes, their families) to return, and at the end of 1945 forcible transfer became, at last, limited to Soviet soldiers from the pre-1939 Soviet Union and proven collaborators with the Germans. Perhaps half a million managed to avoid repatriation.

In 1945 the refugees, 'displaced persons', and surviving inmates of concentration camps and prisoners of war trudged east or west, many seeking their old homes, many searching for new ones, some with nowhere to go. Germany contained about 14 million uprooted people and 3 or 4 million Germans rendered homeless after bombing and bombardment. The most enfeebled were Jewish survivors of concentration camps, nearly half of whom died within a few weeks of their liberation. Together with the Jews coming out of hiding, there were between 50,000 and 100,000 Jews in Germany. Unexpectedly their numbers increased: a year later there were 140,000 Jewish survivors in the western zones, and in 1949 allied-controlled territories in Germany and Italy contained about 250,000. Refugee Jews coming back from the Soviet Union, or ex-prisoners, or Jews emerging from hiding, when they returned to western Russia, Poland, Hungary, Romania, and the rest of eastern Europe, found the old Jewish communities destroyed and unwelcoming newcomers in possession of their former homes. Their return even set off anti-Jewish pogroms—the worst in Kielce, in Poland, where at least forty Jews were killed by hostile mobs. Jewish survivors, therefore, went further west, especially to the US occupation zone in Germany. Return home had proved impossible. Survivors of German persecution felt neither happy nor safe in Germany. Where should they go? From that question and from the horror caused by the fate of the Jews of Europe, which in 1945 was at last fully understood, sprang the independent state of Israel.

After the war the British authorities felt as strongly as ever that they should not offend influential Arabs: privileged access to Middle-Eastern oil became imperative to improve the British balance of payments, while defence of Britain against a hypothetical Red Army advance into western Europe required the ability to strike at the Soviet Union, especially its oil-producing areas, from Middle-Eastern bases, eventually with atom bombs. They therefore opposed any increase in Jewish emigration to Palestine and opposed the creation of an independent Jewish-controlled state. The change in British government from Churchill's wartime coalition to Attlee's Labour government substituted Bevin for Eden as Foreign Secretary, causing only a more emphatic expression of the anti-Zionist views of the Foreign Office. The British Foreign and Colonial Offices, and the military, argued that, with Nazi domination destroyed, surviving Jews could and should resume life in their original homes; if they could not, then they should move elsewhere, perhaps to the United States, the most prosperous society in the world, where Jewish culture flourished. President Truman, lacking the overwhelming prestige of Roosevelt and therefore more sensitive to domestic pressures, and perhaps personally sympathetic to Jewish aspirations, supported the Zionist demand for free entry of Jewish refugees into Palestine. But as Bevin pointed out, in an embarrassing phrase, the President was thus evading the political awkwardness of modifying American immigration practices: 'they did not want too many Jews in New York.' Truman, the British believed, by backing Jewish settlement in Palestine, was trying to win the approval of American Jews without alienating American anti-Semites and xenophobes.

In the summer of 1945, the American representative on the Inter-Governmental Committee on Refugees, after seeing the terrible conditions of Jewish survivors, suggested the admission of 100,000 Jewish refugees into Palestine, and in August Truman asked the British for the immediate entry of 100,000 Jews. The British refused, and the well-publicized problem of the 100,000 Jews drove them out of Palestine. In order to fore-stall American attacks on British policy, Bevin suggested an Anglo-American commission which met to find an agreed solution. It did not recommend a Jewish state but it did recommend the immediate entry of the 100,000, and Truman instantly took up that isolated point. Again, the British refused. As a result the Zionist leaders could use the obloquy Britain's pro-Arab attitude now incurred to overwhelm its position as mediator between Jewish and Arab claims in Palestine. The Royal Navy found itself ingloriously intercepting and turning back overloaded ships, bearing some of the much-publicized 100,000 towards the Jewish home-land; the British army in Palestine was attacked by guerrillas and terrorists whom the Haganah, the official Jewish self-defence force, was morally in-hibited from opposing. On 22 July 1946, Menachem Begin's *Irgun* force blew up the British headquarters at the King David Hotel in Jerusalem.

Zionist leaders, such as Ben Gurion, relied on American acquiescence to enable them to brush aside the British and impose an independent Jewish state on British and Arabs alike. The British authorities would not act with the Jews against the Arabs for fear of losing influence in the Muslim world, or with the Arabs against the Jews because of active Jewish resistance backed by a growing tide of American (and British) opinion. The British economic crisis of early 1947 ruled out any attempt to impose a solution on both sides. On 26 September 1947, the British told the United Nations that they intended to withdraw from Palestine and threw the issue back to the UN as successor of the League of Nations, the original source of British legal authority in Palestine. In November the UN voted for an independent Jewish state in a partitioned Palestine and the British, detaching themselves from this anti-Arab solution, announced that they would finally withdraw on 15 May 1948. On that day Israel emerged, fighting for its life against mutually divided Arab enemies. The suffering of the Jews in the Second World War had made possible and legitimized the fight for a sovereign Jewish state and the suffering imposed on many of the indigenous inhabitants of Palestine.

In Asia and Africa the war hastened the decay of rule by Europeans. In 1942 Churchill proclaimed: 'We mean to hold our own. I have not become the King's First Minister in order to preside over the liquidation of the British Empire.' The war weakened the great colonial empires, however, and in 1947, Indian independence began the evolution and eclipse of the British Empire. The British had long expressed their hope of eventual self-government for India, but its timing and its conditions had remained vague. The war accelerated liberation and weakened British power to dictate its conditions. Everywhere in the east Japanese victories lowered British prestige, which American interference further reduced, while the mobilization of Indian manpower and resources for war changed traditional relationships. Even before Pearl Harbor, Americans seeking to support Britain worried about the hostility felt in the United States towards British imperialism, especially its rule in India. Roosevelt asked Churchill about British intentions in India when they met in August 1941. After the Far Eastern war broke out, the easy Japanese conquest of British colonies brought more pressure for change from the United States, now that an invasion of India seemed possible. In February 1942, Roosevelt again asked Churchill to find some way 'of conciliating the Indian leadership'. In March 1942, the British government promised freedom to India immediately after the war under a constitution worked out by Indians.

Immediately after this declaration, British rule grew stronger. When the Congress Party, representing nationalists, mostly Hindu, who demanded a free but united India, declined to co-operate in the war effort without immediate independence and launched their 'Quit India Now' rebellion in August 1942, the British were able to crush large-scale revolts and lock up the Congress leadership. They succeeded because the administrative machine, the army and the police, most of whose members were non-British, showed cohesion and readiness to obey British orders. At the end of the war those qualities had declined. The promise of independence warned servants of the state that loyalty to the British did not necessarily ensure future reward or security. Mobilization of resources for war diluted all government services: the proportion of British officials and officers fell, sometimes drastically, and so did the time available for Indian recruits to acquire a sense of commitment to their new organization. Moreover, wartime economic stresses, rationing, requisitions, and inflation, brought unpopularity to the pro-British landowning classes on whose support British rule greatly relied, and substituted support for middle-class nationalists. The suppression of the Hindu-dominated all-Indian Congress Party enabled the Muslim League, with its demand for a separate Muslim-dominated Pakistan, to increase its support, with the acquiescence of the British authorities who wished to avoid confrontation with Muslims because of their disproportionately large contribution of manpower to the Indian army. As a result, tensions rose between religious groups, and Indian troops and police, the instruments of British power, became more and more concerned with their own individual fates in a communally-divided society, and less and less reliable in keeping order. After the war, the British could reimpose their position as the final arbiters of the distribution of power in India only by an unacceptable use of British resources, especially troops from the British army. As it was, British rule became increasingly irrelevant, until the British gave short notice of their withdrawal in an attempt to compel negotiated co-operation among their successors. Their rapid loss of power was, in a way, demonstrated by the blaze of friendship towards them that accompanied the coming of independence on 15 August 1947: they no longer inspired fear.

British, Dutch, and French governments faced special post-war problems in trying to reimpose control in their Japanese-occupied colonies. The British had an advantage: they had troops available to take the surrender of Japanese forces. In Malaya and Singapore they did so rapidly, since their invasion of Malaya (ZIPPER) was, in any case, about to begin, and went ahead, perhaps fortunately, after Japanese resistance had ended. In Malaya, even so, the British eventually had to launch an attack on Communist forces they had themselves built up during the war as resisters to the Japanese. In the Dutch East Indies, the Japanese had encouraged indigenous nationalist groups during their wartime occupation, and in 1945, the British did not have enough troops to clear the way for an unchallenged return of Dutch administration, even with the help of their obedient Japanese prisoners. The Dutch were never able subsequently to restore complete military control. They could not enforce a new relationship of their own choosing on the local nationalists, even though the latter, at first, perhaps expecting a more determined and sustained effort from the Dutch, proved eager to negotiate one.

In French Indo-China a similar pattern led to one of the three greatest wars of the years after the Second World War. Here, in the closing months of the war, the Japanese abolished French administration and worked with indigenous nationalists. In Laos and Cambodia the Japanese pushed monarchies into repudiation of French guidance; in Vietnam they encouraged the formation of a grouping of nationalists, including Communists, the Viet-Minh. At Potsdam, the country was divided at the 16 degree parallel into a southern area, where the British came into occupation after the Japanese surrender, and a northern where Chinese had this task. In the south, after the Japanese surrender, the British held back the nationalists and helped the French to return. In the north, Ho Chi Minh proclaimed the Democratic Republic of Vietnam, and although the French came back to North Vietnam with the Vietnamese government's permission, probably to hasten the departure of the corrupt and greedy Chinese, French reassertions of their rights at the end of 1946 met a Vietnamese resistance sufficiently organized to begin a war which drove the French out of Indo-China in 1954. This was followed by another ferocious struggle when the United States intervened to try to check the Vietnamese Communists, despite their earlier support of the anti-French movement. Eventually the new government of North Vietnam, which had seized control after the Japanese had destroyed French power and the Allies had destroyed Japanese power, conquered and made Communist the whole of Indo-China.

In another part of the French Empire, one with closer bonds to France itself, the war transformed relations between rulers and ruled; indeed, the post-war struggle for Algeria can be dated from the very day on which the final German surrender took place, 8 May 1945. Wartime conditions aggravated the social problems brought on by the rise in population that has characterized underdeveloped countries in the twentieth century: after the Anglo-American descent on north Africa in 1942, shortages worsened and price-rises accelerated. The war changed political attitudes: before the war three indigenous Algerian movements existed, a Muslim 'reform' movement aiming at the restoration of Muslim purity, a group seeking full equality with the French in Algeria led by Ferhat Abbas, and a party aiming for independence led by Messali Hadj. The French defeat in 1940 and the appearance of the Vichy regime, which repudiated seventy years of French republican rule, turned out to mean only more rigid conservatism. The Anglo-American invasion at the end of 1942 seemed to signify, therefore, the defeat of conservative France and its replacement by Americans, who appeared all-powerful, and who showed no enthusiasm for French imperial integrity. Early in 1943, Ferhat Abbas wrote to Roosevelt setting out his ambitions and conferred with Robert Murphy, Roosevelt's personal representative in north Africa. In this way, it was with American acquiescence that Ferhat Abbas published, in February 1943, the 'manifesto of the Algerian People' calling for an autonomous Algeria. A year later de Gaulle's provisional French government in Algiers attempted to recover lost ground by proclaiming an equal citizenship which proved more evident in theory than in practical application. In reply, Algerian opponents of French power united in the 'Association of Friends of the Manifesto' which, as the end of the war approached, demanded independence for Algeria. A demonstration, apparently organized to draw international attention, including that of the nascent United Nations organization, unexpectedly set off rioting among poor peasants in an area centred on Setif, 100 miles to the east of Algiers. An attempt at general insurrection followed. Anticipated by the French authorities, they repressed it with violent determination, using aircraft, naval bombardment, and troops flown in from France. About 100 French were killed and perhaps 5,000 Muslim Algerians. From then on, their testimony agrees, Algerian nationalists waited only for a better opportunity for rebellion, which they seized in 1954.

The Second World War, then, was followed by political stability in Europe, and instability in Africa and Asia. European stability derived from a partition effectively agreed between the great powers during the war and maintained after it, albeit with growls and increasingly apocalyptic threats of mutual destruction. Outside Europe the great powers did not agree on spheres of influence, and even if they had, non-European populations were not ready to accept their dictation.

The second half of the twentieth century has been marked by the transformation of Japan and West Germany from enemies into prosperous friends of the western democracies, aligned in opposition to Communist expansion. In the newly expanded Communist world after 1945, expropriation and deportation were the fate of the property-owning class and much of the intelligentsia, to the material advantage of some of the poorer peasantry and of the working-class, while in the industrialised, capitalist west, post-war economic reconstruction proved, unexpectedly, to be only the prelude to economic growth sustained over decades. American grants and loans overcame the checks to economic expansion which post-war shortages of dollars to feed and re-equip surviving economies might otherwise have imposed, and encouraged the political and economic integration of West Germany and Japan into the western world. By the end of 1949, West German industrial production overtook pre-war levels and a new Federal Republic appeared. The American occupation of Japan, under General MacArthur as an enlightened despot, devoted itself for two or three active years to the demilitarization, democratization, and emancipation of Japanese society. Then the fear of Communist expansion shifted the emphasis to economic recovery and even to a reversal, in practice, of the American-drafted constitution's prohibition of military forces. American aid, followed by buying for the Korean war, looked after Japan's balance of payments and stimulated expansion. Pre-war levels of production and consumption were passed within six years after surrender as growth proceeded at an unprecedented rate. The economic hegemony of the United States, which resulted from the Second World War, was now used as a weapon of capitalist liberalism, and helped to launch a post-war prosperity expressed and sustained by the economic miracles enjoyed by the two great losers of the war.

No solemn peace conference marked the end of the Second World War. The great powers, reluctantly and step by step, brought into being the new world of the second half of the twentieth century. A series of complicated negotiations and meetings made the transition from the grand alliance of America, Britain, and Russia to the new alliances directed against the Soviet Union. The formal culmination was at Paris on 23 October 1954. The allied occupation of West Germany ended, British, French, and American troops remained in Germany as friends to help in its defence, and the allies invited West Germany to join Britain, France, and the United States in NATO.

NOTE ON QUOTATIONS

Quotations on p. 123 are from N. Ike (ed.), *Japan's Decision for War. Records of the 1941 Policy Conferences* (Stanford, 1967), 154, 229, 273; on pp. 305 and 326 from N. Hamilton, *Monty, Master of the Battlefield* (Pbk. edn. London, 1985), 778, 800, 804, and cover; on p. 320 from M. Steinert, *Hitler's War and the Germans* (Athens, Ohio, 1977), 263; on p. 401 from M. Bejski, in Y. Gutman and E. Zuroff (eds.) *Rescue Attempts during the Holocaust* (Jerusalem, 1977), 629, and R. L. Braham, *The Politics of Genocide* (New York, 1981), 1124.

THE SECOND WORLD WAR:
A SHORT BOOK LIST

GOOD single-volume works are H. Michel, *The Second World War* (London, 1974); P. Calvocoressi, G. Wint, and J. Pritchard, *Total War* (London, 1989, also in 2 vols. in paperback); M. Gilbert, *The Second World War* (London, 1989); G. L. Weinberg, *A World at Arms* (Cambridge, 1994); and an excellent reference book, I. C. B. Dear and M. R. D. Foot (eds.), *The Oxford Companion to the Second World War* (Oxford, 1995). Shorter studies are G. Wright, *The Ordeal of Total War* (New York, 1968), which concentrates on social and economic themes, and M. Kitchen, *A World in Flames* (London, 1990). For detailed enquiry the most important works are the American and British official histories. The US navy has a fifteen-volume masterpiece by S. E. Morison, *History of US Naval Operations in World War II* (Boston, Mass., 1947–62). W. Craven and J. Cate (eds.) bring together individual studies in *The Army Air Forces in World War II*, 7 vols. (Chicago, 1948–58), and, for the ground forces, the mighty series of volumes in the *The United States Army in World War II* gives a thorough treatment. Individual authors present essays on critical points in K. R. Greenfield (ed.), *Command Decisions* (Washington, 1960). HM Stationery Office has published two main groups within the official *British History of the Second World War*, the *UK Civil Series* and the *UK Military Series*, the former on social and economic problems, the latter including studies of individual campaigns and, in a sub-series of six volumes, valuable surveys of *Grand Strategy*. A British official sub-series by F. H. Hinsley and others on *British Intelligence during the Second World War, its Influence on Strategy and Operations*, 3 vols. in 4 (London, 1979–88) impressively reassesses the European war, using some evidence still kept from public scrutiny. RAF Bomber Command has four volumes by C. Webster and N. Frankland, *The Strategic Air Offensive Against Germany 1939–45*, 4 vols. (London, 1961). Extensive reports by the United States Strategic Bombing Survey have been published and provide information on varied aspects of the German and Japanese war efforts as well as on the allied strategic bombing attack. A selection of these reports were brought together by D. MacIsaac in ten volumes (New York, 1976). There are good official histories commissioned by the British Dominions and India. V. J. Esposito (ed.) in *The West Point Atlas of American Wars*, vol. ii, *1900–1953* (New York, 1959) offers admirable maps with a commentary. Also informative is J. Keegan (ed.), *The Times Atlas of the Second World War* (London, 1989).

In other languages the historical sections of the French army, air force, and navy are producing excellent studies and, more slowly, the relevant Italian ministries. For Germany, the officially supported *Militärgeschichtliches Forschungsamt* publishes more and more studies of the highest quality. The eight-volume German survey of the Second World War is in the process of translation by Oxford University Press. From Japanese work, sets of individual essays have been translated, especially under the aegis of J. W. Morley. The most recent Russian official account of the war is in the twelve volumes of *Istoriya vtoroi mirovoi voiny* (Moscow, 1973–83).

Most of the serious work appearing on the Second World War is noted in two periodicals, one German, the *Vierteljahrshefte für Zeitgeschichte*, and one French, the *Revue d'Histoire de la Deuxième Guerre Mondiale*. Two compilations by A. G. S. Enser give titles of about 10,000 books in English: *A Subject Bibliography of the Second World War, Books in English 1939–1974* (London, 1977) and *Books in English 1975–1983* (Aldershot, 1985).

Origins of the European and Far Eastern Wars

GENERAL:

A. P. Adamthwaite, *The Making of the Second World War* (London, 1979)
P. M. H. Bell, *The Origins of the Second World War in Europe* (London, 1986)
R. Lamb, *The Drift to War 1922–1939* (London, 1989)
G. Martel (ed.), *The Origins of the Second World War Reconsidered. The A. J. P. Taylor Debate after Twenty-five Years* (Boston, 1986)
W. J. Mommsen and L. Kettenacker (eds.), *The Fascist Challenge and the Policy of Appeasement* (London, 1983)
R. J. Overy, *The Origins of the Second World War* (London, 1987)
K. Robbins, *Munich, 1938* (London, 1968)
A. J. P. Taylor, *Origins of the Second World War* (London, 1961)
D. C. Watt, *How War Came* (London, 1989)

GERMANY:

V. R. Berghahn, *Modern Germany* (Cambridge, 1987)
W. Carr, *Arms, Autarchy and Aggression* (London, 1972)
K. Hildebrand, *The Foreign Policy of the Third Reich* (London, 1973)
—— *The Third Reich* (London, 1984)
I. Kershaw, *The Nazi Dictatorship* (London, 1985)
N. Stone, *Hitler* (London, 1980)
G. L. Weinberg, *The Foreign Policy of Hitler's Germany*, 2 vols. (Chicago, 1970–80)

BRITAIN:

U. Bialer, *The Shadow of the Bomber* (London, 1980)

M. Ceadel, *Pacifism in Britain* (Oxford, 1980)

M. Cowling, *The Impact of Hitler* (Cambridge, 1975)

D. Dilks, *Retreat from Power*, vol. i (London, 1981)

N. H. Gibbs, *Grand Strategy*, vol. i, *Rearmament Policy* (London, 1976)

M. Gilbert, *Roots of Appeasement* (London, 1966)

M. Howard, *The Continental Commitment* (London, 1972)

R. A. C. Parker, *Chamberlain and Appeasement. British Policy and the Coming of the Second World War* (London, 1993)

G. C. Peden, *British Rearmament and the Treasury* (Edinburgh, 1979)

D. C. Watt, 'Misinformation, Misconception, Mistrust—Episodes in British Policy and the Approach of War' in M. Bentley and J. Stevenson (eds.), *High and Low Politics in Modern Britain* (Oxford, 1983)

FRANCE:

A. P. Adamthwaite, *France and the Coming of the Second World War* (London, 1977)

R. J. Young, *In Command of France. French foreign policy and military planning 1933–40* (Cambridge, Mass., 1978)

POLAND:

A. M. Cienciala, *Poland and the Western Powers 1938–39* (London, 1968)

Anita Prazmowska, *Britain, Poland and the Eastern Front, 1939* (Cambridge, 1987)

ITALY:

D. Mack Smith, *Mussolini's Roman Empire* (London, 1979)

MacGregor Knox, *Mussolini Unleashed 1939–41* (Cambridge, 1982)

USA:

N. J. Cull, *Selling War* (New York, 1995)

R. A. Dallek, *Franklin D. Roosevelt and American Foreign Policy* (New York, 1978)

W. L. Langer and S. E. Gleason, *The Challenge to Isolation. The World Crisis of 1937–1940 and American Foreign Policy*, 2 vols. (New York, 1952, 1953)

A. A. Offner, *American Appeasement 1933–1938* (Cambridge, Mass., 1969)

D. Reynolds, *The Creation of the Anglo-American Alliance 1937–41* (London, 1981)

USSR:

J. Haslam, *The Soviet Union and the Struggle for Collective Security in Europe* (London, 1984)

—— *The Soviet Union and the Threat from the East 1933–1941* (London, 1992)

G. Roberts, *The Soviet Union and the Origins of the Second World War* (London, 1995)

JAPAN:

N. Ike (ed.), *Japan's Decision for War. Records of the 1941 Conferences* (Stanford, 1967)

A. Iriye, *The Origins of the Second World War in Asia and the Pacific* (London, 1987)

F. C. Jones, *Japan's New Order in East Asia 1937–1945* (Oxford, 1954)

P. Lowe, *Great Britain and the Origins of the Pacific War* (Oxford, 1977)

I. H. Nish, *Alliance in Decline* (London, 1977)

Battles and Campaigns (In addition to official histories)

GENERAL:

J. Keegan, *The Second World War* (London, 1989)

E. von Manstein, *Lost Victories* (London, 1958)

F. W. von Mellenthin, *Panzer Battles 1939–45* (London, 1955)

R. Overy, *Why the Allies Won* (London, 1995)

P. Padfield, *War Beneath the Sea. Submarine Conflict 1939–45* (London, 1995)

A. Seaton, *The German Army 1933–45* (London, 1982)

M. Van Creveld, *Supplying War* (Cambridge, 1977)

H. P. Willmott, *The Great Crusade* (London, 1989)

WESTERN AND MEDITERRANEAN:

S. E. Ambrose, *The Supreme Commander. The War Years of General Dwight D. Eisenhower* (New York, 1968)

C. Barnett, *Engage the Enemy More Closely. The Royal Navy in the Second World War* (London, 1991)

E. Belfield and S. Essame, *Battle for Normandy* (London, 1975)

R. Bennett, *Behind the Battle. Intelligence in the War with Germany* (London, 1994)

B. Bond, *France and Belgium 1939–40* (London, 1975)

G. Chapman, *Why France Collapsed* (London, 1968)

E. M. Gates, *End of the Affair. The Collapse of the Anglo-French Alliance 1939–40* (Berkeley, 1981)

D. Graham and S. Bidwell, *Tug of War. The Battle for Italy 1943–45* (London, 1986)

J. A. Gunsberg, *Divided and Conquered: The French High Command and the Defeat of the West* (Westport, 1979)

N. Hamilton, *Monty*, 3 vols. (London, 1981, 1983, 1986)

M. Hastings, *Overlord* (London, 1984)

J. Keegan, *Six Armies in Normandy* (London, 1982)

R. Lamb, *Montgomery in Europe 1943–45* (London, 1983)

S. Lawlor, *Churchill and the Politics of War* (Cambridge, 1994)

J. Rohwer, *The Critical Convoy Battles of March 1943* (London, 1977)

R. F. Weigley, *Eisenhower's Lieutenants* (London, 1981)

FAR EAST AND THE ATOM BOMB:

C. Blair, *Silent Victory. The US Submarine War against Japan* (Philadelphia, 1975)

R. J. C. Butow, *Japan's Decision to Surrender* (Stanford, 1954)

B. Collier, *The War in the Far East* (London, 1969)

J. W. Dower, *War without Mercy* (New York, 1986)

H. Feis, *Japan Subdued. The Atomic Bomb and the End of the War in the Pacific* (Princeton, 1961)

M. M. Gowing, *Britain and Atomic Energy 1939–45* (London, 1964)

R. G. Hewlett and O. E. Anderson, *A History of the United States Atomic Energy Commission*, vol. I, *The New World* (Washington, 1972)

D. Irving, *The Virus House* (London, 1967)

A. J. Levine, *The Pacific War* (Westport, 1995)

R. Rhodes, *The Making of the Atomic Bomb* (New York, 1986)

THE GERMAN–RUSSIAN WAR:

S. Bialer (ed.), *Stalin and his Generals. Soviet Military Memoirs* (New York, 1969)

P. Carell, *Hitler's War on Russia*, 2 vols. (London, 1964, 1970)

R. Cecil, *Hitler's Decision to Invade Russia* (London, 1975)

J. Erickson, *Stalin's War with Germany*, 2 vols. (London, 1975, 1983)

B. Leach, *German Strategy Against Russia* (Oxford, 1973)

A. Seaton, *The Russo-German War* (London, 1971)

M. Van Creveld, *Hitler's Strategy 1940–41. The Balkan Clue* (Cambridge, 1973)

E. F. Ziemke, *Stalingrad to Berlin* (Washington, 1968)

—— *Moscow to Stalingrad* (Washington, 1987)

THE AIR WAR:

S. A. Garrett, *Ethics and Airpower in World War II. The British Bombing of German Cities* (New York, 1993)

M. Hastings, *Bomber Command* (London, 1979)

R. V. Jones, *Most Secret War* (London, 1978)

A. J. Levine, *The Strategic Bombing of Germany 1940–5* (Westport, 1992)

N. Longmate, *The Bombers. The RAF Offensive against Germany* (London, 1983)

A. C. Mierzejewski, *The Collapse of the German War Economy 1944–5* (Chapel Hill, 1988)

W. Murray, *Luftwaffe. Strategy for Defeat* (London, 1985)

M. Middlebrook, *The Berlin Raids. RAF Bomber Command Winter 1943–44* (London, 1988)

—— *The Battle of Hamburg* (London, 1980)

—— *The Peenemünde Raid* (London, 1982)

R. Overy, *The Air War 1939–45* (London, 1980)

J. Terraine, *The Right of the Line. The RAF in the European War* (London, 1985)

D. Wood and D. Dempster, *The Narrow Margin. The Battle of Britain* (London, 1961)

Churchill, Roosevelt, Allied Strategy and Anglo-American Relations

E. Barker, *Churchill and Eden at War* (London, 1978)

P. Brendon, *Winston Churchill. A Brief Life* (London, 1984)

J. M. Burns, *Roosevelt, the Soldier of Freedom* (New York, 1970)

J. Charmley, *Churchill. The End of Glory* (London, 1993)

W. S. Churchill, *The Second World War*, 6 vols. (London 1948–1954)

R. N. Gardner, *Sterling–Dollar Diplomacy* (Oxford, 1956)

M. Gilbert, *Winston S. Churchill*, vol. vi, *Finest Hour* (London, 1983); vol. vii, *Road to Victory* (London, 1986)

R. M. Hathaway, *Ambiguous Partnership. Britain and America 1944–47* (New York, 1981)

M. Howard, *Grand Strategy*, vol. iv (London, 1972)

M. Jones, *Britain, the United States and the Mediterranean War, 1942–45* (London, 1996)

J. M. Keynes, *Collected Writings*, vol. xxiv, *The Transition to Peace* (London, 1979)

W. F. Kimball (ed.), *Churchill and Roosevelt. The Complete Correspondence*, 3 vols. (Princeton, 1984)

W. R. Louis, *Imperialism at Bay* (Oxford, 1977)

M. Matloff and E. M. Snell, *Strategic Planning for Coalition Warfare 1941–43* (Washington, 1953)

M. Matloff, *Strategic Planning for Coalition Warfare 1943–44* (Washington, 1959)

W. H. McNeill, *America, Britain and Russia 1941–1946* (London, 1953)

H. M. Pelling, *Winston Churchill* (new edn., London, 1989)

K. Sainsbury, *Churchill and Roosevelt at War* (London, 1994)

M. A. Stoler, *The Politics of the Second Front* (Westport, 1977)

C. Thorne, *Allies of a Kind* (London, 1978)

D. C. Watt, *Succeeding John Bull* (Cambridge, 1984)

Economic and Social

J. M. Blum, *V was for Victory* (New York, 1976)

A. Cairncross, *Years of Recovery. British Economic Policy 1945–51* (London, 1985)

A. Calder, *The People's War. Britain 1939–45* (London, 1969)

D. Campbell, *Women at War with America* (Cambridge, Mass., 1984)

J. B. Cohen, *The Japanese War Economy 1937–45* (Minneapolis, 1949)

J. Costello, *Love, Sex and War* (London, 1985)

M. Harrison, *Soviet Planning in Peace and War 1938–1945* (Cambridge, 1985)

S. M. Hartmann, *The Home Front and Beyond. American Women in the 1940s* (Boston, 1982)

M. Kitchen, *Nazi Germany at War* (London, 1995)

S. J. Linz (ed.), *The Impact of World War II on the Soviet Union* (Totowa, 1985)

A. S. Milward, *War Economy and Society* (London, 1977)

—— *The Reconstruction of Western Europe 1945–51* (London, 1984)

W. Moskoff, *Bread of Affliction. Food Supply in the USSR During World War II* (New York, 1992)

R. J. Overy, *Goering, Iron Man* (London, 1984)

R. Polenberg, *War and Society. The United States 1941–45* (Philadelphia, 1972)

H. L. Smith (ed.), *War and Social Change* (Manchester, 1986)

P. Summerfield, *Women Workers in the Second World War* (London, 1984)

US Bureau of the Budget, *The U.S. at War* (Washington, 1946)

N. A. Vosnesensky, *The Economy of the USSR during World War II* (Washington, 1948)

Morale

R. Ahrenfeldt, *Psychiatry in the British Army* (London, 1958)

M. Balfour, *Propaganda in War, 1939–1945* (London, 1979)

J. Ellis, *The Sharp End of War. The Fighting Man in World War II* (Newton Abbot, 1980)

P. Fussell, *Wartime* (New York, 1989)

T. Harrisson, *Living Through the Blitz* (London, 1976)

I. Kershaw, *Popular Opinion and Political Dissent in the Third Reich, Bavaria 1933–45* (Oxford, 1983)

I. McLaine, *Ministry of Morale* (London, 1979)

M. Steinert, *Hitler's War and the Germans* (Athens, Ohio, 1977)

S. A. Stouffer (ed.), *The American Soldier*, 2 vols. (Princeton 1949)

M. Van Creveld, *Fighting Power. German and US Army Performance 1939–45* (London, 1983)

M. K. Wells, *Courage and Air Warfare. The Allied Aircrew Experience in the Second World War* (London, 1995)

Murder of Jews

C. Abramski (ed.), *The Jews in Poland* (Oxford, 1986)

R. Ainsztein, *Jewish Resistance in Nazi-occupied Eastern Europe* (New York, 1974)

R. Braham, *The Politics of Genocide. The Holocaust in Hungary*, 2 vols. (New York, 1981)

C. R. Browning, *The Path to Genocide* (Cambridge, 1992)
—— *Ordinary Men. Reserve Police Battalion 101 and the Final Solution in Poland* (New York, 1992)
H. Fein, *Accounting for Genocide* (New York, 1979)
G. Fleming, *Hitler and the Final Solution* (London, 1985)
M. Gilbert, *The Holocaust* (London, 1986)
R. Hilberg, *The Destruction of the European Jews*, 3 vols. (new edn., New York, 1985)
G. Hirschfeld, *The Policies of Genocide* (London, 1986)
W. Laqueur, *The Terrible Secret* (London, 1980)
P. Levi, *If This is a Man* (London, 1960)
M. R. Marrus and R. O. Paxton, *Vichy France and the Jews* (London, 1981)
E. Mendelsohn, *The Jews of East Central Europe between the World Wars* (Bloomington, 1983)
G. Reitlinger, *The Final Solution* (London, 1953)
B. Wasserstein, *Britain and the Jews of Europe* (Oxford, 1979)
D. S. Wyman, *The Abandonment of the Jews. America and the Holocaust* (New York, 1984)
S. Zuccotti, *The Italians and the Holocaust* (London, 1987)

Origins of the Cold War

T. H. Anderson, *The United States, Great Britain and the Cold War* (Columbia, 1981)
J. Coutouvidis and J. Reynolds, *Poland 1939–47* (Leicester, 1986)
J. L. Gaddis, *The United States and the Origin of the Cold War* (New York, 1972)
B. R. Kuniholm, *The Origins of the Cold War in the Near East* (Princeton, 1979)
W. Le Feber, *America, Russia and the Cold War* (New York, 1967)
M. P. Leffler, *A Preponderance of Power* (Stanford, 1992)
M. McCauley (ed.), *Communist Power in Europe 1944–49* (London, 1977)
V. Mastny, *Russia's Road to the Cold War* (New York, 1979)
R. L. Messer, *The End of an Alliance* (Chapel Hill, 1982)
A. Polonsky (ed.), *The Great Powers and the Polish Question* (London, 1976)
G. Ross (ed.), *The Foreign Office and the Kremlin* (Cambridge, 1984)
V. H. Rothwell, *Britain and the Cold War* (Oxford, 1971)

Effects of the War

J. M. Brown, *Modern India* (Delhi, 1985)
M. J. Cohen, *Palestine and the Great Powers 1945–48* (Princeton, 1982)
A. Dallin, *German Rule in Russia* (London, 1957)
D. W. Ellwood, *Italy 1943–45* (Leicester, 1985)
M. R. D. Foot, *Resistance* (London, 1976)

G. Frumkin, *Population Changes in Europe since 1939* (New York, 1951)

R. F. Holland, *European Decolonisation 1918–81* (London, 1985)

H. R. Kedward, *Occupied France. Collaboration and Resistance* (Oxford, 1985)

D. Killingray and R. Rathbone (eds.), *Africa and the Second World War* (London, 1986)

N. Longmate, *The G.I.'s. The Americans in Britain 1942–45* (New York, 1976)

W. R. Louis, *The British Empire in the Middle East 1945–51* (Oxford, 1984)

P. Lowe, *The Origins of the Korean War* (London, 1986)

M. R. Marrus, *The Unwanted. European Refugees in the Twentieth Century* (New York, 1985)

K. O. Morgan, *Labour in Power* (Oxford, 1984)

R. Ovendale, *The Origins of the Arab–Israeli Wars* (London, 1984)

D. Reynolds, *Rich Relations. The American Occupation of Britain 1942–45* (London, 1995)

C. Thorne, *The Issue of War. States, Societies and the Far Eastern Conflict* (London, 1985)

T. I. Williams, *Howard Florey. Penicillin and After* (London, 1984)

INDEX

OXFORD

MORE OXFORD PAPERBACKS

This book is just one of nearly 1000 Oxford Paperbacks currently in print. If you would like details of other Oxford Paperbacks, including titles in the World's Classics, Oxford Reference, Oxford Books, OPUS, Past Masters, Oxford Authors, and Oxford Shakespeare series, please write to:

UK and Europe: Oxford Paperbacks Publicity Manager, Arts and Reference Publicity Department, Oxford University Press, Walton Street, Oxford OX2 6DP.

Customers in UK and Europe will find Oxford Paperbacks available in all good bookshops. But in case of difficulty please send orders to the Cash-with-Order Department, Oxford University Press Distribution Services, Saxon Way West, Corby, Northants NN18 9ES. Tel: 01536 741519; Fax: 01536 746337. Please send a cheque for the total cost of the books, plus £1.75 postage and packing for orders under £20; £2.75 for orders over £20. Customers outside the UK should add 10% of the cost of the books for postage and packing.

USA: Oxford Paperbacks Marketing Manager, Oxford University Press, Inc., 200 Madison Avenue, New York, N.Y. 10016.

Canada: Trade Department, Oxford University Press, 70 Wynford Drive, Don Mills, Ontario M3C 1J9.

Australia: Trade Marketing Manager, Oxford University Press, G.P.O. Box 2784Y, Melbourne 3001, Victoria.

South Africa: Oxford University Press, P.O. Box 1141, Cape Town 8000.

HISTORY IN OXFORD PAPERBACKS
TUDOR ENGLAND
John Guy

Tudor England is a compelling account of political and religious developments from the advent of the Tudors in the 1460s to the death of Elizabeth I in 1603.

Following Henry VII's capture of the Crown at Bosworth in 1485, Tudor England witnessed far-reaching changes in government and the Reformation of the Church under Henry VIII, Edward VI, Mary, and Elizabeth; that story is enriched here with character studies of the monarchs and politicians that bring to life their personalities as well as their policies.

Authoritative, clearly argued, and crisply written, this comprehensive book will be indispensable to anyone interested in the Tudor Age.

'lucid, scholarly, remarkably accomplished . . . an excellent overview' *Sunday Times*

'the first comprehensive history of Tudor England for more than thirty years' Patrick Collinson, *Observer*

HISTORY IN OXFORD PAPERBACKS
THE STRUGGLE FOR THE MASTERY OF EUROPE 1848–1918

A. J. P. Taylor

The fall of Metternich in the revolutions of 1848 heralded an era of unprecedented nationalism in Europe, culminating in the collapse of the Hapsburg, Romanov, and Hohenzollern dynasties at the end of the First World War. In the intervening seventy years the boundaries of Europe changed dramatically from those established at Vienna in 1815. Cavour championed the cause of *Risorgimento* in Italy; Bismarck's three wars brought about the unification of Germany; Serbia and Bulgaria gained their independence courtesy of the decline of Turkey—'the sick man of Europe'; while the great powers scrambled for places in the sun in Africa. However, with America's entry into the war and President Wilson's adherence to idealistic internationalist principles, Europe ceased to be the centre of the world, although its problems, still primarily revolving around nationalist aspirations, were to smash the Treaty of Versailles and plunge the world into war once more.

A. J. P. Taylor has drawn the material for his account of this turbulent period from the many volumes of diplomatic documents which have been published in the five major European languages. By using vivid language and forceful characterization, he has produced a book that is as much a work of literature as a contribution to scientific history.

'One of the glories of twentieth-century writing.'
Observer

PAST MASTERS

A wide range of unique, short, clear introductions to the lives and work of the world's most influential thinkers. Written by experts, they cover the history of ideas from Aristotle to Wittgenstein. Readers need no previous knowledge of the subject, so they are ideal for students and general readers alike.

Each book takes as its main focus the thought and work of its subject. There is a short section on the life and a final chapter on the legacy and influence of the thinker. A section of further reading helps in further research.

The series continues to grow, and future Past Masters will include **Owen Gingerich** on *Copernicus*, **R G Frey** on *Joseph Butler*, **Bhiku Parekh** on *Gandhi*, **Christopher Taylor** on *Socrates*, **Michael Inwood** on *Heidegger*, and **Peter Ghosh** on *Weber*.

OXFORD PAPERBACK REFERENCE

From *Art and Artists* to *Zoology*, the Oxford Paperback Reference series offers the very best subject reference books at the most affordable prices.

Authoritative, accessible, and up to date, the series features dictionaries in key student areas, as well as a range of fascinating books for a general readership. Included are such well-established titles as Fowler's *Modern English Usage*, Margaret Drabble's *Concise Companion to English Literature*, and the bestselling science and medical dictionaries.

The series has now been relaunched in handsome new covers. Highlights include new editions of some of the most popular titles, as well as brand new paperback reference books on *Politics*, *Philosophy*, and *Twentieth-Century Poetry*.

With new titles being constantly added, and existing titles regularly updated, Oxford Paperback Reference is unrivalled in its breadth of coverage and expansive publishing programme. New dictionaries of *Film*, *Economics*, *Linguistics*, *Architecture*, *Archaeology*, *Astronomy*, and *The Bible* are just a few of those coming in the future.

Oxford
Paperback
Reference

THE CONCISE OXFORD DICTIONARY
OF POLITICS

Edited by Iain McLean

Written by an expert team of political scientists from Warwick University, this is the most authoritative and up-to-date dictionary of politics available.

* **Over 1,500 entries provide truly international coverage of major political institutions, thinkers and concepts**

* **From Western to Chinese and Muslim political thought**

* **Covers new and thriving branches of the subject, including international political economy, voting theory, and feminism**

* **Appendix of political leaders**

* **Clear, no-nonsense definitions of terms such as veto and subsidiarity**

OXFORD

RETHINKING LIFE AND DEATH
THE COLLAPSE OF OUR TRADITIONAL ETHICS

Peter Singer

A victim of the Hillsborough Disaster in 1989, Anthony Bland lay in hospital in a coma being fed liquid food by a pump, via a tube passing through his nose and into his stomach. On 4 February 1993 Britain's highest court ruled that doctors attending him could lawfully act to end his life.

Our traditional ways of thinking about life and death are collapsing. In a world of respirators and embryos stored for years in liquid nitrogen, we can no longer take the sanctity of human life as the cornerstone of our ethical outlook.

In this controversial book Peter Singer argues that we cannot deal with the crucial issues of death, abortion, euthanasia and the rights of nonhuman animals unless we sweep away the old ethic and build something new in its place.

Singer outlines a new set of commandments, based on compassion and commonsense, for the decisions everyone must make about life and death.

FOUR ESSAYS ON LIBERTY

Isaiah Berlin

'*those who value liberty for its own sake believe that to be free to choose, and not to be chosen for, is an inalienable ingredient in what makes human beings human*'
Introduction to *Four Essays On Liberty*

Political Ideas in the Twentieth Century
Historical Inevitability
Two Concepts of Liberty
John Stuart Mill and the Ends of Life

These four essays deal with the various aspects of individual liberty, including the distinction between positive and negative liberty and the necessity of rejecting determinism if we wish to keep hold of the notions of human responsibility and freedom.

'practically every paragraph introduces us to half a dozen new ideas and as many thinkers—the landscape flashes past, peopled with familiar and unfamiliar people, all arguing incessantly'
New Society

POLITICS

Kenneth Minogue

Since politics is both complex and controversial it is easy to miss the wood for the trees. In this Very Short Introduction Kenneth Minogue has brought the many dimensions of politics into a single focus: he discusses both the everyday grind of democracy and the attraction of grand ideals such as freedom and justice.

'Kenneth Minogue is a very lively stylist who does not distort difficult ideas.'
Maurice Cranston

'a dazzling but unpretentious display of great scholarship and humane reflection'
Professor Neil O'Sullivan, University of Hull

'Minogue is an admirable choice for showing us the nuts and bolts of the subject.'
Nicholas Lezard, *Guardian*

'This is a fascinating book which sketches, in a very short space, one view of the nature of politics ... the reader is challenged, provoked and stimulated by Minogue's trenchant views.'
Talking Politics

JUDAISM

Norman Solomon

'Norman Solomon has achieved the near impossible with his enlightened very short introduction to Judaism. Since it is well known that Judaism is almost impossible to summarize, and that there are as many different opinions about Jewish matters as there are Jews, this is a small masterpiece in its success in representing various shades of Jewish opinion, often mutually contradictory. Solomon also manages to keep the reader engaged, never patronizes, assumes little knowledge but a keen mind, and takes us through Jewish life and history with such gusto that one feels enlivened, rather than exhausted, at the end.'
Rabbi Julia Neuberger

'This book will serve a very useful purpose indeed. I'll use it myself to discuss, to teach, agree with, and disagree with, in the Jewish manner!'
Rabbi Lionel Blue

'A magnificent achievement. Dr Solomon's treatment, fresh, very readable, witty and stimulating, will delight everyone interested in religion in the modern world.'
Dr Louis Jacobs, University of Lancaster